*The Tancook Schooners
An Island and Its Boats*

The Tancook Schooners tells the story of a remarkable Atlantic Canadian watercraft, now fast disappearing. The book also records the history of a Maritime coastal community on the brink of the modern industrial age.

The Tancook schooners, or "little Bluenoses," formed the backbone of Nova Scotia's inshore fisheries and short-run coastal trade in the early twentieth century. Wayne O'Leary provides detailed descriptions of how they were conceived and perfected and shows how national and international developments affected the character and uses of the vessel for which Tancook Island became famous. He paints a vivid picture of life on Tancook from the late eighteenth century into the twentieth century, complemented by many stories about individual builders and a wealth of photographs and drawings.

O'Leary's interdisciplinary approach shows how development of the schooner was affected by its social, cultural, and economic context and makes an important contribution to maritime history. *The Tancook Schooners* will be of interest to maritime enthusiasts as well as maritime, economic, and social historians.

WAYNE M. O'LEARY is a research associate in history, University of Maine.

The Tancook Schooners

An Island and Its Boats

WAYNE M. O'LEARY

McGill-Queen's University Press
Montreal & Kingston • London • Buffalo

To my grandfather, Howard Mason, who built these boats, and to his sons, Thomas, Murray, Steadman, Eustace, Emery, Leaman, and Howard, Jr, who sailed them

© McGill-Queen's University Press 1994
ISBN 0-7735-1172-5 (cloth)
ISBN 0-7735-1206-3 (paper)

Legal deposit fourth quarter 1994
Bibliothèque nationale du Québec

∞

Printed in Canada on acid-free paper

This book has been published with the help of a grant from the Social Science Federation of Canada, using funds provided by the Social Sciences and Humanities Research Council of Canada. Publication has also been supported by the Canadian Embassy in Washington, DC.

Canadian Cataloguing in Publication Data

O'Leary, Wayne M., 1941–
  The Tancook schooners: an island and its boats
  Includes bibliographical references and index.
  ISBN 0-7735-1172-5 (bound) –
  ISBN 0-7735-1206-3 (pbk.)
  1. Schooners – Nova Scotia – Tancook Island – History. 2. Tancook Island (N.S.) – History. 3. Shipbuilding – Nova Scotia – Tancook Island. I. Title.
  FC2345.T36O54 1994   387.2'2   C94-900440-5
  F1039.T36O54 1994

This book was typeset by Typo Litho Composition Inc. in 10/12 Palatino.

Contents

List of Figures, Photographs, and Maps   vii

Preface   xi

Prologue: Little Bluenoses   3

1 The Setting   6

2 The Boats   17

3 The Economy   119

4 Last Years   175

Epilogue   182

Figures   183

Appendices   211

Reference Abbreviations   237

Notes   241

Bibliography   267

Index   277

List of Figures, Photographs, and Maps

FIGURES

1 Sail plan of an unidentified schr, ca. 1905–09 185
2 Sail plan of schr *Togo* [?], 1905 185
3 Lines of schr *Comet G.*, 1910 186
4 Sail plan of schr *Comet G.*, 1910 187
5 Revised sail plan of schr *Comet G.*, 1916 187
6 Lines of schr *Blackbird III*, 1910 188
7 Sail plan of schr *Flosie*, 1912 189
8 Sail plan of schr *Dagon*, 1912 189
9 Sail plan of schr *Mianus*, 1912 190
10 Sail plan of schr *Tancook*, 1914 190
11 Sail plan of schr *Haig*, 1917 191
12 Lines of a proposed Stanley Mason schr, ca. 1910–20 192
13 Lines of schr *Green Bow*, ca. 1923 193
14 Lines of schrs *Elsie B. Young* and *Bluebeard*, 1923 194
15 Lines of schr *Sarah Pauline*, 1924 195
16 Lines of schr *Mother*, 1924 196

17 Lines of schrs *Attaboy*, 1928, *Catchalot*, 1929, *Turret*, 1930, *Glendora*, 1931, and *Stormalong*, ca. 1936   197

18 Lines of schr *Patavana*, 1929   198

19 Sail plan of schr *Patavana*, 1929   199

20 Deck plan of a Tancook semi-deck boat, 1929   199

21 Sail plan of schr *Holly C.*, 1929   200

22 Lines of schr *Gerald L.C.*, 1933   201

23 Deck plan of a Tancook deck boat, 1933   202

24 Lines of sloop *Polly Anna*, 1934   203

25 Sail plan of sloop *Polly Anna*, 1934   204

26 Lines of schr *Amasonia*, 1935   205

27 Sail plan of schr *Amasonia*, 1935   206

28 Lines of Cape Island boat *Here We Are*, 1939   207

29 Lines of schr *X10U8*, 1940   208

30 Deck plan of a Tancook hatch boat, 1940   209

31 Lines of an Ervin Cross Cape Island boat, ca. 1960   210

PHOTOGRAPHS

1 Schooners racing off Big Tancook Island, 1911   35

2 Tancook schooners and whalers off Chester, NS, ca. 1907   36

3 Schooners and sloops moored near Little Tancook Island, 1921   36

4 Whalers hauled at Northwest Cove, Big Tancook Island, ca. 1905   37

5 View of Southeast Cove, Big Tancook Island, in the late 1930s   37

6 Big Tancook Island from Southern Head, 1968   38

7 Builder Alfred F. Langille (1839–1926)   38

8 The Joseph Thomas home (built ca. 1870), Big Tancook Island, 1968   39

9 Builder Joshua Mason (1845–1924)   40

ix Illustrations

10 Builder Wesley H. Stevens (1871–1967) 40
11 Builder Amos H. Stevens (1850–1935) 40
12 Builder Stanley G. Mason (1882–1960) 40
13 Builder Howard Mason (1874–1953) 41
14 Builder Reuben Heisler (1874–1946) 41
15 Builder Vernon R. Langille (1888–1979) 41
16 Tancook whaler *Nancy* at Peggy's Cove, NS, in the 1920s 72
17 Stern view of a Tancook whaler, Peggy's Cove, NS, 1920s 72
18 Schr *Adare* (ex *Tacoma*) off Tancook Island, 1969 73
19 Schr *Squanto* of Duxbury, MA, ca. 1902 73
20 Schr *Patavana* under full sail off Tancook Island, 1930 74
21 Schr *Amasonia* off Chester, NS, late 1930s 75
22 Schr *Patavana* coasting with salt, 1939 76
23 Schr *X10U8*, broadside to, Mahone Bay, NS, 1942 76
24 Schr *X10U8* seen from astern, Mahone Bay, NS, 1942 77
25 Schr *Windstark* (ex *Blue Lagoon*) in Albemarle Sound, NC, ca. 1940 78
26 A new Tancook schr preparing for sea, 1920s 78
27 Schr *Nelson L.* moored off Tancook Island, 1929 79
28 A Tancook deck boat ready for launching, 1920s 79
29 Schr *Frances M.R.* at Chester, NS, late 1920s 80
30 Schr *Verna B.* hauled at Big Tancook Island, late 1930s 80
31 The Tancook bow: schr *Patavana*, 1929 111
32 The Tancook stern: schr *Amasonia*, 1943 111
33 The Tancook sheer: schr *Sea Way*, 1949 112
34 The Tancook profile: schr *Patavana*, 1929 112
35 The Tancook transom: schr *Blue Lagoon*, ca. 1935 113

x Illustrations

36 Deck view of schr *X10U8*, looking aft, 1944   113

37 Deck view of schr *Patavana*, 1929   114

38 Preparing the mast, Tancook-fashion: schr *Sea Way*, 1949   114

39 The former S.G. Mason boatyard, Big Tancook Island, 1969   115

40 Stepping the mast, Tancook-fashion: schr *Sea Way*, 1949   116

41 Steaming frames, Tancook-fashion: schr *Shanti*, 1971   116

42 Bending frames, Tancook-fashion: schr *Shanti*, 1971   117

43 Sealing the hull, Tancook-fashion: schr *Amasonia*, 1964   117

44 Hull framing of a Tancook schr: *Amasonia* during reconstruction, 1964   118

45 Schr *Patavana* trawl fishing off Mahone Bay, NS, ca. 1930   147

46 Crew of schr *Patavana* dressing herring, Big Tancook Island, mid-1930s   147

47 The Cape Breton swordfishing fleet, Glace Bay, NS, ca. 1935   148

48 Broadside view of schr *Mianus* swordfishing, ca. World War I   148

49 Bow view of schr *Mianus* swordfishing, ca. World War I   149

50 Hauling the cod trawl of the schr *Patavana* off Mahone Bay, NS, ca. 1930   149

51 Wharf and launchway at low tide, Big Tancook Island, ca. 1960   150

52 Crating Tancook cabbage for export, Halifax, mid-1930s   151

MAPS

1 Nova Scotia and Prince Edward Island   5

2 Big and Little Tancook islands   15

Preface

This book satisfies most of the requirements for a labour of love, having been a personal preoccupation, off and on, for over two decades. It had its genesis in the 1950s and early 1960s, when as a teenager and college student I spent numerous summer vacations fishing and sailing the waters of Mahone Bay with my uncles and cousins and informally absorbed a storehouse of family lore associated with Tancook Island and its famous boats. About twenty years ago, it became apparent that this unique body of historical information would soon be lost if not recorded. The last islanders who had worked under sail in the old manner were aging, and it was obvious that Tancook's oral tradition would not survive their passing. Equally important, the schooners themselves were fast disappearing, surviving here and there in scattered yachting fleets only in substantially altered form. Simultaneously, a generations-old way of life was rapidly being transformed under the inexorable pressures of modernization.

It was at this point that I began to systematically gather half-models, sail plans, and photographs and to interview those individuals – family members and others – who could transmit details about Tancook's technological heritage and traditional fishing-farming-coasting economy. The work proceeded intermittently at first, interrupted at length for the completion of a doctoral degree in history, and then intensified in recent years with an urgent sense of the passage of time. It was also expanded to include formal research in libraries, museums, and archival repositories.

In the meantime, other persons became interested in the Tancook story, particularly those aspects relating to the highly romanticized

Tancook whaler, the island's first important small craft. A number of publications touching on the subject appeared in the 1970s and 1980s, some of them reasonably accurate and others less so, but none managed to present anything approaching a complete history of the island's people, boats, and economy. It is hoped that this book will help to fill that void.

A great many individuals and institutions provided information, assistance, and encouragement during the course of my work. I would first like to acknowledge the late Howard I. Chapelle of the Smithsonian Institution's National Museum of American History, whose pioneering work inspires all those who navigate the turbulent waters of historical naval architecture. "Chap" admired the Tancook schooner and, though cognizant of the pitfalls involved, strongly urged an investigation into its origins. He would have been interested in the results of this study.

I would also like to mention the contribution of Niels W. Jannasch, former director of the Maritime Museum of the Atlantic. Niels read the manuscript in its entirety and provided perceptive commentary and pertinent suggestions that immeasurably improved the narrative. His help and keen interest throughout the project were invaluable.

A special debt of gratitude is owed to my late uncle, Thomas Mason, of Chester, Nova Scotia. Tom spent countless hours over several years' time patiently answering questions and describing the building and operation of Tancook's boats, the character of its fisheries, agriculture, and coasting trade, and the life of its people. His firsthand knowledge, devotion to fact and accuracy, and uncanny memory proved to be unsurpassed. In some respects, this book is as much his as mine.

Two other uncles, Murray A. ("Joe") Mason of Halifax and the late Steadman S. ("Ted") Mason of Chester, both former schooner sailors and natives of Tancook, also submitted willingly to lengthy interviews and provided critical information. To them I owe much of what I know about the island's history and traditions. Their contributions cannot be overemphasized.

Numerous other individuals opened their doors and graciously imparted their knowledge of the subject at hand or granted access to half-models and photographs in their possession. I woud like to express my appreciation to Gerald L. Stevens, the late Perry W. Stevens, Guy B. Stevens, Benjamin Heisler, Mrs Audrey Mosher, Mrs Dorinda Mason, and the late Leslie A. Mason, all of Chester; Murray Stevens, the late David M. Stevens and the late Harold W. Stevens, all of Second Peninsula, Lunenburg; Wesley H. Stevens, Jr, Vincent Stevens, the late Ervin B. Cross, DeWitt Baker, and Mrs Mary M.

Baker, all of Tancook; Cecil F. Langille and the late Vernon R. Langille of Indian Point; Mrs Sadie I. Langille of Martin's Brook; the late Hovey Slauenwhite of Mahone Bay; Donald Langille of Berwick; Mrs Carrie A. Kehoe of Bridgetown; Harry W. Piper of College Park, Maryland; and Mrs Margaret M. McLaughlin of Nashua, New Hampshire.

A number of persons not directly connected to Tancook Island nevertheless helped to facilitate my task. For their timely assistance, I would like to thank David B. Flemming and Mary Blackford, director and librarian respectively, of the Maritime Museum of the Atlantic, Halifax; Heather Risser, curator of the Fisheries Museum of the Atlantic, Lunenburg; Richard Brown, transportation archivist, National Archives of Canada, Ottawa; Peter J. Ady, superintendent of ship registration, Canadian Coast Guard, Ottawa; Katrina J. Naud, assistant registrar of ships, Halifax Customs House; Margaret Campbell, photographic archivist, Public Archives of Nova Scotia, Halifax; Anne Risley and Jamie Nicoll of National Art Works, Ltd, Halifax; Donald Parker, manager of the Provincial Crown Lands Record Centre, Dartmouth; Brenda Mulroney, vice-commodore of the Chester Yacht Club, Chester, Nova Scotia; Nathan Lipfert, curator, Maine Maritime Museum, Bath; William Bayreuther, former curator, Penobscot Maritime Museum, Searsport, Maine; Gerald E. Morris, former director of the G.W. Blunt-White Library, Mystic Seaport Museum, Mystic, Connecticut; David Matheson, formerly of the Mystic Seaport curatorial staff; and Lance R. Lee, former director of the Rockport Apprenticeshop, Rockport, Maine.

Several institutions and government agencies were of particular help in the completion of this project. The efficient and obliging staff of the National Archives of Canada answered numerous research questions on a variety of topics and arranged for me to borrow microfilm copies of critically important Nova Scotia shipping registers. The equally capable staff of the Public Archives of Nova Scotia satisfied several telephone requests for information and aided in my search for historical and geneological data, maps, and photographs. The staffs of the Registry of Deeds for the Municipality of Lunenburg, Bridgewater, and the Office of the Registrar-General, Halifax, gave prompt and courteous assistance in researching the land deeds and vital records, respectively, in their possession. Finally, the staffs of the Lunenburg and Halifax customs houses allowed me full latitude to examine their current ship register books at leisure.

The research phase of this work could not have been completed without the financial help of the Canadian Embassy in Washington, DC, whose academic studies program provided a generous grant for the year 1987–88. I am likewise indebted to the University of Maine's Canadian-American Center for several travel grants over the period 1987 through 1992.

Last but not least, I want to thank my wife, Elaine T. O'Leary, who accompanied me on innumerable trips "down home," helped to take research notes, cheerfully endured endless excursions to boat yards, sail lofts, museums, and archives, and typed the original draft of the manuscript. Her help was inestimable.

A few words should be said regarding the illustrations in this book. The architectural drawings, including whatever imperfections, are my own. The vessel lines were taken directly from builders' half-models, and the sail plans were traced from sailmakers' originals. The deck plans were reconstructed from models, period photographs, and interviews, and are necessarily approximate renderings. Many of the photographs, specifically those depicting the boats of schooner builders Stanley and Howard Mason, are the work of Sadie (Mason) Langille and the late Eustace Mason, daughter and son of the respective builders. Without their interest in preserving a visual record of island watercraft in the 1920s and 1930s, few pictures of working Tancook schooners would now exist.

The Tancook Schooners

Prologue
Little Bluenoses

There's a man I used to know here ... He never went to school. But he learned how to make boats. When he was a young man he crossed over to Tancook Island and studied how they built those light shore-craft over there.

Hugh MacLennan *Barometer Rising*

In the period beginning just prior to World War I and ending roughly with the start of World War II, a span of only three decades, a small island off the Atlantic coast of Nova Scotia created and perfected a remarkable working watercraft the like of which had never been seen before and will never, in its pure form, be seen again. The short life of the Tancook schooner was, nevertheless, long enough to imprint its image indelibly on the counsciousness of Atlantic Canadians and fix its memory in the minds of sailing boat admirers everywhere. For over thirty years, this unique craft dominated the inshore fisheries and short-run coastal trade of much of its home province and influenced yacht and work boat design throughout the Maritimes and beyond. Ubiquitous in its comings and goings, it was an integral part of the waterfront scene of countless outport villages from Lunenburg to Canso.

The historical popularity of the Tancook schooner as a fishing craft may be seen in its sheer numbers throughout the Nova Scotia fleet. During the 1920s, for example, close to one quarter of all fishing schooners registered in the province* were products of Tancook

---

* By count, 75 out of 338 in 1925 and 74 out of 334 in 1927 – in each case, 22.2 percent.

builders.[1] These so-called "little Bluenoses,"[2] superficially similar to the large Lunenburg salt bankers, formed the backbone of Nova Scotia's inshore fishery during the first decades of the twentieth century, providing an intermediate class of vessel to work the inner grounds beyond the reach of day fishermen but too near at hand to capture the attention of the deep-water bankers. As such, they were the critical component of an inshore industry that occupied eight out of nine Nova Scotian fishermen on the eve of the First World War.[3]

The qualities of the Tancook schooner were well known not only to provincial fishermen but also to a host of international yachtsmen who frequented the South Shore in the years between the world wars. The reaction of one was typical. "One day we sailed over to Tancook Island where they build quite a few boats during the winter," wrote Floridian Donald Waters in 1937. "Here we saw one of the cleanest looking little 50-foot schooners it has been ever my pleasure to view."[4]

Some enthusiasts did more than look. Desmond Holdridge, an American adventurer, chose a Tancook-built 31-footer for his perilous voyage to Labrador in 1925. He later described the hair-raising experience of running under bare poles before an October gale in the Gulf of St Lawrence: "I do not know what virtue it is the Tancook model possesses, but it will run in any weather. With a different type of boat it would have been suicidal, but not with one of those."[5]

More demanding still was the celebrated passage of Bermuda-born Richard Maury from Nova Scotia to the Fiji Islands by way of the Panama Canal in 1933–34 aboard a 35-foot Tancook schooner. Maury's *Cimba*, a Vernon Langille creation, survived months of deep-sea voyaging in all manner of conditions, including an Atlantic hurricane, before running aground on a Pacific atoll. Her owner's story has since become a classic in sea literature.[6]

William McCoy – the noted Bill ("the real") McCoy of rum-running fame – also remembered Tancook Island when his battles against Prohibition ended. In 1935, he commissioned the yard of S.G. Mason to refit the island-built fishing schooner *Harold H.* for use as a retirement yacht. The result was the beautiful 49-foot *Blue Lagoon* (see photo 25), a suitable home afloat for a deep-water schooner man who had pursued his glamourous, if illicit, livelihood from the deck of a converted Gloucester fisherman. The *Harold H./Blue Lagoon* eventually sailed out of Coral Strand, St Augustine, Florida.[7]

Closer to home, the founding members of Mahone Bay's Chester Yacht Club, many of them influential Americans and some of literary bent, contributed in no small measure to the growing reputation of

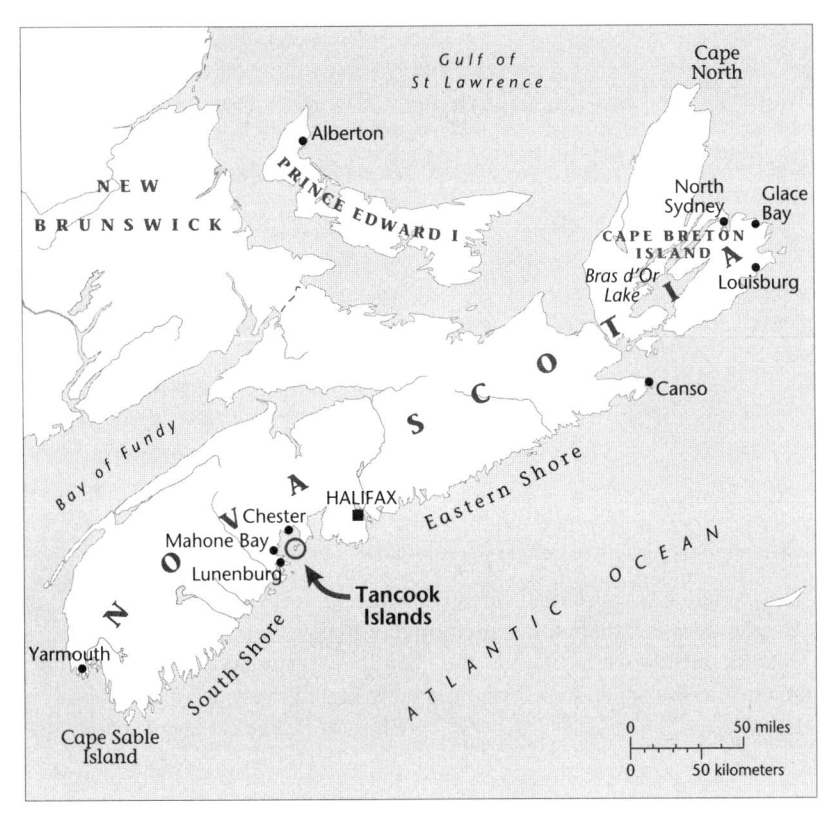

Map 1 Map of Nova Scotia and Prince Edward Island showing the Tancook islands in relation to associated regional locales.

the Tancook schooner after 1910 by adopting and publicizing it as their cruising and racing yacht of choice. Among the prominent devotees of the type was Dr John Finney of Baltimore, internationally known surgeon, whose prized 45-foot Tancooker *Meemie* was considered worthy of extensive mention in his widely read autobiography.[8]

These notable schooners, as well as innumerable lesser known but equally capable Tancook craft, spread the island's fame as a boatbuilding locale far and wide. They were the end product of three generations of experience that began early in the nineteenth century and culminated in the depression years of the 1930s, and their story is, to a large extent, the story of coastal Nova Scotia itself.

1 The Setting

These [Mahone Bay islands] vary greatly in size, from the far-famed Tancook, several miles in extent and settled by hundreds of families – looking from its outside sea location as the great breakwater and protector of the others – to the small ones forming merely bathing rests for a boat.

Thomas R. Pattillo *Sports Afield*, 1908

THE ISLAND

Tancook Island – or, more properly, Great or Big Tancook Island – is situated at the outer edge of Mahone Bay about midway between the Aspotogan and Lunenburg peninsulas that form the bay's mouth. It lies roughly six miles southeast of Chester, ten miles east of Mahone Bay township, and thirteen miles northeast of Lunenburg, the nearest mainland settlements of any size. By sea, it is approximately forty-five miles southwest of the city of Halifax, population center of Nova Scotia and the province's economic hub.[1]

Tancook is the largest by far of Mahone Bay's numerous islands – 365 according to legend – the next largest being nearby Little Tancook, less than half a mile away, with which the main island has long been closely associated. Tancook itself is a mostly oblong land mass slightly less than two and one-half miles long and just under one and one-half miles wide at its maximum breadth. It is predominantly flat lowland, barely reaching fifty feet above sea level except for a large headland at its southern end, which rises to 100 feet and forms a hook or tail on the seaward side of the round main body of the island.[2]

Southern Head, as the curved promontory is appropriately called, also helps form one of Tancook's two harbours, Southeast Cove. Facing the Atlantic, Southeast Cove is one mile wide at its mouth and three quarters of a mile long, ending in a gravel beach. Although it is the island's major anchorage, it is shallow (less than a fathom deep in many places), open to rolling ocean surges, and exposed to storms from southerly and easterly directions.

Northwest Cove, at the opposite end of the island, has deeper water but, being only one third of a mile wide and more a curve in the land than a true inlet, barely qualifies as a harbour. Though shielded from the Atlantic, it affords no protection from the northerly winds of fall and winter.[3] Those familiar with both anchorages recall the alternate surge and undertow at Southeast Cove, which was hard on both boats and moorings, and the wind and short, choppy seas (or "lop") at Northwest Cove, which imposed a pronounced pitching motion on moored vessels.[4] These less than ideal conditions profoundly influenced the types of watercraft eventually developed by local builders.

Mostly barren of trees by the early twentieth century,[5] Tancook was initially heavily forested. Its 559 acres, first surveyed in 1788, were thought to contain 10,000 cords of potential firewood and substantial building timber, including a variety of hardwoods. There were several rivulets and springs affording good drinking water but, as the original survey emphasized, no real harbour and insufficient depth on the ocean side to allow vessels to approach closer than 200 yards off shore.[6]

It was to this land, marginally useful at best from the mariner's viewpoint but with other attributes not immediately visible, that Europeans first came in the eighteenth century. Initially christened Queen Charlotte's Island, and later Royal George Island, the island finally received the name by which it had long been informally known. To the Micmacs of Nova Scotia's South Shore, it was simply Uktancook ("facing the open sea").[7] A more succinct description would be hard to find.

On September 12, 1759, Lieutenant-Colonel Patrick Sutherland, commander of the British garrison at Lunenburg and veteran of the siege of Louisburg in 1758 during the French and Indian War, was given title to both Big and Little Tancook islands by Nova Scotia's Royal Governor Charles Lawrence, perhaps as a reward for his wartime services or possibly in recognition of his role in establishing the Lunenburg settlement.[8] At any rate, Sutherland's tenure was relatively short lived due to a failure to satisfy the terms and conditions of the grant, which required eventual payment of an annual quit rent (beginning in 1769) and the gradual improvement of the land in incremental stages over a thirty-year period.[9] By 1779, clearing and occupation of the main island had proceeded only to the extent of laying out six small plots of land in the vicinity of Northwest Cove and constructing small buildings on three of them. Five years later, even those temporary structures were gone, and the island was once more uninhabited.[10]

By 1792, Sutherland's title to the still-wild Tancooks had reverted to the Crown by escheat, and new claimants were free to apply. On December 17, Lieutenant Governor John Wentworth approved transfer of the islands to John Henry Fleiger, a civil servant, and George Grant, a merchant, both of Halifax. Their grant, which divided Big and Little Tancook between them, stipulated the payment of a nominal annual fee (two shillings per hundred acres) after two years, the clearing or draining of at least six percent of the land, and the acquisition of three head of cattle for every fifty acres within three years – or (if the land was found not arable) the erection of a small house and the employment of one man in mining or quarrying for the three-year period.[11]

Unlike their predecessor, Fleiger and Grant fulfilled the required terms, obtained full title, and began disposing of their speculative grant at a handsome profit. In 1795, Grant sold his eastern half of Tancook for £340 cash to two Lunenburg merchants, who in turn sold it two years later to several Lunenburg farmers named Becker and Krass. In 1796, Fleiger disposed of his western half of the island to another member of the Lunenburg Becker family – Tancook's first permanent settlers – who acquired it through a £500 mortgage that was settled four years later. Little Tancook was transferred from the grantees to working pioneers in much the same fashion, being sold first to merchant interests and then to farming families from the mainland. The first full-time occupant was John George Steebing (1807), whose descendants later appeared on the main island under the name Stevens.[12] By about the turn of the nineteenth century, then, ownership of the Tancooks had passed from grantees to speculators and, finally, to ordinary settlers. It was at this point that the human history of the island truly commenced.

THE PEOPLE

The story of Tancook Island and the schooner that bears its name really began in the forests of the Rhineland. The island was largely occupied by the same "Foreign Protestants" who populated the rest of Lunenburg County in the mid-eighteenth century as part of the British government's policy of creating a buffer against Acadian Catholicism. Those settlers, as Winthrop Bell's definitive historical

9 The Setting

investigations established, were of two ethnic groups. Most were of Germanic origin, migrating either from Germany (principally Württemberg, Hesse-Darmstadt, and the Palatinate) or from the German-speaking regions of Switzerland. A sizeable minority, however, were French Lutherans from the semi-independent principality of Montbéliard, located in what is now the Franche-Comté region of northeastern France and ruled until 1793 as a branch of the German house of Württemberg.[13]

Montbéliard (or, in German, Mömpelgard) is significant in the maritime history of Tancook because two of the island's four principal boatbuilding families, the Masons (Fr. Masson) and the Langilles, originated there. Of the remaining two, the Heislers (Ger. Haussler) came from Baden-Durlach in southwestern Germany as part of the mass Lunenburg migration of the 1750s, and the Stevenses (Ger. Steubing or Steebing) descended from a Hessian mercenary who settled on the South Shore after service in the Halifax garrison during the American Revolution. The other family names prominent in the early settlement of Tancook, including Baker (Becker), Cross (Krass), Young (Jung), Hutt (Hatt), Slauenwhite (Schlagentweit), and Rodenhiser (Rothenhausser), were also German or German-Swiss.[14]

Whatever their precise origins, those pioneering families shared a common background and experience. They had left forest or agricultural homelands near the headwaters of the Rhine, descended the river to Rotterdam, and crossed the Atlantic in English emigrant ships to Nova Scotia. Scottish, English, Irish, Spanish, and Jewish immigrants later gave Tancook a leavening, cosmopolitan mix of peoples,* but the dominant ethnic strain remained German, as did the dominant culture.

According to the first official census, in 1861, the Tancooks[†] contained a population of 379, 69 percent of whom were German or German-Swiss extraction, 12 percent Montbéliard French, 10 percent Jewish, 6 percent Scottish, 2 percent Irish, 1 percent English, and 1 percent Spanish. Four fifths, in other words, were descended from the Foreign Protestant migration of the previous century.[15] The

---

* Well-known Tancook names that were not German or French included Thomas and Crooks (English), Wilson (Scottish), Pearl or Parrel (Irish), Alinard or Linnard (Spanish), and Levy (Jewish). (*See* Can.MsCen, 1871, 1881: Lunenburg County, Nova Scotia, town of Tancook.) (For key to abbreviations, see list, p. 237.)

† Census takers considered both Big and Little Tancook, as well as East Ironbound and two smaller islands, as a single unit or township subdivision. The overwhelming bulk of the population, however, was on the main island. Population figures for 1881 were Big Tancook, 486; Little Tancook, 52; E. Ironbound, 19; others, 15. (*Source*: Can.MsCen, 1881: Lunenburg County, Nova Scotia, town of Tancook.)

Jewish component, the Levy family, thought to have descended from a Philadelphia merchant who went to Halifax in 1759,[16] was concentrated at Little Tancook and produced the smaller island's only family of boatbuilders.

The essentially Germanic population base of the Tancooks – particularly Big Tancook – was maintained throughout the nineteenth and early twentieth centuries (notwithstanding periodic romantic claims of widespread English United Empire Loyalist influence, some of which have found their way into print).[17] Islanders reporting Lunenburg German ancestry comprised eighty-two percent of the population in 1871 and eighty percent in 1881, for instance, and at the turn of the century they still made up two thirds of the total. Interestingly, however, the census takers of 1921 and 1941, whose interviews took place shortly after and during the world wars, found few persons willing to acknowledge a German background. Instead, most islanders were "English."[18] This obvious concession to patriotism and/or war hysteria, combined with the gradual anglicization of island names over time, is perhaps the foundation for the traditions of Loyalist heritage that persist to the present day.

In terms of religion, the various peoples of Tancook were surprisingly homogeneous. Except for a small "Reformed" minority, the southwestern Germans among them had come as Lutherans, as had the Montbéliardians, whose beliefs have been incorrectly labelled Huguenot or Calvinist. The Montbéliardians were quickly assimilated upon arrival into the Church of England by the judicious use of a French-speaking Anglican missionary.[19] However, the failure of both Lutheranism and Anglicanism to provide clergy and places of worship for Lunenburg County's more remote outports in the nineteenth century left a vacuum that was ultimately filled on Tancook by proselytizing Baptists from the mainland village of Chester, who established the first church on the island in 1855.[20] Prior to that time, a variety of doctrinal affiliations had coexisted, varying from family to family and from generation to generation. Both Methodists and Anglicans were strongly represented among Tancook's population at the time of the first Dominion census in 1871, and there were smaller numbers of Lutherans and Presbyterians as well, but the absence of an institutional presence on behalf of those dominations combined with the fervor of the Baptist congregation to produce an overwhelming Baptist dominance – in 1891, no less than 96 percent of the population of the Tancooks – by the late nineteenth century.[21]

It seems that children often rebelled against their fathers' beliefs or (more probably) were baptized in the island's only existing church at the insistence of their mothers. Two Tancook patriarchs, Peter Mason and Alfred Langille, were Methodists whose wives were Baptists and whose children grew up Baptist.[22] The convoluted religious history of the Stevenses is probably typical of most island families. From Dutch Reformed beginnings at Lunenburg in the eighteenth century, they proceeded to become Anglicans for two generations, and finally converted to Baptists by the late nineteenth century.[23] The Langilles followed a similar path of evolution from Anglicanism through Methodism to Baptist conversion.[24]

By the middle of the nineteenth century, the major fishing and boatbuilding families on Tancook were established settlers. Land records indicate that the pioneering Bakers and Crosses of 1797 were followed in short order from the Lunenburg mainland by the Slauenwhites (1801), Langilles (1807), Masons (1819),* Youngs (1823), Heislers (1824), Wilneffs (1826), Hutts (1828), Rodenhisers (1840) and, finally, the Stevenses (1848), last of the families whose story is closely tied to the maritime development of the island. The Levys (1827) arrived at Little Tancook from the Chester side of Mahone Bay during the same approximate period. Most of the first generation of settlers on the main island purchased twenty- or thirty-acre lots from the Bakers, including John David Langille, George Mason, George Heisler, and David Stevens, all progenitors of their lines on Tancook.[25] These and other island forefathers founded a population that grew from thirty families in 1829 to over sixty a generation later in 1861. In 1881, about the time they began to attract attention as a boatbuilding locale, the population of the Tancooks stood at 572, up slightly from ten years before. A period of major growth began shortly before the turn of the century. In 1911, at the start of the schooner era, the population of the two islands peaked at 733. Thereafter, it steadily fell, slowly until the 1920s and then more rapidly, until by 1941, near the end of the schooner-building period, the population was 543, about the same as fifty years earlier.[26]

CREATING A WAY OF LIFE

In 1829, Thomas Haliburton, Nova Scotia's first chronicler, observed that Tancook's inhabitants derived their subsistence "wholly from tilling the land."[27] Haliburton did not know that the island had acquired its first large sailing vessel two years before and was already looking seaward.[28] Yet in essence he was correct. That Tancook began

---

* Geneological sources place the arrival of this family on Tancook at about 1805-10, but no confirming land deeds have been found. (See PANS, CC, Lunenburg County: Canon E. A. Harris geneologies, Mason family.)

as an agricultural community was hardly surprising. A majority of the Foreign Protestant immigrants to Lunenburg County were peasant farmers, and most of the rest held occupations tied in one way or another to the land.[29] Those who migrated to Tancook Island were no exception, although a hint of their eventual skill as boatbuilders may be seen in the fact that the forebears of many of the Montbéliardians among them* had come from forest regions and been employed as lumbermen or wood workers.[30]

The initial migration to Tancook appears to have been solely motivated by agrarian pursuits. Early settlers at Lunenburg on the mainland exhibited no inclination toward fishing, and official correspondence suggests that the offshore islands of Mahone Bay were a desired objective of land-hungry farmers. In Winthrop Bell's view, at least, the islands' good soil and adaptability to animal raising (less need for fencing, for example) made them uniquely attractive.[31] Tancook Island, as it turned out, possessed excellent growing soil in selected areas, a fact not realized (or at least not commented upon) by its first surveyors, and within a decade of its occupation, farming was already well under way on the southwestern side of the island.[32]

Island life appealed particularly strongly to one group of Tancook settlers, the Montbéliardian Mason and Langille families. The original French settlers, as a group, had been settled at Northwest Range, several miles from Lunenburg township, on what one historian has described as inferior or poorly situated land.[33] Frederique Masson, who received lot 38 NW from the British authorities, was one of those presumably dissatisfied landholders. His son Pierre, at any rate, purchased what came to be known as Mason's Island, near Lunenburg's Back Harbour, and moved there in 1794. It was Pierre's son George who, in turn, went to Tancook a generation later. The family's figurative island hopping did not stop there. In 1828, George Mason, comfortably established at Tancook, bought the northern half of Flat Island, an islet less than two miles away. That new possession became a prime site for sheep raising, a major interest for some years to come.[34]

Tancook's exclusive preoccupation with planting and stock raising lasted for about a generation and was premised on an abundance of available farmland. The Tancooks and their associated islands encompassed roughly 1,500 acres, most of which was either arable or suit-

---

* Leopold Frederick Langille (1728–1817), from whom the Tancook Langilles descended, arrived in Nova Scotia in 1752 as a "joiner" and earned a subsequent reputation as a fine craftsman and maker of carpentry tools. (*Source*: PANS, CC, Lunenburg County: Canon E.A. Harris, geneologies, Langille family.)

able for pastures.[35] In 1861, islanders were keeping oxen, bulls, milk cows, pigs, and sheep; they were harvesting hay and apples, making butter, weaving wool cloth, and raising wheat, rye, barley, oats, peas, Indian corn, potatoes, turnips, and "other roots," including the eventual specialty, cabbage.[36] A more selective approach to farming gradually developed over the latter half of the nineteenth century. The Indian corn, rye, and wheat favoured by the first settlers were phased out, the growing of oats and barley declined, and apple harvesting disappeared. Potato production, however, increased nearly fivefold between 1861 and 1891, and hay production more than doubled over the same period. The planting of cabbage, turnips, and other root vegetables also increased, and animal products – wool and butter, for instance – saw phenomenal growth.[37]

Until the mid- to late nineteenth century, Tancook's agricultural richness and diversity permitted the island to largely ignore the sea that surrounded it. The subsistence farming of the first generation gave way to limited cash-cropping as specialization and increased production allowed for some selling to mainland markets. After 1870, sufficient excess crops were being harvested to support a fledgling coasting trade with Halifax. Large vessels from Chester, Lunenburg, and elsewhere began to call at the island to load native cabbage and other produce for distribution to city merchants.[38] Tancook's agricultural health was tenuous, however. It was based on sufficient good land, and as the population grew, that sufficiency diminished.

By the 1870s, the Tancooks had about reached the limits of their agricultural potential. The land under cultivation, which stood at 398 acres in 1861, reached 524 in 1871 but expanded only to 550 during the following decade, a rate of growth one third that of the population itself. On average, cultivated land increased from eight acres per owner in 1861 to nine acres in 1871, and then fell to seven acres in 1881. Aggregate land holdings shrank from twenty-three acres per capita in 1871 to under twenty acres ten years later. By 1881, furthermore, all the occupied land on the islands had been "improved" – cleared, broken up, or otherwise readied for utilization.[39]

This levelling off suggests that a natural barrier had been reached, and that was indeed the case. Instead of acquisition of new land, the subdivision of existing land became the rule. Succeeding generations had less land to work on an individual basis, as fathers were forced to parcel out family holdings to sons coming of age. The number of families sharing the same land grew by half between 1871 and 1911, and the number of houses nearly doubled,[40] necessitating radical adjustments from one generation to the next. Peter Mason was Tancook's largest landholder in 1871 with 110 acres, but he had five sons to claim an inheritance, and by the 1920s and 1930s, one of Peter's grandsons found himself in the position of having to borrow growing land for his cabbage crop and clear the lender's acreage in payment.[41]

Tancook's premium on land was expressed most clearly in the elaborate practices that evolved to govern its conferral and distribution. Although they varied from family to family, these practices were all premised on the understanding that there was not really enough acreage to go around. If just two sons claimed an inheritance, the land was usually apportioned equally, but the island's large nuclear families ordinarily precluded such a simple and obvious solution. As a rule, there were multiple needs to be satisfied or, if need be, deferred. Sometimes, several sons in a large family divided the landed wealth, while several others were left out of the equation entirely. In certain cases, one son – often the youngest – received most or all of a father's land, and his brothers got little or nothing. This was customary in the Langille clan, for example. In other instances, the process was reversed, so that one son in each generation was left landless in order to provide a more equitable division among his brothers. It was not uncommon among modestly affluent families for the youngest son to receive a monetary inheritance and his older brothers allotments of land. The tradition in the Mason family was that the youngest sibling "got the gold," while his elders inherited real estate. On occasion, joint ownership of land was practised, and brothers shared a common parcel of property in much the same way that they might hold joint shares in a fishing vessel.[42]

Whatever the precise formula of land division, however, the result was that an increasing number of islanders found themselves land poor as time passed. Many acquired just enough property to build a house, plant a garden, and raise a little hay for their animals. There was always the option of buying additional growing land, and some disinherited individuals did so, but that was a rare and increasingly difficult recourse.[43] As Tancook's first generation of occupants gave way to the second, and especially as the second gave way to the third, the realities of island life became clear. The occupation of farmer, so natural to people descended from European peasants, was not enough to sustain life on a small speck in the ocean. Other avenues had to be found, and Tancook's people, ever practical, turned to the sea round them.

On the mainland, the transition from husbandry to seafaring was estimated to have taken forty years, so that by 1790 Lunenburg was already emerging as a fishing port and vessel-building centre.[44] On Tancook, the process was delayed by the lure of island land, but was

15 The Setting

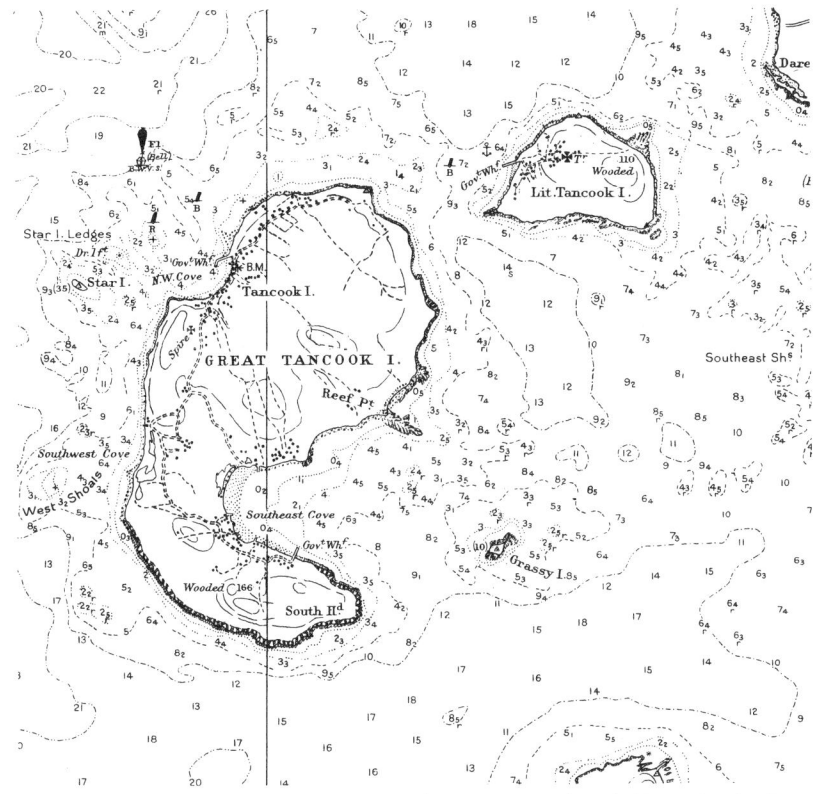

Map 2 Partial chart of Mahone Bay, NS, showing Big and Little Tancook islands and environs. (*Source*: Canadian Hydrographic Service)

well under way by the mid-nineteenth century. The number of islanders who called themselves "fishermen," rather than farmers or fisherman-farmers,* grew from a small minority in 1871 to include almost the entire male work force twenty years later.[45] Simultaneously, the number of watercraft owned at the Tancooks increased at a much

---

* Actual figures, as related to census enumerators, were as follows:

	1871		1881		1891	
Fishermen	27	(25%)	69	(46%)	141	(87%)
Fisherman/Farmers	56	(53)	44	(29)	0	(0)
Farmers	14	(13)	20	(13)	18	(11)
Other occupations	9	(9)	18	(12)	4	(2)
TOTAL	106	(100%)	151	(100%)	163	(100%)

(*Source*: Can.MsCen, 1871, 1881, 1891: Lunenburg County, Nova Scotia, town of Tancook, returns for population.)

faster rate than the growth in population. Between 1861 and 1911, the number of island residents grew by 93 percent (82 percent among males), while the number of fishing boats swelled by nearly 400 percent[46] – a startling indication of the evolution from a primarily agrarian to a predominantly maritime society and economy. In the process, Tancook's unique boatbuilding industry was born.

2 The Boats

> The Tancook boats are noted for their fine qualities, and the men
> for the ability with which they handle them in rough weather.
>
> Mather B. DesBrisay, historian of Lunenburg County, 1895

MYTHS AND ANTECEDENTS

There is no record of the very first boats built at Tancook, but it is certain that the initial settlers needed some form of watercraft, if only for occasional fishing close to shore or for periodic visits to the nearby mainland. The late Howard I. Chapelle speculated that these early craft were probably open skiffs of a double-ended design and lapstrake construction that were taken out to the island from around Lunenburg and later copied by the islanders themselves.[1] Be that as it may, there is no doubt that some rudimentary boatbuilding skills had developed at Tancook by 1827, when the first recorded vessel was built there.

Fittingly, this first register-sized* vessel, a 29-ton schooner, was a product of the Baker family, the island's original permanent occupants. Her builder was John Baker, a first-generation islander, who launched the appropriately named *Three Brothers* at Southeast Cove for himself, his brothers Jacob and Philip, and George Mason. *Three Brothers* was nothing like the sleek schooners for which Tancook later

---

* For an explanation of vessel registration, see note †, page 44.

became famous. She was a rather burdensome affair of blunt proportions, measuring 39'6" × 14' × 5'11" and incorporating carvel planking, a billet head, a square stern and a standing bowsprit – all typical of the type of vessel then in use on the mainland.[2] She does serve, however, to dismantle one longstanding myth associated with Tancook boatbuilding, namely that the first non-lapstrake boat produced there was built by Amos H. Stevens around the year 1900.[3]

The *Three Brothers* was followed by several other derivative island schooners of similar configuration but somewhat large size. First was the *Linnet* of 46 tons (46'4" × 15'7" × 7'4"), built by John Gasper Young at Northwest Cove in 1832 and sold the following year to Jacob Baker and George Mason, who had evidently relinquished their shares in the *Brothers*.[4] *Linnet* was replaced in 1843 a successor of the same name, built by Peter Mason, son of George, for himself, his father and Jacob Baker. This second *Linnet* (38 tons; 47.6' × 14.3' × 7.2') may not have been a success, for she was sold off the island two years later.[5] In 1845, a second Peter Mason-built schooner slid down the ways at Southeast Cove. Christened *Sandwich*, this vessel (31 tons; 50.3' × 15' × 6.9') was the first island boat of record to enter the offshore fisheries, collecting a provincial mackerel bounty in the summer of 1851 for her primary owner, skipper Peter Mason, and a crew of seven.[6] The final products of this first wave of Tancook-built schooners were the *Dolphin* (23 tons; 39.5' × 12.3' × 6.1'), constructed in 1848 by George Baker for himself and John Cross, and the *Patience* (42 tons; 49' × 15.8' × 8.3'), launched the same year for Frederick Slauenwhite of Northeast Cove, who was probably also the builder. The *Dolphin* was later sold (in 1850) to Peggy's Cove.[7]

The last of these early carvel-built and square-sterned schooners were disposed of shortly after 1850 – *Sandwich* was purchased by a Halifax merchant in 1853 – and almost no others of register size were produced at Tancook for the next half century.* That is not to suggest that Tancookers entirely gave up the ownership of large vessels. Shipping registers for the ports of Halifax and Lunenburg indicate that they did not. Islanders did, however, begin to purchase their vessels second hand on the mainland, starting with Walter Pearl's Mahone Bay-built *Isidore* in 1848 and Henry Hutt's Indian Point-built *Ostrich* in 1853.[8] This curious development had two possible explanations. Either the first generation of island builders were dissatisfied

---

* An exception was the 36-ton schooner *Daring* (58' × 17.4' × 7.5') built at Northwest Cove in 1872 by George Slauenwhite for his own use. (*See* NA, HalSR: register of schr *Daring*, 14 May 1872.)

with their handiwork or circumstances beyond their control curtailed their fledgling industry. Available evidence points strongly to the latter.

Tancook, as already mentioned, was once heavily wooded. The first surveyor's map of the island, prepared in 1788, noted that it was "in general good hardwood land" and contained substantial stands of beech, birch, and maple as well as smaller amounts of oak and ash.[9] A survey report, done on behalf of grantees Fleiger and Grant four years later, confirmed that observation and characterized both Great and Little Tancook as "all Wilderness Lands covered principally with hard Wood and a mixture of Spruce and Pine."[10] Yet the 1871 Dominion census described Tancook township as consisting of "five islands on which no timber grows."[11] In the interim settlement had taken place, and the once-abundant hardwood stands and pine clusters best suited to shipbuilding had been cut down. Thomas Mason, a long-time resident of Big Tancook, remembered that by his youth (post-1905), the island retained none of its original pine and very little usable hardwood. A few inferior birch trees could still be found and a handful of gnarled hackmatack survived in isolated swampy areas, but most of Tancook's remaining growth was softwood. The slow-burning hardwood, Mason thought, had been consumed as firewood prior to the age of coal stoves, leaving the fast-burning and therefore less desirable spruce.[12]

Whether the early settlers used up their prime timber for firewood or for boatbuilding and home construction, the fact is that by mid-century supplies had been depleted, and the ability of islanders to turn out large sailing vessels using local resources had been seriously circumscribed. The importation of sawn lumber, a solution resorted to in the early twentieth century,[13] appears not to have occurred to the first generation of island builders or (more probably) was limited to the purchase of lesser and cheaper amounts of wood suitable to the construction of small craft. At any rate, it was not until the early 1900s that vessels large enough to warrant government register were once more being built at the Tancooks in significant number. Throughout the intervening half century, island boatbuilders continued to pursue their art, but their efforts were now geared to producing classes of in-shore fishing boats of limited size that eventually included the fabled Tancook whaler.

The first small craft built in substantial numbers at Tancook, however, were somewhat prosaic and rather unremarkable. These were the so-called "lobster" or "jolly" boats that preceded the more famous whalers by perhaps a generation and were used for general fishing and lobstering close to shore. It is thought that they descended from a ship's yawl-boat of the type hung from stern davits.* Alfred Langille, a renowned island builder, began his professional career by repairing one such boat that had been inadvertently damaged when its mother vessel visited nearby Ironbound Island. Langille, the story goes, rebuilt the badly wrecked craft in the loft of his fish store near Southeast Cove beach and thereby initiated small boat building on Tancook.[14] Since Langille was born in 1839,[15] this first boat would probably have been completed around 1860, by which time there were already eighty small fishing boats of some description owned at the Tancooks.[16] It is fairly certain, therefore, that small craft construction at the islands antedated Alfred Langille's first boat by a number of years, and that jolly boats as a class dated back to at least 1850, if not earlier.

Although there is uncertainty about its origins on Tancook, there is no disagreement about the jolly boat's general appearance. It was an open lapstrake or clinker-built rowing and sailing craft of 18' to 20' overall length and 6-foot beam, incorporating a small forward cuddy and drawing 18" of water. To compensate for extreme shallowness, it normally came equipped (in later years) with a centreboard, and it possessed a removable sloop rig for working under sail. The rig consisted of a short portable mast with gaff mainsail and jib attached, which was set in a hole through a forward seat or thwart and held in place by a jib-stay extending from its top to the boat's stemhead. When not in use, the rig was collapsed (gaff and boom folded against the mast and sails furled around it), unshipped, and stored in dory fashion. The bow of the jolly boat was characterized by a straight, nearly upright stem having less rake than that of a dory but sufficient to avoid the appearance of tumble-home. The stern was a wide, almost vertical transom type that accommodated an outboard rudder.[17]

The jolly boat's signature transom stern was said to be similar to the one on the ship's boat repaired by Alfred Langille,[18] and that fact may clarify Langille's role in its development. It is quite possible that doubled-ended craft of the sort described by Chapelle (see page 17) were the original island boats, and that Alfred Langille simply introduced a transom stern about 1860, thus altering the design and creat-

---

* Howard I. Chapelle provides plans for a typical yawl-boat of the period and for a sailing variation of the type that developed in Newfoudland prior to 1870. Both closely resemble verbal descriptions of Tancook's jolly or lobster boat. (*See* Chapelle, *American Small Sailing Craft*, 222–4.)

ing the jolly boat's final form.* Langille himself, though primarily a builder, was known to have maintained one of these boats for his own use in inshore halibut fishing.[19] His innovation of a wider stern would have made that and similar work considerably easier by providing more space within a given set of dimensions. It is probable that this later type of jolly boat, along with assorted smaller skiffs and dories, formed the bulk of the 96 boats owned at the Tancooks in 1871 and operated by individual fishermen working alone. There were, however, sixteen other boats under register size operated by two men each.[20] These, it would seem, represented the first recorded appearance of the successor to the jolly boat, the larger and better-known Tancook whaler.

THE MYSTERY OF THE TANCOOK WHALER

The origin of the Tancook whaler, a subject of endless fascination, has spawned numerous popular and scholarly articles and at least one book.[21] It has also been mired in controversy and beset by myth and misinformation. The physical appearance of this particular small sailing craft has enthralled generations of marine historians, yacht designers, and boat lovers in general. From its stately clipper bow and sharply raking sternpost to its lapstrake construction and fine lines, the double-ended whaler has always exuded character. Its very name carries an aura of romance. Yet, it was essentially an unpretentious work boat with a very natural evolution rooted in geography and environment.

Several theories have been advanced to explain the beginnings of the Tancook whaler. Its supposed lineal ancestors have included the Viking longship, the New England pinky, and the rowing whaleboat.[22] The first of these deserves little comment and can be dismissed out of hand: transient Norse visitors to North America antedated the era of the Tancook whaler by a thousand years and left no material record of their vessels known to nineteenth-century Nova Scotians. The latter two theories of whaler development, however, warrant serious consideration.

---

* The combination of a squat, sharply turned transom stern of the jolly boat type with lapstrake planking was considered difficult construction on Tancook, much more so than double-ender work. (*Source*: Interview, Thomas Mason, 15 June 1989.) The mastery of this tricky procedure may well have been the original source of Alfred Langille's subsequent reputation as a builder.

The presumed relationship between the pinky and the Tancook whaler is premised, first, on their superficial similarity as clipper-bowed and schooner-rigged double-enders and, second, on the fact that numerous pinkies found their way into Maritime waters during the course of the nineteenth century.[23] There is no doubt that pinkies from Maine and Massachusetts traversed the Nova Scotian coast on their way to the Labrador and Gulf of St Lawrence fishing grounds. Several of them were observed passing through the Strait of Canso in late August 1852, for example.[24] There is also no doubt that the pinky was avidly copied by Canadian builders, especially in the vicinity of Yarmouth and on the Nova Scotia side of the Bay of Fundy.[25] However, there is no evidence that the pinky had any meaningful impact in and around Lunenburg County, where the Tancook whaler developed.

An examination of the 56 recorded building sites of pink-sterned vessels launched in Nova Scotia between 1830 and 1849 indicates that only 2 were located in Lunenburg County (while there were 12 in Halifax County, 9 in Guysborough County, 7 in Shelburne County, and 6 in Digby County). Over one third of the total were situated along the province's Eastern Shore, well beyond Halifax, while nearly one quarter were on the Bay of Fundy. Those scattered along the South Shore were mainly found toward the Yarmouth end of the coast.[26] Closer examination of the Halifax registers for the period 1843 to 1847, when that city's customs officials still registered most Nova Scotian vessels (including those from around Lunenburg), reveals that of the 89 large pink-sterned schooners entered during those five years, only 2 had been launched in Lunenburg County.* The majority (46 or 52 percent) had been built on the Eastern Shore and most of the remainder (31 or 35 percent) at the extreme western end of the South Shore or on the Fundy Coast.[27]

The twin heartlands of double-ender construction in the province during the 1830s and 1840s were the region between Owl's Head and the Bay of Islands east of Halifax – roughly the middle third of the Eastern Shore – and the region between Cape Sable and Lockeport in western Shelburne County, both of which were seventy-five to a hundred miles from Tancook Island. It is unlikely, therefore, that Tancookers had much contact with Nova Scotia's pinky builders during the first half of the nineteenth century, when the pinky reached

---

* One at Lunenburg in 1830, and one at New Dublin in 1846. By way of comparison, the two leading sites, Barrington and Sheet Harbour, built 12 and 10 pinkies, respectively.

the peak of its development. Furthermore, the comparative dimensions of the archtypical pinky – particularly the 1 to 3 or 1 to 3.5 beam-length ratio commonly found among those provincial pinks built prior to 1850[28] – make a transfer of influence improbable. The typical Tancook whaler, as Howard I. Chapelle and others have pointed out (and as register data confirms), had a much more svelte 1 to 4 ratio.[29]

Other differences are evident as well. The whaler did not incorporate the true pink stern, which was characterized by an artificial extension of the bulwarks out over the sternpost so as to create the illusion of an inboard rudder. Nor did the bald whaler clipper bow carry billets, gammon-knees, scrollheads, trailboards, or other appurtenances usually found on pinky bows. Moreover, the loose-footed, overlapping foresail characteristic of the whaler's schooner sail plan was rarely featured in the pinky, which historically favored a boom-foresail. Finally, the pinky had no centreboard, a critical component of whaler design.[30] The pinky was, at best, a very distant relative of the Tancook whaler.

A more plausible case for whaler ancestry can be made on behalf of the whaleboat. There is, first of all, the name, although that forms a very tenuous connection. No whaling was done at Tancook Island, and very little in Nova Scotia as a whole. However, two short-lived whaling colonies were established in the province during the eighteenth century by migrating New Englanders from Nantucket and Cape Cod, first at Barrington near Cape Sable in 1762 and then at Dartmouth on the eastern side of Halifax harbor in 1785.[31] The Dartmouth venture, the more successful of the two, lasted only seven years before being transferred to Milford Haven in Wales, but that would have been long enough to introduce the New England whaleboat, which by then had nearly reached its final form,[32] to the coastal region around Halifax.

As was the case with the pinky, there were superficial similarities between New England whaleboats and Tancook whalers. Both were double-enders powered by sail and oar, and the whaleboat, like the whaler, was noted for speed, seaworthiness, and fine lines. In addition, the sailing qualities of the whaleboat were improved around 1850 by the installation of two whaler-like features: a centreboard and (to replace the steering oar) an outboard rudder.[33] However, Nova Scotia's brief flirtation with whaling had long since ended by that time, and these later technical refinements would have been unknown to local builders. There also remains the problem of beam-length ratios, 1 to 5 in the case of whaleboats.[34] If the pinky was too wide and burdensome to father the whaler, the whaleboat was too narrow (and too shallow). Dissimilarities also appear in the area of construction – lapstrake planking for the original whalers, carvel (or combined lapstrake and carvel) for whaleboats – and in the area of rigging. Whaleboats, unlike either whalers or pinkies, carried single-masted rigs featuring lug or sprit sails.[35] In sum, a whaleboat heritage for the Tancook whaler is extremely unlikely.

Still, there remains an intriguing historical reference to muddy the waters. In partial answer to a letter from M.H. Perley requesting information on Nova Scotia's fishing industry, John E. Fairbanks, a Halifax fish merchant, wrote on November 18, 1850: "The shore or boat fishery, is carried on to a greater or lesser extent, along our whole coast. Whale-boats manned by two or four men, and large sail boats, undecked are used."[36] It is tempting to interpret Fairbanks' reference to "whale-boats" literally, but an observation by Howard I. Chapelle gives pause. The name "pinky," he cautioned, was often loosely applied in Maine to any sharp-sterned boat, whether or not it had a true pink stern.[37] Could not the same have been true of the term "whaler" or "whaleboat" in Nova Scotia?*

The dilemma presented by the Fairbanks letter brings us full circle back to Chapelle's informed opinion that the Tancook whaler did, indeed, descend from a craft called a whaleboat, but one of a decidedly different character. The Tancook boat, Chapelle theorized, was probably based on the so-called Hampton boat developed in the Seabrook-Hampton district of coastal New Hampshire.[38] The Hampton boat, also known as the Hampton whaler (and eventually, in Canada, as the Labrador boat or whaler) – a suggestion of its own possible whaleboat origins – was a partially decked, clinker-built double-ender of sharp design measuring up to 23' overall. It carried a ketch or schooner rig, with or without jib, and was used extensively in New England's nineteenth-century Labrador cod fishery, wherein schooners anchored in coves or harbours and pursued their quarry from small boats (the Hamptons) that were often sold at the end of the season to local Canadian fishermen.[39] George Brown Goode and Joseph W. Collins, writing in the 1880s, elaborated on the involved nomenclature associated with these small craft:

The vessels of the Labrador fleet always carried four or five boats of the pattern now generally known as the "Hampton" boat, but about Newburyport

---

* Mather DesBrisay used the terms "whale-boats" and "whalers" interchangeably when describing fishing boats operating near West Ironbound Island at the mouth of the La Have River in the summer of 1879. (*Source*: DesBrisay, *County of Lunenburg*, 236.)

25 The Boats

still known as the "Labrador" boat. These boats were made at Seabrook, NH, and were often called whale-boats.[40]

Chapelle presents a set of plans for one of these Hampton whalers, and except for the absence of a clipper bow and centreboard, its resemblance to his published lines and sail arrangement for a fully developed Tancook whaler is striking.[41] Provided that Nova Scotia fishermen from the Lunenburg area visited the Labrador coast during the prescribed period, there would seem to be little question that the New Hampshire craft was, as Chapelle believed, the missing link in Tancook whaler chronology. And, in fact, they did.

American schooners first went to Labrador waters for cod in 1794, and their employment of Hampton-type boats or whalers can be documented as early as 1833.[42] By about 1850, fishermen from Nova Scotia, New Brunswick, and Newfoundland were also on the Labrador grounds in substantial numbers and, like their American counterparts, carried on the fishery "entirely in boats."[43] Prominent in the provincial fleet were schooners from Lunenburg. Lunenburg's participation actually began shortly after the start of the century, and its Labrador enterprise was already the most important aspect of the town's fishing industry by the mid-1820s. This continued for the next half-century, and the northern fishery lost its dominant position only with the onset of offshore banks trawling in the 1870s.[44]

It appears that Lunenburg's boatbuilders became acquainted with the Hampton whaler early in the nineteenth century. They probably purchased some used whalers at Labrador from American fishermen, took them to Lunenburg, and copied them locally. Over time, native versions evolved and coalesced into a stock type. The final form may be judged from a set of lines and a sail plan provided by Howard I. Chapelle that show the Labrador whaler as it was built in Lunenburg County after 1890. The plans, drawn by Chapelle in the 1940s,[45] apparently represent a larger version of the whaler designed for local inshore fishing rather than for carrying aboard vessels.* They show, therefore, the type of whaler most likely to have influenced Tancook Island builders. To an even greater degree than its predecessor, the Hampton boat, Chapelle's Labrador whaler bore a close resemblance to the Tancook whaler of the same period. The two-masted rig with

---

* The Chapelle whaler measures nearly 24' in overall length, while those carried aboard Lunenburg's Labrador schooners during the nineteenth century were said to average just 17' overall. In the early 1880s, all boats built at Lunenburg for the Labrador fishery were well under 22' in length. (*Sources*: Hewitt, "History of Lunenburg County," 71; LP, news item, 31 May 1881, 2.)

loose-footed foresail,* the outboard rudder mounted on a sharply raked sternpost, the lapstrake construction and boiler plate centreboard (an apparent later innovation of the Lunenburg builders), and the fine entrance and hollow stern lines all militate in favour of a Tancook connection. Most of all, the Labrador whaler's 1 to 4 beam-length ratio makes it the only regional small craft of the time to approximate the proportions of the Tancook whaler.

The sheer number of Labrador whalers built at Lunenburg suggests that Tancook Islanders must have been aware of them, particularly since they frequented the town's outfitting merchants for fishing supplies from as early as the 1850s.[46] In 1881, well after the Labrador fishery had passed its peak, a report on local boatbuilding activity indicated that during the first five months of that year, eighty-seven standard-sized whalers were produced for the northern cod fleet by the seven Lunenburg firms specializing in that work,† accounting for more than a third of the total value of all small craft constructed in the town. In an ironic turnabout, it was Lunenburg-built whalers that were now in demand on the Labrador coast, and their rapid sale at the end of each fishing season provided a steady stimulus to the industry. "Our boats have evidently acquired a reputation for being well built [and] of sound material" wrote a local observer.[47]

This report on small boatbuilding at Lunenburg provides a further clue to the origin of the Tancook whaler. In addition to supplying the 1881 Labrador fleet, the town's builders turned out a half dozen craft described as "large whalers." These ranged from 22' to 25' long and were specifically intended for local inshore fishing. They did not apparently have centreboards, since one builder distinguished them from a 20' "centreboarder" also constructed, but they otherwise appear to have been closely related to the Chapelle whaler of post-1890 with its optional board.[48]

Ernest A. Bell, whose 1933 article in *Yachting* magazine spurred modern interest in Tancook whalers, maintained that these large Labrador whalers, reaching up to 30' in length and carrying a ketch

---

* The loose-footed foresail was a direct inheritance from the Hampton whaler. Naturalist John J. Audubon, who saw the Hamptons at work off Labrador in 1833, described them as rigged with "lugsails," a term that did not refer to European style dipping lugs with yards but rather to loose-footed sails. Chapelle defines the phrases "lug-fashion" or "lug-footed" as being synonymous in early America with "boomless." (Sources: Audubon, *By Himself*, 228; Chapelle, *American Small Sailing Craft*, 14, 21, 131.)

† A year later, in 1882, the Lunenburg Labrador fleet of 26 schooners carried no fewer than 160 double-enders to northern waters. (Sources: PANS, Bus, Zwicker Coll., MS 129: Export and Clearance of Fish Book, 1882–86, unidentified newspaper clipping for 1882.)

rig, were the basis for the Tancook model.[49] The subsequent career of one of Lunenburg's Labrador whaler builders of 1881 seems to confirm that judgment. Edward Conrad, who with John Anderson was responsible for eighteen of the Labrador boats launched in the winter and spring of that year,[50] emerged a quarter century later as one of the primary builders of a class of exceptionally large "Tancook whalers" produced at Lunenburg. Between 1903 and 1906, Conrad turned out four double-enders of 42' to 48' overall length, including the *Hazel R.*, whose photograph both Chapelle and Robert C. Post have used to represent the general appearance of the Tancook boats.[51] In fact, these large, somewhat burdensome craft were not typical of the final Tancook product and should more properly be categorized as "Lunenburg whalers."* Nevertheless, they present the clearest available evolutionary link between the whalers built at Lunenburg for the Labrador fishery and those later built at Tancook Island for inshore fishing.

The Tancook whaler, then, appears to have indeed descended from the whaleboat, but indirectly and several times removed. Its lineage can be traced from the presumably whaleboat-inspired Hampton whalers of New England through the Labrador whalers carried aboard Lunenburg cod fishing vessels to the larger Labrador-type whalers built at Lunenburg for the general inshore fisheries and, finally, to Tancook Island. The appeal of the Hampton-Labrador model on Tancook is not hard to understand. As Chapelle pointed out with respect to the New Hampshire version, it was a type that could be beached, and that accounted for its popularity among Canadian shore fishermen.[52] Indeed, his drawing of the Lunenburg County Labrador whaler of post-1890 shows a craft that drew just 18" with its board up – no more than the early Tancook jolly boats. Tancook Island, which lacked protected anchorages and was surrounded by shoal water, needed boats that could lie as close to the cover of land as possible when in use and be easily hauled ashore if necessary.

Precisely when and under what circumstances Tancook whalers first appeared on the island has always been a vexing question, but as will be seen, there is little doubt that its basic design came from Lunenburg. Chapelle concluded as much from interviews conducted

---

* Conrad's four Lunenburg whalers were *Hattie*, 1903 (12 tons; 44.4' × 12.3' × 5.7'); *Ellwood*, 1905 (16 tons; 48.5' × 13.5' × 6.1'); *Anita*, 1905 (16 tons; 48.6' × 13.5' × 6.1'); and *Hazel R.*, 1906 (11 tons; 42' × 11.2' × 5.1') (*Source*: NA, LunSR: registers of Schrs *Hattie*, 23 June 1903; *Ellwood*, 13 April 1905; *Anita*, 11 April 1905; and *Hazel R.*, 27 January 1916). *Anita's* published lines (*See* Post, *Tancook Whalers*, 27) show a much fuller body plan and less hollow run than was usual for a true Tancook whaler. However, the general family resemblance is obvious.

on Tancook in the late 1940s, and although unable to establish a specific year or builder of origin, he settled on the decade 1860–70 as the period of its probable introduction from the mainland.[53] More recently, doubts have been raised about Chapelle's determination of a Lunenburg genesis,[54] while explicit claims have been made on behalf of particular builders. At least one writer has credited Amos H. Stevens, a whaler builder of considerable eventual reputation, as being the "father" of the Tancook whaler.[55] Others have pointed with equal certainty to Alfred F. Langille as the originator of the type and to 1880 as the approximate year.[56] The latest formal investigation by Robert C. Post remains cautiously vague about the date of introduction, placing it anywhere from 1840* to 1880, but states categorically that "nobody disputes that the first whaler built on Tancook was the handiwork of Alfred Langille."[57]

Fortunately, Tancook's oral tradition resolves the question of Lunenburg origins and settles the matter of builders and dates in fairly definitive fashion. According to a story related to Howard Mason by his father, Joshua, one of the original whaler builders on Tancook, and passed down to succeeding generations,† the first Tancook whaler was actually produced by John Crooks and a member of the Baker family, who obtained the design from observation in Lunenburg and duplicated it on the island.[58] The date is uncertain, as is the precise identification of one of the building partners, whose name was rendered only as "old man Baker," but both may be inferred with some precision.

The Baker in question was undoubtedly John George Baker (b. ca. 1805–07), known as "Hulty George" because of his predilection for loud talking or hollering (and to distinguish him, island fashion, from other Tancookers of the same name). George Baker was an established fisherman and boatbuilder, having launched the square-stern schooner *Dolphin* in 1848, and he lived into the 1890s, an important consideration in that Howard Mason (1874–1953) knew the elderly builder in his youth and referred to him familiarly as "old man" Baker. Furthermore, Baker's daughter, Adelaide, was married to John Crooks, and in-law relationships on Tancook often carried over into other aspects of island life, including the economic. It is quite prob-

---

* This early date is based on the assumption that Alfred Langille built the first whaler and that he was born in 1821 rather than 1839, as was actually the case.

† Unlike many island tales attributing credit for historic firsts to various individuals, this one earns special credibility from the fact that it makes no family claim on behalf of a relative or ancestor.

able that George Baker, whose home served as the setting for the wedding ceremony, worked with his new son-in-law to produce the first Tancook whaler.

John Crooks (b. 1836) was twenty-four years old when he married Adelaide Baker in the summer of 1860, and given his age, it is unlikely that he engaged in boatbuilding much before that time. The first of his surname to settle on the island, Crooks moved there from the mainland town of La Have shortly before his marriage. If his father-in-law was indeed his building partner, that partnership almost certainly developed following the union of the two families, and the first Tancook whaler, therefore, was not built before 1860. The most plausible date would seem to fall between 1865 and 1870, when John Crooks was entering his mature middle years and George Baker remained young enough to perform physical labour. This chronology is reinforced by Crooks' first recorded purchase of Tancook land, which took place in 1865.[59]

In any case, the Tancook whaler was not a unique Tancook Island design, but an adaptation of the large Labrador whaler then being constructed on the mainland. It is not known what precise stage of evolution the whaler had reached when it came to Tancook. Chapelle suggested that the boats were 24' to 28' long with a cuddy and some decking.[60] They may or may not have had centreboards. The early Labrador boats were without boards, and some Tancook whalers – the first ones according to one source – also lacked this feature.[61] It is possible that the centreboard was a Tancook innovation, but just as possible that it originated with the Lunenburg whaler builders and migrated to the island. Certainly, the installation of a board made sense from the Tancook perspective. It allowed island builders to gradually enlarge their boats for offshore work, while retaining the relatively shallow draft that permitted rowing, beaching, and ease of hauling.

The nature of the first Tancook whaler rig, like the use of centreboards, is unclear. Some large Labrador whalers built at Lunenburg may have dispensed with their original sprit-sail, cat-ketch rig in favour of a schooner arrangement with headsail by the time Crooks and Baker brought the design to the island. One possibility is that the installation of centreboards and the adoption of the schooner rig were related developments. The extra stability provided by a board would have been necessary to accommodate the powerful rig – large jib, overlapping lug foresail, gaff mainsail, and fisherman staysail – eventually seen on the Tancook whaler. The inspiration for that rig, assuming it evolved on Tancook, may well have been the memory of the earlier island schooners of the 1830s and 1840s. In any event, the large schooners of the contemporary Lunenburg vessel fleet would have provided ample precedent for Tancook sailmakers.

The question remains of how the Tancook whaler acquired the graceful, unadorned clipper bow that was perhaps its most admired and distinguishing characteristic. The Labrador whaler, after all, was a straight-stem craft, as was the Hampton whaler that preceded it. So, too, was the Tancook jolly boat. Chapelle is vague on the subject, suggesting in one instance that the clipper bow simply "developed" over time,[62] and in another that "the Tancook model is reputed to have had a bald clipper bow from the first."[63] Traditional boatbuilding terminology on Tancook provides the answer and reveals a subtle British influence on the design of what was in most ways a typically North American craft. Among Tancook Islanders, a clipper bow of the sort found on the Tancook whaler was universally known as an "Aberdeen stem."[64]

The Aberdeen was a very particular type of clipper bow that was formed not by a shaped knee and other supporting timbers superimposed on an essentially straight stem, but by the stem itself curving sharply outward in a hollow sweep followed by the hull planking or rabbet line. It was created in Aberdeen, Scotland, in 1839 as a way to alter register measurements in order to reduce taxable tonnage while at the same time improving sailing qualities. During the 1840s, the design gradually spread throughout the British Isles among builders of fast sailing ships, particularly tea clippers, and eventually found its way abroad.[65] David R. MacGregor, who chronicled its development, has discovered examples of the Aberdeen bow as far afield as northern Europe and North America. In the 1850s, it appeared in Nova Scotia. The bark *Stag* of Halifax, built at La Have in 1854, exhibited what MacGregor calls "an extreme form of Aberdeen bow adopted by some copyists."[66]

The *Stag*, a vessel noted for fast passages, was the work of Ebenezer Moseley, whose yard on the La Have River near Bridgewater operated from 1853 to 1864 and produced everything from merchant barks and brigantines to fishing schooners and yachts.[67] The Moseley yard was not far from either Lunenburg township or Tancook Island, and the reputation and appearance of its Aberdeen-bowed vessels, including the record-breaking *Stag*, would have been well known to marine interests throughout Lunenburg County. Contemporary ship paintings suggest that other regional builders also adopted the British fashion in vessel design during the 1850s. A rendering by Halifax artist John O'Brien of the highly regarded brigantine *Ocean Bride* (built at Chester by Herbert Young in 1854 and owned there until 1857) shows a sharply raked, Aberdeen-type bow.[68] The village of Chester was at Tancook's very doorstep.

Gradually, after 1854, the Aberdeen bow was modified by alterations in British vessel tonnage laws, and by the mid-1860s, it had evolved into the standard clipper bow of the late nineteenth century.[69] In the meantime, however, there seems little doubt that the original form, with its long, flaring overhangs, was copied in miniature by boatbuilders in Lunenburg County, changing the profile of some larger version of the Labrador whaler to resemble what we now know as the Tancook whaler.* This was the first instance of large vessel design influencing Tancook's small craft; it would not be the last.

THE FIRST GENERATION

It is possible that the introduction of the Aberdeen stem took place on Tancook itself, rather than on the mainland, and that this design feature eventually found its way back to Lunenburg, along with the centreboard and schooner rig, to be incorporated in the Lunenburg whaler of later years – a kind of reverse pollination. If that was indeed the case, there can be no doubt that Alfred F. Langille (1839–1926) was the man primarily responsible. Langille, called "Gaundy" (a child's corruption of "grandfather"), was a revered, almost mythic, figure on the island, and his name is more closely associated than any other with the beginnings of whaler building there. He was Tancook's wood worker nonpareil, a man who excelled as a lathe operator and built houses, furniture, and burial caskets as well as boats.[70] His skill and versatility can still be seen in the scrollwork that decorates his former home at Southeast Cove, as well as in numerous Victorian chairs and spool beds that survive in scattered South Shore locales. But it was as a builder of boats that Alfred Langille earned his most enduring fame. He was Tancook's first professional boatbuilder,† the first to construct fishing craft for other islanders. He also initiated off-island contracting and is known to have built whalers on the mainland, around Chester, on that basis.[71] Since he lived across Southeast Cove from John Crooks, the supposition is that Langille observed the launch of the first primitive island whaler, copied and improved on it, refined its distinct look, and became the chief builder of the type.[72]

---

* MacGregor cites two distinguishing hallmarks that set the original Aberdeen bow apart. These were the rake of the stem, which leaned forward at a 50° angle, and the curve of the stem rabbet, which followed the exact profile of the stem. Both features were faithfully reproduced in the Tancook whaler bow, as an examination of existing plans and photographs makes clear. (*Source:* MacGregor, *Tea Clippers*, 43, 46.)

† In 1871, at the start of the whaler era, Langille gave his occupation to Lovell's provincial directory as "boat builder," the only Tancook resident to claim that trade. (*Source: Nova Scotia Directory for 1871*, 20.)

Altogether, there were five primary island builders of the Tancook whaler in the latter third of the nineteenth century. Besides Alfred Langille,* they were Joshua Mason, Amos Stevens, Alvin Stevens, and (on Little Tancook) Henry Levy.[73] Among the five, Joshua Mason (1845–1924), known as "Old Bluff" due to his brusque manner, was Alfred Langille's closest contemporary in terms of age and probably the second man on Tancook to take up whaler building extensively. Like Langille, he worked on the Southeast Cove (or back) side of the island, where whaler construction began, and built his boats in a small shed attached to his barn on the family homestead. Langille maintained a separate shop nearer the shore below his house. Amos H. Stevens (1850–1935) and his brother Alvin G. Stevens (1864–1920), who started somewhat later, came to dominate whaler building on the Northwest Cove (or front) side of Tancook. Their adjacent shops were located below the main road just beyond the cove, along a section of the island known as "Backalong." Henry Levy (b. ca. 1872), youngest of the major builders, worked near the main settlement of Little Tancook.[74]

These respective geographic locations, especially those on the larger island, had a marked impact on Tancook boat design and construction over the next generation or so. Distinct differences emerged between the builders of Southeast and Northwest coves and their boats. The former, comparatively isolated and facing seaward, were more insular and slower to change. Whatever external influences affected their work came from the direction of Lunenburg, and after the initial introduction of the Labrador whaler, these were relatively few. The Northwest Cove builders, on the other hand, possessing (until 1908) the island's only public landing and facing the nearer mainland, were more exposed to outside influences and new ideas, particularly from the yachting and resort centre of Chester. At least until World War I, this quirk of geography meant that innovations generally originated on the northwest side of Tancook and then gradually spread to the other, more conservative side of the island.

Nevertheless, at the very beginning of the whaler period, the reverse was true. A possibly apocryphal tale, yet one with a certain ring of truth, relates how whaler building migrated from Southeast Cove, where it began, to the opposite side of Tancook. According to the story, one of Amos Stevens' brothers, a fisherman at Northwest Cove, needed a whaler and proposed that Alfred Langille build it. At the last moment, he and Amos, who was an aspiring builder, decided to

---

* Among the minor whaler builders was Langille's brother Benjamin (1843–1918), who turned out a few double-enders at his farmstead near Southeast Cove. (*Sources*: Interview, Benjamin Heisler, 22 June 1989; Langille, *South Shore Langilles*, 48.)

save money by doing the job themselves. Since they had never built a whaler, and since Alfred Langille had one under construction, they entered his shop surreptitiously to examine the work in progress, take measurements, and learn how the older man carried out certain techniques. Too proud to ask openly for help, the brothers gained access to the locked shop at night through a window and obtained the rudimentary knowledge that launched Amos Stevens on his career as a builder. However, a Langille neighbour* saw the brothers and their lantern and later told of the incident.[75]

If this story is true, the affair probably took place in 1876 or 1877, following Amos Stevens' return from living in Halifax and after his brief sojourn on Flat Island in Mahone Bay. Stevens married at Tancook in 1870 and moved with his wife and son a year or so later to Halifax, where he worked for a time as a teamster hauling glass. Family tradition relates that he engaged in a fight one evening and fled the city to avoid involvement with the police. This was not before 1875 because Stevens registered the births of twin daughters in Halifax in January of that year. Upon his return to Tancook, he went to live on Flat Island off Southeast Cove, presumably for lack of available housing on the main island and perhaps also to put further distance between himself and the Halifax constabulary.† He remained there for thirteen months, returning in mid-1876 at the earliest but certainly prior to late 1877 when another daughter was recorded as being born on Tancook. Stevens family sources agree that Amos Stevens' career as a builder began shortly thereafter and that his first effort was a whaler.[76]

Beyond its value as an entertaining morality play, the Langille-Stevens affair points up one of the interesting features of Tancook boatbuilding, the manner in which technical knowledge was obtained and transmitted. Almost none of the island's first generation of whaler builders could depend on great reservoirs of previously accu-

---

* The neighbour was Amos Stevens' uncle Edward Stevens (1832–90), who lived next door to Alfred Langille and was married to Langille's sister. His son Charles told the story some years later to Emery Mason, a grandson of Joshua Mason and Alfred Langille, from whom it passed to other members of the Mason family. There is more than one version of this incident, another being that Edward Stevens merely saw a light in Langille's shop and inquired the next day as to why he was working so late. Since Langille was not, in fact, working, he investigated and learned the truth. (For relationships, see Stevens and Stevens, *Stevens Familes of Nova Scotia*, 78, 89–90, and Langille, *South Shore Langilles*, 48.)

† Amos Stevens' wife was Augusta Mason, whose father, Peter, owned Flat Island. An alternative explanation of Stevens' return to Tancook holds that he was fired from his Halifax job for fighting and left the city for that reason, not for fear of the police. A lack of living space at the family homestead then dictated the move to Flat Island. (*Source*: Interview, Perry W. Stevens, 2 October 1989.)

mulated learning. Instead, they depended to a remarkable degree on their own resources.

As far as is known, only Joshua Mason, whose father Peter (1813–97) had been among the early builders of square-sterned schooners on Tancook, started with the advantage of a family heritage in boatbuilding. Yet even he was only three years old when the last of the island's first group of large schooners was launched in 1848, and only eight when his father's last vessel was sold. Alfred Langille, the dean of Tancook's whaler builders, must have been naturally gifted and largely self-taught, for there is no record or tradition that his father, John David, was a builder. Like Joshua Mason, he was very young when the last of the early carvel schooners were launched. Likewise, Amos Stevens' father was not a known builder. Amos learned, furtively if we are to accept island tradition, from Alfred Langille, and then taught his younger brother Alvin.

Sailmaking developed in much the same manner. Islanders initially cut and sewed their own canvas.* Joshua Mason and Benjamin Langille were among the early builders said to have made suits of sails for their boats.[77] As building activity increased, however, specialization in this work became a practical necessity. Joseph Pearl (b. 1845), a sometime fisherman and cobbler of the same generation as the original whaler builders, was Tancook's first professional sailmaker. Apparently self-taught, he eventually made most of the sails for the boats on the northwest side of the island, including those of Amos Stevens. He later passed his skills on to Stevens' son Randolph.[78]

The spontaneous nature of Tancook's early boatbuilding industry explains much about why the building of the island's whalers proceeded as it did. All authorities agree – and available photographic evidence supports them – that until their last years, the Tancook whalers were universally clinker-built or lapstrake planked.[79] At first glance, this seems an anomaly, since register data indicates that the island schooners built between 1827 and 1848 were without exception carvel-built.[80] However, nearly a generation separated those carvel schooners from the first whalers, and the memory of earlier construction methods appears to have dimmed. The whaler builders must have relied on Labrador whaler techniques borrowed from Lunenburg and from what they had learned or devised building the smaller lapstrake jolly boats.

---

* This tradition never completely died. As late as 1933, fisherman Willis Crooks of Southeast Cove sewed the sails for his new schooner *Gerald L. C.* (*Source*: Interview, Thomas Mason, 1 October 1989.)

Photo 1   Schooners racing off Northwest Cove, Big Tancook, in the summer of 1911, during the annual Mahone Bay fishermen's regatta. The photo was probably taken from a large observer vessel, and the immediate backdrop is that part of Tancook known as "Backalong." The Aspotogan Peninsula appears in the distance. On the far left of the island, partially hidden by a small bluff, are the Amos and Alvin Stevens boat shops, and in the center-right of the picture is the island's main government wharf. Several fish houses are scattered along the shore, and a number of schooners, some of them whalers, are at their offshore moorings. The racers are seen at the start, sailing on a reach in a southwest wind. The leading boat (white hull) is believed to be the eventual winner *Hollo*, built and owned by Alvin Stevens. The boat on the far right is the Amos Stevens-built *Black Nance*, which lost a mast during this memorable contest. [Author's collection]

Photo 2 Tancook schooners and whalers at the start of one of the annual Mahone Bay fishermen's regattas off Chester, Nova Scotia, ca. 1907. The boats are ghosting along in light airs with their lofty fisherman staysails set to catch the capricious inshore breeze. The leader, a knockabout with novel crosscut sails, displays the distinctive knuckled McManus stem of the early Tancook round-bow schooners. [Courtesy Perry W. Stevens]

Photo 3 Several knockabout-rigged Tancook schooners and sloops laying to their moorings near the government wharf at Little Tancook Island on a hazy summer morning in August 1921. Big Tancook may be seen in the background. Crewmen are in the process of boarding their craft to go fishing. [Courtesy Maritime Museum of the Atlantic, Halifax, NS, Canadian Department of Public Works photo]

Photo 4   Five Tancook whalers and an Aberdeen-stem Tancook schooner hauled on their launchways at Northwest Cove, Big Tancook Island, in about 1905. The island's government wharf is just out of sight to the far left, and the small building in the upper right corner approximates the future location of the Reuben Heisler boatyard. The nearest whaler clearly exhibits the lapstrake planking traditionally associated with the type, and all are painted white in typical fashion. Note also the tall pole mainmasts to accommodate their fisherman staysails. The partially obscured dark-hulled vessel (fourth from the top) may be the well-known *Black Nance*, the island's first counter-stern schooner. [Courtesy Perry W. Stevens]

Photo 5   View of the southern shore of Southeast Cove, Big Tancook Island, in the late 1930s, showing the unique mooring poles used by islanders to secure their boats. A small scallop sloop can be seen in the foreground, while a motorboat and two schooners lie closer inshore. [Courtesy Thomas Mason]

Photo 6 Big Tancook Island in 1968, little changed from a generation earlier. The view is facing northwest from Southern Head and shows Southeast Cove, the island's major anchorage, to the right. The South Shore mainland around Chester and the inner islands of Mahone Bay may be seen in the distance. [Photograph by author]

Photo 7 Legendary boat builder Alfred F. Langille (1839–1926) on Tancook Island at about age 85. [Courtesy Thomas Mason]

Photo 8 A typical late nineteenth-century Tancook home, the Joseph Thomas house (ca. 1870) at Southeast Cove, as it appeared in 1968. Many aspects of island life are in evidence. A vegetable garden is in the left foreground. Beyond it, overlooking the water, is the roof of the owner's underground cabbage house. In the right background lies Southern Head, Tancook's highest point of land. On the horizon to seaward is neighbouring East Ironbound Island. And, next to the house, in lieu of indoor plumbing, is the ubiquitous outhouse. The electric pole in the right foreground, a concession to the modern era, would have been installed after the Second World War. [Photograph by author]

Photo 9 Whaler builder Joshua Mason (1845–1924) in early middle age, ca. 1890. [Courtesy Mrs Sadie I. Langille]

Photo 10 Schooner builder Wesley H. Stevens (1871–1967) in his late years, ca. 1965. [Courtesy Gerald L. Stevens]

Photo 11 Boat builder Amos H. Stevens (1850–1935) in a posed portrait taken in 1907. He is holding the half-model of a straight-stem Tancook schooner. [Courtesy Perry W. Stevens]

Photo 12 Stanley G. Mason (1882–1960), schooner builder, toward the end of his career, ca. 1940. [Courtesy Mrs Dorinda Mason]

Photo 13 Boat builder Howard Mason (1874–1953) at the tiller of his schooner *Patavana*, ca. 1940. [Author's collection]

Photo 15 Schooner builder Vernon R. Langille (1888–1979) posing for a studio portrait in about 1913 at age 25. Note the strong hands of the professional craftsman. [Courtesy Maritime Museum of the Atlantic, Halifax, NS]

Photo 14 Schooner builder Reuben Heisler (1874–1946) in middle age, ca. 1930. [Courtesy Mrs Audrey Mosher]

Lapstrake and carvel really represent two separate building traditions. The former was essentially shell construction – planking first, followed by framing – while the latter was basically skeletal construction, wherein the frames or "skeleton" preceded the planking. Lapstrake work was done mostly by eye or rule of thumb, and carvel more typically with the aid of scaled half-models or (most recently) drawings. Both traditions existed and intertwined on Tancook.

Certain things are known about the early construction methods used by islanders. First, there is no record of their employing half-models prior to 1900. Joshua Mason, one of the leading whaler builders, never worked from models; neither, so far as is known, did Alfred Langille. The usual procedure followed by these and other whaler builders was to shape their boats from three removable framing moulds representing bow, stern, and midship sections. These moulds, which were used over and over again, served as rough guides for planking and (later) framing. The rest was done "by eye." The position of the moulds could, of course, be adjusted to accommodate changes in length from boat to boat, and they could be padded as well to allow for alterations in depth or beam measurement.[81] As Howard I. Chapelle pointed out, lapstrake hulls with bent frames – which was the practice on Tancook – required few moulds, since the planking was essentially used to shape the boat.[82] In building from a few moulds without benefit of models or drawings, Tancookers were following a time-honoured technique in lapstrake construction, one widely practised in the British Isles, Scandinavia, and the northeastern United States during the nineteenth century.[83] It was the American mould-building tradition, no doubt, that reached Tancook Island from the nearby mainland by way of the New Englanders who settled the South Shore in the 1760s.*

Precisely when moulds came into use at Tancook is unknown, and it is conceivable that the earliest whalers were built completely by rule of thumb without even the aid of moulds for guidance, as was the case with other lapstrake double-enders of the same period, in-

---

* Chester, the first permanent non-German settlement in Lunenburg County, was founded in 1760 by New Englanders from coastal regions of Massachusetts, New Hampshire, and Maine, and by 1767 boatbuilding was well under way there. Other county townships, including Lunenburg itself, also had small but significant New England populations by 1767. (*Sources*: DesBrisay, *County of Lunenburg*, 57, 262, 264, 317; Haliburton, *Historical and Statistical Account*, 2:128–9. For the New England influence in this part of the province, see also Brebner, *Neutral Yankees of Nova Scotia*, 19–27, 43–4, and McCreath and Leefe, *Early Nova Scotia*, 251–2.)

cluding the herring sloops of Denmark, and the Block Island boats of southern New England.[84] Since most authorities agree, however, that building with moulds is foreign to lapstrake construction in its purest form and is probably a latter-day borrowing from carvel or skeletal construction,[85] it is possible that moulding was an indirect inheritance from the original carvel schooners built on the island prior to 1850. Little is known about those early vessels. If any models ever existed, none have survived. Nevertheless, carvel work could be carried out by a rule-of-thumb method in which one or more ribs, starting with a centre rib moulded from the body of an existing craft, were raised and faired by eye before planking.[86] That is the probable procedure used by Tancook's first builders and perhaps the source of the three-mould technique of full-size designing employed by the whaler-building generation.

The use of half-models on Tancook almost certainly occurred in conjunction with the transition from lapstrake back to carvel planking (or, as islanders called it, "seamwork" construction[87]), which took place around the beginning of the twentieth century. Those who have examined the role of scale models in boat production are in general agreement about the close association between modelling and carvel work. Unlike clinker building, which may be carried out entirely by eye if necessary, carvel construction must start with some prior notion of the shapes of frames. For builders unschooled in the subtleties of marine drafting, that means models.[88]

Several factors prompted the switch from clinker to carvel and, not coincidentally, to the use of half-models on Tancook. One of these was size. As time passed, the need grew for larger boats able to venture farther offshore. Clinker construction, as Douglas Phillips-Birt and Basil Greenhill have demonstrated, had inherent limitations: it was impractical beyond a certain point because it demanded relatively thin and narrow planking unsuitable for large craft,* and it was comparatively inflexible in terms of shaping and forming hulls.[89] The latter made it especially inappropriate for the new counter or "transom" stern Tancook schooner models of post-1900 with their more

---

* Lapstrake Tancook whalers were planked with boards of ⅝" thickness or less, while the island's later carvel-built schooners were planked with boards ¾" and up. Thinner planking was installed in the smaller whalers in order to keep them light for rowing and hauling, but also because thicker planks were harder to lap. Conversely, boards of less than ¾" thickness were considered too thin for planking on edge, carvel fashion. (*Source*: Interview, Thomas Mason, 25 September 1987.)

sharply curved after sections and flatter runs. Furthermore, larger lapstrake hulls, if built, required ever wider planking,[90] and the wider stocks necessary for constructing bigger whalers were increasingly unavailable, both on and off the island.

As a result, the lapstrake Tancook whaler was of necessity a small craft rarely built above certain limited dimensions. In the latter stages of its development, its average length was 35' to 38' overall.[91] Even the largest Tancook whalers did not exceed 45', and the few approaching that size were carvel-planked boats built after the turn of the century, at the tail end of the whaler era.* References to supposed big whalers in the 50' range pervade the existing literature,[92] but there is no record that any that large were ever built. Whalers over 40' in length were rare. The largest one owned on Big Tancook was a 45-footer belonging to David ("Old Shops") Baker, a part-time storekeeper who lived on the northwest side of the island, and she was built on the mainland at Mahone Bay by Obed Hamm.[93] Canadian government shipping registers, which recorded most provincial vessels of more than 10 tons (or about 40' length and over),† documented just twenty-seven whaler schooners up to 1915, when the last large example of the type was built at West Dover near Peggy's Cove. Only three of those exceeded 45', all of them Lunenburg-built, and none reached 50' overall.[94]

The Lunenburg whalers were essentially a separate species. They were what Tancook Islanders derisively referred to as "bulky" boats, burdensome craft carrying their maximum beams well fore and aft.[95] The beam-length ratios for those found in the registers averaged

---

* The exception that proves the rule is the Lunenburg whaler *Oreda*, a 44-footer whose register indicates a carvel hull, but whose published photograph shows her to have been clinker-built. This vessel tested the outer limits of lapstrake construction. (*Sources*: Post, *Tancook Whalers*, 41; NA, LunSR: register of schr *Oreda*, 4 April 1904.)

† Under "An Act relating to shipping and for the registration, inspection and classification thereof," passed by the Second Parliament in 1873 – and later incorporated into the comprehensive Canada Shipping Act – all decked Dominion sailing vessels over 10 tons were required by law to be registered. Registration was optional for completely open sailing craft and those of 10 tons or less, many of which were nevertheless enrolled for reasons of vanity or pride of ownership. Registration was further stimulated after 1882 by the desire of owners to qualify for the tonnage portion of the federal fishing bounty, which applied only to officially documented craft of 10 or more tons (see note, page 125). Throughout the period under consideration, therefore, virtually all Tancook-built boats over 10 tons, as well as a handful under that size, were duly entered in government lists. (*Sources: Can.S*, 36 Vict. (1873), chap. 128, sec. 7; *Can.RS*, 6 Edw. VII (1906), chap. 113, sec. 5; *Can.RS*, 18 Geo. V (1927), chap. 186, sec. 5; *Can.RFB*, 1883, lxxiii–lxxiv; ibid., 1898, 10–11.)

1 to 3.76, compared with 1 to 3.96 for several built at the Tancooks.*
The few authentic Tancook whalers registered – those actually produced by island builders – were nine in number, the largest being the 13-ton *Willie Roy* launched at Little Tancook in 1906 by Henry Levy. She measured 44' in overall length. The biggest whalers built by Alfred Langille and Alvin Stevens, the *Elma M.* and the *Mildred Baker*, were 10-ton 40-footers launched in 1905 and 1907, respectively. More to the point, except for two 34-footers turned out by Amos Stevens in 1893–94, all of those documented double-enders were carvel-built.[96] In short, the size of the Tancook whaler has been greatly exaggerated, and when efforts beyond the 40' range were tried, the traditional lapstrake planking was abandoned.

In addition to increased size requirements, another factor influenced the transition from lapstrake to carvel construction (and modelling) on Tancook. This was the development of yachting on the nearby mainland. The original whalers were simple work boats. Most were built for fisherman-farmers like William Stevens of Big Tancook, who commissioned Joshua Mason to build him a 35-foot whaler around the turn of the century and delivered a cow in payment.[97] The idyllic simplicity reflected by that transaction was being altered to some degree, however, by the arrival of sport and its associated motivations: competitiveness, the desire for speed under sail, and the demand for the latest in technological innovations appearing in the yachting fleets.

Organized sailing races started in the Mahone Bay area in 1885 with the first of many annual regattas at Chester that included whaler contests.[98] Three years later, the *Lunenburg Progress* reported that

---

* The slim 1 to 4 ratio of the true Tancook whaler, though copied from the proportions of the Labrador whaler, was probably governed in part by the sorts of timber available locally or regionally for planking. Clinker-built hulls lapped in softwood were necessarily sharp ended and narrow beamed because of the resistance of pine, spruce, and similar coniferous species to steam bending. These less flexible stocks were overwhelmingly abundant along the South Shore of Nova Scotia and were certainly used in building the early Tancook boats. White pine was the preferred planking wood on the island from the 1890s to the 1930s, while the limited hardwood available was mostly reserved for the frames and backbones of vessels, particularly for the former where steam bending was essential. In marked contrast to the narrow Tancook boats were the lapstrake double-enders of nineteenth century Denmark, whose steam-bent oak planking permitted beam-length ratios that were commonly in the 1 to 3 range. (*Sources*: Chapelle, *Boatbuilding*, 360, 442–4; Chapelle, *American Small Sailing Craft*, 166–7; Fader, "Reminiscence," 4; interviews, Thomas Mason, 29 September 1986 and 14 June 1989; Nova Scotia, Royal Commission, *Provincial Economic Inquiry*, 174, 176; Nielsen, *Wooden Boat Designs*, 3–158, passim; *Can.CenInd, 1917*, pt 4, sec. 1: Lumber Statistics, 7.)

"Tancook can boast of the best and smartest fleet of boats in the province," and that "any body who has plenty of money and wants to have a race can soon find an opponent."[99] The 1888 Chester regatta, held in August before two thousand spectators, featured a whaler race between island boats that was hailed as the closest and most exciting match of its kind ever witnessed on the South Shore.[100] By the 1890s, centreboard yachts, in addition to working whalers, were being built at Tancook for area sportsmen, including members of the Royal Nova Scotia Yacht Squadron (RNSYS) in Halifax.[101] Finally, in 1901, the Chester Yacht Club (CYC) was founded, adding immeasurably to the outside influences affecting boat design and construction on the island. These included exposure to the most recent developments in British and American yacht architecture, which reached Chester by way of the prestigious RNSYS (more advanced than its local counterpart) and were carried to Tancook by island natives serving as professional skippers* for members of the newly formed CYC.[102]

Yachtsmen were keenly interested in novel hull shapes, new trends in design, and the latest construction techniques. Consequently, they were enthralled by models and plans, which were the best ways to visualize those new ideas, and by carvel construction, the most adaptable building method for implementing changes in marine architecture.[103] Those enthusiasms soon found expression on Tancook, and the man most responsible for transmitting them was Amos H. Stevens.

Stevens, by all appearances an ordinary designer and builder,† was a superb publicist and promoter and a great innovator. He cultivated contacts in the yachting community early on, and by 1893–94 was al-

---

* The Chester Yacht Club was noted in early years for its extensive use of professional, rather than amateur or "Corinthian," skippers, and working aboard CYC yachts provided lucrative part-time employment for many skilled island boatmen.

† The lines of his Tancook schooner *Comet G.* (1910), taken from the only surviving Amos Stevens half-model, show a rather unattractive, slab-sided hull with an overly long mid-section and abruptly turned buttocks, resulting in a very short run (see fig. 3). This boat's contemporary reputation for speed must be attributed to her radically slim, shallow shape – the most extreme yet found on any Tancook model in terms of beam-length ratio – and to her abnormally large sail plan, which was later cut down considerably for fishing (see figs. 4, 5). These features, well calculated for summer racing on Mahone Bay's protected inner waters, did not translate into a well-rounded schooner. The lines of a widely known Stevens whaler model published by Ernest Bell in 1933 are much better, but no vessel was ever built from them, the model being purely decorative. In 1986, furthermore, the late Harold W. Stevens, grandson of Amos Stevens, informed the author that the builder's son Randolph had actually finished the model in question. (*Sources*: Bell, "Passing of the Tancook Whaler," 56; interview, Harold W. Stevens, September 1986.)

ready providing clinker-built racing whalers to RNSYS members in Halifax.[104] The following year, carvel-planked pleasure boats were first built at Chester for the growing tourist trade and shortly thereafter found their way into the local yachting fleet. Amos Stevens was in the forefront of that change, building racing sloops for two prominent members of the Chester yachting fraternity in 1898. It was at about this time that he reintroduced carvel building on Tancook, his first seamwork effort being a yacht for David Freda of Chester.[105] Not long after (probably around 1900), he launched the first carvel-built working whaler* for Stephen or Reuben Cross of Big Tancook.[106] It was yacht building, however, that principally occupied Amos Stevens during this phase of his career and gained him renown. In the years immediately after 1900, according to a founding member of the Chester Yacht Club, he "built a number of good boats and helped materially in building up the prestige of the CYC."[107] By 1907, Stevens' reputation has spread across the Atlantic, and one of his carvel-built centreboard sloops was shipped to Cowes on the Isle of Wight, the very centre of English yachting.[108]

Sometime during this period, half-models first appeared on Tancook, inspired by the changeover to carvel building and the increased interest in speed and hull shape engendered by yacht racing. One knowledgeable island source credits either Amos Stevens or his son-in-law and apprentice Reuben Heisler with being the original modeller on Tancook.[109] The older man, with his mainland yachting connections and early conversion to carvel construction, seems the likelier candidate. At any rate, the half-model was essentially a tool of the next era in Tancook boatbuilding, the schooner period. No genuine builders' models of bona fide Tancook whalers exist; the only known examples of this type are models of double-enders built on the mainland around Lunenburg and Mahone Bay after 1900.[110] Thomas Mason, whose grandfathers were whaler builders Joshua Mason and Alfred Langille, never saw or heard of whaler models during half a lifetime spent on the Southeast Cove side of Tancook.[111] Author Desmond Holdridge did recall seeing supposedly authentic whaler half-models carved by Amos Stevens when he visited the old man in

---

* Islanders possessed a sardonic sense of humour. This first carvel whaler was not a particularly stiff sailer, a characteristic some blamed on her novel seamwork construction, which was thought to lack the grip on water afforded by traditional lapwork planking. When the boat's owner finally decided to dispose of his floating white elephant, he was offered a back-handed compliment on his good sense by a relative, who allowed that one thing could always be said of him, "If you have something that's no good for nothing, you get rid of it." (*Source*: interview, Thomas Mason, 14 June 1989.)

1925 at his retirement home on Second Peninsula near Lunenburg.[112] Those models no longer exist, but unless they were decorative pieces produced after the fact, they almost certainly represented carvel whalers built around the turn of the century.

By the time carvel construction and modelling replaced clinker building and the three-mould system, the day of the Tancook whaler had about ended. The last of the breed built on the island slid down the ways before 1910. Among the original builders, Joshua Mason built his last whaler with the aid of his son Howard sometime between 1900 and 1905, thereafter retiring to a farmer's life.[113] Alfred Langille, who managed to make the transition to carvel work and schooner building, launched his last sizeable whaler in 1905. Alvin Stevens continued to produce whalers at his shop near Northwest Cove until 1907, and Henry Levy kept on at Little Tancook until 1908.[114] Both younger men subsequently turned to schooner building. Elsewhere, builders and fishermen clung to the whaler design for a few more years. As late as 1915, Daniel Publicover turned out an 11-ton, 38-foot whaler at West Dover,[115] but by then the type had all but disappeared from Tancook Island, where it had been nurtured and developed. The island fishing fleet gradually phased out its whalers in favour of counter-stern schooners during the years leading up to World War I and sold the last of the older boats to resort interests on the mainland for service in the summer tourist trade.[116] By the eve of the war, only two registered double-enders remained actively fishing under Tancook ownership.[117]

THE SEARCH FOR THE TANCOOK SCHOONER

For all of the romance associated with their name, the Tancook whalers were much less historically significant than the counter-sterned Tancook schooners that succeeded them. The schooners were built in greater numbers, and more of them were owned on the island at the height of their influence.[118] The schooners were also larger vessels, by and large, and they ventured much farther afield than their predecessors. They were more versatile as well, serving in more varied and demanding occupations than the essentially one-dimensional whalers, which were almost exclusively fishing craft. Yet the schooners, perhaps because of their unremarkable name and less striking appearance, have never received the acclaim due them. They were, quite simply, the ultimate expression of Tancook Island's boatbuilding genius and the pre-eminent small craft produced in the Maritimes during the first half of the twentieth century.

The Tancook schooner went through several stages before it reached its final and most recognizable form, which was characterized by a round or "spoon" bow and a counter stern with an oval or elliptical transom. The first step in the process was simply to superimpose an overhanging counter stern on the basic whaler design that had served islanders for so many decades. The resulting Aberdeen-stem/counter-stern schooner appeared shortly after the turn of the century, and, as is the case with so many innovations in Tancook boatbuilding, there is uncertainty about its precise origin.

Steadman Mason, who worked for Amos Stevens' apprentice Reuben Heisler once he had become an independent builder, remembered Heisler's telling him one version of the story of the adoption of the counter stern. Heisler (1874–1946), born Joseph Reuben, was prominent among the younger generation of island builders who came to the fore after 1900 and were instrumental in the transition from whalers to schooners. According to his story, he himself introduced the idea of the counter stern, or what islanders imprecisely called the "transom stern," to Tancook. The event was said to have taken place when Heisler was fourteen or fifteen years old and working as a deckhand aboard a Mahone Bay dory trawler. While his vessel was visiting Canso for bait, he saw an American schooner with a counter stern, remembered it, and drew a sketch of it when he returned home. Heisler either showed that sketch to his future father-in-law, Amos Stevens, then the leading builder at Northwest Cove, or used it some years later himself to form the basis for the first Tancook schooner.[119]

This tale is suspect for several reasons. In the first place, Heisler's age at the time of the occurrence places the date at about 1888–89, but by then, the counter stern, which was introduced to the fisheries in its shorter form prior to 1870 and lengthened to a somewhat longer overhang in the 1880s, was already quite common among vessels in the Nova Scotia banks fleet, including those sailing out of Mahone Bay.[120] Tancook Islanders would not have needed to discover it on a visiting New England schooner. Second, there is the inexplicable gap between the supposed first sighting of the counter stern and its reproduction on the island well over a decade later, a time lapse that defies logic. Furthermore, as will be seen, the Heisler story is strikingly similar to accounts relating to the origin of the round bow on Tancook and may have been confused with them. In any case, what would have been new to island boatbuilders in the 1890s was not a counter stern per se but a narrow or tapered counter stern, particularly one applied to small sailing craft. That was shortly to change.

Edmund A. Fader, who was intimately familiar with the Chester yachting scene, recalled that in the spring of 1895 a builder named Andrew Walker launched the first two boats built locally with "overhanging sterns and the rudder head through the deck."[121] These were, in other words, the first counter-stern craft of non-vessel size built in the Chester area. As trend setters, they certainly came to the attention of Amos Stevens, who was heavily absorbed in yacht building by that time and aware of developments in the region's leading resort centre. He appears, at any rate, to have mastered counter-stern construction by the late 1890s, when he employed it in two racing sloops built for Chester parties.[122]

In the meantime, Stevens and other island builders were becoming aware of the "*Fredonia* model" in large fishing schooners, which combined a raking clipper bow with a lighter and narrower counter stern than had previously been seen in banks vessels. This model, inspired by the Boston schooner *Fredonia* designed by Edward Burgess in 1889, became the prevailing style in large fishermen and remained so until replaced by the round-bow type in the early 1900s.[123] New England schooners built on the *Fredonia* model were common in Nova Scotian waters after 1890*, and Lunenburg County vessel builders gradually began to copy their most obvious features. By the turn of the century the raked clipper bow and longer, yacht-like counter were typical of the large bankers being built along the South Shore.[124]

These graceful vessels were no doubt admired on Tancook, and the desire to duplicate the *Fredonia* "look" seen in the regional offshore fishing fleets likely led Amos Stevens – after experimenting first with small racing sloops – to adapt the stern construction techniques he had copied from mainland yachts to the whaler hull form, thus creating the first Tancook schooner. This scenario fits with the testimony of the builder's grandson Perry W. Stevens, who claimed that Amos Stevens produced Tancook's first counter-stern schooner, the *Black Nance*, around 1903.[125] This boat, a 38-foot clipper-bow model, was

---

* The counter stern said to have been seen at Canso by Reuben Heisler may have been a *Fredonia* counter, in which case his story was true but his dating off by several years. This is entirely possible, since it is known that Heisler fished on the banks for several seasons in the early to mid-1890s. (*Source*: Interview, Benjamin Heisler, 4 October 1989.) *Fredonia* and her sisters began calling at Canso during the fishing season of 1891, and their appearance would have caused a sensation among Tancook observers used to the short, wide counters then carried by Canadian schooners. The idea for a Tancook counter may have germinated sometime during the early 1890s, but could not be fulfilled until island building techniques caught up later in the decade. (*See Can.RFB, 1891*, pt 2: *Report on the Fisheries Protection Service*, 22–3.)

owned by Wesley Young, an island fisherman, who used his novel craft (among other mundane chores) to haul scallops to Halifax. Significantly, however, the *Nance* was also a noted racer that participated in Chester's annual fishermen's regattas,* additional evidence of the close connection between design innovation and competitive sport on the northwest side of Tancook.[126]

Only a handful of Aberdeen-stem/counter-stern schooners were built on Tancook – probably not more than eight or ten at most. The majority of the boats originated on the northwest side of the island. Besides the *Black Nance*, Amos Stevens built the *Beulah W.*, a 40-footer, for Charles Wilson and Herbert Young of Big Tancook. The other clipper-bow schooners owned at Northwest Cove were unidentified, and were probably too small to be registered. Just two of the type were launched at Southeast Cove, and they were also the last produced on Tancook. Albert ("Allie") Stevens built the 38-foot *Vernie S.* for his own use in 1907,† and Howard Mason built a small Aberdeen schooner in the 34' to 38' range a year or two later, which he used briefly for fishing and then sold to Gabarus in Cape Breton County. By the time of World War I, these unique boats, like the whalers that preceded them, were gone from the island.[127]

The next step in Tancook schooner development was the straight-stem model, in which the newly adopted counter stern was retained, while the original whaler bow was straightened to eliminate its curvature but left at the same approximate angle of rake. The new bow profile was, in effect, a brief evolutionary pause midway between the concave clipper bow and the convex round bow yet to come. Its origins are obscure, but it seems to have been an approximation of some latter-day version of the famous "*Gloriana* bow" seen in local yachting fleets. Created by American yacht designer Nathaniel G. Herreshoff in 1891, the *Gloriana* bow – basically a straight, raking stem with a cutaway underwater profile – was an attempt to take advantage of existing class racing ratings by maximizing overall length on a fixed waterline measurement. The bow was formed by projecting a straight, sharply angled cutwater from billet to keel that eliminated the hollow forefoot then found on conventional clipper-bowed

---

* In the period prior to World War I, annual racing regattas featuring island fishing craft were held each August at either Chester or Tancook. The participating boats were originally whalers and, in later years, schooners. (*Sources*: Allen, "Chester Yacht Club," 2; Fader, "Reminiscence," 1–3.)

† This schooner was an entirely homemade affair. Her owner not only did the designing and building, but also sewed his own sails, made his own blocks, and did his own ironwork. (*Source*: Interview, Steadman S. Mason, 17 June 1989.)

yachts.* The result was hailed as a great departure and became a widely imitated fashion in boat design.[128] As L. Francis Herreshoff, the originator's son, later observed, "The 'Gloriana's' bow was copied throughout the world and in the next ten years it was seen on everything from catboats to three-masted schooners."[129]

On Tancook, the raking, straight-stem schooner appeared in about 1905–06, two or three years after the clipper-bow model, and briefly became the preferred style in the island fisheries. There were even fewer straight stemmers than Aberdeen schooners, and only two are known by name. One was the 38-foot *Black Lize*, an Amos Stevens creation built for the Youngs or the Wilsons of Northwest Cove. The other was the *Tacoma*, a 40-footer modelled by Reuben Heisler for Alexander ("Sandy") Wilson, Jr of Big Tancook and built at Northwest Cove in 1906. The *Tacoma*, which went through innumerable owners and at least one major rebuilding, has survived into the 1990s as the yacht *Adare*, prominent in the Nova Scotia Schooner Association.[130] An accompanying photograph (see photo 18) illustrates her modern appearance.

The short-lived straight-stem schooner, no models of which have survived, remained in vogue for only a year or two before giving way to the round-bow type. Fortunately, a half-model of one featured in a posed 1907 photo portrait of builder Amos Stevens clearly shows the schooner's salient characteristics, including the distinctive bow profile (see photo 11). The chief legacy of the straight-stem schooner was its slightly less concave entrance, an inevitable result of its cutaway stem and a departure from the hollow waterlines formed by the earlier Aberdeen or clipper bow. Those fuller lines distinguished the mature Tancook schooner from its whaler ancestor and probably contributed to its buoyancy and seaworthiness.

The shape of the transom or stern plank on the early Aberdeen and straight-stem schooners is of some interest, since it varied considerably from the oval form eventually adopted. All or most of the first

---

* A modified *Gloriana* bow also appeared on some *Fredonia*-type New England fishing schooners after 1891, taking the form of a straight (or nearly straight) raking stem rabbet combined with a flaring, clipper-style, gammon-knee cutwater. A number of these vessels, including one perhaps not coincidentally named *Gloriana*, frequented Nova Scotia fishing ports around the turn of the century, and they may have indirectly influenced design developments on Tancook, since copies could be seen soon after in Lunenburg County's vessel fishing fleets. However, it is more likely that exposure to the cutaway straight stem came via the yachting community, especially the Royal Nova Scotia Yacht Squadron in Halifax with its American contacts and interest in international design trends. (*Sources*: Chapelle, *American Fishing Schooners*, 185–92, 197–8, 208–15; *Can.RFB, 1901*, 271–4; Armour and Lackey, *Sailing Ships of the Maritimes*, 195; Stephens, *American Yachting*, 115–16, 161–2; Erhard, *First in Its Class*, passim.)

Tancook schooners had what was known as a "V-stern." This was a counter stern incorporating a very narrow, triangular-shaped transom with straight sides and top that, because of its appearance, was sometimes called a "fan" transom. Amos Stevens installed a fan stern plank in his initial clipper-bow / counter-stern schooner and continued with variations of the style for several more years.[131] The accompanying plan of the early round-bow schooner *Blackbird III*, designed and built by Stevens' understudy Reuben Heisler in 1910 (see fig. 6), provides an example of a modified fan transom with more-than-usual width and curvature mounted on a typically elongated counter of the period. The narrowness and small size compared to later forms is obvious despite an absence of the usual sharp corners and flat crown.*

The angular V-stern was relatively simple to construct and required minimal expertise in woodworking compared to the skills needed to shape and finish a stern with an elliptical transom.[132] That was certainly part of its appeal to boatbuilders who, like those on the northwest side of Tancook, were just starting to experiment with counter sterns. For builders already familiar with whaler construction, the V-stern was a natural progression, resembling as it did a double-ender stern lopped off a few feet inboard from the top end of the sternpost and planked over. The V or fan may also have owed something to the small, semi-elliptical, V-shaped transom popularized in the vessel fishing fleets by the famous *Fredonia*.[133] The *Fredonia* model was widely copied in all respects, and numerous Nova Scotia salt bankers adopted its counter V-stern in the 1890s. It appeared on vessels of the Lunenburg fleet through the end of the century and well into the next decade.[134]

Although common everywhere on Tancook for a time, the V-stern was basically a Northwest Cove form, and it became a signature feature of the Stevens and Heisler boats built on that side of the island.[135] Eventually, after 1910, it disappeared in its purest manifestation – small, sharply angled, triangular transom affixed to a long, narrow counter – but traces remained in the rather less rounded and less finely sculpted elliptical transom normally found on schooners produced at Northwest Cove boatyards. According to register documentation, the pure V-stern reached its peak of popularity on Tancook in 1908 and then fell rapidly out of favour. Its last practitioners were Alvin Stevens and Reuben Heisler.[136]

---

* The flat crown associated with the fan transom was largely the result of a lack of camber or transverse curvature in the decks of the Northwest Cove schooners that introduced it. The later oval transom followed a deck line that was more sharply cambered as a rule. (*Source*: Interview, Thomas Mason, 18 June 1989.)

The final stage in the evolution of the Tancook schooner was the creation of the familiar round-bow/counter-stern model incorporating an elliptical or semi-elliptical transom. This development was the culmination of a brief but extraordinarily fertile period of technological experimentation on the island that lasted less than a decade and transformed the physical appearance of the local fishing fleet. The transition from clipper bow to straight stem to round or spoon bow took no more than five years and was characterized by considerable overlap in designs and forms of construction. From about 1905 to 1910 – roughly the period of introduction for the Tancook schooner – several types of island craft coexisted side by side, including old-style whalers and Aberdeen, straight-stem, and spoon-bow schooners. Almost as many stern types as bow shapes mingled simultaneously as well, ranging from the pure V to the pure elliptical stern, with many gradations between.[137] Ultimately, a consensus emerged as to the most attractive and practical design, and by 1910, the round-bow model had come to the fore. Over the next decade, it displaced all other types to become the quintessential Tancook schooner.

Like so many other Tancook innovations, the introduction of the round- or spoon-bow schooner is clouded in confusion and contradictory opinion concerning precise dates, circumstances, and persons to be credited. Howard I. Chapelle supposed that the round bow did not appear until after 1910, perhaps between 1912 and 1915,[138] an estimate that erred badly. At the other extreme, some former islanders have placed the time as early as the mid-1890s,[139] well before the actual date of inception. As to the builder responsible for introducing the round bow, reputable sources disagree, but they do concur that it was either Amos Stevens or Reuben Heisler.

Emotions have been known to run strong on this matter, and they are exacerbated by the in-law relationship that existed between the two builders. As was the case with so many island building families, including the Masons and Langilles of Southeast Cove,* the Stevenses and Heislers were related by marriage – specifically the marriage of Reuben Heisler and Amos Stevens' daughter Celest. While such an event might be expected to strengthen the bond between families, the reverse appears to have occurred in this case, and it combined with the former master-apprentice relationship of the two principals to

---

* These two pioneer whaler-building families were united around the turn of the century by the marriage of Joshua Mason's son Howard and Alfred Langille's daughter Bridget. A generation earlier, Amos Stevens had married Joshua Mason's sister, Augusta, thus complicating kinship matters further. Such interrelationships explain much about island rivalries in the boatbuilding sphere. (*Sources*: Langille, *South Shore Langilles*, 49; Stevens and Stevens, *Stevens Families of Nova Scotia*, 103.)

produce a boatbuilding rivalry of considerable magnitude.[140] Personalities no doubt played a part. According to those who knew them, both men were proud, wilful, and somewhat short tempered. David Stevens recalled that his grandfather Amos was a gruff, preoccupied workman who had no patience with youngsters like himself around the boat shop and guarded his tools jealously.[141] Steadman Mason, once employed by Reuben Heisler, remembered Heisler as a fair but hard taskmaster who tolerated no frivolous talking among his workers and fired those who broke the code of silence.[142] The competition between these two rival Northwest Cove builders carried over into succeeding generations in the form of conflicting claims over their comparative abilities and their respective roles in the development of the Tancook schooner.

One consequence of the Stevens-Heisler rivalry has been to complicate the search for the origin of the round-bow model. Each side has had its family loyalists and outside adherents. Reuben Heisler's son Benjamin, for instance, insisted that his father built the island's first spoon-bow schooner, a 35- to 40-foot boat launched sometime in the late 1890s or early 1900s.[143] Builder Vernon Langille, certainly an unbiased source, agreed that Heisler probably deserved credit for this particular innovation, and Steadman Mason concurred.[144] Conversely, members of the Stevens family, including David and Perry Stevens, held that their grandfather Amos was the person responsible, and Thomas Mason, a reliable and impartial observer, was inclined to share that view.[145] It is significant, however, that some doubt existed in the minds of those individuals not directly related to the builders in question. In contrast, no such doubt existed for two writers who committed their opinions to print well after the fact. Desmond Holdridge, who was greatly influenced by the Amos Stevens mystique, wrote in 1939 that Stevens "introduced the spoon bow to Nova Scotia."[146] Half a century later, Robert C. Post repeated the assertion that Stevens was the first on Tancook to experiment with the spoon bow, making the additional erroneous but understandable assumption that he copied the idea from large schooners sailing out of Lunenburg.[147]

The truth, as usual, is somewhat more complex. Both the Stevens and Heisler versions of the origin of the Tancook round bow have the same basis: that it was first seen on an American banks schooner in Canadian waters and subsequently duplicated on Tancook.[148] This provides the initial clue to unravelling the puzzle. Claims that the original round-bow Tancook schooner was built in the 1890s may be dismissed. The convex curved stem first appeared on fishing schooners in 1898, when Boston naval architect Thomas F. McManus introduced it in a class of vessels that, because they were named for

Indian chiefs, were called "Indian Headers." Their design was characterized by a snubbed round bow with short overhang, a counter stern with elliptical or semi-elliptical transom, and a rounded or "rockered" keel. A considerable number of these schooners entered the Massachusetts fleet between 1898 and 1904, but none of them visited Nova Scotia before 1900.[149] In that year, another noted Boston designer, Benjamin B. Crowninshield, refined the round-bow look in the new schooner *Rob Roy* by adding a longer, less knuckled, forward overhang and a short, straight keel to create the classic "fisherman profile" of the next three decades. He produced plans for several more vessels on the same model between 1900 and 1907.[150] Finally, in 1902, the first "knockabout" fishing schooner, the *Helen G. Thomas*, was built to a McManus design. She carried the round-bow concept one step further by replacing the standard spike bowsprit with a radically extended bow overhang, which brought all headsails inboard. The knockabout slowly gained acceptance in the New England fleet between 1902 and 1906 and then blossomed in popularity after 1907.[151]

It was these three round-bow types – the first two combined under the catchall term "semi-knockabout" – that, to one degree or another, influenced the development of the spoon-bow schooner on Tancook. Initially at least, the new island boats owed little to the large bankers sailing out of Lunenburg, Mahone Bay, and other regional ports. South Shore vessel builders were slow to abandon the *Fredonia* model. The first round-bow schooner to join the Lunenburg fleet was the semi-knockabout *Henry L. Montague* (96 tons), built by Solomon Morash for W.C. Smith & Company and launched in October 1906.[152] She remained the only representative of her type until joined by the McManus-designed *Clintonia* (96 tons) and the *Vivian C. Walters* (86 tons), launched at Lunenburg's Smith and Rhuland yard in March and May of 1908, respectively.[153] Shortly after, in June of the same year, the *Minnie H. Mosher* slid down the ways at the A.C. Zwicker yard in Mahone Bay. This 73-ton vessel, designed by Obed A. Hamm, was billed as the first large banker of the semi-knockabout variety to be built in Nova Scotia from other than American plans.* The pride

---

* The practice of building fishing schooners in Nova Scotia shipyards from American plans was a common one, especially in the early years of the round-bow era. Thomas McManus of Boston developed a particularly thriving business with the Shelburne yards, and at least four semi-knockabouts were built there to his designs between 1908 and 1911. One of these was the *Artisan* (1911), which Chapelle mistakenly assumed was designed by her builder, John McKay. (*Sources*: HH, news items, 19 March 1908, 9; 14 November 1910, 9; and 7 November 1911, 9. See also Chapelle, *American Fishing Schooners*, 263, 284–5, 296.)

of Atlantic Fish Companies, Ltd, she was quickly proclaimed queen of the Lunenburg fleet.[154]

It took several more years for the pure knockabout design (round bow minus bowsprit) to find its way into the Nova Scotia offshore fisheries. During the interim, Lunenburg builders like Smith and Rhuland concentrated on perfecting the semi-knockabout and adapting it to local requirements. By 1912, they had developed the *Delawana* type, a moderately fast, all-around schooner suitable for winter coasting as well as summer banking.[155] A native version of the large knockabout finally appeared six years later, a decade after its full acceptance by American fishermen. This was the *General Haig* (109 tons), launched at Lunenburg by Smith and Rhuland in February 1918.[156] She was followed within four months by a virtual sister ship, the *Shepherd King*, and over the next two years several more knockabouts were built at Lunenburg, completing the institutionalization of the round bow in the region's banks fleet.[157]

The Lunenburg builders were less reluctant to experiment among smaller classes of fishing schooners. Spoon-bow boats in the 20-ton range were being modelled and built at local yards as early as 1907.[158] Tancook builders, however, had seized upon the new bow shape even before then, anticipating mainland boat and shipyards by a year or more. The date cannot be precisely determined, but by correlating scattered strands of Tancook's oral tradition with known facts it is possible to make a fairly close estimate. The round-bow model, it appears, was introduced on the island between 1904 and 1906, 1905 being the most likely year.

According to a story passed down through the Stevens family and related by David M. Stevens, Amos Stevens' son (and David's father) Randolph went to either the Grand or Western banks as a crewman aboard a mainland fishing vessel sometime around the turn of the century. Reuben Heisler may have accompanied him on the trip, since the two men were shipmates on the banks at some point in their early careers. While on the fishing grounds, young Randolph saw an American round-bow/counter-stern schooner and was much taken with her appearance. He saw the same vessel again when in port at "Canso or someplace," drew a profile on a piece of paper or a board, and took the sketch home to show his father. Thus the concept of the round-bow Tancook schooner was born. The skipper of the vessel that took Randolph Stevens to the banks was Adam ("Addie") Knickle, a native of Heckman's Island near Lunenburg, who was Stevens' uncle by marriage and who signed his nephew on as crewman for several years in succession. It was on one of these annual voyages that the sighting occurred, the American schooner being a "Crowninshield type" with spoon bow and bowsprit.[159]

The Stevens story was familiar to other islanders. Benjamin Heisler told a similar tale, placing both Reuben Heisler and Randolph Stevens aboard as crewmen, but crediting his father, Reuben, with being the crucial observer and sketch maker. Thomas Mason, who endorsed the broad outlines of the Stevens account, was able to add confirmation and fill in crucial gaps. Adam Knickle was, indeed, the captain of the Lunenburg County banker, and his crew on the trip in question included both Reuben Heisler and Randolph Stevens, the former serving as cook and the latter working as a dory fisherman. The American schooner, however, was thought to have been "a knockabout."[160]

Captain Adam Knickle emerges as a key figure in the round-bow story. He was a long-time fisherman who visited the offshore grounds in the 1880s as master and part owner of the Lunenburg banker *Nova Zembla*. In 1891, he sold his shares in that vessel and disappeared from the list of active owners for more than a decade, but in 1903, he entered the industry once more as skipper and managing owner of the new *Fredonia*-type schooner *Hispaniola*, launched at Lunenburg in March of that year. Knickle collected a fishing bounty with the *Hispaniola* for the next four years until he and his partners sold her to a Newfoundland merchant house in February 1907.[161] In the meantime, Randolph Stevens courted and, in January 1904, married Knickle's niece Evelyn Slauenwhite, thereby establishing a personal and familial relationship with the veteran skipper, whom the Stevens family came to know as "Uncle Addie."[162] It was sometime during this four-year period (1903–06) that Randolph and Reuben Heisler sailed out of Lunenburg for their rendezvous with the Yankee round-bow schooner, for by 1907, Adam Knickle was no longer commanding his own banker, and by the following year, Heisler and Stevens had embarked on careers ashore in the boatbuilding and sailmaking businesses.[163]

The questions remain of what vessel, or type of vessel, the Tancookers saw and where they observed it. It was certainly not a knockabout, for official port records show no American knockabouts at all fishing off Dominion shores until 1907, and none appearing in significant numbers until 1908–09.[164] Howard I. Chapelle, who was unfamiliar with the circumstances surrounding the voyage of the *Hispaniola*, nevertheless concluded (quite accurately, as it turned out) that "the round bow Tancooks were obviously inspired by the Indian Headers."[165] Indeed, the first American round-bow fishing craft to appear in northern waters were McManus-designed semi-knockabouts. These vessels came, for the most part, as participants in the Western Banks trawl fishery off Nova Scotia's Altantic coast.

With the late nineteenth century onset of dory trawling, which required constantly replenished stocks of fresh bait and ice, numerous ports along the province's southern and eastern shores became important supply depots for American as well as Canadian schooners working nearby Quereau and Sable Island banks – the so-called "Western Banks." These included, among others, places like Shelburne, Liverpool, Canso, and Arichat.[166] Canso's strategic location, jutting well out into the Atlantic and readily accessible from the fishing grounds, made it a particularly favoured entrepôt. In the 1900 season alone, New England bankers made 1,009 recorded stopovers at Maritime ports, 168 of them at Canso.[167] The technological interaction permitted by these brief "baiting up" visits was critical in the transfer of American ideas in naval architecture to the Canadian fishing fleet after about 1885 when, as Chapelle pointed out, Canadian trends in schooner design began to closely parallel United States practice.[168] The round-bow episode was just one example of this phenomenon.

The first American round-bow schooner to put in at a provincial baiting station was the Indian Header *Juniata*, which called at Shelburne during the seasons of 1900 and 1901. In 1902, she was joined by two more semi-knockabouts, including Crowninshield's *Rob Roy*, which made the initial visits by a round-bow schooner to settlements east of Halifax. By 1903, Adam Knickle's first season in the *Hispaniola*, 11 New England round-bows were recorded entering Nova Scotia ports, 9 of them McManus-designed Indian Headers. An even dozen appeared the following year, and thereafter the number increased rapidly, from 19 in 1905 to 25 in 1906. Nearly all were Indian Headers. At Canso, no fewer than 34 of the 38 entrances made by semi-knockabouts between 1903 and 1906 were by vessels carrying the McManus stamp. If Randolph Stevens and Reuben Heisler were in port there from the Western Banks when the reputed sketch of the round-bow profile was made – a reasonable assumption – there is little question that an Indian Header was the subject, most likely the McManus-designed *Squanto* (see photo 19), which frequented Canso several times each season during these years and recorded more than a quarter of all the visits made by vessels of her class.[169] It is probably no coincidence that one of the very first spoon-bow schooners built on Tancook (by Alfred Langille for his son Owen) was also christened *Squanto*,[170] a name rich in American historical symbolism but one having no particular meaning to islanders except as a reference to a familiar vessel.*

---

* Squanto was the Massachusetts Indian who befriended the Pilgrims during their first winter at Plymouth colony in 1620. (*Source*: Encyclopedia Americana, 1988 ed., s.v. "Squanto.") It is exceedingly doubtful that Alfred Langille had ever heard of him.

The position of Thomas McManus as the stepfather of the round-bow Tancook model was solidified by the discovery of two early sail plans of island schooners found in the loft of the old Randolph Stevens sailmaking establishment at Second Peninsula, Lunenburg, in 1969.* The plans, since redrawn (see figs. 1, 2), displayed the characteristic McManus stem of the Indian Header period – very short overhang, abrupt knuckle, and plumb top with a hint of tumblehome. Although undated, they were obviously prepared prior to 1910 and thus represent the earliest known renderings of Tancook schooners.

The first of the two plans was for an unidentified 35-foot schooner built (probably by Amos Stevens) for Benjamin Levy, a fisherman at Little Tancook. The second of the two, also unidentified, bore the inscription "Randolph Stevens" on the waterline, a location usually reserved by the sailmaker for the names of his owner-customers. It is possible, therefore, that this plan, carefully drawn with more than usual detail, outlined the sail arrangement for the *Togo*, built in 1905 for Randolph Stevens as a racing fisherman by his father, Amos.[171] The overall hull measurement, indicating a 42-footer, was a reasonable approximation of *Togo*'s official register length (43'), and the McManus bow was the type said to have been adopted for the Stevens schooner.[172] If the plan did indeed portray the *Togo*, as would seem to be the case, it probably also showed the first round-bow schooner built on Tancook, establishing Amos Stevens as the originator of the type.

The likelihood is that Randolph Stevens, who became acquainted with Adam Knickle through his marriage to Knickle's niece in the winter of 1903–04, accompanied his new father-in-law to the banks the following summer, where he saw his first round-bow schooner. Returning home, he described the vessel, an Indian Header, to his father, Amos, and urged the elder Stevens to build him a two-master with a similar bow profile.† The result, launched 20 May 1905, was the

---

* The Stevens sail loft was moved from its original Tancook location to Second Peninsula in 1919 or 1920. (*Sources*: Interview, Harold W. Stevens, July 1969; NS, article, 31 May 1986, 4; Stevens and Stevens, *Stevens Families of Nova Scotia*, 129; unidentified newspaper clipping in the possession of Perry W. Stevens.)

† Amos Stevens would have had little difficulty duplicating the McManus stem, since he had already built Tancook's first round-bow boat, the small keel sloop *Jennie S.*, for his own use around the year 1900. This experimental craft, inspired no doubt by contemporary sloops of the RNSYS, and used initially for day fishing and later for racing in Chester – she won the first officially sanctioned race of the CYC in 1901 with Reuben Heisler at the helm – provided her builder with sufficient experience to undertake a large round-bow creation (*Sources*: Interviews, Perry W. Stevens, 16 June and 3 October 1989; unattributed notes of a conversation with Randolph B. Stevens, spring 1955, 1.)

Togo, whose sail plan Randolph devised himself, incorporating the knockabout rig seen on local yachts. Reuben Heisler, who also observed the Yankee schooner, may have produced a round-bow replica of his own the same year, but if he did, it was not of register size. Official documentation indicates that Heisler built no sizeable boats until the following year, at which time he was still modelling straight-stem schooners – witness the *Tacoma*, launched in April 1906.[173] Thus, Stevens' *Togo* was most probably the first round-bow Tancook schooner, and she was certainly the first to be registered.

Whether or not the second of the two unidentified sail plans actually depicted the *Togo*, it is certain that both plans dated from no later than about 1905–09, for they betrayed a recent whaler legacy in the form of overlapping lug foresails, which were not seen on Tancook schooners after 1910. Like their whaler precursors, the two schooners also carried club-headed fisherman staysails and single jibs, but in a significant departure the latter were set entirely inboard, knockabout fashion. Since Stevens and Heisler could not have seen a knockabout fisherman at Canso or anywhere else prior to 1907 (and assuming that the plans in question do indeed reveal the original appearance of the Tancook schooner, circa 1905), it appears that the spritless headsail rig developed on Tancook independent of large-vessel influences. It was probably copied from a popular class of one-design knockabout racing sloops adapted from American plans by the Royal Nova Scotia Yacht Squadron in the late 1890s, an example of which was taken to Chester around 1903.[174] If, on the other hand, the plans postdate 1907 and do not represent the initial Tancook round-bows, it is conceivable that the rig was borrowed from visiting American bankers observed after the round bow with bowsprit had already been introduced on the island. The big McManus knockabout *Arethusa*, for example, was at Lunenburg at 1908, and her sister *Pontiac* was there the following year.[175]

In either case, the Nova Scotia knockabout schooner was a Tancook creation that anticipated mainland design in the fisheries by at least a decade. Besides the two Stevens schooners described above, island boatyards turned out a number of other fishing knockabouts prior to World War I. These included Mason and Langille's *Elsie C.* in 1910, Henry Levy's *S.F. Levy* in 1911, Vernon Langille's *Cecil V.L.* and Amos Stevens' *Mianus* in 1912, and an unidentified schooner built by Stevens for Sebastian Cross of Southwest Beach, Tancook.[176] A few knockabout schooners were also built for area yachtsmen during this period, appearing prominently in the racing fleet of the Chester Yacht Club.[177] In addition, an island knockabout named *Zaida* (builder unknown) found her way into the Royal Nova Scotia Yacht

Squadron in 1910, where she "not only proved a handy and comfortable craft, but fast enough, especially in a breeze and sea, to make it interesting for the best of the handicap fleet."[178]

The lug foresails shown on the early Stevens knockabout plans were not unique among Tancook's first generation of counter-stern schooners. One of the pre-1910 schooners built by Howard Mason at Southeast Cove carried one, and others on that side of the island did as well. Prior to the adoption of engines in the 1910s, schooner builders also followed the whaler practice of equipping their boats with oarlocks and sweeps for motive power in case of calms. Other vestigial remnants of the whaler era included centreboards, commonly installed in schooners until World War I and in some cases after that time.[179]

These reversions to older building practices point up one of the seldom acknowledged truths about the Tancook schooner, that although it may have superficially copied some of the design fashions of its time it remained, at bottom, a genuine product of Tancook Island and not a scaled-down version of some larger type of craft. Its above-water bow and stern profiles, for instance, may have come from mainland fishing vessels or yachts, but its essential body shape and proportions remained true to its island heritage. A perusal of the recorded dimensions of the registered Tancook schooners built after 1904 makes clear that the classic 1 to 4 beam-length ratio of the earlier double-enders was steadfastly maintained (see Appendix 1), and a glance at the accompanying lines drawings (see figures, throughout) shows that the whaler-building technique of calculating the maximum draft at approximately half the maximum beam[180] was never abandoned.* The perpetuation of traditional forms was exemplified by the work of schooner builder Howard Mason, who used his father's old bow and midship whaler moulds in the construction of his earliest transom-sterned boats, creating new shapes only for the obviously variant after-sections near the counter.[181]

The changeover from whalers to schooners was undertaken with some wariness on Tancook. What had worked was not easily abandoned. Islanders wanted to be up to date and to emulate the latest model features introduced at Northwest Cove, but the fundamental

---

* The similarities may be clearly seen in a statistical comparison of Alfred Langille's last registered whaler, the *Elma M.* (10.21 tons; 40.2' × 10' × 5.2'), built in 1905, with one of his first schooners, the *Oriole L* (10.43 tons; 39.4' × 10' × 5'), built in 1909. The former had a beam-length ratio of 1 to 4.02, the latter a beam-length ratio of 1 to 3.94. Depth-beam ratios were 1 to 2.00 and 1 to 1.96, respectively. Proportionately the two boats were virtually identical. (*Sources*: NA, LunSR: registers of schrs *Oriole L.*, 13 July 1911, and *Elma M.*, 27 June 1913.)

motivation for change went beyond style. Second-generation builder Stanley Mason summed it up quite succinctly. The schooner supplanted the whaler, he said, "because there was more room on deck."[182] The counter-stern schooner was, quite simply, a more practical working vessel, and practicality was the ruling ethic on Tancook. Nevertheless, the pragmatic impulse for improvement did not mean a total rejection of the past. There were firmly established island traditions, based on experience, as to the proper configuration of a boat, and much that set the whaler apart – its low freeboard to ease net hauling and rowing, for instance – was retained. To those who cared to look closely, the lineage of the Tancook schooner was unmistakable.

THE SECOND GENERATION

The similarity of the early Tancook schooner to its whaler predecessor was natural, given their common origins. With one or two exceptions, the first schooner builders on the island were members of the whaler-building generation. The initial counter-stern boats were built by Amos Stevens, who maintained his yard until 1919 before retiring to Second Peninsula on the mainland. Joining him in the transition to schooner building were his brother Alvin, who remained active until about 1917, Henry Levy, who launched schooners at Little Tancook until the outbreak of World War I, and Alfred Langille, who also worked until the eve of the war.[183] The Stevens brothers' careers ended on a sad note. Alvin died relatively young in 1920 at the age of fifty-five, and Amos' long career was terminated in 1919 by a haying accident* in which he lost a foot to a mowing machine.[184] Henry Levy's days as a boatbuilder likewise concluded prematurely, when he closed his yard and moved to Halifax to engage in house carpentry during the wartime construction boom, thereby ending schooner building at Little Tancook.[185]

Alfred Langille's years as a builder came to a close in more gradual, serene fashion. Perhaps the most remarkable of the pioneer schooner builders, he is generally thought to have been the third man on Tancook (after Amos Stevens and Reuben Heisler) – the first at Southeast Cove – to make the transition to the round-bow model.[186]

---

* An ox-drawn mower severed the builder's leg above the ankle. He recovered, but gave up boat work in favour of running a general store and post office on Tancook. Stevens subsequently retired to Second Peninsula in the early 1920s, where he lived with his son Randolph.

Langille made the conversion from whalers to schooners in his midsixties, a time when most men are contemplating retirement or, at the very least, are mired in old habits and established ways of thinking. He finally built his last counter-stern schooner, the 40-footer *Bernice*, for his son James in 1912[187] and then gave way to younger builders at the age of 73, after a career of half a century.

By the second decade of the twentieth century, a new generation of Tancook builders, most of them born between 1875 and 1890, had appeared on the scene. It was these craftsmen, possessing only tenuous connections to the whaler era, who carried the Tancook schooner to its final development. The first of the new generation to achieve prominence was Reuben Heisler. Next to Amos Stevens, Heisler was the leading builder at Northwest Cove. During a Tancook career that encompassed the years 1906 to 1923, he launched thirty-six register-sized schooners, second only to the forty-two built by Stevens between 1904 and 1919. These included the *Silver Oak* (42 tons; 62.4' × 16' × 8') in 1917, the largest Tancook schooner ever built.[188] Heisler was the second among his peers to convert to the counter stern and one of the first two to adopt the spoon bow. His shop was located on the left-hand side of Northwest Cove facing the water, opposite the present public wharf.[189]

An imposing figure who stood six feet tall and weighed two hundred pounds, with sufficient command and presence to serve as sailing master of the champion schooner *Bluenose* during her 1921 elimination races, Reuben Heisler was the first of his family to build boats.* He learned his trade over several years from a number of established island craftsmen. In his youth, he received instruction in laying a keel and setting a boat up in frame from the old master whaler builder Joshua Mason, thereby gaining the necessary knowledge to turn out his first craft, a Tancook jolly boat.[190] During the last whaler years, he worked in Amos Stevens' shop, along with the builder's sons, Randolph, Wesley, Ernest, and Ervine and refined his skills and techniques under the older man's tutelage. With that preparation, Heisler was able to start his own business around 1905–06, building first in borrowed locations, including barns and fish stores, and after 1910 in his own shop at Northwest Cove. His work force was among the island's best, and his employees included at various

---

* Tancook produced only one other Heisler builder of note who practised his trade on the island. That was William ("Will") Heisler, Reuben's first cousin, who built a few small boats at Northwest Cove as a young man before migrating to Gifford Island near Indian Point. (*Source*: Interview, Thomas Mason, 18 June 1989.)

times such accomplished boatwrights as Melvin and Perry Stevens, Howard Mason – from whom Heisler learned the exacting art of stern work – Alexander Wilson, and (from Chester) George Smith.[191]

Reuben Heisler's boats, as exemplified by *Blackbird III* (see fig. 6), typified the early Tancook schooners. His designs showed substantial sheer, a long, sharp entrance, a narrow rising stern, and a comparatively high length-to-beam ratio. In common with his mentor Amos Stevens, he also favoured a rather shallow model, particularly in the forebody, and one that exhibited considerable deadrise under the quarters, a feature reminiscent of the old whalers of the past.

Heisler's shop at Northwest Cove burned down in the fall of 1923, and rather than rebuild at the same site, he moved his boatbuilding operations to Chester the following year. This change of venue was probably economically inspired. Lumber supplies were closer at hand on the mainland, and Chester provided an opportunity to generate increased income by building yachts for summer residents, a line of work to which Heisler quickly applied his talents.[192] According to some reports, however, there was a darker side to the transfer of Heisler's business. The outspoken builder, whose ego was said to match his size, was rather controversial on Tancook and unpopular in some circles. Despite the likelihood of spontaneous combustion, rumours persisted for years that his shop was intentionally set on fire and that he left the island to avoid further trouble.[193] Whatever the motive, Heisler's success on Tancook was duplicated at Chester, and in 1927 he launched one of his largest vessels, the 32-ton schooner *Pearl M. Pettipas*, at his new Back Harbour location.[194]

Reuben Heisler's departure from Tancook, following closely on the heels of Alvin Stevens' death and Amos Stevens' retirement, ended the great days of boatbuilding on the northwest side of the island. Until 1920, about two-thirds of all Tancook schooners launched came from the hands of Northwest Cove builders – about three quarters if Little Tancook's production is not counted. After that date a total reversal occurred, three quarters of the launchings taking place on the Southeast Cove side. Vessel registrations indicate that during the first schooner-building phase (pre-1920), 143 boats exceeding 10 tons were built, 90 of them (or 63 percent) at Northwest Cove and vicinity, 31 (22 percent) at Southeast Cove, and 21 (15 percent) at Little Tancook.*

---

* There was little difference in hull design between the schooners built at Big and Little Tancook, respectively, but those produced at the smaller island exhibited cruder workmanship. Henry Levy's boats, which were well modelled but roughly finished, inspired a popular saying on the main island: "She's built by Henry Levy; take her home and plane her down!" (*Source*: Interviews, Thomas Mason, July 1969 and 12 June 1986.)

Of the total, well over half were products of the dominant Stevens and Heisler yards.[195]

That Northwest Cove dominance was never approached again, but construction did continue, after a fashion, on the front side of Tancook. No additional building of any consequence was done at Northwest Cove proper following the demise of the Heisler yard. Farther "backalong" on the island, however, the two Stevens yards remained in operation. Amos Stevens' establishment was taken over by his eldest son Wesley (1871–1967), and Alvin Stevens was succeeded by his sons Melvin (b. ca. 1892) and Byron (b. ca. 1900).[196] Both shops turned out a substantial number of schooners through the 1930s, although neither came close to reaching former levels of production. Wesley H. Stevens, trained by his father, built several sizeable fishing schooners and schooner-yachts between the middle 1920s and late 1930s (see figs. 16, 17, 22), including the highly regarded *Mother* in 1924 and the large swordfisherman *Gerald L.C.* in 1933, which later became the first Chester-to-Tancook ferry. Melvin H. Stevens, who honed his skills as a worker for Reuben Heisler and Stanley Mason, built (with his brother Byron) three large schooners on his own account between 1928 and 1931, including the 44-foot *Dorothy and Ella*, as well as other boats too small to be registered.[197]

Along with its most well-known and productive builders, Northwest Cove lost its sail loft – the only one on Tancook – after 1920. Upon the retirement of the island's original sailmaker, Joseph Pearl, shortly after the turn of the century, Reuben Heisler had encouraged his brother-in-law Randolph B. Stevens (1881–1962) to enter the business in order to maintain a convenient source of sails for himself and Randolph's father, Amos.[198] Sometime around 1909, after receiving instruction from the elder Pearl, Randolph had followed that advice by setting up a modest loft backalong near the Stevens homestead.* His building was sufficiently small that sails for large schooners had to be laid out and cut on the winter ice at nearby Hutt's Pond prior to sewing.[199] That inconvenience, plus his father's retirement and

---

* In late 1909, Amos Stevens formally transferred a parcel of Stevens land "known as the sail loft lot" and its structures to his son Randolph, whose occupation was recorded as "sailmaker." (*Source*: NS.LunRD, registry bk. 72, 257: deed dated 19 February 1910.) The younger Stevens started in business prior to that time, however, for his original sails (ca. 1905–08) were sewn in the sitting room of his Tancook home. Randolph himself claimed to have begun making sails in 1899 at the age of eighteen – perhaps the start of his apprenticeship with Joseph Pearl – while his son Harold dated the establishment of the family sailmaking enterprise from 1908. A daughter, Mary, recalled the construction of a new loft at the backalong site shortly before 1911. (*Sources*: PE, article, 5 February 1964, 5, in conjunction with Stevens and Stevens, *Stevens Families of Nova Scotia*, 129; CH, article, 21 December 1976, 21; unidentified newspaper clipping in the possession of Perry W. Stevens.)

the likely desire to be closer to mainland supplies and customers, motivated Stevens to purchase a farm at Second Peninsula near Lunenburg in 1919 or 1920 and construct a larger sailmaking facility there.[200] During the formative years of the Tancook schooner, however, he was the primary island sailmaker,* as Joseph Pearl had been during the whaler era, and deserves much of the credit for devising the sail and rigging arrangements for the new vessel type.

Schooner builders on Tancook ordinarily took specific dimensions for required sails to the Stevens loft, but on occasion they would leave the entire plan to the discretion of the sailmaker.[201] The inscription on a crude sail plan for a semi-knockabout schooner found at Second Peninsula in 1969, and evidently drawn in the early years of the century by a fisherman-builder, suggested how the procedure was often carried out. "Randolph, aney [sic] thing you See for the Better, Change," urged the customer. "You know about how many yards for a Boat 35 over all, 8½ feet beam, 50 inches deep."[202]

Following the closure of the Stevens sail loft on Tancook, islanders at Northwest Cove and elsewhere were left with two sources for professional canvas work. They could patronize either Randolph Stevens' new establishment at Second Peninsula or the large-vessel sailmakers at Lunenburg. Most builders and boat owners exercised one or the other of these options.[203] There was a third choice, however, and that was to use what were, in effect, homemade sails. Randolph Stevens' brother Wesley, who remained in the building business on Tancook, made his own sails for the schooner *Glendora*, a 36-footer he launched in 1931. A few years later, he hired Bridget Mason, wife of the builder Howard, to sew the sails for a sister ship, the *Stormalong*.[204] The employment of island women in this work was not uncommon in the 1920s and 1930s. Stanley Mason, the leading builder at Southeast Cove during those years, is known to have hired local female help on occasion, althought most of his sails were made at Lunenburg on the mainland, where prices tended to be cheaper than at the yacht-oriented Stevens loft and where the heavy canvas needed for larger vessels was most readily available.[205]

Stanley G. Mason (1882–1960), younger son of whaler builder Joshua Mason, was the most prolific of the second-generation schooner builders on Tancook. Working first in consecutive partnerships with Vernon and David Langille and later on his own, "Stan" Mason was, quantitatively at least, the island's premier producer of schoo-

---

* Another sometime sailmaker active during this period was Hibbert L. Langille (1869–1957), who periodically cut and sewed sails for dories, sloops, and small schooners at Southeast Cove from the 1910s through the 1930s. He rarely turned out canvas work for boats over 30' long, however. (*Sources:* Interview, Thomas Mason, 25 June 1990; Langille, *South Shore Langilles*, 50.)

ners and other craft. Notwithstanding the latter-day designation of Amos Stevens as "the master builder of Tancook,"[206] Mason surpassed Stevens both in number of registered sailing vessels (48 to 42) and in recorded tonnage (832 to 686). He was also responsible for three of the four island schooners over 60' in registered length,* and his *Nelson L.* (40 gross tons), launched in 1929, was exceeded in tonnage only by Reuben Heisler's *Silver Oak* (42 gross tons), built in the war year of 1917.[207]

The Mason boatyard was located on the north side of Southeast Cove in a part of Tancook known informally as "Canvas Town." Its main buildings, until recently a local landmark, stood clustered before a backdrop of evergreens facing one of the cove's few adequate mooring grounds. Stanley Mason started a small shop there in 1907, primarily building boats under 40' in length. He initially worked alone and then, beginning in 1909, in partnership with Vernon Langille. That brief association dissolved in 1911, when Langille elected to build independently. Within a year or two, Mason formed a second partnership with David Langille, Vernon's second cousin, and with his new partner began to construct larger vessels under the firm name Mason and Langille. Upon David Langille's untimely death in 1926, full ownership reverted to the senior partner, and he continued to operate the business as S. G. Mason until his retirement† at the end of 1945.[208]

Originally, all work in the Mason shop was done by hand in the traditional manner. During the Mason and Langille years, however, a concession to changing times was made in the form of a table saw for cutting planking. Later, the partners installed a stationary engine and winch to haul boats and to operate the table saw at greater efficiency. A planing machine was added during World War II, when business turned from fishing schooners to the mass production of naval patrol craft, but in the schooner-building era work mostly proceeded in time-honoured fashion – skilled craftsmen carrying out selected tasks without the aid of machine tools. In addition to the partners themselves, Mason and Langille usually employed three or four other

---

* The three Mason vessels were *Sarah Pauline*, 1924 (37 tons; 60' × 17' × 9'); *Nelson L.*, 1929 (40 tons; 60' × 17.2' × 9'); and *Morning Star II*, 1931 (31 tons; 60' × 16.5' × 8.5').

† Stanley Mason's son David succeeded him in business and maintained building operations at Southeast Cove for several more years before moving the enterprise to Ontario in 1952. David Mason launched the Mason yard's last working fishing schooner, a 34-footer for an Eastern Shore owner, in 1946 and also built two schooner-yachts in 1946–47. These were the last two-masters constructed at this location. (*Sources*: Interviews, Thomas Mason, July 1969, and Murray A. Mason, 21 June 1989; Sail Plan Record Book, Stevens sail loft, Second Peninsula, Lunenburg, Nova Scotia.)

men, who where paid an average of 20¢ per hour;* occasionally, when building large vessels, they hired as many as five or six – for a total work force of six to eight men. These included specialized shipwrights for difficult tasks, such as trimming (with adz), planking, finishing, and caulking, as well as few "rough carpenters" for general work. Among those employed at the yard in the early 1920s were such well-known island workmen as Percy Young, Hibbert Langille, Melvin and Roland Stevens, and Rufus Wilson.[209]

The peak period for schooner building at the Mason yard was the decade from 1923 to 1932, when 30 boats of register size were launched there,† about two thirds of all the large two-masters produced on Tancook during those years. That figure compared favourably to the 35 schooners built by Amos Stevens from 1907 to 1915 and the 30 turned out by Reuben Heisler between 1908 and 1918, during Northwest Cove's heyday of boat construction.[210] It was an output that received its initial impetus from Mason's partner David W. ("Davey") Langille (1890–1926).

David Langille, grand nephew of the famous Alfred, was responsible for most of the designs created by the Mason boatyard in the years when it established its reputation as a quality enterprise. Stanley Mason was an excellent builder and shrewd businessman, but judging from existing half-models, his schooners, though workmanlike, lacked a certain flair and elegance and were not designed with a high potential for speed under sail. The lines of one of his models, which was not built from (see fig. 12), illustrate his penchant for burdensome schooners, heavy on the quarter, with substantial carrying capacity. Mason did model the 50-footer *White Birch* (launched in 1918), as well as other early boats, and handled all the firm's designing after the death of his partner, but during the critical period between the end of the war and the mid-1920s, it was David Langille who modelled most of the fine schooners turned out by Mason and Langille.

---

* That was about the standard wage for Tancook boat carpenters between the world wars. Reuben Heisler also paid his best workers 20¢ per hour, although the less skilled earned just 15¢. At the turn of the century, however, Heisler himself took home only 65¢ per day as an apprentice to Amos Stevens. (*Source*: Interview, Benjamin Heisler, 22 June 1989.)

† Among these was the *Sarah Pauline* (1924), which measured 65' overall and had to be built outdoors, alongside the firm's shop, because the existing building was too small to accommodate her dimensions. This prompted an expansion and enlargement of facilities in the late 1920s so that two later boats of similar size could be built indoors. The building order for the *Sarah Pauline* had originally gone to Reuben Heisler, but was turned over to Mason and Langille upon the loss of Heisler's shop in 1923. Her construction marked the establishment of the Southeast Cove firm as the dominant boatyard on Tancook. (*Sources*: Interviews, Thomas Mason, 23 June 1988, and 22 June 1989, and Steadman S. Mason, 21 June 1986; see also HH, news item, 17 April 1924, 13.)

Among his known creations were *Elsie B. Young* (1923), *Bluebeard* (1923), *Sarah Pauline* (1924), *Tyrienne S.* (1924), and *Frances M.R.* (1925). He modelled the fast Cape Island boat *Jazz Vamp* during this time as well.[211]

Langille, whom his good friend Hovey Slauenwhite described as "smart as an eagle,"[212] must be ranked with Howard Mason, Vernon Langille, Wesley Stevens and Reuben Heisler as one of the premier schooner designers of the younger generation on Tancook. His boats (see figs. 13, 14, 15) were characterized by a pronounced sheer, short counter, fine wineglass sections, and a deep heel or sternpost combined with a shallow bow. The latter feature, which was thought necessary to achieve quickness in stays, required Langille's schooners to be trimmed by the bow, or in Tancook parlance "tripped by the nose," in order to gain sufficient stability for efficient windward work.[213] This need for forward ballasting was considered by some to be his chief failing as a designer,[214] but it did not detract from the appearance of his boats, which were among the island's most attractive.

David Langille was one of the tragic figures in Tancook's boatbuilding history. His association with Stanley Mason was just fifteen years old when he died in early January 1926 at the age of thirty-five, after a brief illness. The circumstances surrounding his death are strange – even bizarre – and speak to one of the shortcomings of island life during that period, the woeful lack of proper medical care. Langille, it seems, developed a severe winter cold or a case of influenza and devised a home remedy consisting of dark rum mixed with black pepper, a not-surprising recourse in the rum-running era. Instead of curing his condition, the lethal brew precipitated or exacerbated an undiagnosed gastrointestinal problem that proved fatal. It was later concluded that the builder had probably suffered from a ruptured appendix.[215]

With David Langille's death, Tancook lost one of its most promising craftsmen and, as it turned out, the last of his family to pursue the art of boatbuilding professionally on the island. David's father, Joshua C. Langille (b. 1864), a sometime builder of the earlier period, had launched his last large schooner in 1914,* and David's cousin

---

* Joshua Langille was a noted, if minor, island builder, who specialized in small schooners and scallop sloops and may have built whalers in his early career. His shop, attached to his barn, was located a slight distance inland from Alfred Langille's establishment at Southeast Cove. He built the *Sealer* (1908), one of the first Tancook schooners, and two other registered boats prior to the outbreak of World War I, finishing his career shortly after his uncle, Alfred. It was said that Joshua kept only one set of moulds for his boats and could build any size craft from them. (*Sources*: Interviews, Thomas Mason, 5 February and 14 June 1989; NA, LunSR: registers of schrs *Sealer*, 17 August 1911, *Delia H.*, 28 May 1912, and *Elva M.Y.*, 29 June 1914.)

Vernon had left the island to pursue his trade elsewhere a short time later. Like David, Vernon R. Langille (1888–1979), was for a time a worthy successor to his grandfather Alfred. In just two years following the dissolution of his partnership with Stanley Mason in 1911, he built five registered schooners in his own right and established himself as one of the most important builders at Southeast Cove.[216] Hovey Slauenwhite, who knew him well, considered Langille second as a craftsman only to Reuben Heisler, who was "hard to beat." Slauenwhite and his brother Clements, island fishermen during these years, purchased Langille's *Cecil V.L.* (1912), a fast 41-foot knockabout Langille himself considered his finest schooner. She was copper-fastened throughout – a rarity on Tancook – and, as Slauenwhite remembered three-quarters of a century later, a "wonderful" boat.[217] Her reputation suggests that the *Cecil V.L.* may well have been the best of the prewar schooners on the island, although Amos Stevens' *Comet G.* also earned contemporary notice.

Both Alfred Langille (who originally instructed him) and Howard Mason are known to have assisted Vernon Langille in his early building career, and it seems likely that the elder Langille, in particular, was partially responsible for some of the schooners bearing his grandson's name that emerged from their shared Southeast Cove shop in 1912 and 1913.[218] The largest of these, the 44-foot *Howard Stanley*, launched in June 1913,[219] was also the last. Vernon owned no boatbuilding property of his own at Southeast Cove, and when his first wife, an island woman, died in late 1912, his ties to Tancook were sharply diminished. After a few years spent fishing, he moved to Indian Point in 1916, remarried, and resumed his building operations at that mainland location,[220] where he earned a richly deserved reputation as a builder of fine fishing boats and yachts based on Tancook schooner lines.

The last of the important builders of the younger generation was Howard Mason (1874–1953), eldest son of whaler builder Joshua Mason and brother of Stanley. He began his career around the turn of the century, first assisting his father in the construction of double-enders and later building schooners and sloops on his own account. Mason worked alone or with one or two of his sons in a barn adjacent to his house at Southeast Cove. Over a period of four decades (ca. 1909–49), he built a dozen boats, including the famous *Patavana*, a 43-foot knockabout generally considered the finest all-round fisherman in the Tancook fleet during the 1930s.[221] His designs (see figs. 18, 26, 29) featured a bold, straight forward sheer, a relatively deep forefoot, a long, flat run, and graceful, yacht-like lines.

Mason was widely known for his ability to "put a stern on a boat," an arcane skill much in demand after whalers gave way to counter-

Photo 16   Tancook whaler *Nancy*, a typical representative of her type, moored at Peggy's Cove, Nova Scotia, probably in the 1920s. Note the bald clipper or "Aberdeen" bow, the peaked double-ender stern, the low freeboard, and the absence of a fore-boom, all standard features. [Courtesy Public Archives of Nova Scotia, Halifax, W.R. MacAskill Collection]

Photo 17   The rakish stern of a Tancook whaler hauled at Peggy's Cove, Nova Scotia, in the 1920s. This boat is carvel planked, unlike the original clinker-built whalers, and shows an adaptation for auxiliary power – a propeller aperture cut in the base of the reinforced outboard rudder. Otherwise, she exhibits the distinctive, sharply angled sternpost and long tiller that marked her class. [Courtesy Public Archives of Nova Scotia, Halifax, W.R. MacAskill Collection]

Photo 18 Schooner-yacht *Adare* (ex *Tacoma*) sailing off Tancook in 1969. This boat, designed by Reuben Heisler in 1906 as a fisherman, shows the appearance of the straight-stem Tancook schooner that preceded the round-bow model. Her narrow "V" stern is typical of island craft of that vintage, as is the pure gaff rig with large single jib. [Photograph by author]

Photo 19 Schooner *Squanto* of Duxbury, Massachusetts (built 1902), probable stylistic prototype for the round-bow Tancook schooners. [Courtesy Peabody and Essex Museum, Salem, MA/Peabody Museum Collections]

Photo 20 Knockabout schooner *Patavana* under full sail off Tancook in the spring of 1930. Her marconi or Bermudian mainsail was the first to be carried by a Tancook fishing boat. [Author's collection]

Photo 21 Schooner-yacht *Amasonia* under sail off Chester, Nova Scotia, in the late 1930s. Built by Howard Mason in 1935, she displays the wider stern, overhanging spoon bow, and marconi rig of the last Tancook schooners. [Courtesy Thomas Mason]

Photo 22 Tancook schooner *Patavana*, rigged as a semi-knockabout, carrying a load of salt home from Lunenburg in 1939. The boat is working to windward in a stiff northeast breeze. Her forward cuddy cabin and open main fish hatch are clearly visible. [Author's collection]

Photo 23 Tancook knockabout schooner *X10U8* under full sail on the starboard tack in Mahone Bay in 1942. The open deck arrangement of a typical, small island hatch boat, featuring forward cuddy, after engine housing, and fish hold amidships, may be seen. Note the marconi mainsail carried by several of the last Tancook fishermen. [Courtesy Murray A. Mason]

Photo 24 The small (33-foot) hatch boat *X10U8* beating out to Tancook from nearby Chester in 1942. The wind is southwest, and the builder, Howard Mason, stands in the cockpit watching the set of the schooner's sails. His son Thomas mans the tiller, which exhibits the weather helm common to knockabouts in windward work. [Author's collection]

Photo 25 Tancook schooner *Windstark* (ex *Blue Lagoon*) lifts her bow to southern waters in Albemarle Sound, North Carolina, around 1940. Originally built as the fisherman *Harold H.* by Stanley G. Mason in 1929, this powerful and attractive vessel was refitted in 1935 as a yacht for blue-water sailor William ("Bill") McCoy of rum running fame and began a notable second career as a pleasure craft. [Courtesy Harry W. Piper]

Photo 26 A new Tancook schooner, recently launched from the S.G. Mason yard in Southeast Cove, preparing for sea in the late 1920s. A dory is alongside. [Courtesy Mrs Sadie I. Langille]

Photo 27 The large (63-foot) hardwood-built deck boat *Nelson L.* moored at Southeast Cove, Tancook, shortly after her launch from the S.G. Mason yard in 1929. Two of her five "bastard" dories are nested between the masts, which exhibit the crosstrees used in rigging Tancook's bigger schooners. The vessel's sails are loosely furled and ready for raising. Note the rope lanyards securing her multiple wire shrouds. This schooner fished out of Canso and North Sydney for several years before being lost in a storm off Port Bickerton, Nova Scotia, in 1938. [Courtesy Mrs Sadie I. Langille]

Photo 28 A Tancook deck boat of the 55-foot class ready for launch at the S.G. Mason yard, Southeast Cove. Probably the *Marion C.* (23 tons), built in 1927. Among visible details are the anchor windlass, wheelbox, stanchion rails and scuppers, and double rigging with deadeyes. Note as well the sled under the vessel's port bilge to aid in launching and the mast hoops encircling her rough-hewn spruce spars. This schooner also displays an after cabin and a quarter rail, unusual for a Tancooker. [Courtesy Mrs Sadie I. Langille]

Photo 29 A large Tancook hatch boat at anchor off Chester, Nova Scotia, in the late 1920s. Believed to be the 45-foot *Frances M.R.*, built by Mason and Langille in 1925. [Courtesy Mrs Sadie I. Langille]

Photo 30 *Verna B.*, one of the last Tancook schooners, hauled on the launchway of her owners, fishermen Ainsley and Percy Baker, Backalong, Big Tancook Island. Built by Murray Wilneff in the late 1930s, this boat exemplified the transition of the island schooner from a pure sailing craft with auxiliary engine to essentially a motor-sailer in the years just prior to the adoption of the fully motorized Cape Island boat. [Courtesy Mrs Mary M. Baker]

stern schooners in the early 1900s. The transition from the double-ended to "transom" stern greatly increased the difficulty of shaping the after sections of vessels. Whaler construction, as builder David Stevens recalled, was a simple proposition involving straight planking, while schooner work presented the problem of getting around "the tuck" – the place near the top of the sternpost where the counter met the bottom timbers.[222] A facility for this task, as well as an eye for properly formed transoms and a fine touch in finishing hulls, were Howard Mason's hallmarks as a craftsman. He tutored Vernon and Thomas Langille and Reuben Heisler in building schooner sterns, and spent a year in Heisler's employ as a specialist in stern work.[223]

Howard Mason, like a number of other Tancook builders (Wesley Stevens and Joshua Langille among them), was not a professional boatbuilder. He was what Agnes McGuire, one-time staff writer for the *Canadian Fisherman*, called a "fisherman-carpenter." In a perceptive 1917 article on Lunenburg County's shipbuilding industry, she made the following observation:

There have in some small communities, notably at Tancook, been some exceedingly fine crafts turned out [by fisherman-carpenters] with blacksmith work, carpenter work, and sailmaking complete. These men are able to turn their hand to anything and would laugh at the idea of having to go to one of the larger shipyards for their trim little schooners ... It is passing strange that [such] small places can compete with much larger ones in a craft requiring much constructive skill, and the application in practice of scientific principles, but it is a fact and an incontrovertible one at that.[224]

Howard Mason accurately fits that profile of the fisherman-carpenter. He was an archtypical jack-of-all-trades who fished, farmed, coasted and also builts boats; and his boats, more often than not, were intended for his own use or that of his sons. He did occasionally perform contract work – he built one schooner, for example, as a subcontractor to Reuben Heisler[225] – but considered building more of an avocation to be pursued when more pressing work was completed.

The building of Howard Mason's *Patavana* typified the manner in which part-time builders constructed countless small Tancook schooners. This boat was built over a two-year period between late 1927 and late 1929 by the elder Mason and his son Thomas, who carried on the work during lulls between the planting and harvesting of crops. Wood was acquired from Mahone Bay, and the keel laid in the family's unheated barn,* where construction proceeded sporadically in the spring, summer, and early fall when temperatures were tolerable. *Patavana* was completed in November 1929, just in time for the winter coasting season, and had only to be launched. This would normally have been a simple procedure, but unlike his brother, who inherited ample shore property, Howard Mason had to work a considerable distance from salt water, and launching was an exercise in ingenuity and fortitude. A tackle attached to the bow, and puncheons (large fish barrels) placed horizontally under the 11-ton schooner's bilges, were used to drag and roll her by hand from the builder's barn, through his fields, and out onto the Southeast Cove road. This remarkable feat was accomplished by two men working alone. A wooden sled was then set under the vessel, and a borrowed team of oxen hauled her, canted to one side, over log rollers down to the water's edge several hundred yards away. The schooner's completed masts were likewise transported by hand to the launchway on the shoulders of the builder and his son, one man at each end of a spar.[226]

Despite the handicaps under which fishermen-carpenters like Howard Mason laboured, and the limited number of boats they produced, their contribution to the development of the Tancook schooner was critical. The major professional builders – Amos Stevens, Reuben Heisler, Stanley Mason, and others – built as many as half a dozen boats per year and, at least by Tancook standards, were interested in mass production. As a result, their work, while good, was not always finely honed on an individual vessel basis. The best of the fisherman-carpenters, on the other hand, treated their few boats as labours of love or works of art. Inordinate thought and planning went into their design, and exacting effort into their construction. They were an extension of their builders' personalities and a source of

---

* Howard Mason's barn, like those of other Tancook builders who combined boatbuilding with farming, was a specially designed, dual-purpose structure. Windows were installed for working light, and the floor plan was arranged so as to maximize the space available for laying down a vessel. The central threshing floor remained intact in its usual location, but substantial alterations were made elsewhere. The stable, which traditionally occupied the entire lower part of one end of the building, was reduced in size and moved to one side, while the main hay mow, which normally dominated the opposite end from roof to ground level, was converted into a loft with work space below, thus allowing full use of the barn's length. In addition, temporary extensions or annexes were periodically added to the building to accommodate the construction of extra large craft. (*Sources*: Interviews, Thomas Mason, 3 October 1989 and 25 June 1990, and Murray A. Mason, 26 June 1990.)

83 The Boats

pride. More than that, they were the keys to their livelihood and survival.*

All of Howard Mason's schooners were, with few exceptions, living laboratories in which he worked on a daily basis. The faults and strong points of each boat were noted by the designer-builder, who observed the performance of his handiwork firsthand in all conditions. How did the craft sail to windward versus off the wind? Was she stiff or "cranky"?† Was she balanced properly – "slung right" as islanders termed it?‡ Did she respond quickly when tacking? Was she confortable and dry in rough weather? These and a myriad of other questions were answered by hard experience over a period of months or years, and what was learned found expression in the half-model carved for the next boat built, wherein the progressive trial and error process continued. Perhaps the builder would make his new creation a little fuller forward or deeper aft to correct some perceived flaw, or perhaps retain some other feature that had seemed to augment performance. In this step by step manner, multiplied several times by the experience of numerous builders, an optimum design slowly evolved that combined practicality with appearance. By the 1930s, perfection within the limits of intended usage had been attained, and the Tancook schooner reached its final form.

Estimates on the total number of island schooners built have ranged from 100 to 200 boats.[227] The actual figure was well over 200, but a complete tabulation can never be made due to incomplete documentation. Official records, based on vessel registrations, show that in the thirty-two-year period 1904 to 1936, 193 schooner-rigged vessels of 10 or more tons were launched at the Tancooks, 169 of them at the main island. Of these, 7 were double-ended whalers, leaving a

---

* In terms of speed and seaworthiness, the best schooners owned on Tancook in the 1920s and 1930s, respectively, were thought to be Wesley Stevens' *Mother* and Howard Mason's *Patavana* (see figs. 16 and 18). Both were products of fisherman-carpenters, and both were built as fishing and coasting vessels for their builders' personal use. Vernon Langille's vaunted *Cecil V.L.*, probably the best of Tancook's prewar schooners, was also owned for several years by her builder. (*Sources*: Interviews, Thomas Mason, July 1969 and 15 June 1986; NA, LunSR: registers of schrs *Cecil V.L.*, 15 June 1912, and *Mother*, 21 July 1924; Can.LCH, LunSR: register of schr *Patavana*, 28 November 1929; see also HH, marine lists, 1925–40, passim, and Stevens and Stevens, *Stevens Families of Nova Scotia* ,127.)

† In island terminology, a "cranky" boat was one that was weak or tender – unable to stand up to a strong breeze. (*Source*: Interview, Thomas Mason, 3 October 1988.)

‡ A reference to the vessel's sail plan and the positioning of her masts. A boat that was not "slung right" might, for example, carry a weather helm. (*Source*: Interviews, Thomas Mason, 29 September 1987 and 3 October 1989.)

total of 186 true Tancook schooners.[228] However, my own independent search has uncovered at least 30 more that, because of their size, were never registered; there were doubtless many others built as well. In general, customs records did not list boats of less than 40' registered length.* (Only 14 such craft built on Tancook were documented.) Since island schooners were turned out in lengths as short as 28', however, it is obvious that a sizeable percentage were never recorded. This was particularly true before World War I, when the average length of a Tancook schooner was about 38' to 40' overall.[229]

Changes in island rigging practices after the war added to the raw numbers of small schooners, even though average schooner size increased during that period. As far back as the whaler era, large sloops were common on Tancook. Besides the standard schooner-rigged whaler and the small jolly boat, a whaler sloop called a "ram boat" was used by island fishermen who preferred an intermediate-sized craft. This clipper-bowed sloop, a gaff-rigged double-ender with a centreboard, was approximately 28' to 30' long overall.[230] In the early years of the twentieth century, the ram boat was replaced by another 30-footer with a relatively straight stem, a deep transom stern, and an outboard rudder. This class was followed in turn by a counter-stern sloop of 32' to 34' which incorporated a round bow. Around the beginning of the First World War (ca. 1912–14), the demand for large single-masters diminished, and a smaller, more easily handled type, the Tancook scallop sloop (or "scallop boat"), was developed. This shallow-draft, round-bow craft, which averaged 26' or 27' overall and drew only two to three feet of water, remained popular for inshore fishing, lobstering, and scalloping until about 1940 and may still be seen in unrigged form today. It was roughly modelled on the larger schooner (see fig. 24), but was usually built without a heavy keel or centreboard, and its light weight and minimal underbody allowed for daily launching and hauling in the winter months. The scallop sloop really replaced the nineteenth century jolly boat in the island hierar-

---

* Registered length was measured from the front of the stem to the after side of the sternpost on deck. Double-ended whalers, therefore, were registered according to their overall lengths, while counter-sterned schooners were registered at less than their full dimensions. The schooner *Harold H.*, for example, was listed at 45.6' register, but actually measured 49' overall. Discrepancies arose in the recorded lengths of many schooners due to the fact that tonnage, which was derived from hull measurements, determined a vessel's fishing bounty. Owners, who assisted in the measuring, often succumbed to the temptation to maximize tonnage by stretching the tape a few inches or more. On rare occasions, overall length was substituted for length to the sternpost. (*Sources*: Can.LCH, LunSR: register of schr *Harold H.*, 1 May 1929; *Lloyd's Register of American Yachts, 1939*, 475; interview, Thomas Mason, 30 September 1986.)

chy of watercraft, and consequently the new, postwar intermediate type became the small schooner. After 1918, any Tancook boat over 27' long was routinely rigged as a schooner,* and small two-masters became commonplace.[231]

The upshot was that innumerable pocket-sized Tancook schooners built both before and after the war were never officially listed. Howard Mason, who turned out close to a dozen two-masters during his lengthy career, registered only one because the rest were all under 10 tons. His smallest was a 30-footer built in 1923.[232] Similarly, Wesley Stevens' name appeared in the registers just three times as a builder, but a rudimentary investigation uncovered a half-dozen more boats in the 34' to 36' range built under his supervision,[233] and there were probably others. It is possible that in addition to those documented, another hundred or so schooners were built by island craftsmen, bringing Tancook's total production to nearly 300 boats.

Judging only from register data, it appears that about one third of the schooners built at the Tancooks between 1904 and 1936 (when the last one was recorded) were for island owners, and about two thirds for outside ownership. Unsurprisingly, most of the latter were products of the professional builders, chiefly Amos and Alvin Stevens, who worked almost entirely for off-island customers, and Stanley Mason, who sold a majority of his considerable tonnage output to buyers from "away." The leading individual markets were Big Tancook itself (53 schooners or 28 percent of the total), Blandford (27 or 15 percent), Indian Harbour (17 or 9 percent), Canso (9 or 5 percent), Little Tancook (9 or 5 percent), Terence Bay (8 or 4 percent), Lunenburg (6 or 3 percent), and Halifax (5 or 3 percent). However, requests for schooners came from 40 locales throughout Nova Scotia, primarily from fishing communities along the South Shore and Eastern Shore in Lunenburg, Halifax, and Guysborough counties. Among the more distant markets, the Canso connection was particularly fruitful for island builders, and it accounted for sales of some of the largest Tancook boats, including the 60-foot dory trawlers *Sarah Pauline* (1924), *Nelson L.* (1929), and *Morning Star II* (1930), built by the Mason yard for Captain Frank C. Lohnes.[234]

Eventually, through the resale of older boats, the fame of the Tancook schooner spread well beyond the immediate confines of coastal Nova Scotia. Secondary owners came to include fishermen

---

* By the early 1930s, former island builder Vernon Langille was turning out Tancook-type knockabout schooners as small as 27' overall at his Indian Point shop. (*Source:* Sail plan dated September 1933, Stevens sail loft, Second Peninsula, Lunenburg, Nova Scotia.)

throughout Atlantic Canada. An examination of the ultimate disposition of the nearly 200 registered island schooners indicates that while a third ended their days working out of neighbouring South Shore ports between Liverpool and Halifax, another third finished their careers on the Eastern Shore and in Cape Breton Island, and still another third found their way to such places as Prince Edward Island, Newfoundland, Quebec, Ontario, New Brunswick, the United States, and even St Pierre and Miquelon.[235]

The peak period for the construction of Tancook schooners was just before the start of World War I, and the leading year was 1912, when no fewer than 30 large boats of register size slid down the ways, 19 at Northwest Cove and backalong, 8 at Southeast Cove, and 3 at Little Tancook. Stimulated by the immediate pre-war fishing boom, Tancook's brief "golden age" in schooner building lasted from 1908 to 1913, when 101 recorded launchings took place. Substantial, if reduced, production was maintained through most of the prosperous war years, but after 1917, a severe post-war decline set in that lasted until 1923. No large boats at all were built in 1920 or 1921, and only one the following year. Starting in the early middle years of the 1920s, however, island boatbuilding experienced a late revival predicated on a revived fishing industry, the growth of the Halifax coasting trade, and the sudden phenomenon of rum running. These factors created a demand that lasted until the Great Depression, when economic activity of all kinds, including boat construction, suffered a decade-long collapse. This second period of sustained production lasted from 1923 to 1931 and brought the Tancook schooner to its final form and ultimate development.[236]

FORM AND FUNCTION

A number of changes took place in the design and construction of the round-bow Tancook schooner during the quarter century following its introduction. A few were purely stylistic, but most were outgrowths of the work for which the vessel was intended and the means chosen to best accomplish the required tasks. The most obvious change was in overall boat size.

The early Tancook schooners, like their whaler predecessors, were relatively small sailing craft. Prior to World War I, most of them measured 40' or less on deck, but by the 1920s they commonly ranged from 45' to 47'.[237] Statistics culled from customs records indicate that among registered schooners alone, the average length grew from 42' for boats built between 1905 and 1909 to 47' for those built between 1930 and 1934 – a 12 percent increase. Average tonnage increased from 14 to 18 gross tons over the same period* – a rise of nearly 30 percent.[238]

Most of the growth in size took place between 1910 and 1920, when Tancook's fisheries, and those of the South Shore generally, underwent significant changes. Islanders had always known that the farther out one fished, the bigger the fish and the better the fishing. That was one reason for replacing the double-ended whaler with the somewhat larger counter-stern schooner around 1905.[239] The whaler, moreover, had been essentially a herring boat designed for net fishing along the adjacent coastline where the herring schools gathered, and it rarely ventured far off shore. The schooner, on the other hand, while quite adaptable to herring or mackerel netting, was primarily intended as a hand-line, cod-fishing vessel, and was designed with offshore work foremost in mind.[240]

Beginning in 1910, Tancook's salt cod fishery, which had been nearly moribund for several years, increased dramatically and entered a period of sustained growth. Almost simultaneously, the island's salt herring fishery, mainstay of the local economy for decades, went into a marked temporary decline.[241] It was this shift in fishing priorities from herring to cod that generated the burst in schooner construction which made the three years starting in 1910 the greatest boatbuilding period in Tancook history.[242] Official figures from the Canadian Department of Marine and Fisheries show that by 1912, the Tancooks had a combined vessel-fishing fleet of 16 schooners in excess of 10 tons each, up from none at all the year before.[243] Unofficial figures compiled from register data, which in this case present a more accurate picture, indicate an increase between 1909 and 1912 of from 8 to 21 registered schooners owned at the two islands.[244]

Two factors stimulated the upsurge in cod fishing and the concomitant rise in the number and size of schooners. First was the drop in the price of herring realized by Tancook fishermen, which fell by over a third between 1910 and 1912 and did not return to previous levels until 1916. This encouraged the alternative pursuit of cod, the price of

---

* The average gross tonnages and dimensions of registered Tancook schooners built during consecutive five-year periods beginning in 1905 were as follows:

1905–09 – 14.11 tons; 42.4' × 11.2' × 5.8' (35 schooners)
1910–14 – 16.42 tons; 44.4' × 11.6' × 6.1' (85 schooners)
1915–19 – 17.60 tons; 44.9' × 11.8' × 6.2' (22 schooners)
1920–24 – 18.30 tons; 45.7' × 12.8' × 6.5' (10 schooners)
1925–29 – 17.85 tons; 45.8' × 12.8' × 6.6' (22 schooners)
1930–34 – 18.11 tons; 47.0' × 13.1' × 6.7' (10 schooners)

(Sources: NA, LunSR; NA, AriSR; Can.HCH, HalSR; Can.LCH, LunSR; and Can.SRD, CanSSR: registers of Tancook-built schooners, 1905–45.)

which remained steady through 1912 and then increased sharply over the next several years.²⁴⁵ Concurrently, the onset of steam or "otter" trawling (i.e., dragging), which began in Nova Scotia in 1910, impelled inshore cod fishermen from Tancook and other South Shore ports to go farther off the coast to obtain a decent catch. Mass-production steam trawlers, making short, frequent trips and marketing fresh, increasingly depleted the closer inshore grounds and forced the smaller sailing vessels to abandon their traditional haunts close to home.²⁴⁶ The need to venture ever farther afield reinforced the already growing trend among shore fishermen at Tancook and elsewhere to acquire larger craft.

Additional developments over the decade after 1910 continued to spur the growth of the provincial cod fishery and to indirectly encourage the building of bigger schooners at Tancook. The Underwood Tariff, enacted by the United States Congress in 1913, reduced duties on imported Canadian fish and created greater demand and higher prices* for the production of Nova Scotia's inshore operators.²⁴⁷ A year later, the war in Europe began, and one of its economic side effects was a growing meat shortage that stimulated seafood consumption among Canada's civilian population. As a result, the South Shore fishing ports realized unprecedented high prices for their cod and other groundfish that lasted through 1918.²⁴⁸

There was one other factor bearing on the size of Tancook schooners after 1910, and it was technological, not economic. This was the coming of the internal combustion engine. The gasoline engine had a profound impact on the island's boats and on its fishing industry, but that impact has been generally misunderstood. The Tancook schooners, first of all, were not originally auxiliary craft, and they were not initially intended to accommodate inboard motors, although their shape proved adaptable to that innovation.† The first schooners preceded the introduction of gasoline engines by at least a half-dozen years, and in most respects, their construction paralleled that of the older, engine-less whalers. Like the whalers, the early schooners had narrow sternposts that could not support propeller apertures. When engines first appeared, holes were cut in the rudders of the schooners (and some of the whalers) in order to accommodate propeller blades without weakening essential structural timbers. Later, wider sternposts were used, and the necessary holes were cut in the posts them-

---

* The prices Tancook fishermen received for their cod rose by 38 percent during the treaty's first year of operation. (Sources: Can.RFB, 1912/13, 128; ibid., 1913/14, 98–9.)
† The schooners had an advantage over the whalers in this regard because their counters and transoms dictated wider after sections than were found in the narrow-sterned double-enders.

89 The Boats

selves or in the adjacent deadwood.[249] Many counter-stern schooners did not acquire engines, however. Of the 186 registered schooners over 10 tons built after 1904, 34 (all of them launched prior to 1915) never had engines, and another 32 were built without engines but had them installed in later years. Over a third of all registered Tancook schooners, in other words, were designed purely as sailing craft.[250]

Nevertheless, engines did eventually alter the appearance of island schooners in significant ways. One was to contribute to the increased size of the vessels. If the gasoline motor did not create the Tancook schooner, it did encourage the building of larger boats able to fish farther from shore. The old whalers and the early schooners, it must be remembered, were rowing as well as sailing craft. Their range was circumscribed by the practical distance they could be powered by sweeps if the wind fell, and to be rowed effectively they had to be fairly small. Contrary to some stated opinion,[251] the island whalers rarely, if ever, worked as far as thirty miles outside Tancook. Their effective range (and that of the original schooners) was only half that distance. Most fished the so-called "first ridge," an underwater shoal running parallel to the coastline about twelve to fourteen miles seaward of Southeast Cove.* In terms of time and expended energy, that was about the farthest two crewmen could reasonably be expected to row a 35-foot boat to the fishing grounds in morning calms, even with the sails up (the usual practice) to take advantage of occasional cat's paws or wisps of wind.[252]

The gasoline engine removed the restrictions imposed by geography and nature. It freed Tancook fishermen to move beyond their traditional fishing grounds and permitted them to build the bigger boats needed to fish farther off shore.† By the 1910–20 period gasoline-powered island schooners, operating under sail and motor, were regularly working the "second ridge," eighteen to twenty miles from Tancook or about five or six miles farther out than before. By the 1920s, they were venturing to "the peak" or Dunn's Ridge, an angular extension of the second ridge that jutted another five miles out into the Atlantic, or approximately twenty-five miles outside Tancook.[253]

The larger schooners of the post-1910 years, which easily accommodated the 4- to 5-foot long "engine room" that replaced oarlocks and

---

* That was approximately the same working distance (ten to fifteen miles) cited in 1850 by John E. Fairbanks for Nova Scotia's early shore-fishing "whale-boats." (*Source*: Perley, *Sea and River Fisheries*, 247).

† In late 1910, an observer of Lunenburg County's fishing industry wrote: "The conditions of our inshore fishermen in regard to boats and other implements used in their vocation, are infinitely better than formerly. Their boats are larger, and many of them gasolines as well as sail." (*Source*: HH, article, 31 December 1910, 14.)

sweeps and had sufficient bulk to withstand the increased buffeting of wind and wave, enabled island fishermen to add another dozen or so miles to their normal cruising radius. As will be seen, those motorized craft also, for the first time, permitted lengthy voyages to more distant fishing grounds and entry into the regional coasting trade. This was a striking break with the past, and it permanently altered island fishing practices and the island economy. The introduction of the auxiliary engine had much the same impact elsewhere. In 1915, the *Canadian Fisherman* described the revolutionary changes recently wrought by motor power in the inshore fisheries of Scandinavia:

Previous to the general use of the motor, the Swedish fishermen ... had to take whatever fish happened to be in the locality; they set their gear wherever wind and oar would take them ... When the internal combustion motor came into use ... the fishing areas were broadened. The fishermen went further offshore. They followed the fish and made more trips and incidentally more money in the course of a season.[254]

Tancook fishermen were among the earliest in their part of Nova Scotia to experiment with engines, after overcoming the common belief that the noise would drive fish out to sea. It is said that Charles Cross installed the first motor in an island boat, a small, round-stern model of uncertain description.[255] This was probably not long after 1905. The first Tancook-built boats of register size to have engines, however, were three steam-powered vessels turned out in 1907–08 by Alvin Stevens near Northwest Cove, the *Grace* (1907), the *Hilford* (1908), and the *Seacrest* (1908), all produced for Halifax merchants and the only steamers known to have been built on the island.[256] Among registered sailing schooners, the first to come equipped with an auxiliary motor was the *Sealer*, built at Southeast Cove in 1908 by Joshua Langille for Amos Levy, a Cross Island fisherman. She was followed by the *Dan Patch* and the *Laura M. Levy* in 1909, both of them Amos Stevens creations intended for Lunenburg ownership. Not until 1910 did island fishermen begin putting gasoline engines in their own schooners, starting with the *Elsie C.*, launched by Mason and Langille in March of that year for William Cross of Big Tancook.[257]

The year 1910 marked the real beginning of the auxiliary schooner era at the Tancooks, although it was not until 1911 that more island-built craft were registered with engines than without. By 1912 almost every new schooner launched had a motor, and for the first time, owners of older boats began to have them installed in large numbers. During the war years, the trend became almost universal. On Tancook itself, very few boats had used engines prior to 1911, but by 1915 nearly every resident boat owner had one.[258]

Well over half the engines used in Tancook-built boats came from two sources, the Lunenburg Foundry Company and the Chester firm of Hawboldt and Evans. The latter partnership was particularly linked with the fortunes of the Tancook schooner. Formed in 1906 by Forman Hawboldt (1876–1951) and his brother-in-law Harry Evans, it operated for several years out of a barn on the Hawboldt premises, where initial experiments with internal combustion were carried out and where casting was done. By around 1910, the partners had developed a light gasoline engine known as the "Canadian Standard," and in 1912, they set up regular production in a bona fide machine shop. Their most popular model among fishermen was a single-cylinder, twelve-horsepower, "make and break" affair that could push a 40-foot schooner at speeds of up to six knots. Most of the engines employed in Tancook schooners were of this type – one or two cylinders, ten to fifteen horsepower, and maximum speeds of six knots or a little better – and to minimize costs, many were installed used.[259]

Some of the engine manufacturers, including the Lunenburg Foundry Company and the Acadia Gas Engine Company of Bridgewater (but not Hawboldt and Evans), maintained commission agents in the fishing villages to hawk their wares. Boatbuilder Stanley Mason of Southeast Cove was the representative for Lunenburg Foundry on Tancook, and in that capacity he endeavoured to have the firm's "Atlantic" model installed in as many of his own boats as possible. A neighbour, Stephen Cross, represented the rival Acadia Company on the island.[260] Such an aggressive, wide-ranging sales network certainly accelerated the adoption of auxiliary motors, but in reality, the fishermen needed little incentive.

It has been suggested that the introduction of these small, relatively inexpensive engines precipitated the decline of Tancook's fisheries by driving low-capital fishermen from the industry,[261] but that is incorrect. Thomas Mason, an island native intimately familiar with the operation of the local fisheries, recalled that most Tancookers were quite able to make the transition to auxiliary power and that those who did not managed to survive economically without it.* New engines cost $300 to $400 in the 1920s, but used ones could be had for about $200.

---

* The failure of a few individuals to acquire engines was not a matter of economics but aesthetics. One island fisherman who disliked the new mechanical device intensely would not take a tow from any boat with a motor, even if becalmed or disabled. Noise was doubtless a factor in creating some resistance. Island native Benjamin Heisler had vivid memories of the nerve-jarring racket produced when several of the early "one lung" engines were fired up simultaneously on otherwise quiet Tancook mornings. (*Sources*: Interviews, Thomas Mason, 29 September 1986, and Benjamin Heisler, 22 June 1989.)

Although that was not an inconsiderable sum, it was nevertheless manageable, and the purchaser was paid back in decreased time and effort and in larger catches of fish.[262] Since the average price of a contemporary 40-foot schooner was $400, sails and rigging included,[263] a motor added about one-third to the overall investment,* a significant additional outlay, but one most islanders made regardless of the sacrifice. As an observer of Sweden's comparable inshore fishery noted, fishermen invariably found a way to acquire an engine, even if it meant investing their last penny: "Every man who owned a boat put an engine into her and the results were beyond expectations."[264] On Tancook, the same psychology applied, and it contributed to the greatest flurry of boatbuilding and fishing activity in the island's history. Gasoline-powered boats of various kinds – schooners, sloops, and motor launches – grew from 8 in 1910 to 50 four years later, and the value of the island catch leaped from $28,000 to $55,000, its highest in almost two decades, over the same period.[265]

In addition to increasing the size and range of the Tancook schooners, the internal combustion engine caused significant changes in their basic design. The most fundamental of these was the final elimination of the iron "boiler plate" centreboards inherited from the old whalers. Until the coming of gasoline power, most schooners (especially those under 40' long) still retained boards that were used in windward sailing to compensate for the boats' comparatively shallow drafts. After motors were adopted, the need for those boards diminished, since fishermen could simply turn on their engines when going against the wind, saving their sails for reaching and running.[266] This was eminently practical for the more sluggish boats – "dummies," as they were called[267] – and for the majority of early ones that lacked true keels. The owners of some of these older schooners removed their centreboards entirely when engines arrived on the scene, planking over the area below the casing to seal the hulls. This was done eagerly and without regret for the most part. Centreboards had always been a problem on Tancook. Their cases leaked and were in the way when loading cargo, and they would occasionally be struck and cracked by fish or sauerkraut barrels. By eliminating the need for boards, engines ended those annoyances.[268]

With the phasing out of centreboards after 1910, the Tancook schooners became genuine keel boats. The 12"-wide (but only 2"-deep) plank keels or "shoes" they had shared with the whalers were replaced by 6"-wide vertical wood keels that typically measured

---

* In 1913, builder Reuben Heisler could turn out a 45-foot schooner, complete with Hawboldt engine, for $650. (*Source*: Interview, Benjamin Heisler, 22 June 1989.)

8" or 9" deep forward, 12" in the middle, and 18" aft near the heel. While rock or iron inside ballast continued to furnish basic stability,* these new keels supplied the lateral resistance formerly provided by boards. The boats themselves also became gradually deeper in proportion, so that windward work under sail alone remained a feasible option.[269] The schooners of the 1920s and 1930s averaged a foot more in depth than those of the prewar years, an increase 4 percent greater than that in hull length.[270] Plans of the prewar schooner *Comet G.* (1910) and the comparably sized postwar *Patavana* (1929) illustrate the changes (see figs. 3, 18). Both sets of lines were taken from the builders' half-models and represent the appearance of the boats to the inside of the planking and minus their keels. The *Patavana* plan shows a vessel similar in beam measurement but shorter by several feet and drawing several inches more water than her opposite number of a generation earlier.

One builder who was instrumental in the creation of a deeper schooner model was Howard Mason of Southeast Cove. Most postwar Tancook designers favoured the shallow-bow/deep-heel profile, which was thought to produce a boat that was nimble in tacking due to her cutaway forefoot and short keel but also efficient in windward sailing because her depth near the sternpost provided holding power. Mason rejected this theory and turned out several schooners after 1929 that emphasized forward depth or "gripe."† He also reversed the traditional shaping of the Tancook schooner keel, which was normally shallow near the bow and gradually tapered aft to its deepest point at the sternpost. In the small knockabout fisherman *X10U8*, launched in 1940, Mason projected a keel of the same depth fore and aft that, combined with a deeper-than-usual forefoot, produced a schooner noted for both quickness in stays and a windward ability nearly comparable to some area racing sloops.[271]

Although keel boats became almost universal on Tancook after World War I, a few schooner owners remained loyal to the centreboard. These included Steven Alinard, a well-known Southeast

---

* Rock ballast was the norm for island boats, but pig iron was sometimes used instead. Iron ballasting was introduced by American yachtsmen belonging to the Chester Yacht Club, who installed it in several of their Tancook racing schooners around 1910–12. (*Sources*: Pugsley, "Chester, Nova Scotia," 11, 24; Hilchie, "Chester Yacht Club," 3.)

† The shallow bow/deep heel profile developed shortly after World War I following the adoption of full keels. Tancook's prewar centreboard schooners had been relatively shallow both fore and aft with profiles similar to their whaler predecessors, whose keels nearly paralleled their waterlines. The newer shape dominated Tancook schooner design until challenged by the deeper bow concept in the 1930s. (*Source*: Interview, Thomas Mason, 12 August 1990.)

94   The Tancook Schooners

Cove fisherman.* Alinard was an old-fashioned owner who grew up with the board and refused to convert to keel construction, even after the introduction of engines. The two centreboard knockabouts he had built at the Mason yard in the 1920s – the last of their type – were essentially throwbacks to an earlier era. The first of these was the 32-footer *Green Bow*, launched by Mason and Langille in 1923 or 1924 and probably modelled by David Langille. Her board, set just forward of the mainmast, whaler-fashion, with the after end of the case positioned in the overall center of the boat, extended 3' to 4' below the plank keel when fully down.[272] *Green Bow*'s lines (see fig. 13) show the shallow hull characteristic of much earlier schooners, such as the *Comet G.*, built almost a generation before.

This first Alinard boat was lost off Dover while carrying a load of coal home from Cape Breton at the conclusion of a swordfishing trip in 1928.[†] Her owner-skipper survived, however, and immediately commissioned a second centreboard schooner, the *Green Bow II*[‡], a 37-footer modelled and built by Stanley Mason in 1929. After a twenty-year career, this craft was rescued by Howard Mason from a beach where she lay rotting and abandoned, becoming his last project (see photos 33, 38, 40) as well as the last true Tancook schooner built. She was substantially refashioned, lengthened at both ends, and relaunched in 1949 as the 40-foot keel schooner-yacht *Sea Way*, later well known in South Shore racing circles as the *Airlie*.[273]

Next to the elimination of centreboards and the resultant deepening of later schooner models, the most noticeable impact of the gasoline engine on Tancook schooner design related to sail arrangements. Some modification in this regard had already taken place prior to the coming of motors. The overlapping lug foresails carried by the earliest counter-stern boats disappeared sometime before 1910, but the first-generation schooners were otherwise rigged quite similarly to their whaler predecessors, the elongated pole mainmast and large, club-headed fisherman staysail figuring prominently in their sail

---

* Another devotee of the centreboard was Zenas Rodenhiser of Southwest Beach, who owned the 38' Reuben Heisler-built centreboarder *Sea Gull* in the early 1920s. Rodenhiser never installed a motor in his schooner and remained an inveterate board sailor to the end. (*Source:* Interview, Thomas Mason, 17 June 1989.)

† This was one of the few instances of a Tancook schooner's being lost at sea. The vessel was heavily laden with loose coal at the time and succumbed to a "smoky sou'wester" that caused her to lay out on her side, fill, and sink. The crew reached the nearby mainland in a dory. (*Source:* Interview, Thomas Mason, 17 June 1989.)

‡ Steven Alinard was a superstitious swordfisherman who believed that the surface-schooling fish were frightened away by lightly or brightly colored boats. He therefore painted the topsides of his white-hulled schooners dark green as far back as the fore rigging – hence their names. (*Source:* Interviews, Murray A. Mason, June 1985, and Thomas Mason, 17 June 1989.)

plans (see figs. 1, 2, 4, 9, 11). The adoption of engines after 1910, however, meant less dependence on light weather sails like the staysail. When the wind dropped, fishermen could now turn on their auxiliaries, and the use of sails was increasingly reserved for moderate-to-heavy conditions. As a result, schooner rigs were cut down following the introduction of the motor. Masts were shortened, and the staysail was eliminated, a procedure called "flat-roofing" the vessels.[274]

This was a gradual process, of course, and it was not completed until the postwar years. Amos Stevens' *Comet G.* (1910) and *Mianus* (1912), neither of which had engines, were both rigged with staysails, but so were the *Tancook* (1914)* and the *Haig* (1917), two Stevens schooners that had engines from the start.[275] Flat-roofing depended on when the owners of existing boats chose to install engines (some did not do so until the 1920s[276]) as well as on the uses to which the boats were put. Those venturing to the fishing grounds off Cape Breton or to the Gulf of St Lawrence tended to maintain more extensive suits of sails for emergencies (engine breakdown, for instance) or for economy on long voyages. Wind was cheaper than gasoline, after all.

Another offshoot of the internal combustion engine was the increased popularity of the knockabout rig on Tancook. Although the island's very first round-bow schooners were probably knockabouts, the type did not become common until the era of the gasoline motor. The Tancook knockabout had only one stemhead jib, a perfectly adequate arrangement for auxiliary schooners but not for the pure sailing schooners of earlier years. For speed and efficiency, the latter needed not only their powerful lug foresails and fishermen staysails but also the large single jibs or two smaller jibs a bowsprit allowed them to set.[277] It was no accident that the years 1910–12, following the introduction of engines, saw an upsurge in knockabout building among islanders. This is not to say that knockabouts were without problems. Natural imbalances in their rig made them difficult to steer in strong winds, and most of those produced on Tancook carried heavy weather helms in such conditons.† A bowsprit and two jibs arrangement, it was found, balanced infinitely better.[278]

---

* The 64' (overall) *Tancook*, largest of the prewar island schooners, mounted a standard topmast, vessel style, to help hoist her big club-less fisherman staysail. She appears to have been the only Tancook schooner to carry such a removable mast extension, which islanders referred to as a "false topmast." (*Sources*: Sailmaker's sail plan, Stevens sail loft, Second Peninsula, Lunenburg, Nova Scotia; interviews, Thomas Mason, 8, 14 June 1989.)

† As Halifax naval architect William J. Roué, designer of the *Bluenose*, described the knockabout problem: "Vessels of this type are generally hard to steer as the centre of effort is as a rule too far aft making the vessel in some cases round up in the wind in spite of the rudder being across the boat's course." (*Source*: HH, article, 30 December 1922, 8.)

The annoying weather helm common to knockabouts was probably the reason so few of large size were built on Tancook. It may also explain why not many appeared in the pre-engine era after the first experimental attempt to combine the rig with the lug foresail. The biggest island knockabout, at any rate, was the *Holly C.* (17 tons; 46.6' × 12.4' × 6.6'), built by Manson Langille* in 1929. Next in size were Amos Stevens' *Mianus* (15 tons; 45.2' × 10.8' × 6') and Howard Mason's *Patavana* (11 tons; 43' × 11' × 5.4'), launched in 1912 and 1929 respectively, both of which later had bowsprits installed.[279] As a rule, the Tancook knockabout rig was restricted to schooners under 40' in overall length, and it was universally applied to those under 35' overall. Boats measuring between 35' and 40' did ordinarily have bowsprits, but they rarely carried two headsails. One large jib set at the end of the bowsprit, whaler-style, was the usual arrangement for this intermediate class, typified by the 1912 Stanley Mason-built *Flosie* (see fig. 7). Twin jibs normally came into play on Tancook schooners when boat length exceeded 40', and, with few exceptions, all those over 45' long were so rigged.[280]

The last important alteration to Tancook sail plans came at the beginning of the final decade of the schooner era. This was the incorporation of the marconi (or Bermudian) mainsail, which was introduced at Southeast Cove in late 1929. The first island fishing schooner to carry the novel sail was Howard Mason's *Patavana*, launched in November of that year. She was followed in 1930 by Stanley Mason's *Morning Star II*, one of that builder's 60-footers, and by several smaller boats built in the 1930s.[281]

Howard Mason, who brought the marconi to Tancook, never returned to the gaff mainsail, putting a Bermudian main on all three of the schooners he subsequently built. Thomas Mason, the builder's son, believed his father conceived the idea for a triangular mainsail by observing the sails of marconi-rigged sloop yachts at nearby Chester and being impressed by their appearance and simplicity. His reasons for adapting it to his own boats were pragmatic, however. First, it was easier to lower in emergencies than a gaff sail, having only one halyard. Second, it could be reefed faster because of its smaller size. Third, its shape made it a better riding sail than the gaff main when drifting or "droguing" for herring. Finally, the absence of a heavy gaff

---

* Manson W. Langille (1902–70), brother of the noted builder David Langille, was a Southeast Cove fisherman who dabbled in boatbuilding. There is no record of his producing schooners other than the *Holly C.*, which was completed with the help of Howard Mason. (For relationship, see Langille, *South Shore Langilles*, 49.)

swinging to and fro made it easier on both boat and rigging in terms of everyday wear and tear.[282]

The marconi mainsail did require certain adjustments in setting up a schooner's masts. In the whaler era, Tancook builders had placed their mainmast considerably aft of the middle of the boat – about 55 percent of the distance on deck from bow to stern – in order to clear the after part of the centreboard case and allow room for the massive lug forsail, the whaler's chief driving sail.[283] When the gaff-rigged keel schooner came into vogue, the foresail was de-emphasized and the mainmast moved closer to the centre of the boat. The normal procedure was to set the mainmast half way between the stem and stern, or just slightly beyond that point.* The appearance of the Bermudian sail reversed the process once more and caused the mainmast to be placed several feet closer to the stern in order to maintain proper sail balance. Retaining the midship position with a marconi rig would have brought the head of the mainsail too far forward and produced the dreaded lee helm, a condition islanders despised because it prevented boats from rounding into the wind, or heaving-to, during squalls.[284] Howard Mason's marconi-rigged schooners avoided that problem by having the mainmast positioned 55 to 60 percent of the distance aft of the stemhead – 57 percent was the average for three of them – compared to 50 to 55 percent for the traditional gaff-rigged Tancook schooners.[285]

The marconi main, which came to typify the Tancook schooner rig in the vessel's last years, was certainly not an island innovation. It is said to have been introduced in the American yachting fleet shortly after World War I by designer Nathaniel G. Herreshoff, who first installed it on the schooner *Queen Mab*.[286] By the late 1920s, it was commonly seen on small East Coast schooner-yachts, particularly those designed by the famous Boston schooner advocate John G. Alden,† who introduced a popular class of 43-foot marconi-rigged two-masters in 1926.[287] Whether Tancook builders observed any of these

---

* The average proportionate distance from the bow for six representative gaff-rigged Tancook schooners built between 1910 and 1917 was found to be 52 percent of overall length. (*Source*: Sailmaker's sail plans, schrs *Comet G.*, *Flosie*, *Dagon*, *Mianus*, *Tancook*, and *Haig*, Stevens sail loft, Second Peninsula, Lunenburg, Nova Scotia.)

† Alden's smaller "fisherman-type" schooners, including the early *Malabars*, were the closest approximation of Tancook schooners appearing in the yachting fleets of the time. They were of comparable size and similar sail plan, but were generally deeper and beamier for their length and of higher freeboard. While superb cruising boats, they lacked the long ends, fine lines, and graceful appearance of the Tancook boats, and were probably not so fast in most conditions. (*See* Carrick and Henderson, *John G. Alden*, passim, especially 31–9, 72–3, 96–8, 134–41).

boats in Nova Scotia waters is uncertain. What is certain is that the marconi-rigged Tancook schooner was the first North American work boat to adopt this particular sail arrangement and that the marconi brought island sail plans to their final and most efficient form.

There were other modifications in Tancook schooner design after 1910 that had little or no connection with the internal combustion engine and were motivated primarily by style and appearance. One of these was the incorporation of the elliptical or, more properly, semi-elliptical transom. The semi-elliptical form, which replaced the fan shape associated with the narrow V-stern of circa 1905–10, may actually have owed something to the coming of motor power in that it was mounted on a somewhat wider counter stern more in keeping with the space requirements of inboard engines. That is speculation, however, and it is likely that the attractive oval transoms then appearing on the large Lunenburg and Mahone Bay bankers had an equal, if not greater, influence. Be that as it may, the oval or semi-elliptical Tancook transom was essentially the creation of the Southeast Cove builders, whose trademark it became.

It is not known who built the first semi-elliptical transom stern on the back side of Tancook, but it was quickly adopted and perfected by David and Vernon Langille and Howard and Stanley Mason. Their counterparts at Northwest Cove, meanwhile, continued to turn out variations of the original fan transom developed by Amos Stevens that eventually approximated – but never quite duplicated – the true Southeast Cove semi-oval. By the 1920s and 1930s, the semi-oval had become the archtypical Tancook schooner transom.[288]

The Southeast Cove transom was designed by a unique compass process in which identical intersecting circles of desired diameter were drawn on the proposed stern plank boards to form the sides and top, thereby guaranteeing evenness on both outside edges of the counter. The "compass" was either a piece of string or a flat stick of wood of proper radius with a pencil attached to one end. The opposite end was made stationary by a driven nail, which held the string or stick in place and formed the pivot. The string or stick was rotated to inscribe the circles, being always sure that their centres remained in horizontal alignment. The curved top was then completed free-hand, and the straight bottom portions connected using a straight-edge.[289] Photographs of the schooners *Blue Lagoon* and *Amasonia* (see photos 32 and 35) illustrate the classic Mason-Langille transom that resulted, which differed markedly not only from the early Northwest Cove fan transom but also from such other regional forms as the "half barrel-head" shape favoured for small Lunenburg schooners.[290]

If the origin of its semi-elliptical transom is somewhat uncertain, there is no uncertainty at all about the source of the final stylistic change that effected the appearance of the Tancook schooner after 1920. That change was the elongated overhanging bow, a direct result of the influence of the highly publicized *Bluenose* and the other large racing fishermen of the 1920s. The Tancook round bow had begun to slowly evolve toward a longer spoon shape almost from the start. The short, snubbed Indian-Header stem originally copied from the early McManus schooners was phased out shortly after 1910.* The Amos Stevens-designed *Tancook* of 1914 (see fig. 10) was one of the last to display it. Most island schooners built between 1910 and 1920 exhibited a moderate spoon bow that was really a stretched version of the pre-1910 form with an easier, more gradually upward-sweeping curve (see figs. 3–8, 11).

After 1920, and particularly after the launching of the famed *Bluenose* in 1921 and her subsequent success in international racing, the Tancook schooner bow took on a much longer, sleeker, yacht-like appearance reminiscent of the racy overhangs of the great Lunenburg banker and her Canadian and American contemporaries – *Haligonian*, *Henry Ford*, *Columbia*, and others. In some cases, the *Bluenose* look was complete even to the distinctive slight knuckle near the top of the stem that resulted from last-minute alterations in the Lunenburger's forward sheer to increase her accommodations.[291] Photographs of several boats built by Howard Mason and Mason and Langille, for example, show this feature (see photos 29, 33, 34, 45). The racing-fisherman profile may also be clearly seen in the plans of the island schooners *Green Bow* (ca. 1923), *Bluebeard/Elsie B. Young* (1923), *Sarah Pauline* (1924), *Attaboy* (1928), *Patavana* (1929), and *X10U8* (1940) (see figs. 13, 14, 15, 17, 18, 29).

The extent of the *Bluenose*'s influence on Tancook schooner design is illustrated by Hovey Slauenwhite's account of the building of his *Tyrienne S*. Slauenwhite, a Southeast Cove fisherman who appreciated fast boats with good lines (he had earlier owned Vernon Langille's *Cecil V.L.*), went to Mason and Langille in early 1924 to order a new schooner. Stanley Mason, the firm's senior partner, offered to build the boat from one of two or three existing half-

---

* A photograph of Tancook schooners and whalers racing at Chester in about 1907 (see photo 2) clearly shows this short-lived style of bow, which was found on many of the early, engine-less schooners that carried fishermen staysails. A similar bow profile may be seen in two views of the schooner *Mianus*, built by Amos H. Stevens in 1912 (see photos 48 and 49).

models, but Slauenwhite objected, asking that a new model be made. He had a particular type of craft in mind, one with long overhangs "like the *Bluenose*." The builder refused to comply, however, and Slauenwhite was about to approach a competitor, Reuben Heisler, when his friend (and Mason's partner) David Langille intervened and agreed to carve a new model to the desired specifications. Langille produced exactly the design required, and Mason and Langille launched the boat, a 52-footer, the following summer. Slauenwhite, who was highly pleased with the result, later repaid Langille for the custom-made model with money he received from a cabbage sale.[292]

THE FINAL PRODUCT

The scaled half-model was, of course, the essential first step in the construction of a Tancook schooner. In lieu of drawings and blueprints, which were never used in island boatbuilding until the late 1940s,* it provided the basic design of the vessel. Tancook half-models were block models carved from soft wood, usually pine. Occasionally a single block of wood was employed, but normally the work was done using two blocks glued together, the intersection of the pieces marking the proposed boat's load waterline. Some builders varnished or painted their models after the completion of construction, but for building purposes, they were usually left unfinished to accommodate the pencil markings representing mould locations and other pertinent details. The models were relatively small (typically 1' to 2' long) and were made to a scale of either ⅜" or ½" to the foot. The ½" scale was sometimes reserved for small schooners or scallop sloops, and the ⅜" scale for large schooners, but that was not universally the case. Stanley Mason and David Langille always worked to the ½" scale, for example, while Amos and Wesley Stevens and Reuben Heisler favored the ⅜" scale. Howard Mason, on the other hand, used both, depending on the circumstances.[293]

Once the model was completed, its lines were transferred to a piece of paper or (more typically) a small board for use in the building shop. This was done by tracing the sheer and deck profiles in pencil and erecting perpendiculars to represent the locations of frame moulds. The various mould shapes were lifted from the model by means of a fitted piece of bevelled pine or (in later years) a thin bar

---

* David Mason, who acquired some training in naval architecture, designed the last schooners built at the S.G. Mason yard after World War II without the aid of half-models. (*Source*: personal knowledge.)

of soft lead, and were also drawn on the board.* Full-size stem and sternpost moulds and frame templates were then made from scaled-up lines laid down in pencil on large, clean boards placed together over a section of the shop floor.† For large schooners, six or seven frame templates were made, but for small sloops, three generally sufficed. Once the templates or moulds were completed, construction could begin.[294]

Framing up was the most critical part of the construction process. It began with the placement of the moulds that determined the boat's basic hull shape. These framing moulds, called "frames" on Tancook, were initially sawn and pieced together, but in the early schooner era (ca. World War I), they began to be steam-bent to shape, as were the frames themselves, in order to save time and work. Later, steamed moulds were often left in the boat as extra frames. If six were used, for example, three (two bow moulds and a stern mould) might remain in place permanently. In contrast to the moulds, the actual frames of a Tancook schooner, collectively referred to as the boat's "ribs" or "timber," were always steam bent from the whaler period onward. These steam-bent frames gave the island boats structural flexibility and made them naturally easy in a seaway. Their insertion was a crucial and anxious moment for the builder, since the steamed timbers had to be placed quickly and made to conform to the moulded hull shape before cooling and hardening. Size was also a factor in their construction. The largest individual frames employed in Tancook schooners were 1½" thick by 2½" wide – the maximum practical for steam bending. Big vessels in the 55' to 65' range, therefore, often had double laminated or layered frames that were placed one atop the other and nailed through for added strength.[295]

---

* Some builders used a different technique in the formative years of modelling. Alvin Stevens, whose career ended prior to 1920, sawed his half-models completely through at the mould stations and traced the exposed sections on paper. Consequently, no evidences of his work have survived. Howard Mason, who later preserved his models, employed a similar process on at least one occasion prior to World War I, tracing the sawn model sections for an Aberdeen-stem schooner on a board. Despite its accuracy, attested to by the noted Mahone Bay craftsman Obed Hamm, this method of scaling up lines was subsequently abandoned by islanders. Amos Stevens, who appears to have initiated modelling on Tancook, used the shaped wood method exclusively, as did Stanley Mason, his successor as the dominant builder on the island. (*Sources*: Interviews, Perry W. Stevens, 16 June 1989, and Thomas Mason, 15 June and 22 June 1989.)

† Tancook tradition holds that some early whaler builders shaped their moulds on barn doors, removing the doors temporarily for the purpose and later re-hinging them. Benjamin Langille of Southeast Cove is said to have used this expedient. (*Source*: Interview, Benjamin Heisler, 22 June 1989.) The procedure is plausible inasmuch as a number of the first island builders were part-time farmers who worked in their barns rather than in bona fide boat shops.

The hull planking of a Tancook schooner was carried out in fairly routine fashion following standard plank-on-edge practices introduced from the mainland at the turn of the century. Only board thicknesses varied, ranging from ¾" for the smallest hulls to 1⅜" for the largest (⅞" was about average), and galvanized nails were used throughout as fastenings.* Deck work, however, followed one or the other of two quite distinct procedures, depending on the size of the boat. Small schooners of less than 50' overall length were decked with wide, thin boards using tongue-and-groove construction. These boards measured 10" to 12" in width and less than 1" in thickness and were bought from area lumber mills in unfinished condition. The matched tongue-and-groove work was carefully carried out by hand on the island using match planes to ensure a proper fit and watertight decks. The schooner *Patavana* illustrates the appearance of this type of decking (see photo 37). Since the exacting tongue-and-groove method was too time consuming and labour intensive for large vessels, schooners over 50' were decked with narrower but thicker planks of 4" to 5" width and 1¼" to 1½" thickness. These were laid side by side and caulked at the seam to prevent leaks, an added step that was unnecessary with matched and fitted boards.[296]

Caulking, whether of hulls or decks, was usually done on Tancook using strands of thin cotton wicking called "candlewick," rather than the oakum preferred for large mainland vessels. Candlewick, which came in balls and resembled a soft wrapping twine, was twisted as it was placed between hull seams and then sealed with a mixture of white lead and putty. This last step was preceded by a priming of the outer planking with an oil-based paint in order to prevent the putty overlay from losing its own natural oil to the surrounding timbers and thus drying out and cracking before its time. For large island boats with extra-wide seams, two intertwined strands of candlewick instead of one was the rule, and, if necessary, double-caulking was employed – two sets of interwoven wicking, one inserted atop the other.[297]

The wood used in Tancook schooners was almost entirely imported from the mainland, since the island was bereft of most types of useful timber except spruce by the early twentieth century. Most lumber came in sawn from and was carried on the decks of schooners from Lunenburg County sawmills located in Mahone Bay, Oakland, and

---

* The only other fastenings used in Tancook schooners were galvanized carriage bolts of ⅜"–½" diameter, which were occasionally employed in large island boats to attach knees, deck beams, and the like.

(especially) Martin's River. For the stem, sternpost, keel, and keelson (or "backbone") of an island vessel, secondary hardwoods like beech, yellow birch, and rock maple were preferred, although in later years red oak was sometimes used. Frames were almost always made of indigenous red oak because it would take steam bending, while decks, cabins, and planking were usually white pine or, on rare occasions, red pine. The latter timbers held their shapes and were therefore especially valued for exterior hull work. Tancook's native spruce was reserved for masts and also for floor timbers abutting the keelson, for the insides of gunwales, and for stringers supporting deck beams or bilge timbers.[298] The variety of species employed in building the schooner *Patavana* in the late 1920s typified the mixed-wood construction of most island boats at that time. They included maple (keel), beech (keelson), oak (frames), pine (deck and planking), spruce (deck frames and masts), and birch (house coamings).[299]

A minority of Tancook schooners were so-called "hardwood-built" vessels. This did not mean that they were constructed of hardwood timbers throughout, but rather that their outer hulls were planked in more durable species than the usual pine. In other respects, their components were similar to those of most island boats. Hardwood planking, normally rejected by Tancook builders because of its tendency to warp and create leaks, was built into a number of large schooners intended for winter coasting and fishing since it provided superior protection from the threat of ice. In all, there were seven hardwood-built Tancook schooners, each over 50' in length and most of them produced at the Mason yard in Southeast Cove: *Petawawa* (1912), *Silver Oak* (1917), *White Birch* (1918), *Sarah Pauline* (1924), *Marion C.* (1927), *Nelson L.* (1929), and *Morning Star II* (1930).[300]

Tancook boat builders followed one disconcerting South Shore practice that was common even at large shipyards in Lunenburg and Mahone Bay. They did not always build exactly to the model. It was natural for craftsmen whose forebears had worked by eye to make small adjustments or improvements as they went along. A mould would often be moved or changed ever so slightly in shape if its original positioning or curvature did not look quite right upon framing up. It was common procedure to stretch a boat out beyond its designed length, either to gain more room or simply to improve the flow of the lines. Howard Mason's *Patavana*, for instance, was modelled as a 39-footer; when launched, she actually measured close to 43' overall. The difference resulted from a lengthening of the boat's midsection during construction. It was also not unusual for schooners of different sizes to be produced from the same model. This was the case with the 43-foot *Elsie B. Young* and the 48-foot *Bluebeard*, which Mason and Langille built simultaneously from one design in the spring of 1923.[301] Sometimes the half-model was used only as a rough guide. Of five schooners built from a single Wesley Stevens model between 1929 and 1936, only two followed the carved lines closely, while three incorporated substantial changes.[302]

Upon completing construction of a Tancook schooner, there remained the task of painting the vessel. Island boats had certain prescribed colour schemes. Originally, all Tancook boats were white-hulled craft, but in later years, darker colours became fashionable. Green was the most common, followed by black, which was used for the last few schooners built and was copied from the large Lunenburg bankers.[303]

The change in the colour patterns of Tancook boats appears to have been linked to the transition from pure sailing craft to auxiliary-powered vessels. The original island whalers had white topsides and cream, buff, or light yellow decks. The earliest schooners were likewise white from waterline to rail, although there were some exceptions to the general rule, notably the aptly named *Black Nance* (ca. 1903) and *Black Lize* (ca. 1905). Dark coloured hulls did not become common, however, until about 1910, when gasoline motors made their appearance. It is therefore probable that the conversion to green or black hulls was an expedient adopted to cover rust streaks caused by discoloured water draining from inboard engines through exhaust holes at the sterns of the boats.[304]

Generally speaking, black topsides were reserved for large Tancook schooners over 50' in length, while most smaller boats were dark green from the waterline up. Standard Lunenburg vessel-building practices were followed in painting the bigger island craft, which were given gray or dull red decks like the offshore bankers. The majority of smaller schooners, which were not completely decked over, evolved a quite different painting scheme. Their dark green topsides were combined with white exterior coamings (or waterboards) and cabin sides, light gray or off-yellow fore and after decks, washboards, and cabin tops, light green interior coamings and upper bulkheads, and dull red (i.e., reddish brown) floors and lower bulkheads.* A few

---

* A more detailed painting scheme for a typical Tancook schooner built at Southeast Cove in the 1920s or 1930s would have been as follows:
topsides – dark green
bottom – copper
decking (fore and after decks, washboards) – light gray or yellow; white for very small boats
waterboards (coamings) – white exterior; light green interior
rails – dark green exterior; white interior

fishermen expressed personal idiosyncracies in painting their boats and insisted on using only one colour (the small scallop sloops *Gray Bear* and *Red Huntz*, were entirely light gray and dull red, respectively), but most owners adhered to the standard colour combinations established by island builders.[305]

After painting the vessel and raising her softwood masts, the next step in the creation of a Tancook schooner was the preparation of sails and rigging. Following the departure of the island's pre-eminent sailmaker, Randolph Stevens, in 1920, Tancookers were for the most part obliged to have their sails sewn on the mainland, especially for schooners of substantial size.* The devising of sail plans and the preliminary laying out and cutting of cloth remained a local activity for some years, however.

The firm of Mason and Langille, leading builder on the island after the First World War, continued its longstanding practice of cutting much of its own canvas until the mid-1920s, particularly for its largest schooners. During the winter, the frozen surface of Southeast Cove Pond, which bordered Southeast Cove beach and had once been part of the cove itself, served as a convenient, if uncomfortable, setting for this work. In keeping with Tancook tradition, the shape of a proposed sail was laid out on the ice using string and nails, and 22"-wide strips of (typically) seven- or eight-ounce canvas were unrolled side by side over the pattern, marked for location, and trimmed with shears. The fitted and cut strips were then taken to Lunenburg with a scaled drawing of the sail plan for sewing by professional sailmakers. In warmer weather, the Southeast Cove breakwater served as a laying-off location, and cleared spaces on the firm's own shop floor also served for small sails. After 1925, however, little patterning and cutting was done on Tancook, virtually all canvas work being contracted to sail lofts on the mainland.[306]

Unlike sailmaking, the rigging of Tancook boats continued to be carried out on the island until the end of the schooner era, although

---

rail caps (large boats) – white
cuddy cabin – white sides; light gray or yellow top; white or gray interior except for varnished ceiling
ceiling (inside hold under deck) – light green
upper bulkheads – light green
lower bulkheads – dull red
floors – dull red
masts – buff or light yellow with white mastheads
booms – buff or light yellow with white ends

* For exceptions to this general rule, see p. 67 and notes, pp. 34, 67.

working materials, such as rope, wire, and wooden blocks, were usually purchased in Lunenburg. The basic standing rigging, made of galvanized wire of ⅜" to ⅝" diameter and adjusted by lanyards of Manila rope, was arranged in two ways according to the size of the vessel. All small schooners (and, in earlier years, whalers) under 40' overall were equipped with "single rigging," that is, a single wire shroud on each side of both spars extending roughly parallel to the mast from the deck rail to within a few feet of the masthead. Most boats over 40' long, and all of those exceeding 50', had "double rigging" – two shrouds on each side of both spars set in various configurations.[307]

There were two fundamental forms of double rigging. Schooners between 40' and 50' long that were equipped with long mainmasts for handling fisherman staysails had their shrouds set piggyback style, so that one extended about three quarters of the way up the mast, while its partner, starting from the same place on deck, continued on a wider angle to the top of the masthead itself. Similarly sized flat-roofed* boats without staysails had both of their twin shrouds attached together well below the masthead and run side-by-side to the rail in inverted-V fashion, diverging slightly at deck level.

The largest Tancook schooners – those exceeding 50' overall length – used a combination of double riggings that could almost be called triple rigging. Three shrouds were set on each side of both masts, two joined together part way up the mast as on smaller flat-roofed vessels and one carrying to the top of the mast via crosstrees or "spreaders" placed slightly below the masthead. On occasion, three lower shrouds were set on each side along with one upper shroud, making for four in all. In addition to crosstrees, which did not appear on smaller island boats, large schooners also incorporated deadeyes made of lignum vitae into their rigging in place of the simple iron thimbles used by the majority of island boats to secure their rope lanyards to the external hull chain plates that replaced primitive eyebolts in the post-whaler era. By the 1930s, modern turnbuckles were not unheard of, but were generally reserved for the new schooner-yachts turned out by island builders.[308]

When ready for sea, new Tancook schooners fell into three classes according to their sizes, deck arrangements, and intended fisheries. Those over 50' long were called "deck boats" because they were completely decked over except for small forward cuddy cabins, twin fish hatches amidships, and hatched engine compartments aft (see fig. 23).

---

* See page 95.

They carried two to four dories nested between their fore and mainmasts and fished with crews of four to nine men. Deck boats were essentially miniature bankers, engaging in dory trawling for cod and other groundfish and salting their catch on board. They came equipped with stanchion rails similar to those found on large vessels, hawsepipes and windlasses for hauling their anchors, and steering wheels mounted on wheelboxes in place of tillers.[309]

Island schooners under 50' long (the vast majority) were mostly classified as "hatch boats," a designation based on the prominence of hatches in their deck construction. Aside from small forward decks and cuddies and narrow, peripheral washboards, they were essentially open boats having several loose, abutting hatches (usually two to four) that fitted around their mainmasts and covered their cockpits (see fig. 30). Hatch boats carried no dories, and their typical three-man crews fished on board. They functioned for the most part as net boats, drifting for herring or mackerel and occasionally hand-lining for groundfish.[310]

Although some large ones were built,* most pure hatch or net boats were under 40' long. The partial size gap this left was filled by the so-called "semi-deck boats," a compromise class of 40' to 50' schooners combining some of the features of the other two types (see fig. 20). The semi-deckers were all-round craft that normally operated like hatch boats but were superior for coasting because of their additional deck space and more protected holds. They were also capable of fishing off shore if the occasion demanded. Some, like the *Mother* and the *Patavana*, were basically small deck boats with after steering cockpits. Others, like the *Bluebeard* and the *Elsie B. Young*, each of which incorporated six or more cockpit hatches end to end, were essentially big hatch boats with extra wide washboards to accommodate dories. Semi-deckers usually carried a single dory that was towed or stored on one after-quarter and used for added fishing room when hand-lining, for setting inshore trawls, or for tending stationary mackerel nets. They had spike, rather than stanchion, rails, steered with tillers, and did not employ windlasses.[311]

The typical Tancook schooner was without question the hatch boat. Hatch boats were the most common and popular island craft for several reasons. For one thing, their size and deck configuration made them especially convenient when unloading fish. Because of

---

* The 45-footer *Frances M.R.*, built by Mason and Langille in 1925, was an example of a large hatch boat. She engaged extensively in herring netting and therefore needed to be undecked. Her size was about the maximum practical for such work. (*Source*: Interview, Thomas Mason, 1 October 1987; see also photo 29.)

Tancook's shallow coves, most boats – scallop sloops were an exception – could approach the island's small wharves only at high tide, and catches of fish were ordinarily transported to shore in dories from schooners moored well away from the land. In the case of hatch boats, individual crewmen could easily stand in the open holds and pitchfork fish directly into dories tied alongside. Decked and semi-decked boats, on the other hand, required two men for the task, one working in the hold and one stationed on deck, and transferring catches to the waiting dories was a two-step process.[312]

The small size of their multiple hatches was another advantage hatch boats possessed, and it created added operational flexibility. During the fishing season, hatches were rarely carried on board. The boats brought their catches home fresh for salting and curing and did not stay long at sea. The open hatchways permitted standing room for hand-lining and net hauling, and there was little need to cover the fish for short periods of time. Occasionally, herring droguers took their portable hatches along if they planned to stay out for several days. In such cases, the covers were used to shade the catch from the sun and also to preserve the stored nets from heat-generated rot as they lay piled in the hold.[313]

During the fall coasting season, hatch covers served to protect cabbage and other island cargoes from the elements, and in wintertime, they kept interiors free of ice and snow. The latter function was especially important in the schooner era, when former methods of winter storage were of necessity abandoned. The double-ended whalers of earliers years, which did not participate in coasting, were completely open boats with no cockpit coverings, but their construction allowed the smaller ones (those under 40' in length) to be turned upside down for winter storage. That expedient was made possible by an absence of engines and by the fact that whaler rails were simply gunwale extensions of the hulls themselves. The schooners, however, had engines that could not easily be removed, as well as attached rails that could be damaged or loosened if the boats were inverted.* Upright storage, therefore, was the only off-season option, and sealed decks and closed hatches the solution to winter precipitation. Owners of a few of the smallest island schooners and scallop boats even dispensed with hatches and permitted their craft to fill with snow. In such in-

---

* Most island schooners under 50' long came equipped with spike rails, which were basically boards standing on edge, end to end, with evenly spaced, semi-circular water courses cut through at deck level. As their name suggests, they were nailed or spiked to the decks. Large deck boats over 50' long had more conventional stanchion rails with hardwood rail caps and water courses abutting either side of each stanchion or wooden support pillar. (*Source*: Interview, Thomas Mason, 23 June 1988.)

stances, the boats were shovelled out after major storms, and salt or pickle was periodically added to their bilge water to loosen ice and keep the interiors from freezing up. Islanders never considered canvas tarpaulins because of their cost and limited durability.[314]

The natural limitations on island boatbuilding enhanced the popularity of the hatch boat type of Tancook schooner. Hatch boats were relatively easy to haul and launch. Deck boats, however, presented a special problem. At 50' to 65' overall, they were the largest craft that could be practically built on Tancook because of its shoal waters. The biggest of them drew 9' or 10' at the post and could only float to their designed load waterlines well off shore.[315] In order to build these outsized craft, island builders were forced to devise ingenious modes of launching.

At Northwest Cove, Reuben Heisler launched his deck boats using a wheeled cradle and sled system. Boats were hauled upright from the shop in customized cradles that incorporated wheeled posts measuring 10" by 10". The wheels ran on planks laid at righ angles to rollers facing the launchway. Upon reaching the ways, vessels were transferred from cradles to standards sleds or "sleighs" for launching on their bilges at high water.[316] At Southeast Cove, Stanley Mason employed sleds exclusively. Vessels were hauled stern first down the launchway on their sides as far as the low-water mark. They were then maneuvered into upright positions and stabilized by two to four empty forty-five-gallon gasoline drums strapped under their quarters. When the tide came in, the buoyant drums lifted the vessels' sterns, floated them off the ways, and allowed them to be towed by motorboat to deep-water moorings. There, men in dories cut the drums loose.[317]

Once the boats were built, painted, rigged, and launched, only the final treatment of their sails remained to be done. Traditionally, islanders had tanned their canvas to a brown color in the process of preserving it from rot and mildew. During early years, the dye used was a boiled mixture of pine tar and black spruce, logwood, or hemlock bark.[318] Toward the end of the whaler period, sails were treated with a tanning solution made from a commercial wood extract called "cutch" (for catechu), which came in cakes and was mixed with water and a little oil.[319] In the schooner era, tanning went out of fashion, and only a handful of island fishermen continued to dye their sails. Instead, a salt water and lime solution was used. It was generally applid with a broom while the sails were spread on a rock beach and possessed the advantage of protecting the white duck against rot without discolouration. White canvas remained the rule on Tancook for the balance of the age of sail.[320]

This, then, completes the story of the evolution of the Tancook schooner from its inception through the various changes in its design and construction to the final product that appeared throughout Maritime waters and elsewhere during the 1920s and 1930s. It is only part of the story, however. Still to be told is how this unique boat was used by the men who built it and how it influenced and shaped their way of life. For an understanding of that process, it is necessary to examine the economic history of Tancook Island, beginning with its most basic industry, the fisheries.

Photo 31   The Tancook bow. Schooner *Patavana* just prior to her launch in 1929. [Courtesy Thomas Mason]

Photo 32   The Tancook stern. Schooner-yacht *Amasonia* (built in 1935) being loaded aboard a rail flat car at Lunenburg, Nova Scotia, for transport to the Great Lakes during World War II. Note the exceptionally long, clean run. [Author's collection]

Photo 33   The Tancook sheer. Sleek schooner-yacht *Sea Way* at anchor in Chester's Back Harbour in 1949. This boat was the rebuilt swordfisherman *Green Bow II*, originally launched at the S.G. Mason yard in 1929 and reconstructed twenty years later by island builder Howard Mason. She survives today (1993) as the yacht *Airlie*. Note the racing-fisherman bow profile and long overhangs characteristic of the later Tancook schooners. [Courtesy Thomas Mason]

Photo 34   The Tancook profile. Knockabout schooner *Patavana* ready for launching at Southeast Cove, Tancook, in November 1929. Note her "*Bluenose*" bow. Note also the use of single wire rigging with chain plates and rope lanyards. The boat's propeller aperture is visible just forward of the sternpost. Her rudder has not yet been shipped. [Author's collection]

Photo 35   The Tancook transom. Stern view of the schooner *Blue Lagoon* (ex *Harold H.*), ca. 1935, showing the distinctive Southeast Cove oval transom in its final form. A perceptive observer sent the photo to the builder, Stanley G. Mason, with the inscription, "This is a great stern. Can you duplicate?" [Courtesy Mrs Sadie I. Langille]

Photo 36   Deck view of the Tancook hatch boat *X10U8*, looking aft from the fore-deck. The cuddy slide is in the foreground and beyond are the main hold for storing fish and nets, the enclosed engine compartment, and the steering cockpit. Note the standard spike rails, the engine exhaust pipe, and the fore and main sheet horses. [Courtesy Thomas Mason]

Photo 37   Deck view of the semi-deck boat *Patavana*, prior to launch in the fall of 1929. The builder's granddaughter is seated on the engine hatch next to the main boom, which rests atop the engine hatch slide. Farther forward are the two fish hatches, the forecastle break, and the cuddy. Farther aft is the steering cockpit sporting a temporary cover designed to keep out winter snow. The schooner's tongue-and-groove deck planking, rope lanyards, and spike rail are clearly visible. [Courtesy Thomas Mason]

Photo 38   Preparing the mast, Tancook-fashion. Finishing the mainmast for the schooner-yacht *Sea Way*, formerly the fishing schooner *Green Bow II*, at Southeast Cove, Tancook, in 1949. At the far left, supervising his last project, is island master-builder Howard Mason, age 75. [Courtesy Thomas Mason]

Photo 39 The Stanley G. Mason boatyard at Southeast Cove, Big Tancook Island, as it looked in 1969. The scene is typically foggy. To the left is the original flat-roofed shop where the keels of several dozen schooners were laid between the world wars. The small pond in the foreground served as a convenient place to soak oak planks intended for deck boat frames, keeping them soft and pliable for eventual steam bending. [Photograph by author]

Photo 40 Stepping the mast, Tancook-fashion. Raising the foremast for the rebuilt schooner-yacht *Sea Way* (ex *Green Bow II*) at the Mason yard, Southeast Cove, Tancook, in 1949, using sheer poles and a hoisting tackle. The principals are (left to right) Eustace, Earl, and Thomas Mason. Partially obscured is the master builder, Howard Mason. [Courtesy Thomas Mason]

Photo 41 Steaming frames, Tancook-fashion. Heating the frames or "ribs" for a schooner in the traditional manner prior to insertion into the hull. A hardwood frame is being removed from the steambox in ready condition for bending during the rebuilding of the schooner *Shanti* at Chester, Nova Scotia, 1971. [Photograph by author]

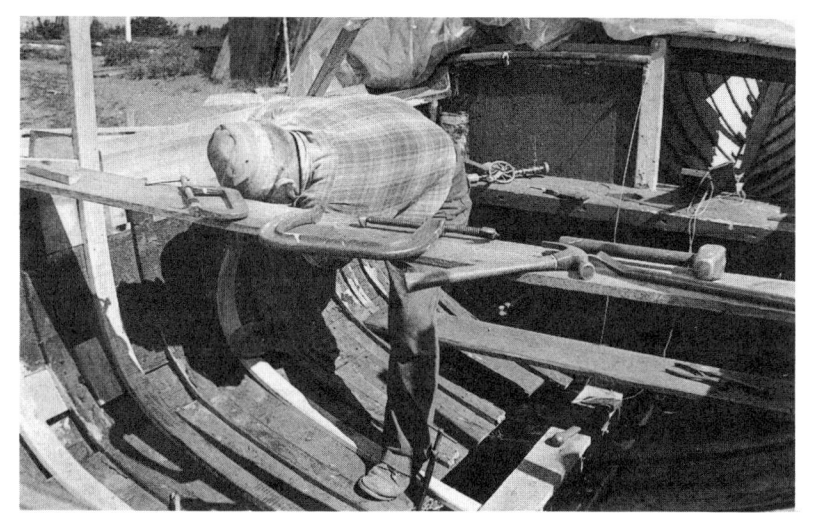

Photo 42   Bending frames, Tancook-fashion. Inserting a flexible, steamed frame into the partially planked hull of the schooner *Shanti* during rebuilding in 1971. The builder is bending the new "rib" to conform to the pre-existing hull shape before nailing it in place. [Photograph by author]

Photo 43   Sealing the hull, Tancook-fashion. Builder Thomas Mason applying cotton "candlewick" caulking to the seams of the Tancook schooner *Amasonia* (built 1935) during reconstruction in 1964. Note the traditional hand tools – wooden caulking mallet and caulking iron. [Photograph by author]

Photo 44   The hull framing of a Tancook schooner, also known as the boat's "ribs" or "timber." This is the interor of the yacht *Amasonia*, looking aft during reconstruction in 1964. Note the increased curvature of the steam-bent frames as they approach the counter. The horn timber is visible where it joins the sternpost. [Photograph by author]

3 The Economy

I've just arrived from Tancook
And the folks they are all well,
We have a load of sauerkraut
Which we would like to sell.
We're lying up to Silver's wharf
In the schooner *Pauline Young*,
The summer we go sword fishing,
In the spring we bring our dung.

Sauerkraut Song (sung at Tancook)

LOCAL WATERS

The Tancook fishing industry began soon after the island was populated, though for some time it was subordinated to the primary activity of farming. Fishermen did not have far to go for a catch. Blunt's *American Coast Pilot* described Nova Scotia's South Shore in 1850 as teeming with cod, haddock, halibut, and mackerel within three to ten miles of the coastline, as well as herring and Atlantic salmon that schooled in as far as the immediate bays and harbour entrances.[1] Island fishing started close to shore. Locally tended floating weirs or "traps" were a standard item of equipment from the earliest settlement days onward,* providing an annual salmon catch in the spring

---

* These trap nets were set just off shore in particular berths reserved for individual fishermen or families. Their locations were established by law and passed from one generation to the next. Most were on the seaward side of Tancook in the vicinity of Southeast Cove and Southern Head. As many as nine traps were still set near the island in the 1920s and 1930s and were tended by men in dories.

and herring in the summer months. The salmon ceased to appear after 1910, but herring trapping continued well into the 1930s.[2] Groundfish and mackerel were initially pursued in or adjacent to the relatively protected waters of Mahone Bay itself, where the islanders' small, sloop-rigged jolly boats could be used to advantage. Around mid-century, however, the offshore fisheries beckoned, and in 1851 Peter Mason and a crew of seven made the first recorded deep-water voyages from Tancook in the schooner *Sandwich*, line fishing for mackerel* and collecting a provincial bounty in the process.[3]

By that time shore fishermen all along Nova Scotia's Atlantic coast had begun to visit the nearer offshore fishing grounds up to a dozen or so miles beyond land, using "whale-boats" or large, undecked sail boats.[4] It may be assumed that they were quickly joined by Tancook's fisherman-farmers, who were able to venture beyond the confines of Mahone Bay on a regular basis once they had developed their schooner-rigged whaler in the 1860s. With this larger craft, islanders began to frequent portions of the outer ridges, a series of contiguous fishing shoals that ran parallel to the South Shore roughly twelve to twenty-five miles from the coastline.[5] For the next three quarters of a century, "the ridges" remained the primary focus of Tancook's inshore industry.

The earliest first-hand observations of Tancook's fisheries date from 1870, when Dominion fishery department officials first visited the island. Daniel Dimock, regional overseer for eastern Lunenburg County, described its marine economy to his superiors in the following manner:

The Island of Jancook [sic], about seven miles from Chester, appears to be well calculated for prosecuting the fisheries as any place along the coast. There are about ninety men engaged in the fisheries, who reside on the island; most of them have small farms, on which, with female help, they manage to raise a supply of vegetables, etc.[6]

The federal census taken a year later recorded 22 vessel and 127 boat fishermen actively pursuing the industry on a full- or part-time basis at Big and Little Tancook and East Ironbound islands,

---

* Mackerel fishing with hook and line remained a lesser pursuit for a few Tancookers until the end of the nineteenth century. It was carried on in the fall from whalers and jolly boats, whose crews used a chum or rising bait composed of chopped herring and fish oil (called "progy") to attract their catch. After about 1900, this minor activity ceased altogether and mackerel were taken exclusively with nets. (*Source*: Interview, Thomas Mason, 17 June 1989.)

which were statistically grouped together. These men maintained a fleet of 4 schooners over 10 tons and 111 smaller whalers, sloops, and other boats, as well as equipment that included 21,000 fathoms of fishing nets. Their catch for the 1870 season consisted of 1,016 quintals* of cod, 833 quintals of haddock, pollock, and hake, 1,612 barrels of herring, 1,821 barrels of mackerel, and 2,041 gallons of fish oil. About two thirds of the total production (in processed pounds) was comprised of schooling species captured by net, and one third of groundfish taken by line, a proportional distribution that was maintained for several decades to come.[7]

The four large schooners based at the Tancooks in 1871 all hailed from the main island. They were the *Sea Slipper* (41 tons; 59.3' × 17.4' × 7.8'),[†] owned by Benjamin Mason and Timothy Hebb; the *Bella Young* (35 tons; 53.6' × 17.8' × 6.8'), owned by Henry Hutt and David Stevens; the *Highland Lass* (15 tons; 37' × 12.9' × 5.2'), owned by Gaspar Levy, Edward Young, and Charles and John Cross; and the *Sky Lark* (27 tons; 50' × 17.3' × 6.8'), owned by George, Daniel, Ephraim, Isaac, and Joshua Mason, and George Cross. Each was a square-sterned, carvel-planked vessel built on or near the mainland – at Young's Island, Lunenburg, Mahone Bay, and La Have, respectively.[8] That was in keeping with a tradition established some years earlier of purchasing the few large boats required by islanders at other locales. It was not until well after the turn of the twentieth century that Tancookers began once more to construct their own register-sized craft, as they had before 1850. There were never more than four of these large vessels owned on the island at any one time prior to the onset of the schooner era in 1905, and usually there were only one or two.[9] They served as coasters as well as fishermen, transporting produce to Halifax and fish to Lunenburg. One of them, the Chester-built *Bella Barry* (41 tons; 59' × 20' × 7.4'), even undertook a summer voyage from Tancook to Boston by way of Lunenburg in 1879 under the command of her managing owner John Pearl, perhaps with a portion of the island's cured spring catch.[10] More typically, however, islanders were content to let Lunenburg's wholesale merchants dispose of their fish production, most of which went to the West Indies.

---

* The quintal (qtl), the traditional measure for dried fish, was equal to 112 pounds, while the hundredweight (cwt) used in most government statistics was equal to 100 pounds. (*Source: Can.RFB, 1915/16,* 152.)

† This vessel, which carried a crew of fourteen, was responsible for over half (598 quintals) of Tancook's cod catch in 1870. Her skipper and part owner, Timothy Hebb, was an experienced banks fisherman from Heckman's Island near Lunenburg.

Lunenburg was the focus of the Tancook fisheries from the very beginning. In 1859, island shore fishermen were already purchasing their salt and other outfitting necessities there,[11] and by the mid-1870s, the town's merchants were virtually the sole recipients of Tancook's catch, as well as those of neighbouring Little Tancook, Ironbound, Deep Cove, and Blandford.[12] This remained the dominant marketing pattern for the next half century or more. Except for a small proportion of Tancook's pickled herring and mackerel, which found its way to Halifax aboard large coasting schooners in the late nineteenth century,[13] the island's salted catch was sent exclusively to Lunenburg for resale or export. That was increasingly the case as time passed and Halifax buyers became preoccupied with Tancook's agricultural products. By the post-1900 period, nearly all of the island's annual fish output was being carried to Lunenburg in the late summer and early fall (August through October) prior to the start of the Halifax cabbage-coasting season. After 1910, much of the catch was shipped in shallow-draft scallop sloops, which were small enough to tie up to the island's undersized fish wharves and shoal enough to approach those in Southeast Cove for loading at mean or low water.[14]

The natural environment played a constant role in shaping the Tancook fisheries. Daniel Dimock, who evaluated the island as a potential fishing station in 1870, accurately assessed the difficulties under which its fishermen laboured: "The great inconvenience they have to contend with," he wrote, "is the want of a harbor[,] and the last heavy gale destroyed a number of their boats and nets to the value of hundreds of dollars. If the government would construct a place of refuge for their boats, it would facilitate the fishing business very much." Tancook was so well situated geographically, Dimock thought, that numerous additional deep-sea fishermen would be drawn there to settle, "if there was a harbor."[15] Within three years, a breakwater was, indeed, built at Northwest Cove with federal and provincial monies, affording some modest security for fishing craft owned on that side of the island and providing a landing place for coasting vessels.[16] Unfortunately, no comparable public improvement was made at larger Southeast Cove until near the end of the first decade of the twentieth century, when the Dominion Department of Public Works finally erected a combination breakwater-wharf there. Its purpose was to protect small fish wharves and other property lining the southwestern side of the cove from storm damage and to provide moored boats with a modicum of shelter from heavy southeast winds and seas. However, the barrier did little good, since the open

Atlantic surged over and around it with impunity when sufficiently provoked and eventually (ca. 1960) washed it away altogether.[17]

The lack of any breakwater at Tancook's one substantial inlet prior to 1908, and the existence of a largely ineffective one thereafter, meant that local fishermen were forced to meet nature on its own terms and adapt. One recourse was to move boats from one side of the island to the other, depending on prevailing winds and seas. Generally speaking, the Northwest Cove, or front, side of Tancook was the more secure anchorage, especially in the spring months, and more schooners were kept there than on the opposite ocean side. It was susceptible to the northwest winds of fall, however, and during the storms of that season its fishermen habitually abandoned their moorings and anchored in the safety of Southeast Cove. The back side of the island, though, had its own drawbacks. It was shallow, and southeast storms savaged it, sending tidal surges rolling directly up the unprotected cove. Therefore, Southeast Cove boat owners sought mooring locations along both sides of the inlet where the limited deep water was found, avoided the treacherous "Sile" (Seal) Rock in the centre of the cove, and hugged the shoreline as much as possible to gain some minimal protection from the headlands at the mouth of the anchorage. Many of them also maintained two permanent moorings, one on each side of the island, and shifted their craft from one to the other as circumstances dictated.[18]

The lack of secure, protected anchorages for their boats impelled Tancook fishermen to devise a unique mooring system. Islanders moored their whalers, and later their schooners, to long poles attached by links of chain to large rocks that rested on the ocean bottom. The rocks, appropriately called "boat rocks," varied in size according to the size of the vessels they secured, but were typically 4' to 5' square. They were found along the shore or labouriously dug from Tancook's stony soil. Shape was important for stability. Boat rocks had to be rectangular with more width than height, since insufficient flatness could cause them to turn over and drag during storms.

Once located, a promising mooring rock was holed by means of a hand drill and hammer, and an iron rod was inserted and made fast. This rod was then attached to three 16" chain links, which, in turn, were attached to a long, buoyant, spruce pole, 5" to 6" in diameter, designed to protrude above water at high tide. The pole, tapered at the top end, resembled a boat mast. Its length varied according to the depth of the proposed anchorage, and because Tancook vessels were often moored well off shore, that length could be quite extraordinary. At relatively shallow Southeast Cove, poles were 16' to 20' long, with

18' being about average. At deeper Northwest Cove, somewhat longer ones were used, and at exposed Southwest Beach,* halfway between Northwest Cove and Southern Head on the front of the island, 30' poles were common. The above-water portion of the pole was equipped with wooden cleats, nailed in place 4' or 5' from the top so as to accommodate a boat hawser. The rope hawser, which had floats attached, was fastened to a chain leading to the foredeck of the moored craft. On large deck boats, the hawser chain was taken through a hawsepipe and made fast to the anchor windlass, while on smaller semi-deck or hatch boats, it was brought in through a bow chock next to the stem and secured to a mooring post or eyebolt on the foreward deck. Occasionally, it might be looped around the foremast for added security and then belayed. The "play" or freedom of movement needed to allow for the action of wind and tide was provided by the critical links of chain connecting the mooring pole to its anchoring rock resting on the sea bottom.[19]

Like so many Tancook activities during the sailing era, the process of dropping or retrieving a mooring was done largely by hand. Twin dories and a Spanish windlass were the only aids. The boat rock and its linked pole were attached by a single rope looped through the rock's aperture to the windlass, which was balanced between the two dories sitting at the water's edge. The entire arrangement was next hauled off the beach and into the water between the floating dories, which were rowed to the selected mooring location by two men, each manning the outside oar of one dory. A third man then slowly lowered the suspended rock and pole using the windlass and cut the rope at the proper moment. Moorings were retrieved the moved by reversing the process.[20]

The natural disadvantages under which Tancook fishermen were forced to work stunted the growth of the industry there during the island settlement's first half century. As Daniel Dimock remarked in 1870 with reference to the shore fishermen of eastern Lunenburg County in general, "The great part work their farms and fish only when there is no farm work to do."[21] In Tancook's case, that began to change with the diminishing of readily available agricultural land and with the direct industry involvement of the newly created

---

* Southwest Beach was the least desirable of the island anchorages. It possessed no wharves or launchways, and boats were hauled up directly over the beach rocks. The normal greased pole launchways used elsewhere on Tancook were impractical there due to periodic storms that drove rocks ashore and filled any slips that might be built, rendering them useless. Large craft moored at this location were hauled for the winter at one of the island's two main coves. (*Source:* Interview, Thomas Mason, 18 June 1989.)

125 The Economy

Dominion government in Ottawa. Dominion participation was especially important and resulted in the initial boom period of the island's fisheries. The stimulus for that boom was the federal fishing bounty law enacted in 1882, which provided for annual payments* to boat owners and crews engaged in the cod, mackerel, herring, and other sea fisheries for at least three months of the year.[22] Together with the flowering of Nova Scotia's salt fish trade to the West Indies, much of it out of Lunenburg,[23] subsidization provided the incentive needed for a rapid expansion of the Tancook fisheries. From 275,000 processed pounds in the last pre-bounty year of 1881, the annual catch at the Tancooks more than doubled to 592,000 pounds in 1882. It doubled again to 1,359,000 the following year, and nearly doubled once more in 1884, when it reached 2,373,000 pounds,† the third highest combined production in the island's history.[24]

The initial flush of expansion in the new bounty era lasted for a little over a decade and turned the Tancooks into bona fide fishing communities. By 1891, there were 141 self-proclaimed full-time fishermen in residence there compared to 69 (and 44 "fishermen-farmers") ten years earlier.[25] In 1896, aided by a record herring catch, the islands enjoyed their most productive year ever, with 2,921,000 pounds of fish landed and marketed. Shortly thereafter, however, the impetus provided by government subsidies began to wane in the face of declining exports and falling market prices, and the Tancook fisheries levelled off and declined during the first decade of the new century. A slow recovery then began around 1906 and gained momentum after 1910, ushering in a second period of expansion. By 1914, the industry revival had produced the second greatest fishing year in island

---

* For vessels over 10 tons, payments were exclusively on a tonnage basis from 1882 to 1895, the per-ton rate changing from year to year. Half the subsidy went to the owners, and the crew divided the other half. After 1895, vessel owners were compensated at an annual rate of $1.00 per ton (up to 80 tons), and their crewmen on an individual payment basis that varied according to the number of claimants sharing the yearly allocation of bounty funds (originally set at $150,000 per annum and later raised to $160,000). For boats 10 tons and under, payments in varying amounts were made on a per-man basis in 1882 and 1883 and on a per-boat basis from 1884 to 1888, the owners receiving one-fifth and the crews dividing four-fifths. After 1888, owners received $1.00 per boat, and crewmen got equalized individual payments based on the total claimants in a given year. Between 1882 and 1916, bounties ranged from $5.00 to $7.60 for vessel crewmen and from $3.50 to $4.30 for boat crewmen. As the number of fishermen declined after World War I, individual payments rose substantially. In 1927, a typical postwar year, vessel fishermen realized $8.00 each for the season, boat fishermen $6.60. (Sources: Can.RFB, 1882–1916/17, annual statistics on fishing bounty payments; Canada, Royal Commission, Report Investigating the Fisheries, 54, 96.)

† Valued at $104,000, the highest return ever recorded for an annual island catch.

history (2,506,000 pounds marketed) and the most valuable catch in twenty years.[26]

Two already mentioned external factors fueled the post-1910 boom in the Tancook fisheries. The first was the Underwood-Simmons Tariff of 1913, which eliminated most duties on Canadian fish imported into the United States and its possessions, including long-standing levies on pickled herring and mackerel and on the salt cod favoured in the Puerto Rican market. The reduced barriers resulted in an immediate revival of Nova Scotia's previously slumping inshore fisheries and boosted demand throughout the province for both dried and pickled fish to satisfy expanded exports.[27] The second and more important factor in the expansion was World War I, which began a year later and created a brief golden age for the provincial fisheries from 1914 to 1918 based on unprecedented food demands at home and abroad and accompanying high fish prices of unparalleled levels.[28] The status of Lunenburg County's inshore industry during the war years was suggested in a report in *The Halifax Herald* at the end of 1918:

The shore fishermen ... had a great run of luck in the past season. The catch of herring was enormous, fully 14,000 bbls. being landed at this port [Lunenburg] valued at approximately $140,000. Mackerel was also taken in large numbers, some $43,000 of this highly esteemed fish being brought here; these brought as high as $30.00 per barrel.[29]

Tancook fishermen fully shared in the good economic times. By most measures, their industry reached its peak development during the early stages of the war before military enlistments and rising outfitting costs began to offset increased market prices. The average annual value of the island catch for the period 1914–16 ($52,000) was the greatest for any three years since the mid-1890s,* and in 1914, the number of registered island vessels collecting the federal fishing bounty reached its highest level in the more than thirty-year history of government subsidies. Between 1909 and 1916, the number of island wharves and piers doubled, the number of fish houses tripled, the number of hand lines increased fourfold, and the number of trawls and nets grew by eightfold and tenfold, respectively. Simultaneously, the value of island boats, enhanced by increased size and the installation of gasoline engines, multiplied by a factor of six to $47,000, a figure never before approached.[30]

---

* In 1916, the last war year for which market values are available, Tancook's combined catch registered a higher dollar return per pound than at any time in the previous forty years.

Statistics for 1914 provide a picture of the Tancook fisheries at or near the height of their wartime prosperity. Islanders at that time owned 23 large schooners of register size (the most ever), all but 5 of them moored at the main island. Of the 23, 18 collected fishing bounties that year totalling $620, $252 of which went to the owners and $378 to the crewmen at a rate of $6.40 per man. The 59 crewmen, who constituted the largest number ever to go vessel fishing from the islands in schooners over 10 tons, made up about one third of the fishing work force of the Tancooks. Another 110 manned the 300 or so smaller craft – unregistered schooners, sloops, launches, and dories – that comprised the balance of the island fleet. In addition to vessels and boats, Tancook's industry resources included an estimated 60 smoke or fish houses for processing and storing the catch, 40 small wharves, a lobster cannery, and an ice house. The equipment owned or in use consisted of 800 nets, fish traps, and seines, 185 trawls, 600 hand-lines, and 4,000 lobster traps. The catch itself was a mixture of groundfish, net fish, and shellfish. Scallops, a relatively new species, was the largest component in pounds landed and in market value, followed closely by the traditional herring, cod, haddock, mackerel, and lobster. Altogether, the catch returned $55,371, or $328 per fisherman, the highest average per capita earnings recorded since the prosperous days of the early bounty era in the 1880s.[31]

    Although Tancook Islanders continued to sail in search of fishing riches for another generation, the good times exemplified by the 1914 season never returned, and in the postwar era fishing once more became an economic struggle to survive. After 1918 and especially after 1919, an industry recession took hold throughout the province, caused by overstocks of fish, price deflation, dislocations in the traditional Caribbean markets, and increased competition from revived peacetime fisheries in Europe and Newfoundland. Outfitting costs for fishermen remained at or near their inflated wartime highs, while glutted markets forced product prices back to their prewar levels. Fish became virtually unsaleable at Lunenburg for a time, and shore fishermen had great difficulty disposing of their catches. Dried cod, which had brought nearly $14 per quintal during the last year of the war, fell to less than $7 per quintal in the early 1920s. Pickled herring, a Tancook specialty, also plummeted in price as exports fell by two thirds over the same period.[32]

    Problems caused by the natural workings of the postwar economy were accentuated by changes in public policy that took place far from Tancook Island. In late 1922, a Republican-controlled Congress in the United States overturned the low tariff rates established under the Underwood-Simmons Act of 1913, which had done so much to energize Nova Scotia's fishing industry during the "free trade" years of the Democratic Wilson Administration. Under the new Fordney-McCumber Tariff, articles of export crucial to the economic health of South Shore fishermen at Tancook and elsewhere returned to their pre-1913 impost levels and, in some instances, exceeded them.* Among items that had lately been duty-free, salted and dried cod went to 1¼¢ per pound, and pickled herring and mackerel to 1¢ per pound, rated that in the case of herring amounted to an effective 30 to 35 percent surcharge.[33] One result was a substantial decline in provincial fish exports to the United States and a concurrent loss of industry manpower to other occupations. Another, more generalized result was an accentuation of the already severe postwar recession of the early 1920s, which among other things initiated a heavy migration of population out of the Maritimes and to the more prosperous New England states.[34]

Big and Little Tancook were among the many Maritime communities affected by the recession-driven exodus of the 1920s.† The islands, which had reached a population peak of 733 in 1911, lost one quarter of their people over the next two decades, including 18 percent of their male work force.[35] Most of that loss was absorbed in the postwar era and manifested itself in the gradual decline of the local fishing industry. Ownership of registered vessels, for example, which had peaked at 23 schooners in 1914 and averaged 20 per year throughout the war, fell to an average of 16 in the 1920s and to 14 in the 1930s.[36]

Those islanders who remained at home after the war struggled to maintain their fisheries and way of life in the face of more or less constant economic dislocation. The modest recovery from the recession of the early 1920s was followed almost immediately by the calamitous Great Depression of the 1930s, which once more decimated fish markets and imperilled the island economy. At Lunenburg, cod prices fell to one quarter what they had been during the wartime boom.[37] Nevertheless, through it all the Tancook fisheries survived, and the traditional island economy remained intact, if diminished, until World War II, when it finally changed forever.

---

* This state of affairs continued for well over a decade. The destructive tariff law of 1922 was succeeded by the equally debilitating Smoot-Hawley Act of 1930, which maintained intact or increased the high American import duties on Canadian fish. (*Source*: US.SL, vol. 46 (1930), pt 1, chap. 497, sec. 1.)

† Three of my uncles, sons of the schooner builder Howard Mason, were among those who left Tancook for the United States during the postwar decade, one because he had "no land to farm and no boat to fish." Two of the three never returned.

During all these years, good and bad, certain constants worked to shape and define the Tancook fisheries, giving them their own unique character. It is appropriate at this point to examine the operation of the island industry in greater detail, in order to understand how it endured. First, Tancook fishing in the whaler and schooner eras was almost entirely salt fishing. The catch was either salted and sun dried or pickled in brine. This was basically because of a lack of cold storage facilities at Lunenburg, the islands' chief marketing outlet.[38] Cold storage and its attendant activity, fresh fishing, did not come to Lunenburg until 1926–27, and then only in a limited way.[39] Islanders always carried on some fresh fishing for immediate consumption or for sale to resorts and retail markets in nearby Chester, of course. Fresh salmon, lobster, and halibut were valued adjuncts to the predominant salt fisheries almost from the beginning. In the 1890s, flounder, haddock, and Tom-cod became important fresh catches for a time, and just before World War I, these were joined by swordfish and scallops.* Taken in its entirety, however, the islands' fresh production never exceeded a small fraction of the whole, usually not more than 10 percent of the entire catch until after 1910, when it occasionally rose to as high as 25 percent.[40]

Throughout their history, the Tancook fisheries were dominated by three species: cod, mackerel, and herring. Although other interests were periodically pursued, these catches were the primary focus of island fishermen year-in and year-out, accounting for the majority of landed pounds taken in 34 of the 41 years between 1876 and 1917 for which detailed statistics are available. Since two of the three (herring and mackerel) were schooling surface fish captured mostly in nets, net fishing became the signature mode of operation at the Tancooks. On a pound basis, net fishing for herring and mackerel (and, to a more limited extent, for salmon) provided about two thirds of the fish marketed by island fishermen over the years, and line fishing for cod and its associated bottom-feeding species (including haddock, hake, pollock, flounder, and halibut) accounted for about one quarter of the total. The comparative emphasis on these different modes of fishing

---

* The regional scallop beds were found near Chester and in the western half of Mahone Bay. They were tapped with the aid of gasoline motors, which permitted six-foot-long iron scallop rakes to be dragged efficiently for the first time from the sterns of small boats. Large-scale scalloping under power began about 1912 and coincided with the establishment of a winter fishing season and the creation of a wholesale market for shucked scallops at Chester. In prior years, the few island scallopers who worked under sail, dragging their rakes in strong winds under jib and mainsail, had fished summers and peddled their small catches in the shell in Halifax. (*Sources*: Interviews, Thomas Mason, 30 September 1986 and 14, 15 June 1989; Pugsley, "Chester, Nova Scotia," 9.)

varied little from decade to decade, although net fishing was deemphasized somewhat after 1900 when schooners replaced whalers and began to seek increasingly valuable groundfish catches farther off shore.* The twentieth century appeal of more exotic seafoods like lobster, scallops, and swordfish also made inroads in the preoccupation with net fishing, but never supplanted it.[41]

The seasonal movements of their main quarries created certain patterns of activity Tancook fishermen faithfully followed for decades. Early May marked the appearance of the first herring and mackerel schools off the coast and, for the island's hatch and semi-deck boats, the start of the fishing season. Except for a brief interlude to plant cabbage and make hay, May and June were given over to net drifting (or "droguing") for herring or mackerel and intermittent hand-lining for cod on the ridges. Those fishermen who did not devote their summer to farming and trap tending, or to a lengthy swordfishing voyage up the coast, typically spent July and August salt fishing for cod and other groundfish on the ridges or, in the case of small scallop sloops, just off the island. September brought the spawn herring season, and for about a month islanders set stationary nets for these young fry outside of neighbouring East Ironbound Island, three miles away, and tended them daily. Setting mackerel nets or cod trawls off Pearl (formerly Green) Island, about seven miles seaward of Tancook, was a supplemental fall activity. Mid-October saw the beginning of the coasting season, which followed the agricultural harvest and interrupted fishing for a time. The men then returned briefly to net fishing for mackerel until early December (when most boats were hauled for the winter) or embarked on several months of inshore scalloping.† The following May, the cycle began once more.[42]

Of all these activites, none was historically more important than herring fishing. Although it reached a peak in the 1890s, it remained the basis of the island fishery well into the twentieth century. Herring was the leading catch at the Tancooks in a majority of the years between 1876 and 1917, and it provided over half the fish marketed from the islands during most of that time.[43] The bulk of this impor-

---

* The Tancook netted catch as a percentage of the whole declined from 75 percent in the 1870s to 53 percent in the 1910s.
† Because of the harshness of the season, winter scalloping was primarily an activity for the islands' younger fishermen, aged 20 to 40 years. After about 1912, some families maintained two boats, a schooner for general fishing from May to October and a smaller sloop for scallop dragging from November to April. In such cases, the older men ran the schooners, while their sons took charge of the scallop sloops. (*Source*: Interview, Thomas Mason, 14 June 1989.)

tant catch was taken in the summer and fall by stationary traps and nets, but the most distinctive form of herring fishing was carried on by the perennial spring droguers, whose techniques remained essentially unchanged until the mid-1930s.

Despite being equipped with a motor after 1910, the Tancook schooner always operated under sail when droguing.* A typical trip saw the vessel leave her island anchorage about 3 P.M. She reached the inner ridge twelve to fifteen miles south of Tancook around 6 P.M., after a straight windward beat of about three hours against the prevailing southwest wind.† Upon arrival, the first order of business was the setting of drift gill-nets. These finely meshed nets, used for both herring and mackerel,‡ were 40' long and 8' to 10' deep. When in use, anywhere from 10 to 30 of them were attached end to end and run out from the vessel. (The semi-deck boat *Patavana* set 10 or 15 nets at a time in the early 1930s). They hung vertically from the surface of the water, kept in position by cork floats at the top balanced by rock sinkers at the bottom. The entire arrangement was secured by a long line to the bow of the boat, which lay facing the wind with her mainsail up and sheeted tight to serve as a riding sail. In this fashion, the schooner drifted or "drogued"§ throughout the night. The next morning, the nets were hauled, and if the catch was sufficiently large, the schooner sailed directly to the Lunenburg market. Otherwise, she anchored for the day to line fish for cod and haddock, using a portion of the herring for bait, and then reset her nets in the evening. The

---

* Engines were normally reserved for the fall net fishing season, when daily trips had to be made and conditions were less conducive to comfortable sailing (*Source*: Interview, Thomas Mason, 12 June 1986.)

† In the whaler period, Tancook herring boats often ranged the coast from Port Medway on the South Shore to Port Bickerton on the Eastern Shore, fishing close to land. It was common for them to work just off Halifax Harbour, using Herring Cove as a base of operations.
In the schooner era, island net boats fished farther out to sea – typically the first and second ridges, 15 to 20 miles off Tancook – but they did not parallel the coastline so far in a southerly or easterly direction. (*Source*: Interviews, Thomas Mason, 30 September 1986, and David M. Stevens, 20 June 1988.)

‡ Tancook droguing nets were intended primarily for herring and were more finely meshed, as a rule, than common mackerel netting. One expedient occasionally used to capture both species simultaneously was to weave a net with large mesh at the top for the surface-schooling mackerel and small mesh at the bottom for the deeper-schooling herring. (*Source*: Interview, Thomas Mason, 17 June 1989.)

§ The term "droguing" was peculiar to Lunenburg County and, especially, Tancook fishermen. Most other Nova Scotians referred to this form of fishing as "drifting" and to the boats as "drifters." The origin of the term among islanders is unknown, but a drogue was a sea anchor, and in this instance, the herring or mackerel nets approximated the sea anchor's function. (*Sources*: Interview, Thomas Mason, 24 June 1988; see also *HH*, letter to the editor, 22 August 1927, 11, and ibid., news items, 5 June 1931, 15, and 8 June 1931, 13.)

same procedure was followed for two or three days and nights, and when the hold was full, the boat returned to Tancook, this time running before the wind. Upon reaching home, that portion of the catch not sold fresh in Lunenburg – usually most of it because the town's cold storage facilities were limited, and boats were often turned away or offered too low a price – was dressed and salted, placed in barrels, and stored in fish houses for pickling and eventual marketing at the end of the fishing season.[44]

Tancook schooners generally went droguing twice a week from mid-May to early or mid-June. It was dangerous work. The boats working the outermost ridges were close to the Halifax-New York shipping lanes that paralleled the coast, and crews could often see the lights of steamships passing nearby on foggy nights. Watches were sometimes posted, but most skippers simply hung a lantern and trusted to Providence. Thomas Mason, who crewed aboard the droguing schooner *Patavana* in the early 1930s, recalled that a gun was carried aboard the boat as a warning device in place of a bell. On one occasion the men were roused from their bunks by the noise of an approaching ship. Scrambling on deck, they could see the lights and outline of a large steamer through the fog. Several shots were fired into the air, and the vessel veered off. Close calls of this sort were commonplace, but miraculously no Tancook boats were ever run down.[45]

The food served aboard the droguers was regular island fare, plain but nourishing. A typical schooner of the 1920s or 1930s stocked whatever could be prepared quickly and with little difficulty so as not to disrupt the shipboard work routine. This usually included salted herring, potatoes, bread, cake, milk, butter, molasses, and eggs for frying. Occasionally the menu was varied by boiling a cod or haddock caught during daytime hand-lining, and often a boiled dinner was prepared in which everything was thrown into the pot. The boiled meal was also a dietary staple aboard Tancook schooners during the fall and winter coasting season. At that time of year, dinner typically combined salt meat or herring, turnips, and potatoes. Sleeping arrangements for fishing or coasting consisted of four bunks located in the forward cuddy cabin of the schooner, which also contained the boat's cook stove. The stove, secured atop a low storage locker and tended sitting down, was almost invariably the dependable, wood-burning "Little Cod" model manufactured by the Hillis Foundry of Halifax. Essentially a rectangular, cast iron fire box (18" × 12" × 12") with two burners, the Little Cod served most island schooners of the under 50' class from the whaler period onward. Larger deck boats that engaged in winter coasting and spent several weeks at sea during the fishing season favoured the Lunenburg Foundry's fully lined "Atlantic Fisherman" coal-burning stove, which contained a baking oven and provided superior heating below deck.[46]

Droguing as an island fishing technique came to an end around 1935-37, when Tancook fishermen turned exclusively to so-called stationary nets. The main reason for the change was an increased preoccupation with mackerel fishing, which was better adapted to secured gill-netting gear, but the opportunity to return home each evening was also a factor. Despite their name, stationary nets were not immobile, but neither were they attached to drifting schooners. Instead, they were held in place by long anchor lines running from the sea bottom to surface buoys, which marked their locations. One end of each collection of nets was fastened to the upper portion of an anchor line, while the opposite end drifted free. The tops of the nets were floated by corks and the bottoms suspended downward by weights, as with drift nets. Hauling and resetting was done by schooners that sailed out from Tancook on a daily basis* for that specific purpose.[47]

Next to herring netting, cod fishing was the chief preoccupation of Tancook fishermen during the age of sail. It was the one other constant that could be depended upon from one year to the next. Unlike mackerel catching, which fell off significantly after 1890, cod fishing consistently maintained an important position in the island fisheries throughout the nineteenth and early twentieth centuries (except for a brief downturn between 1905 and 1909) and came fully into its own with the introduction of the larger, gasoline-powered schooner after 1910. With the exception of the bounty-inspired catches of 1885-86, the 4,500 hundredweights of dried cod marketed in 1911 was the largest amount taken by island fishermen to the end of World War I, and if haddock, pollock, and other related species are included, that year was the greatest for groundfishing in Tancook's history, with 5,580 hundredweights dried. By the 1910-16 period groundfishing, long the poor relation in the island's industry, had attained a position of near equity with net fishing in dollar value, and the annual cod catch was worth almost as much as the dominant herring catch.[48]

Unlike Tancook's herring and mackerel fishing, which was concentrated in a few short weeks of hectic activity in the spring and fall,†

---

* Sunday was an exception. Island fishermen, being strict Baptists, would not violate the Sabbath to tend their nets unless a storm threatened their gear. By contrast, their Blandford neighbours, who were mostly Anglicans, had no compunctions about Sunday fishing. (*Source*: Interview, Thomas Mason, 17 June 1989.)

† Except for the intermittent summer trap fishing by those who did not follow the Cape Breton swordfishery. (*Source*: Interview, Murray A. Mason, 21 June 1989.)

cod and other groundfishing spread over several months. It was pursued in conjunction with net droguing in the spring, when the catch was carried home fresh, and as a separate occupation in the summer, when the fish caught by hand line on the offshore ridges were salted on board to prevent spoilation in the warmer temperatures. Cod were sought in the fall as well, using trawls or long-lines set in the vicinity of Cross* and Green (Pearl) islands, eight or nine miles beyond Tancook. In the 1930s, the semi-deck boat *Patavana* trawled one fall season with a three-man crew just outside Cross Island, setting a single trawl each evening, sheltering in Cross Island harbour at night, and hauling her line the following morning.[49]

Most cod fishing by Tancook schooners of the common hatch boat variety was hand-line, rather than trawl, fishing. The bait chosen varied according to the locale fished. Fishermen working the outer grounds preferred fresh squid but normally used fresh herring or mackerel. Those day fishing on the inner grounds near Tancook usually made do with fresh clams, the least effective but most readily available bait. Schooners bound for the outer ridges exercised one of two options. They either purchased their herring from the island's trap fishermen or caught it themselves on the fishing grounds in the course of droguing. Non-droguers employed small herring or mackerel nets called "bait nets" for the same purpose and sometimes hand-lined squid. Those wishing to preserve their bait in ice could purchase a supply at East Ironbound Island, and for a few years beginning in 1913, the boatbuilding firm of Mason and Langille also maintained an ice house at Southeast Cove. Since most Tancook boats stayed out for only two or three days at a time, however, ice was not a necessity. Fishermen using clams dug their own from area beaches, working at low tide, and stored them off shore near their moorings in holed wooden crates, to be used as needed. Any Mahone Bay island with a sand beach could provide bait clams, but the favourites were Heckman's, Sacrifice, and Fifty Acre islands at the outer, western edge of the bay and Meisner's Island not far from Chester.[50]

A typical hatch-boat crew of three arranged themselves in a particular manner when seeking groundfish. One man stood in the steer-

---

* Cross Island, a large but sparsely populated land mass located off Lunenburg Bay, was commonly used as a fishing base in sailing days. It contained a half-dozen houses in the 1920s and 1930s and was inhabited by families named Smith, Baker, and Levy, the latter two having migrated there from Big and Little Tancook, respectively. The native Cross Island fishermen periodically patronized Tancook's Southeast Cove boatyards for their schooners.
(*Sources*: Interview, Thomas Mason, 1 October 1988; see also NA, LunSR: registers of schrs *Sealer*, 17 August 1911, *Rakwana*, 25 May 1912, and *Scamper*, 16 May 1917.)

ing cockpit near the tiller, another in a hatchway just forward of the mainmast, and a third just aft of the cuddy near the foremast. Each controlled two hand-lines, one on either side of the boat, and tended them alternately. If a fourth man was present, he stood in a dory tethered to the schooner. The use of a dory was common aboard Howard Mason's *Patavana*, a somewhat larger semi-deck boat whose crew often consisted of the owner/skipper and three of his sons. When groundfishing during droguing operations, the main hold between the masts was reserved for herring or mackerel nets, and the forward hand-liner stood inside on a hatch cover atop the nets. The second man worked in the after portion of the same hold and positioned himself on a platform specifically built for hand-lining. The third man, usually the skipper, fished from the steering cockpit at the stern, and the fourth from the towed dory. The cod or haddock catch was stored in the second and smaller of the boat's two fish hatches, located abaft her mainmast and just forward of her engine room.[51]

Upon a spring droguer's return to Tancook, the groundfish portion of her catch was gutted, cleaned, and pickled in brine. It then sat in kegs inside the fish house for two months or more before being removed, resalted, and spread on beach rocks to dry in the sun. This usually took a week and was ideally done in September or October, when the sun's rays were not direct enough to overexpose or "burn" the fish. Turk's Island sea salt, brought from the Caribbean by Lunenburg coasting vessels, was used in the cure, and 200 pounds of it produced 1,000 pounds of dried cod. After drying, the processed catch was packed in large casks called puncheons, which held 100 gallons of liquid or, in this case, 1,000 pounds of fish. It was then ready for marketing in Lunenburg. The island herring and mackerel catch was mostly split and pickled – a process taking about one month – and similarly packed in barrels for shipment, but the containers for pickled fish were smaller and usually weighed 300 pounds, 100 pounds of which was brine or "pickle," and the rest fish. So-called half-barrels holding 100 pounds of fish were occasionally used for herring, but 200 pounds per barrel was the most common measure.[52]

Upon sale of a Tancook schooner's catch in Lunenburg, the seasonal profits were divided between the owner and crew according to the size of the boat and the relationships of the men involved. In whaler days, sharesmen were a common feature in the island fisheries. There were normally two men in a whaler crew, the owner of the boat and a non-owning sharesman who agreed to "double up" with the skipper in exchange for a set percentage of the returns. The sharesman was typically unrelated to the owner and not always an island resident. In the schooner era (post-1905), doubling up became less common because the larger families of that period permitted a working boat owner to take his brothers or sons on as crewmen. A family crew often dispensed with a formal division of the profit into shares and simply deposited the season's returns in a common pot. (Sons seldom received a separate share unless they were married.) Ordinarily, however, a schooner owner took at least one fifth to one third of the catch proceeds – the "boat's share" – if he had supplied the nets, lines, puncheons, and other fishing necessities. Large island deck boats almost always fished "at the quarters," the owner(s)* taking one quarter of the profit remaining after expenses (bait, salt, gasoline), and the crew dividing the rest equally as per the Lunenburg, dory-trawling system. If an outsider signed on as a traditional sharesman – a rare occurrence by the 1920s and 1930s – he was fed by the owner and allotted a prearranged percentage of the proceeds. Small boats with two crewmen generally operated on the basis of an equal contribution to outfitting expenses and an equal share in the catch.[53]

DISTANT SEAS

While the pursuit of cod, mackerel, and herring in local waters absorbed most of Tancook's fishermen and the majority of its boats, other, more far-ranging fishing interests came to the fore after 1910 and claimed an increasing share of attention. The successful integration of the internal combustion engine with the newly evolved schooner design in the second decade of the twentieth century gave islanders the security and flexibility to expand their economic horizons. The larger, auxiliary-powered Tancook schooner, quickly dubbed a "gasoline schooner" by waterfront observers,[54] brought distant seas suddenly within reach and turned formerly insular shore fishermen into bona fide deep-water mariners. Fishing grounds hundreds of miles from home were drawn into the island's sphere of operations, and places like Louisburg, Glace Bay, North Sydney, and Alberton became part of the island consciousness.

---

* Tancook schooners often had more than one owner, especially if they were large enough to be registered. Two owners was about the average for boats in the 40' to 45' category, but those over 45' registered length (the deck boat class) usually had three and sometimes four. Ownership shares were divided into 64ths, and equal partnerships ($32/64$ ea.) were the rule among two-owner boats. Large schooners with multiple owners also had their shares divided equally, although the managing owner, usually the skipper, took an extra share ($1/64$) as his prerogative. Boats with two or more owners were often family affairs in which shares were held by fathers and sons or brothers. About half of Tancook's registered schooners were in this category, and brother partnerships were particularly common. (Sources: NA, LunsR; Can.HCH, HalsR; and Can.LCH, LunsR: registers of Tancook-owned vessels, 1905–36.)

The schooners behind this geographic revolution in the Tancook fisheries were the large deck boats, which entered the island fleet around the time of World War I.* Their size (over 50') and capacity made long ocean voyages to the coasts of Cape Breton and Prince Edward Island practical from both a seafaring and an economic standpoint. Larger crews and bigger cargo holds meant that the comparative dangers of extended voyaging were offset by greater catches and higher returns. As a result, the Tancook deck boats evolved their own seasonal cycle of fishing activities that differed from the one followed by the island's hatch and semi-deck boats. In May and June, when the smaller schooners went droguing, the deck boats sailed to Cape Breton or the Gulf of St Lawrence for a month or more of dory trawling for cod, salting the catch on board for later drying.† After curing and marketing their groundfish, they returned to northern waters in July for a summer of swordfishing off the southeastern shore of Cape Breton. September was spent closer to home, trawling for cod and haddock off Tancook or Halifax. Early October brought the coasting season, and the deck boats then joined the balance of the Tancook fleet in carrying the island's produce to Halifax.[55]

The first of the distant deck-boat fisheries pursued from Tancook was the Prince Edward Island spring cod fishery, which got under way at the beginning of World War I. The initial participant was the big Amos Stevens-built schooner *Tancook* (38 tons; 59.4' × 16.4' × 7.6'), which went north on her maiden voyage in the spring of 1914 under the command of skipper and part-owner Ernest ("Ernie") Covey. The *Tancook* and her crew of five reached the selected fishing grounds off the northern coast of PEI by way of the Strait of Canso, after a brief layover at Port Hawkesbury. The port of Alberton near the northwest tip of the island was chosen as a base of operations, and day fishing was carried on from there. A catch of five hundred quintals, the vessel's full capacity, was the reward for several weeks' work.[56]

---

* Although a number were built earlier for outside owners, the local precursor of the deck boat type was the *Lobelia L.* (1913) of Little Tancook, the first modern 50-footer owned at the islands. She was followed in 1914 by the 59' *Tancook* (64' overall), first of the very large island-owned deck boats. Several more schooners of this seagoing class were built for Tancook owners before the end of the war. (*Source*: NA, LunSR: registers of schrs *Lobelia L.*, 23 September 1913, *Tancook*, 30 April 1914, *Silver Oak*, 21 April 1917, *Haig*, 25 April 1917, *White Birch*, 21 May 1918, and *Blanche M. Stevens*, 29 May 1918; see also figures 10 and 11.)

† From the first, a minority of the deck boats remained at home in the spring prior to swordfishing season and trawl fished near Tancook, setting their trawls just outside of Pearl and Cross islands. In later years, when the swordfishery became their major focus, most deck boats followed that practice. (*Sources*: Interviews, Thomas Mason, 25 September 1987, and Murray A. Mason, 16 June 1988.)

Among the *Tancook*'s crew was young Hovey Slauenwhite, who had gained the experience necessary for the trip two years earlier when, at the age of seventeen, he had gone to sea in the Lunenburg banker *Alhambra*.[57] Service in the regional banks fleet became the standard means by which Tancookers acquired the knowledge and skills to undertake their own deep-water voyages. The pattern was established early in the 1890s when Hibbert and James Langille (Alfred Langille's nephew and son, respectively) and Reuben Heisler went on banking voyages out of Lunenburg. Later in that decade, they were followed by Howard Mason, who crewed aboard the *Nova Zembla* of Mahone Bay on a trip to Labrador and subsequently skippered his own schooner in the Cape Breton fisheries. Shortly after the turn of the century, another islander, Randolph Stevens, visited the Western Banks in the *Hispaniola* of Lunenburg.[58] A vessel trip to the offshore fishing grounds eventually evolved into a virtual rite of passage for Tancook's young men. It was something almost every island fisherman did once in his life,* and it developed a level of seafaring competence that proved indispensable in the expansion of the island's own fisheries.

The first excursion to Gulf waters by the *Tancook* in 1914 set a precedent that was followed almost immediately by other island schooners. Until the postwar decline in cod prices removed the economic incentive behind the PEI voyages around 1920, a small Tancook fleet went there each year. It consisted mostly of deck boats but included

---

* In 1920, nearly two dozen residents of Big and Little Tancook were among the crews of the Lunenburg banks fleet. The men and their vessels were as follows:

Schooner	*Frank Baxter*	– Percy Young and Eli Young
"	*Helen M. Coolen*	– Albert Langille
"	*Mary H. Hirtle*	– Thomas Levy (L. Tan.)
"	*Aranoka*	– Avery Langille and Lindsay Stevens
"	*Frank J. Brenton*	– Gordon Levy (L. Tan.)
"	*Lois A. Conrad*	– Irwin Langille, Wilfred Wilson, and Jordon Cross
"	*Dorothy Adams*	– Ellsworth Wilson
"	*Donald L. Silver*	– Basil Levy
"	*Gilbert B. Walters*	– Demus Young, Jessen Mosher, and Gurney Young
"	*Ada Westhover*	– Angus Langille (L. Tan.)
"	*Bernice Zinck*	– James Langille
"	*Marion Elizabeth*	– Allen Langille, Perry Stevens, Percy Levy, Charles Hubley, and Willard Langille

(*Source*: HH, article, 31 December 1920, supp., 13–16.)

Among islanders who went banking in succeeding years were: Steadman Mason, schooner *Bernice Zinck*, 1923; Thomas Mason, schooner *Bluenose*, 1923; and Wesley Stevens, Jr, schooners *Jean Smith* and *Isabel J. Corkum*, dates unknown. (*Sources*: Interviews, Steadman S. Mason, 4 October 1986, Thomas Mason, 1 October 1988, and Wesley H. Stevens, Jr, 22 June 1988.)

139 The Economy

a few smaller schooners with adventurous owners, the 41-foot *Cecil V.L.* and the 42-foot *Steward D.S.* among them. One of the last double-ended whalers, an engine-equipped 40-footer, also made the trip. The brief appeal of the Gulf fishery led directly to the building of Tancook's largest schooner, the mammoth *Silver Oak* (42 tons; 62.4' × 16' × 8'), in 1917 and to one of its first 50-footers, the *White Birch* (28 tons; 49.8' × 14.2' × 7.5'), in 1918, both of which were launched expressly for northern voyaging.[59]

Participants in the Gulf fishery all followed a similar routine. They established an operating base, which was usually Alberton, and day fished from that location, working the small banks north of PEI or, on occasion, the eastern New Brunswick shore near Shippegan. They typically set their cod trawls fifteen to twenty miles from shore during the daylight hours, came in to port for the night, and returned to haul and reset their lines the next day.[60] The setting and hauling was done from dories of a special Tancook design. Nicknamed "bastard dories" because of their unusual size, they were 14' to 16' long on the bottom* – midway between the 12', one-man, hand-line dories preferred for inshore fishing and lobstering and the 18' banking dories seen on the large Lunenburg trawlers. Unlike the other two classes, which were purchased used from Lunenburg vessel owners as needed, Tancook's odd-sized bastard dories were constructed on the island and were designed to fit the peculiar specifications of the local deck boats that carried them. They were large enough to accomplish the necessary tasks but small enough to nest comfortably between the masts of a 50' schooner. In addition, they were constructed of heavier than normal timbers and came equipped with a false bottom that permitted them to be hauled fully loaded up island launchways when landing fish.[61]

The PEI cod fishery came to an end as suddenly as it had begun. Three of the largest schooners built to engage in it, the *Silver Oak*, the *Blanche M. Stevens*, and the *Tancook*, were sold to Newfoundland owners between 1919 and 1922, and another, the *White Birch*, went primarily into coasting. Thereafter, a majority of the island deck boats remained in home waters during the spring fishing season, departing only when hay making ended in late June and the summer swordfishery began off Cape Breton.[62] Another springtime alternative to the Gulf cod fishery, however, continued to draw Tancook fishermen, even during the postwar economic doldrums. That was the Cape Breton cod fishery. Exactly when island vessels began to visit the

---

* Overall length was about 17 to 18 feet, and the beam measured just under 5'. (*Source:* Interview, Thomas Mason, 24 September 1987.)

Cape Breton shore for cod is uncertain, but Clements and Hovey Slauenwhite's *Cecil V.L.*, which went there sometime between 1916 and 1918, may have been the first.[63] Another was Ernest Covey's *Tancook*, which made a Cape Breton voyage shortly before being sold in 1922. Steadman Mason, who was a member of *Tancook*'s crew that year, recalled the details of the trip.

    The big deck boat departed Tancook in early June with a crew of seven men – the skipper, a cook, and five fishermen. She sailed up the Eastern Shore with a following wind, keeping to the ship channel twenty miles off the coast, and reached Canso (the normal baiting station for Cape Breton-bound schooners) in about thirty-six hours, having maintained a good average speed of five knots for this longest leg of the trip. Not finding the desired squid bait available, the vessel continued on to Queensport on Chedabucto Bay, a half day's sail away, where a sufficient supply was obtained. She then preceeded to Glace Bay, her chosen base of operations, by way of the convenient inside passage through Bras d'Or Lake. The actual fishing, which occupied the next six weeks, was carried on almost within sight of Glace Bay itself. Trawls were set five to eight miles off the mouth of the harbour, good results inshore making excursions farther from port unnecessary.* The crew worked from three dories, two men to a dory, while the cook stayed with the vessel. Day fishing was the rule, as in the PEI cod fishery. Each day's catch was dressed and salted on board the schooner while returning to port for the night, and rebaited trawls were left to be hauled the following day. Evenings were given over to preparing the main meal of the day, which was eaten in harbour, and to occasional excursions about town. The *Tancook* ultimately sailed for home with 350 quintals of salt fish to show for a voyage that encompassed over a month and a half. The size of the catch precluded drying it at Tancook;† instead it was taken to a flake yard at Second Peninsula and, from there, to Lunenburg for marketing.[64]

    The Cape Breton cod fishery continued into the 1930s and remained a chief springtime occupation not only for Tancook's own deck boats,

---

* In later years, Tancook deck boats working the southeast coast of Cape Breton tended to fish off Louisburg, usually making trips of about four weeks. They were often forced to set their trawls as far as twenty-five miles from shore when day-fishing, in order to obtain a catch. (*Sources*: Interview, Murray A. Mason, 17 June 1986; HH, news item, 19 September 1930, 3.)

† Since Tancook had no flake yards of its own, island deck boats returning from PEI and Cape Breton patronized professional fish dryers at Second Peninsula, Lunenburg South, and the Ovens. Smaller schooners could dry their cod on flat beach rocks in the immediate coves, but there was insufficient space for larger catches. Furthermore, beach drying was risky due to the heat generated by the rocks, which could easily burn untended fish. (*Source*: Interview, Thomas Mason, 15 June 1989.)

but for those built on the island for fishermen from other South Shore villages as well.[65] Its economic importance paled, however, next to the geographically related seasonal activity that followed it: the Cape Breton summer swordfishery. Commercial swordfishing was virtually unknown among Nova Scotia fishermen until 1909. In that year, the federal fishery inspector for the district east of Halifax reported that "quite a number of these [sword] fish were taken on the Atlantic coast this year, which is an unusual thing."[66] The fishermen seeking swordfish for the first time in 1909 included those operating off Cape Breton in the vicinity of Cape North and Isle Madame, but their catch was small, almost incidental. The following season swordfish were landed in considerable numbers at Louisburg, where activity eventually centred, but the Cape Breton fishery remained largely undeveloped and economically insignificant until the middle years of the First World War, when it suddenly flowered and became (by war's end) the dominant source of Canadian swordfish.[67]

Tancook fishermen entered the swordfishery for the first time in 1910, working close to home and landing their catch on the island. They were drawn by the market price, which exceeded that obtained for any other seafood product per pound except lobster, and for a half-dozen years – particularly in 1912 and 1913 – the local swordfishery was an important adjunct to Tancook's other, more traditional activities.[68] The fishing grounds were off the mouth of St Margaret's Bay, where the waters literally swarmed with swordfish for a time. Periodically, the fish could be seen schooling off Tancook itself, and as many as 90 of them were landed in one day at nearby Indian Harbour and shipped immediately in ice to the Boston market. As a result of their growing popularity with American consumers, swordfish were converted almost overnight from a menace second only to dogfish as destroyers of nets and catches to an industry staple in their own right. Just as suddenly, however, this migratory species deserted Lunenburg County waters for a more congenial gathering place off Cape Breton's southeast coast,* and by circa 1917 their pursuit had become a distant sea fishery for Tancook fishermen.[69]

---

* Swordfish schooled northward up the Atlantic coast from southern regions beginning in late spring as waters warmed to above 50°F, appearing off New Jersey and southern New England in May and June and reaching Maine and Nova Scotia in July and August. They returned southward as ocean temperatures cooled in the fall. The species was acutely sensitive to alterations in the marine environment, and their desertion of the South Shore for a more easterly summer rendezvous off Cape Breton around 1917–18 may have been due to slight but abrupt changes in inshore water temperatures. Another possibility is that they were drawn eastward in pursuit of more abundant sources of food. (*Sources*: Ackerman, *New England's Fishing Industry*, 44–5; Goode, *Fisheries and Fishery Industries*, sec. 1, 1:344, and sec. 5, 1:317.)

As a commercial enterprise, the Cape Breton swordfishery came into its own during the postwar period. The number of participating boats grew from an estimated 130 in 1922 to over 200 nine years later, and by the mid-1930s, over 300 were said to be involved.[70] The landed catch for the entire province went from 434,000 pounds in 1917 to an average of 1,060,000 pounds a year for the ten years 1925–34, and the 1935 catch, which broke all previous records, reached 2,220,000 pounds. The bulk of that total – close to two thirds in 1935 – was taken along the shore of Cape Breton between Louisburg and Glace Bay, and smaller amounts off the coasts of Victoria and Guysborough counties. The catch brought into Glace Bay alone rose from 10 fish in all of 1918 to 100 a day in 1932.[71]

By the mid-1920s the old French military outpost of Louisburg had been transformed into the headquarters of the Cape Breton swordfishery, with Glace Bay and North Sydney playing important but secondary roles.[72] Almost the entire catch was boxed in ice and exported fresh to the United States, principally Boston, by express rail via Sydney or by fast steamer. American wholesale fish firms stationed their buyers on the Louisburg waterfront to meet the fishermen as they unloaded their catches at the town wharf each evening. Swift transactions and immediate shipment were essential in this precarious long-distance fresh fishery, and Canadian National Railway facilities were often taxed to the limit. On occasion, even baggage cars were commandeered to accommodate daily shipments to Boston. In the hectic summer of 1932, nearly a half-million pounds of iced swordfish was processed and transported in this manner.[73]

Tancook Islanders entered the Cape Breton swordfishery during the war years and quickly established themselves among the leading South Shore participants. For the next two decades, a sizeable fleet of island vessels went down east each year, as many as 20 to 30 schooners making the 250-mile trip during peak seasons. The majority fished off Louisburg or Glace Bay, although a few worked as far afield as Cape North and Dingwall.[74] For the most part, these were deck boats, but there were exceptions. Unlike the northern cod fisheries, which called for vessels large enough to stay on the grounds for extended periods in order to salt down sizeably worthwhile fares, the northern swordfishery did not require boats of extraordinary capacity, since the fresh catch was landed and weighed out at regular intervals. That fact and the potentially high monetary returns to fishermen persuaded many owners of small Tancook hatch boats to make the long voyage to Cape Breton.* Among those who did so in the early 1920s were Howard Mason in the 36-foot *Rita* and Stephen Alinard in the 32-foot *Green Bow*. Later in the decade, Charles Hutt went in the 35-foot *Oda B.H.* and Harvey and Foster Stevens in the 34-foot *Salada*. In the early 1930s, they were joined by Raymond and Wesley Stevens, Jr, in their 36-foot *Turret*.[75]

The Cape Breton swordfishing season ran from mid-July to mid-September, with August being the busiest month. Until then, most of the Tancook fleet was occupied with spring cod fishing, although in the 1930s, a few large deck boats elected to anticipate the summer fishery by meeting the swordfish on Georges Bank in June as they schooled northward. In late July, Tancook's entire contingent of sworders, large and small, departed the island for Louisburg or Glace Bay, often outfitting at Halifax on the way. Upon arrival, they day-fished up to thirty miles off shore,[†] or as many as four hours sail from port, and spent the night aboard ship in harbour. The workday was from dawn to dusk, and the fishing was normally done either under sail or sail and power combined, depending on wind conditions. In some instances boats used power exclusively, the sails being reserved for commuting to and from the inshore grounds each day. Techniques approximated those employed in whaling. The schooling fish were spotted by one or more lookouts stationed atop the mastheads, some schooners stepping extra tall foremasts for that purpose. Once located, the swordfish were pursued and harpooned from the bows of the vessels, and empty rum kegs, affixed to the ends of the harpoon lines, were thrown overboard to slow and tire the wounded prey and mark their respective locations. Several fish were harpooned at one time by each schooner and were later retrieved by men in dories, who hauled them to the waiting vessels where they were killed (if neces-

---

* Until 1930, only schooners made the annual summer trek to Cape Breton, but after that time, a handful of large Cape Island motor boats also joined the Tancook fleet. The first was probably the 45-foot *Ramona II*, owned by Hovey and Clements Slauenwhite, which went in 1931. Another was the 40-foot *Here We Are* (see fig. 28), built for swordfishing in 1939 by Raymond, Guy and Wesley Stevens, Jr. The last Tancook boat to venture to Cape Breton (ca. 1946) was a Cape Islander commanded by Warren V. Pearl. (*Sources*: Interviews, Thomas Mason, 25 September and 1 October 1987; Hovey Slauenwhite, 30 September 1987; and Guy B. Stevens, 20 June 1988; HH, marine list, 1 August 1931, 21; Can.LCH, LunsR: register of motor boat *Ramona II*, 31 July 1930.)

† The schooner *Tancook*, which swordfished off Louisburg in the early 1920s, normally operated about 10 miles from the coast but sometimes went out as far as 20 or 30 miles and occasionally harbour-fished just a mile or so from port. (*Source*: Interview, Steadman S. Mason, 17 June 1989.)

sary), boated, de-sworded, and taken to port for dressing and cleaning. They were later marketed by the pound, and their swords taken home for ornaments. The typical three-man crews – mastheadman, steersman, and harpooner – shared the monetary returns equally after deduction of expenses.[76]

Swordfishing was challenging, exhilarating work, and the methods employed by Tancook fishermen in the 1920s and 1930s differed little from those used by other Atlantic fishermen a half century earlier.* The formidable quarry was an immense fish with a long, sharp beak ("sword") and weighed anywhere from 250 to 500 pounds.[77] Its capture necessitated a harpoon with a detachable head that weighed up to 18 pounds (pole, shank and head included) and a harpoon line 50 to 150 fathoms in length. The hardwood pole, 15' or 16' long, was manually launched from a semi-enclosed plank platform called a "pulpit," which was mounted on the schooner's bowsprit. Usually sighted from the masthead when two or three miles away, the swordfish was quietly stalked from behind until within 6' to 10' of the vessel. At that point, the harpoon was thrust into its back beneath the dorsal fin, the pole pulled from the detachable head, and the line permitted to run out with the fleeing fish. The line was then passed to a man in a small boat or (as was the practice in the 1920s) attached to a keg buoy, which was towed through the water by the fish until it died or exhausted itself, thus marking the location for the dorymen. Upon retrieval, the catch was killed by lancing it through the gills and hoisted aboard the vessel tail-first by means of a block and tackle rigged in the shrouds.[78]

The stealthful yet periodically feverish activity could be carried on only under optimal weather conditions. The powerful and elusive swordfish was most vulnerable on calm, clear days, when it rose or "bellied up" to the surface of the water to sun itself. In that unsuspecting moment, it could be taken by swift, skilful fishermen. Adverse weather, however, could disrupt the fishery to the point of rendering it profitless. Even under the best of conditions, it was a hit-or-miss endeavour with definite sporting overtones, "among the most thrilling of fishing operations," as one observer characterized it.[79] Sword-

---

* Swordfishing began on the American coast during the mid-nineteenth century and was a common pursuit in New England waters by the late 1870s. Over the next fifty years the major technological advancement in the fishery was the invention of a device that allowed lookouts to steer their vessels from the mastheads rather than relay instructions to steersmen in the after cockpits below. The new device was introduced in 1928, and by the following season, boats from Big and Little Tancook were using it. (*Sources*: Goode, *Fisheries and Fishery Industries*, sec. 1, 1:348, and sec. 5, 1:323–4; HH, news item, 30 July 1929, 11.)

fishing could also prove dangerous and expensive to the men involved. Instances of fish attacking and holing boats were not uncommon, and damage to motors and propeller shafts during the chase was an accepted risk.[80]

Occasionally, more serious incidents took place. At least one Tancook schooner, Howard Mason's *Rita*, was lost while swordfishing. This small 36-footer was deliberately oversparred to obtain maximum lookout proficiency (a common practice), mounting an old mainmast with topmast extension in place of her regular foremast. Equipped of necessity at minimal expense, like most Tancook boats, she also sailed with a second-hand mainsail intended for a larger schooner and no shifting board to hold her loose rock ballast in place. In the summer of 1922, while cruising for swordfish near Louisburg harbor in tricky conditions that combined a northwest wind with a southeast groundswell, the *Rita* was struck simultaneously by a broadside sea and sudden squall and capsized when her ballast shifted. The two men aloft at the time managed to extricate themselves from the entangling rigging and were pulled safely from the water. Attempts were then made to have the stricken craft towed to the nearest beach, but she filled and sank en route. *Rita*'s skipper, like the majority of Tancookers, carried no insurance and was forced to absorb the loss of a schooner he had built himself two years earlier. He thereafter abandoned swordfishing.[81]

For Tancook fishermen in general, however, the Cape Breton swordfishery provided a partial economic answer to the severe decline in the market value of their traditional salt fish products after World War I. Dried cod prices, for instance, never fully recovered from their postwar downturn, while fresh swordfish prices, which had shot upward during the last year of the conflict, remained strong into the 1930s[82] – a reflection of the gradual turning away of consumers from the preserved fish that had long formed the basis of the island fisheries. The best years were in the 1920s. Steadman Mason, who was mastheadman aboard the deck boat *Tancook* in the early part of that decade, recalled a season in which sixty-five swordfish were taken, one of them alone bringing $100 in the Louisburg market.[83] Reuben Heisler, who went down east about the same time in the schooner *Peggy*, realized $600 as his one-third share of the boat's earnings, which were based on a landed price of 10¢ per pound.[84]

The swordfishery, along with all other branches of the industry, eventually fell victim to universal hard times. The per-pound price realized by fishermen marketing their catch in Cape Breton County dropped from nearly 12¢ in 1931, where it had hovered for more than a decade, to 4¢ in 1932 and remained well below the level of the 1920s for the balance of the Great Depression.* By 1935 prices had only rebounded to 6½¢ per pound.[85] Those were averages. Prices obtained by some fishermen at certain times and places were even less. Wesley Stevens, Jr, of Big Tancook, who fished Cape Breton waters for six summers during the 1930s in the schooner *Turret*, remembered receiving just 1½¢ per pound from swordfish dealers at the height of the Depression. Based on the boat's usual harvest of 30 fish per season, that meant a return of no more than $200 (before expenses) to be divided among the crew for two months' work.[86] Still, despite the vagaries of the fishery and the substantial weakening of its price structure after 1930, swordfishing helped enable islanders to survive the bleak years of the interwar period with their fishing economy intact – no mean accomplishment in those times.

As an antidote to the recession of the 1920s and the depression of the following decade, the Tancook swordfishery was reinforced by a related activity, the island's self-contained Cape Breton coal trade. Glace Bay, North Sydney, and Louisburg were not only fishing ports, they were also coaling stations. The first two were situated in the very centre of Cape Breton's mining district and had immediate access to supplies. North Sydney's coal docks were served by the nearby Old Sydney Mine, the region's most extensively worked bituminous pit, and as many as a half-dozen Tancook schooners could be seen coaling there at one time in the late 1920s.[87]

Louisburg, which was twenty-one miles away from the nearest coal, was connected to the mines by the Sydney and Louisburg Railroad, built by the Dominion Coal Company between 1893 and 1895. Louisburg was chosen as a rail terminus because of its status as the only ice-free port in the region, a fortuitous circumstance for the majority of Tancook fishermen who made it their swordfishing base. By the 1920s, the coal company maintained a seven-hundred-foot wharf on the town's waterfront able to accommodate rail traffic and capable of servicing vessels of up to 26' draft. Large colliers and small craft like Tancook schooners were loaded at this location by means of numerous elevated chutes operating from 37' and 22' levels and positioned on either side of the wharf. These chutes funnelled coal directly into the holds of the waiting vessels from hoppers that were filled by continuously arriving rail cars.[88]

The existence of the Cape Breton coal ports was a boon to Tancookers about to depart the swordfishing grounds at the close of

---

* From 1918 to 1931, yearly province-wide swordfish prices ranged from 7¢ to 15¢ per pound and averaged 11¼¢. From 1932 to 1939, they ranged from 4¢ to 11¢ and averaged 8¢. (*Source:* Urquhart and Buckley, *Historical Statistics of Canada*, 394–5.)

Photo 45 Tancook schooner *Patavana* trawl fishing for cod off Green (Pearl) Island, Mahone Bay, ca. 1930. She is operating under foresail alone and is about to pick up her single dory, which has just tended the trawl. Cut tire halves are being placed over the side to serve as rubber bumpers for the dory while unloading fish. Note the schooner's rubbing strake, or "outside gunwale" as it was called, which protected the topsides from quays and wharves. [Author's collection]

Photo 46 Just in from a spring droguing trip, the crew of the schooner *Patavana* are dressing herring at their launchway, Southeast Cove, Big Tancook, in the mid-1930s. Two men are splitting the fish, and two are gutting or "gibbing." The catch will later be salted in barrels. The boat's skipper, Howard Mason, is on the right. His family crew consists (left-to-right) of sons Howard, Jr, Eustace, and Thomas. [Courtesy Mrs Carrie A. Kehoe]

Photo 47   The swordfishing fleet, including Tancook boats, in from the grounds at Glace Bay, Cape Breton Island, ca. 1935. Crewmen are posing for the camera. Note the extra tall masts, some equipped with ratlines to aid the mastheadmen in going aloft for lookout purposes. [Courtesy Mrs Sadie I. Langille]

Photo 48   Broadside view of the Tancook schooner *Mianus* of Indian Harbour, Nova Scotia, swordfishing in home waters, ca. World War I. She carries a crew of four – harpooner, steersman, and two lookouts or mastheadmen. This trim schooner was built as a knockabout in 1912 by Amos H. Stevens and was later fitted with a bowsprit to accommodate the "pulpit" used in swordfishing. Note the short, knuckled Indian-Header stem profile of the first round-bow Tancook schooners. [Courtesy Public Archives of Nova Scotia, Halifax, W.R. MacAskill Collection]

Photo 49 Bow view of the Tancook schooner *Mianus* swordfishing, probably near St Margaret's Bay, Nova Scotia, ca. World War I. It is perfect weather for the enterprise with light wind, calm seas and warm sunshine to lure the quarry to the surface. The boat is towing her dory, which will be used to retrieve the catch. Note the harpooner, ready in his pulpit, and the mastheadmen perched in the fore rigging. [Courtesy Public Archives of Nova Scotia, Halifax, W.R. MacAskill Collection]

Photo 50 Crew members of the Tancook schooner *Patavana* hauling the vessel's cod trawl off Green Island, Mahone Bay, ca. 1930. They are bringing a good-sized catch into their Lunenburg banks dory. [Courtesy Thomas Mason]

Photo 51   A typical small Tancook Island wharf and launchway viewed at near-low tide with most of the pole skids exposed. A fishing dory is hauled on the right, and a Cape Island boat, successor to the island schooners, is tied to a neighbouring wharf on the left. The scene is Southeast Cove, ca. 1960. [Photograph by author]

Photo 52   Crating Tancook cabbage for shipment to the West Indies on the south side of DeWolf's Wharf, Halifax, in the mid-1930s. Three crewmen of the schooner *Essie M.L.* are making and packing wooden crates, while a fourth man aboard the vessel (far right) passes up heads of cabbage. The man on the far left is watching the work. [Courtesy Mrs Margaret M. McLaughlin]

the summer season. Their holds were empty, each day's catch having been sold on the spot, and coal was not only a convenient return cargo, but an essential one. The island's slow-burning hardwood had been exhausted by the early twentieth century, and imported coal became the substitute winter fuel. It was available from two sources, Halifax, where it was purchased from retail coal merchants,* and Cape Breton, where it could be obtained direct from the wholesaler. Cape Breton coal was obviously cheaper, and teams of island oxen hauling wagon loads up from the shore were a common sight on Tancook in the 1930s when the swordfishing fleet returned home each fall.[89]

Coal became the preferred heating fuel on Tancook because it provided a warmer, longer-lasting fire than wood, and by the interwar period, islanders used wood only for starting their coal-fired stoves and for cooking in warm weather. For the most part, the coal burned in heating stoves was the soft, relatively inexpensive bituminous variety from Cape Breton. It produced excessive dust, however, and those with the financial means often substituted cleaner-burning American coke or "hard coal" (anthracite), which was imported to Halifax from New York. In such cases, a cook stove fed by soft coal or wood was maintained in the kitchen, while a self-feeding baseboard stove using hard coal was set up in the living room for all-night heating. Throughout the 1920s and 1930s, however, the single bituminous-burning kitchen stove was the arrangement in most Tancook homes, and it was kept supplied by the Cape Breton coal trade.[90]

DEMON RUM

Another, less legitimate, maritime trade also helped support the struggling Tancook economy in the depressed period between the world wars. For a small minority of islanders, liquor prohibition opened a new avenue of economic opportunity in the 1920s, and illicit rum running became a part-time vocation for a number of Tancook schooners.

Prohibition came to Nova Scotia in limited form during the last two decades of the nineteenth century, when more than a dozen provin-

---

* From at least World War I Halifax was supplied with bituminous coal by sail and steam colliers operating year-around out of Louisburg. Some of that coal found its way to Tancook aboard schooners returning from coasting trips to the city. It was transported from the coal docks in burlap potato sacks islanders saved for that purpose. (Source: HH, news items, 27 October 1917, 15, and 12 January 1918, 11; Keith, "Ben Heisler," 4-C; interviews, Thomas Mason, 30 September 1986 and 17 June 1989.)

cial counties voted themselves "dry" under the local option provisions of the Canada Temperance (or Scott) Act of 1878. This initial burst of moral enthusiasm had little immediate impact at the Tancook islands, since neighbouring Halifax County remained officially "wet" until 1910. In that year, however, the passage of the Nova Scotia Temperance Act abolished retail liquor sales everywhere in the province outside of the municipality of Halifax, and in 1916, prohibition was extended to include the city itself. Almost simultaneously, the provincial ban on retail liquor sales was reinforced by temporary wartime restrictions on importation, transportation, and manufacturing imposed by the Dominion government in Ottawa. Federal controls ended with the war, but in 1920, Nova Scotia voted in referendum to permanently reimpose the lapsed ban on liquor importation as of February 1, 1921. It was then that full-scale prohibition really began in the province, accompanied by increasingly widespread problems in enforcement. By 1929, voters had tired of the temperance experiment, and a new referendum replaced outright prohibition with government sale of alcoholic beverages, effective with the creation of the Nova Scotia Liquor Commission in April 1930.[91] During the intervening decade, however, the phenomenon of rum running reached full flower and created a new chapter in the maritime history of the province. In the process, it prompted novel and unanticipated uses for the Tancook schooner.

Nova Scotians were of two minds concerning the liquor question. On the one hand, the province was historically a prohibitionist stronghold. It had the first temperance organization in Canada and a record of strict licensing laws at the local level. It was also the first of the Atlantic Provinces to enact a comprehensive ban on alcoholic beverage sales.[92] On the other hand, parts of Nova Scotia adopted a decidedly "liberal" view of the subject. Among these was the South Shore county of Lunenburg. Lunenburgers not only resisted prohibition for some years under the Scott Act, they also provided a considerable number of the vessels in the Canadian rum running fleet of the Prohibition era, as well as a large share of the crews who manned them.[93] It was estimated that in 1924 as many of Lunenburg's fishing schooners were engaged in rum running as were actually fishing on the banks. No fewer than seventy-five of the town's schooners were thought to have been active to some degree in the rum trade during that peak year.[94]

There was more than one reason for Lunenburg County's prominent involvement in the transport and importation of illegal liquor during the 1920s. To begin with, it had a long history of alcohol consumption that went back to the founding of the original German colony in the 1750s. Licensed taverns were among the first public buildings erected by the early Lunenburg settlers, and until the midnineteenth century heavy drinking was socially acceptable on community holidays, at sessions of court, and during house raisings. The issuance of daily rum allowances to workingmen in fields, shipyards, and elsewhere was commonplace as well, and the importation of the dark liquid was long a cornerstone of Lunenburg's West Indies trade.[95] Furthermore, the county's status as one of the last wet strongholds in a dry province suggests that it was at best a lukewarm supporter of legalized prohibition. Lunenburg voters did not outlaw local liquor sales until 1894,* nearly a decade after voters in most Nova Scotia counties had done so.[96]

In addition to a lingering cultural tolerance for spirits, Lunenburg County's coastal environment did nothing to discourage participation in alcohol smuggling. This particular section of the South Shore was a virtual rum runner's paradise. In the words of Ted R. Hennigar, "The area from Hubbards to Bridgewater is dotted with hundreds of islands offering concealment for boats and hiding places for liquor on the beaches, in the swamps, and in the woods. The sandy beaches were easy to dig into and the waters of the bay [Mahone] were navigable and not too rough."[97]

Tradition and geography were further reinforced by what was undoubtedly the most important factor in the decision to undertake rum running: economic need. Prohibition, it should be remembered, coincided almost precisely with the postwar downturn in Nova Scotia's fishing economy, which was substantially based in Lunenburg County. By the mid-1920s, Tancook Islanders who chose to crew aboard large Lunenburg vessels carrying rum and bottled liquors from Demerara or St Pierre and Miquelon to Rum Row off the Middle Atlantic coast of the United States could make $65 to $75 per month in wages.† That was double what could be earned fishing, and it was

---

* Oddly, prohibition sentiment was unusually strong on Tancook – more so than elsewhere in Lunenburg County – due no doubt to the pervasive influence of the local Baptist Church. In 1845, 60 island residents, a large minority of the population, became members of a proselytizing mainland temperance society, and in 1894, when the county as a whole voted for prohibition by roughly two to one, the vote at the Tancooks was an overwhelming 72 to 4 in the affirmative. This sentiment was somewhat ironic in light of later developments. (*Source:* DesBrisay, *County of Lunenburg*, 411–12.)

† American prohibition was in force from 1920 to 1933, and running rum to East Coast locations off Long Island and New Jersey was an attractive alternative to the provincial rum trade. It was more remunerative for the crewman involved and also less risky from an enforcement standpoint, since the vessels stayed outside United States territorial waters and transferred their cargoes to smaller boats for delivery ashore. It also carried less social stigma than more localized bootlegging. Most Tancook Islanders regarded long-distance rum running in vessels to be simply another form of coastal trading that required skilled seamen. (*Source:* Interview, Thomas Mason, 17 June 1989.)

the principal reason so many took up rum coasting.[98] Even islanders who limited their smuggling activities to the local fleet of boats that off-loaded ship cargoes outside Canadian waters at night and ran them to selected South Shore rendezvous made up to $35 per month, a more than decent wage by Tancook standards.[99]

It was this latter activity that provided an especially useful role for the Tancook schooners. A few island boats did engage in long-haul rum running, although mostly under off-island ownership. The 65' deck boat *Sarah Pauline*, for instance (see fig. 15), was purchased after a short fishing career by the well-known New Brunswick rum runner Harry Ingalls, who employed her from 1929 to 1931 as one of his fleet of vessels supplying the South Shore with alcohol from St Pierre and Miquelon. She was eventually seized and impounded at North Sydney by customs officials.[100]

More typically, Tancook schooners were used as contact boats that secretively ferried liquor from large vessels anchored in international waters (three to twelve miles off the coast) to transfer points along the South Shore. Three Tancook families, the Youngs, Hirtles, and Wilsons, were particularly active in this work. Most prominent were Percy, Clarence, and Ernest Young, who operated four rum-running schooners in succession during the 1920s, and Clyde and Ralph Hirtle, who operated two.* Wilfred Wilson also ran a boat in the trade. The Young schooners *Gloria Swanson* and *Wildcat*, deck boats of the 55-foot class, were suitable to the St Pierre run and made some passages to and from the French liquor colony. The *Swanson* was ultimately lost off Sambro under mysterious circumstances while rum running in 1927.† The remaining Tancook rum schooners were smaller 45-foot boats exclusively engaged in transshipping the prized Black Diamond or Demerara brands from supply ships laying off Mahone or St Margaret's bays.[101]

In appearance, these craft were identical to most workaday island fishing schooners, and that, along with their traditional low-slung sil-

---

* The Young schooners were *Lucille B. Young* (built in 1919), *Elsie B. Young* (1923), *Gloria Swanson* (1926), and *Wildcat* (1928); the Hirtle schooners were *Opal June* (1918) and *Gloria P.H.* (1924). The *Opal June* and *Lucille B. Young* were built by Reuben Heisler and Amos Stevens, respectively, while the other four boats were products of the Mason yard in Southeast Cove. (For construction details, see NA, LunSR: registers of schrs *Opal June*, 6 May 1918, *Lucille B. Young*, 30 July 1919, and *Gloria P.H.*, 19 May 1924; Can.LCH, LunSR: registers of schrs *Gloria Swanson*, 27 January 1927, and *Wildcat*, 4 August 1928; and Can.HCH, HalSR: register of schr *Elsie B. Young*, 15 May 1923.)
† Unsubstantiated rumours suggest that there was foul play aboard this vessel prior to her loss and that she was purposely set on fire and destroyed to cover up the incident, which involved the death of a French supercargo. (*Sources*: Interview, Thomas Mason, 17 June 1989; Hennigar, *Rum Running Years*, 62.)

houettes, was the key to avoiding detection and capture by government patrol vessels. The only clues to their secret trade lay hidden below decks in the form of unusually large and powerful engines. Island contact boats relied on motors when delivering a cargo, and their power plants, while paltry compared to those of the swift gasoline launches that replaced them after 1930, were considerably above the norm for fishing boats. The 43-foot Percy Young schooner *Elsie B. Young* mounted three separate engines and propeller shafts, while Ralph and Clyde Hirtle's *Gloria P.H.*, a 45-footer, boasted two engines with a combined total of 28 horsepower, twice that needed by a typical schooner of her size.[102]

Percy W. Young of Big Tancook was perhaps the most notorious of the island rum traffickers, and his most celebrated vessel was the slippery David Langille-designed *Elsie B. Young* (see fig. 14). Her career spanned the years 1923 to 1926, when rum running in schooners reached its peak. Guile and trickery were the rum smuggler's stocks in trade, especially in the schooner years, and Percy Young was no exception. The *Elsie* was painted black to blend into the darkness, and her skipper draped the vessel's topsides with white canvas when offloading cargoes in daylight hours in order to disguise her identity from any watching patrol craft. The 16-ton schooner was able to transport 100 to 150 10-gallon kegs of rum (1,000 to 1,500 total gallons), which was typically brought under cover of night to Rafuse Island in western Mahone Bay, a sandy islet not far from Tancook, where it was buried and later excavated for distribution.[103]

The *Elsie B. Young* was a lucky vessel and was never apprehended by Canadian authorities. The same was not true for another noted island rum runner, the *Gloria P.H.*, a 20-ton schooner built by Mason and Langille in 1924. For several years, she operated successfully as a part-time contact boat,* delivering illicit liquor to various South Shore distribution points and even unloading, on occasion, in the very centre of Halifax, using the Northwest Arm and the National Seafood Wharf as places of debarkation. Like other Tancook rum runners, the *Gloria P.H.* was supplied by large vessels and often rendezvous at sea with the tern schooner *D.D. McKenzie*, a Lunenburg merchantman that regularly appeared outside Cross Island, within striking distance of her own home port. The *Gloria P.H.* averaged three thousand gallons per trip and earned her owners a dollar on

---

* Most of the Tancook rum-running craft were smugglers by avocation. They fished and coasted like normal schooners during much of the year and illegally supplemented their income as the occasion arose.

each gallon delivered,* a tidy sum, but her luck ran out in 1929. On a calm, foggy night in late May, while attempting to bring her usual cargo into St Margaret's Bay, she was located and chased by the fast motor patrol boat *Beebe*, commanded by feared prohibition enforcer Captain John ("Machine-Gun") Kelly. Damaged by gunfire and abandoned by her crew (who made Indian Harbour by rowboat), the schooner was seized by customs officials and later auctioned off to a Halifax buyer.[104]

By the time of the capture of the *Gloria P.H.*, Tancook schooners had largely outlived their usefulness as liquor smugglers. Between 1928 and 1930, speed replaced stealth as the illegal trade's primary mode of operation, and specially designed and constructed motor launches displaced fishing boats and sailing craft in the last years of rum running.[105] Nevertheless, a few schooners continued in the trade for several more years despite the competition from legal liquor (after 1930) and despite the trend toward ever-faster contact vessels and patrol craft. These were mostly locally built boats that were sold off the island. One was the 47-foot knockabout *Holly C.* (see fig. 21), purchased by Joshua Young of West Dover from her original Tancook owners a few months after her launch in 1929. Under Young, the *Holly C.* had a notable rum smuggling career until early 1935, when she, too, was run down by Machine-Gun Kelly and driven on the ledges off Pennant Point while trying to escape capture.[106]

The combination of legalized liquor sales and more efficient enforcement of restrictions against unauthorized imports gradually put an end to rum running along Nova Scotia's South Shore in the 1930s. A second coastal carrying trade, however, continued to occupy Tancook schooners in considerable numbers for another decade after the end of Prohibition. That was the traditional commerce in agricultural produce, an activity in which the island schooners made their last stand.

CABBAGE AND 'KRAUT

Tancook's traffic in farm products actually began in the last third of the nineteenth century and coincided roughly with the construction of a government wharf and breakwater able to accommodate large vessels, which was completed at Northwest Cove shortly after

---

* Most of the profit in the trade went to the operators of the supply ships, however. The rum delivered by Tancook's contact boats ultimately sold for $25 per five-gallon keg, or $5 per gallon, when it reached shore. (*Source*: Interview, Steadman S. Mason, 17 June 1989.)

1870.[107] There is no record of cash cropping prior to that time, and what little exporting the island's subsistence farmers did was geared to the Lunenburg market, where they sold their fish and outfitted their boats. In 1870, however, two mariners from nearby Chester, Daniel and Charles Baker, purchased the schooner *British Lady* (19 tons; 40' × 14.6' × 6') at Martin's River and initiated an agricultural carrying trade between Tancook and Halifax that lasted for three quarters of a century. The first two voyages took place in December of that year. The cargoes are not recorded, but since they were delivered at the end of the fall harvest season, there is little doubt as to the content.[108]

The following year, the *British Lady* and two other Chester schooners, the *British Tar* (41 tons; 57.6' × 18.3' × 7.5') and the *Hero* (35 tons; 50' × 17.9' × 6.6'), made six trips from Tancook to Halifax. The first voyage by an island vessel, the La Have-built two-master *Sky Lark* (27 tons; 50' × 17.3' × 6.8'), owned by the Mason brothers (George, Daniel, Isaac, Ephraim, and Joshua) and Charles Cross, raised the number to seven. Purchased for coasting the previous spring at St Margaret's Bay, *Sky Lark* made her pioneering departure for the city produce market in mid-December 1871. Three months later, Henry Hutt's and David Stevens' Lunenburg-built *Bella Young* (35 tons; 53.6' × 17.8' × 6.8') became the second island schooner to make the Halifax run.[109]

Thenceforth, the number of annual coasting trips from Tancook increased rapidly, exceeding a dozen each year by the mid-1870s and remaining at that level for the balance of the century. On average, four vessels per year serviced the island, each making several departures between September and December and, beginning in the 1880, continuing throughout the winter. For the most part, these were comparatively large schooners of 30- to 40-tons register, about half of them hailing from mainland ports like Chester and Lunenburg and about half built on the mainland but owned at Tancook.[110] By the turn of the century, they were joined – and supplanted to some extent – by steamboats operating between Mahone Bay or La Have and Halifax, which stopped at the island for produce en route to the city and whose ranks included, among others, the 168-ton S.S. *Kinburn* of Lunenburg, a regular visitor at Tancook for several years in the period immediately before World War I.[111]

At first the cargoes shipped the city merchants varied considerably in content. Cabbage and sauerkraut were most prominent from the start, but in the 1870s and 1880s these were accompanied by significant amounts of beets, turnips, potatoes, eggs, butter, and pickled herring and mackerel. In the succeeding decade, numerous head of cattle were added to the manifests, as well as some apples and occasional lumber products, such as shingles, hoops, and barrels.[112] The cargo delivered by the schooner *Albertina* of Chester in late December 1874 was rather typical: 400 dozen cabbages, 6 barrels of sauerkraut, 39 bushels of turnips, 4 bushels of beets, 400 pounds of butter, and 7 dozen eggs.[113] Although small by later standards, the cabbage portion of Tancook's nineteenth-century agricultural commerce was overwhelmingly dominant – and that domination increased with time. During the season of 1890–91, for example, five large schooners made a total of eight trips to Halifax between mid-November and early April carrying 1,910 dozen cabbages (nearly 23,000 head). Sauerkraut, the chief derivative of cabbage, was the second most important item with 275 half-barrels (27,500 pounds) shipped.[114]

Cabbage became the key item in Tancook's agricultural economy for several reasons. First, its natural characteristics were well adapted to the island's marine environment. Cabbage grew best in cool, moist conditions on soil that was rich and well fertilized with natural manures.[115] Nova Scotia's rainy, foggy South Shore provided a conducive climate, and Tancook's growing land, constantly enriched with a natural compost of lobster shells, fish waste,* stable manure, and seaweed, offered an ideal setting.[116] Cabbage also possessed properties that made it a prime cash commodity for islanders. It was an excellent native source of ascorbic acid or vitamin C – one of the few such sources in a part of North America lacking easy access to citrus fruits and most other scurvy-preventing vegetables – and it was also an above-average provider of calcium.[117] The nutritional value of cabbage, as well as its low cost,† made it a staple food item for several generations of ordinary Nova Scotians and an easily saleable product for Tancookers. Finally, its resistance to frost and its keeping qualities meant that cabbage could be stored and marketed at leisure over a considerable period of time. In proper storage cellar conditions (32°F and 90–95 percent humidity), it lasted for up to four months – or, in the case of crops harvested in November, for most of a winter.[118]

For all these reasons, raising cabbage for export became a natural, and increasingly valuable, sideline for Tancook Islanders. One other

---

* Remains before rotting. In the 1930s, fish waste was imported to the island from Halifax each year prior to planting season as a substitute for local fertilizer, which was not immediately available because the start of Tancook's spring fisheries exactly coincided with the annual cabbage seeding, preventing the stockpiling of fish remains. (*Source*: Interviews, Thomas Mason, 24 September 1987 and 15 June 1989.)

† At the height of the Great Depression in 1931, cabbage wholesaled for less than a nickel a head in the Halifax produce market. (*Source*: HH, news item, 27 November 1931, 12.)

ingredient was necessary, however, to fully establish the island's cabbage trade: a sufficient regional market. The rapidly growing city of Halifax provided the necessary outlet. Lunenburg, Tancook's primary fish market, raised its own cabbage and had little need for the island's produce, but Halifax had depended from its very beginnings on imported foodstuffs. Founded as a garrison town and later populated by landless immigrants, the city looked to Lunenburg County for its vegetable supply from at least 1760 onward.[119] Lunenburg township itself had developed a flourishing maritime trade with Halifax in cattle, firewood, and produce by the middle of the nineteenth century, and much of that carrying trade was in cabbage, a common item of export as early as the 1820s.[120] Fifty years later, Tancook Island, populated by large numbers of hereditary German cabbage growers, was ready to succeed Lunenburg and other mainland locales as the primary supplier of the capital city's needs.

A major reason for Tancook's ability to wrest control of the Lunenburg County cabbage trade from mainland exporters (in addition to its convenient location near the edge of the coastal shipping lanes) was the quality of its product. Tancook cabbage was, first of all, larger than most cabbage grown in the region. While mature head cabbage normally reached seven to ten pounds, individual heads of fifteen and even twenty or twenty-five pounds were not unheard of on the island.[121] Tancook cabbage was also of superior shape and texture and possessed a better flavour than mainland varieties, resulting in, among other things, a finer and sweeter grade of sauerkraut. The flat-headed cabbage commonly grown around Lunenburg tended to be wider, shallower and less compact than the round, solid, more closely grained Tancook type. Islanders grew what was known as Danish round-head or "bald-headed" cabbage, a late-maturing and hardy strain admirably suited to winter storage – an advantage in marketing.[122] Its inherent advantages were accentuated by the unique manner in which it was grown. Islanders raised and planted their own seeds, selecting only the best heads for seeding purposes. Combined with a richly fertilized soil and abundant rainfall, this provided a variety of plant that stored well, had an attractive appearance, and acquired a reputation for taste that was second to none.[123]

Like most economic endeavours on Tancook, the cultivation of cabbage was ruled by a strict adherence to nature and its seasonal cycles. Activity began in late April when the ground thawed and seeds could be planted in gardens. Around mid-June, the small cabbages were transplanted to full-scale cabbage fields, where they grew and ripened. Harvesting usually ran from mid-October to mid-November. The October cabbage was sent directly to Halifax along with small amounts of early sauerkraut, while those heads gathered in November prior to the winter freeze was transferred to specially constructed underground "cabbage houses" or to the cellars of homes for protection from the elements until eventual shipment. Once the bulk of the cabbage was harvested and housed in late November, the sauerkraut-making season began in earnest, and winter produce cargoes sent from the island included substantial amounts of both sauerkraut and the dominant head cabbage.[124]

By the early twentieth century, almost everyone on Tancook was raising at least some cabbage because of its commercial value even if, as often happened, they had to borrow growing land. Annual production ranged from 2,500 to 4,000 head (a single schooner load or slightly more) for the smaller growers to as much as 15,000 to 20,000 head for the biggest.[125] Certain individuals specialized in cabbage farming and as a result largely neglected the fisheries. For the most part, they tended to have inherited substantial family land under the island's Byzantine system of property allocation. Families whose holdings had not been greatly subdivided over time – the Crosses and Slauenwhites, for example – produced Tancook's most prominent farmers, while others families concentrated their energies more heavily on fishing and boatbuilding.[126]

The commercial cultivation of large amounts of cabbage on a small land area meant that strict rules of soil usage had to be observed. There was a harvest each year, but never from the same growing land. Despite annual composting, consecutive plantings generated a condition known as "club root," which stunted full growth and resulted in immature cabbage heads or "shuttles." To avoid this undesirable eventuality, caused by leaving the stumps and leaves of the plant in the ground during harvesting, cabbage lands were rotated every seven years so as to allow time for root decomposition. The lands did not lie fallow in the interim, however. Soil that could not support cabbage in a given year could support other crops, and islanders devised an ingenious system to satisfy their secondary agricultural needs while allowing recovery time for their primary cash crop. In consecutive years, a typical patch of Tancook land grew cabbage in the first year, followed by potatoes; grain, barley, or oats; hay seed; hay; hay again; and (in the seventh year) cabbage once more.[127] Alternating commercial and subsistence crops in this manner created a delicate balance that allowed two distinct kinds of farming to coexist and contribute to a unique style of island life.

Although more than ninety percent of Tancook's cabbage was marketed by the head, a small but important portion was turned into the island's other famous agricultural commodity, sauerkraut. Like cabbage, "'kraut" was a rich source of vitamin C; that and its compactness gave it a prominent place in the outfitting provisions of vessels sailing to the offshore fishing banks from Lunenburg in the nineteenth century.[128] The chief appeal of sauerkraut, however, appears to have been its flavour, a sweet-sour tanginess that endeared the product to generations of Lunenburgers whose forebears had brought it from Germany, as well as to countless other Nova Scotians who cultivated the necessary acquired taste.

Sauerkraut was essentially pickled cabbage in shredded form, and it was made by adding salt to the natural juices and allowing the mix to "work" or ferment, a process that usually took a week to ten days.* On Tancook, the production and sale of sauerkraut was considered a subsidiary by-product of the main cabbage trade, and only the smallest heads – those not large enough to attract wholesale produce buyers – were used. About three dozen of these small "'kraut cabbage," measuring 4" or 5" in diameter, were required to produce a standard half-barrel (100 pounds) of the finished product. The cabbages were first shredded with a special knife and then placed in the half-barrel in layers interspersed with about two to three pounds of sprinkled Turk's Island salt to generate brine. As the container was filled, the shredded heads were pressed – first by hand and later by tramping with bare feet – so as to mix the pickle and stimulate fermentation. This filling and pressing exercise, which was eventually made more efficient by the use of a mechanical press, took roughly twenty to thirty minutes. Upon its completion, the half-barrel (a product of Western Shore) was covered, the barrel head holed to allow excess pickle to escape, and the aging process began.[129]

Until the era of the Tancook schooner (ca. 1910–40), the island's produce trade with Halifax was important but limited. Most fisherman-farmers grew just enough cabbage to satisfy their own needs through the winter months and to make a little 'kraut on the side.[130] This pattern began to change around the time of the First World War, when several key developments took place. The war itself was an important factor, creating instant food shortages and boosting produce prices. Tancook cabbage sold for twice as much during the war years as it had previously, and sauerkraut reached record wholesale levels that were never approached again.[131]

Simultaneously, the creation of the hatched or decked Tancook schooner, larger than its indigenous island predecessors and equipped

---

* In the early part of the season (September), five days was sufficient time to produce 'kraut, but in colder weather fermentation often took three weeks.

equipped with an auxiliary engine, provided a more efficient, less expensive way to get cabbage and 'kraut to the Halifax market. Rather than pay others to deliver their produce, as in the past, islanders began to carry it in vessels they built and operated themselves. The first to do so were residents of Little Tancook, who anticipated their neighbours on the main island by three years, starting in a limited fashion during the 1911–12 season.[132] In 1913–14, the Henry Levy-built deck boat *Lobelia L.* (25 tons; 48.8' × 13' × 7.8'), skippered by Charles Levy of Little Tancook, became the first bona fide Tancook schooner to engage in extensive winter coasting, making five trips to Halifax between December and March and monopolizing the seasonal cabbage trade.[133] Thereafter, however, Big Tancook took control of its own shipments and proceeded to dominate coastwise commerce from the islands on an annual basis.

To some extent, the new, self-contained trading system arose out of sheer necessity. Tancook's ancient class of second-hand coasting schooners, acquired in the late nineteenth century, had long since left the scene. The last of them, John Pearl's *Florence B.* and Freeman Young's *W.E. Wier*, had ended their island careers in 1899 and 1901, respectively.[134] For a time, their place on the Halifax run was taken by the scheduled coastal steamers that had begun making regular weekly or biweekly stops at the island. These steam packets temporarily provided a dependable marketing outlet for Tancook's small farmers, who mostly patronized them, the island's larger producers continuing to ship in bulk by way of intermittent, mainland-based freighting schooners. The steamer captains routinely brought orders from Halifax for specific amounts of cabbage, which were filled on a first-come, first-served basis. Growers packed their produce in large flour barrels for shipment and accompanied the cargoes to the city, returning on the next scheduled trip with their remuneration. Although steamer traffic was initially limited to Northwest Cove, the site of Tancook's first docking facility, vessels began to call at Southeast Cove as well upon completion of the wharf and breakwater there in 1908, giving all islanders convenient access to service. Unfortunately, that access was brief. With the onset of war in 1914, the steamers were gradually dispersed and assigned to other, more strategically important routes. By the end of 1917, their visits to the island had ceased – the last were made by the Halifax and La Have Steam Packet Company's converted tug *La Have* – and steamer shipments became a thing of the past.[135]

This disruption in service left a gap that was filled by Tancook's own native schooners, beginning with the deck boats *Tancook* (1914),

Bleucher C. (1916), *Hurry Up*,* *Steward D.S.* and *Silver Oak* (1917), and *White Birch* (1918). Originally built for summer dory trawling in the Gulf of St Lawrence (a response to the dramatic wartime rise in fish prices), these large schooners were also eminently suitable, it was soon realized, for off-season coasting. Their size made them practical substitutes for both the absent steamers and the dwindling transient sailing coasters. Most important, they possessed engines, which made cabbage freighting an easier and safer proposition in the fall and winter months. The added security of engines made self-contained coasting practical on a large scale and eventually brought smaller Tancook schooners into the cabbage trade in substantial numbers after the war, ensuring that the island would no longer be dependent on outside carriers for its water-borne agricultural commerce.[136]

Radically increased and broadened domestic markets were part of the wartime environment that stimulated the growth of Tancook's cabbage trade. Halifax, which experienced an economic boom as it was transformed into a key naval base and embarkation point for convoys,[137] saw its population swell by 12,000 during the war decade. That growth in potential produce consumers continued into peacetime, resulting in an overall population increase of 51 percent between 1911 and 1941, roughly double the percentage increase of the previous 30 years.[138] Domestic markets outside Halifax also emerged during this period, chief among them the Cape Breton market at Sydney. Beginning in 1918 and continuing for the next two decades, schooner loads of Tancook cabbage were periodically delivered to CNR Piers 2 and 3 in Halifax for rail shipment farther down east. Sydney merchant Charles Mason, distantly related to the Tancook family of the same name, was the main conduit for this trade, which absorbed two to three rail car loads of cabbage (1,200 to 1,800 dozen head)† per season by the 1930s. In addition to the Cape Breton shipments, a few cargoes of island cabbage began simultaneously to be transshipped from Halifax to various places along the Eastern Shore; this practice continued sporadically throughout the interwar years.[139]

Despite the rapid expansion of the domestic market after 1910 and the concurrent appearance of an improved class of island boats

---

* This aptly named schooner barely escaped the famous Halifax explosion of December 6, 1917. Having completed delivery of a cargo of cabbage the previous day, she departed the city at 6 o'clock on the morning of the disaster. Three hours later off Dover, halfway to Tancook, her crew felt the shock of the blast and saw the pillar of smoke that accompanied it. (*Source*: Interview, Thomas Mason, 22 June 1989.)

† A standard rail car held about 600 dozen head of cabbage, or the full cargo of a large Tancook deck boat of the 60' class.

able to accommodate that expanding market, the major impetus for the development of Tancook's cabbage trade came from the phenomenal growth in foreign produce exports from Halifax following World War I. This commerce, focused almost entirely on the British West Indies, actually had its roots in the nineteenth century. The Caribbean had likely been a sometime consumer of Tancook cabbage as far back as 1889, when the first lines of mail and cargo steamships to the tropics were established with the aid of government subsidies. Early coasting schooners from the island regularly frequented the city wharves of Pickford and Black, the private firm contracted that year to initiate a monthly service between Halifax and the Crown colonies of Turk's Island and Jamaica.[140]

In 1899, the sailings became fortnightly and were broadened to connect Halifax with virtually all of Britain's Caribbean possessions, but regular hemispheric commerce between the Empire countries developed slowly until a series of bilateral trade agreements introduced a system of mutual tariff preferences. The first of these took effect in 1913 and included a 20 percent impost reduction on Canada's agricultural products. More significant was the succeeding agreement negotiated in 1920, which reduced standard tariff duties on Canadian goods by between 33 and 50 percent, beginning in late 1921. Four years later the Dominion's major commercial policy accomplishment of the postwar period, the Canada-British West Indies Trade Agreement of 1925, gave permanence to the new economic relationship. Under its provisions, tariff reductions of 50 to 67 percent were granted for twelve years on Canadian fish, lumber, and agricultural commodities, and in return Ottawa agreed to substantially lower duties on incoming West Indies goods and to provide improved steamship service to the Caribbean region under direct government auspices. The shipping portion of the agreement was implemented by passage of the Canadian National Steamships, Act of 1927, which created Canadian National Steamships, Ltd (CNS) and undertook the building of a new class of larger, more modern passenger/cargo ships with expanded cold storage capacities – the famous "Lady Boats," named for the wives of noted British admirals.[141]

These public sector initiatives brought immediate results. Under the first two trade agreements, Canada's exports to the British West Indies tripled in value and peaked in the late 1920s following implementation of the comprehensive third agreement.[142] Metropolitan Halifax, and indirectly its surrounding hinterland, shared in the economic benefits. The city's merchants, who had called for tariff negotiations with the Caribbean islands as early as 1907 in the hope of stimulating their nascent foreign agricultural trade, saw their vegetable exports climb to nearly $1 million annually by the immediate postwar period.[143]

The localized impact on places like Tancook was even more striking. Cabbage shipments from the island began to increase immediately after the second trade pact went into effect. Starting with the 1922–23 season the number of schooners on the Halifax run doubled, and their total visits to the city tripled to two dozen per year.[144] Islanders agree, however, that it was the coming of the CNS Lady Boats in the late 1920s that truly energized the cabbage trade, permitting exporters to absorb up to half the entire Tancook crop over the course of the ensuing decade when production reached its peak.[145]

Between July and November 1928, the five 7,500-ton liners Ottawa had ordered for the Indies trade were delivered by builders at Birkenhead, England, and by the end of the year three of them – *Lady Nelson*, *Lady Hawkins*, and *Lady Drake* – had already instituted bimonthly service from Halifax to the eastern portion of the British Caribbean.[146] All were extensively equipped with refrigerated compartments for their primary intended cargoes of perishable fruits and vegetables, and their itineraries included such wide-ranging destinations as Bermuda, Demerara, the Bahamas, Jamaica, British Honduras, Trinidad, and the many small islands of the Windward and Leeward chains. Of special interest to provincial shippers was a winter schedule that began in late November and featured twenty-four departures from Halifax.[147] The start of these sailings exactly coincided with the South Shore agricultural harvest – a fortuitous circumstance for Tancook growers – and the same ships that carried tropical bananas north each year throughout the tourist season returned south laden with crates of island cabbage for Caribbean consumers.

Tancook's shipments to Halifax began to increase markedly during the season of 1927–28 in anticipation of the expected inauguration of Lady Boat service, which was the subject of optimistic public speculation for months before the fact.[148] When the long-awaited sailings finally got under way the following season, nearly two dozen Tancook schooners – twice the previous number – were active in the produce trade, making a combined total of 38 trips to the city between October and April. That year of 1928–29 saw the largest number of island boats to ever engage in coasting (21 schooners and 2 Cape Island motor boats), but actual deliveries increased in the 1930s as fewer boats made more voyages. Annual arrivals in excess of 40 cargoes became common during the depression decade, and the total cabbage shipped approached 100,000 head per year.[149]

The cabbage trade largely offset te severe decline in fishing income suffered by islanders after World War I. It replaced losses in the traditional fisheries beginning with the recession of the early 1920s and partially compensated for lower prices realized from swordfishing in subsequent years. It also offered an alternative form of employment for those who had previously earned their livings in the boatbuilding industry, which, like most aspects of the island economy, slumped after 1930.[150] Throughout the Depression, cabbage marketing accounted for roughly half Tancook's total annual income. It provided, in the words of one islander, "a way to survive."[151]

The trade reached its mature form in the late 1920s and 1930s. By then, it was almost purely a cabbage and 'kraut trade, and little else was shipped. The exceptions were small amounts of new potatoes, carrots, and parships, which were carried in fifty-pound burlap sacks, and a few dozen eggs, which were taken in wicker baskets holding five or six dozen each. Even those few extraneous items gradually disappeared from Halifax-bound cargoes as competition from PEI farmers (especially potato growers) became increasingly acute. Fortunately, there was little to challenge the island's cabbage and 'kraut in the Halifax produce market except a limited annual supply from across the harbour in Dartmouth, and that source was rarely a factor after the fall season.[152]

In contrast, Tancook was able to provide city consumers with cabbage throughout the long winter. Its boats began to coast in October and continued into early April. On average, about fifteen schooners and one or two Cape Islanders were involved in the fall months, most of them smaller craft primarily transporting their owners' own crops and making only a few trips. The majority were hatch boats hauled for winter storage in December, but a handful (three or four) were decked or semi-decked-boats that continued through the winter months,* delivering cargoes for large farmers or for those without schooners of their own. These bigger carriers made multiple voyages, sailing whenever conditions permitted, and levied a standard freight charge for the service (10¢ per dozen for cabbage and 15¢ pr half-barrel for 'kraut). Their return cargoes consisted of miscellaneous seasonal necessities such as coal, kerosene oil, gasoline, animal feed, flour, and selected groceries. For the most part the winter coasters were fully decked vessels of 50' or more, but at least two, the *Mother*

---

* Fully or partially decked schooners were better adapted to coasting than the smaller hatch boats, especially in winter. They kept cabbage cargoes in a warmer, more protected condition and also possessed added peripheral deck space for storing barrels of 'kraut, which were too heavy to be placed atop hatch covers. (*Source*: Interview, Thomas Mason, 1 October 1988.)

and the *Patavana*, were semi-deckers that barely exceeded 40' overall. The latter schooner became a familiar sight to an entire generation of islanders, remaining in the water for all but one winter season from 1929 to 1940 and averaging a dozen cabbage trips per year during that span.[153]

By the 1920s, Tancookers had evolved a fairly systematic means of transferring their main crop to market. The first step in the process involved the island's ubiquitous oxen. Selected cabbages were transported by ox cart from the cabbage house to the shore or, alternatively, to one of the government wharves. At Northwest Cove, which was not subject to heavy groundswells, wharf loading was always the standard procedure, but on the back side of the island a cabbage cargo was more typically transferred to a half-dozen dories and rowed out to a schooner moored off shore,* where the individual heads were passed up to men on deck and carefully placed one at a time in the open hold. Southeast Cove's shallowness and the small size of its fishing wharves precluded loading a vessel at the owner's launchway. At the same time, the cove's government breakwater was rarely used except by small boats, which could lay alongside in tidal surges without excessively pounding or straining their lines. In the late 1920s, when smaller coasters increased in number, loading at the Southeast Cove wharf became more common, but for years loading by dory was the universal rule.[154]

Once aboard, the cabbage was loosely stowed below in a prearranged manner. If the schooner was carrying a cargo belonging to several parties, a head count was made beforehand to ensure proper compensation to the individual owners after sale in Halifax. The heads were then stacked in rows, separated by owner as much as possible but ultimately marketed in a somewhat mixed condition. The size of the cargo varied according to the size of the vessel. Large deck boats averaged 400 to 500 dozen head per trip,† while medium-sized semi-deckers averaged 200 dozen. Small hatch boats carried fewer still. When the cabbage portion of the cargo was secure below deck, the sauerkraut was taken aboard packed in half-barrels that stood 3' high, held 10 to 11 gallons, and weighed (when full) 100 to 130

---

* On more than one wintry occasion at Southeast Cove, dories were placed on sleds, hauled from the shore to the cabbage house, loaded and covered, and then hauled back to the launchway to be slid directly into the water. This unusual short-cut procedure protected the vulnerable cabbage heads from undue exposure and kept them from freezing during the loading process. (*Source*: Interview, Thomas Mason, 1 October 1989.)

† The largest recorded island cabbage cargo was the 600 dozen (7,200 head) taken to Halifax in January 1918 by Tancook's biggest schooner, the 42-ton *Silver Oak*. (*Source*: HH, marine list, 8 January 1918, 9).

pounds. These containers were sometimes placed on their sides in the hold, but were more typically stowed on deck, either lying end to end or (if the vessel's rail was sufficiently high) standing side by side in upright positions. A deck boat loaded with upwards of 500 dozen head of cabbage below deck might carry as many as 200 half-barrels of 'kraut topside, while 20 to 25 barrels was a typical deck cargo for a semi-decker with 200 dozen cabbages in her hold.[155]

After loading, the schooner made an immediate departure for Halifax to conserve her sensitive cargo, proceeding under power and sail for maximum efficiency. A fast trip was a prime concern, since the first fall cargoes to arrive generally commanded the highest prices. Vessels leaving the island together in the early part of the season heavily laden with cabbage – or "filled to the gunnels," as the saying went – often raced to market in the hope of securing a few additional cents per dozen from the wholesalers. These informal contests took on an importance that went far beyond money. The respective merits of the boats and their builders' reputations were at stake, and comparisons were made and remembered. By the 1930s, auxiliary motors were always operated on the passage, and sails were routinely raised if there was a favourable following wind. The 11-ton schooner *Patavana*, for example, employed a twelve-horsepower Lathrop engine capable of six knots as well as three sails (jib, fore, and main) that steadied the vessel and provided additional speed. Heavier canvas was used in winter, and a removable deck house was installed around the boat's steering cockpit to provide some protection from the seasons's harsh winds, blowing snow, and icy spray.[156]

Under optimum conditions, a coasting voyage to Halifax normally took six hours, although it could take a bit longer if head seas were encountered or if the habitually strong breezes off St Margaret's Bay swung to an easterly or facing direction. When forced to battle head winds, boats sometimes left their sails up and pursued a zigzag course under power, gaining just enough angle on the wind to be "full and by" and thereby retaining the advantage of their sails. After safely rounding Cape Sambro, the schooners, whose decks were often virtually awash from the weight of their cargoes, headed directly up Halifax Harbour past McNab's and George's islands and made for one of several commercial wharves situated close together opposite Dartmouth Cove at the approach to the Narrows. The preferred wharves were Black and Flinn's, DeWolfe's, and Silver's.* Their

---

* Tancook schooners began unloading at DeWolfe's and Silver's wharves during World War I and at Black and Flinn's and Cronan's shortly thereafter. (*Source*: HH, news items, 14 November 1917 and 8 January 1918, 9, and marine lists, October to April 1918–20, passim.)

Upper Water Street location was not far from the foot of Cogswell Street, just north of the present-day Historic Properties. A fourth, smaller wharf in the same vicinity, Cronan's, was also sometimes used.[157]

Although they primarily handled large vessels delivering such bulk items as salt and sand, these wharves were chosen by Tancook's coasters because they were conveniently near the city's cabbage and 'kraut buyers and because they usually had ample spare space available for small schooners. For a flat flee of $2 per visit, island boats could tie up for unlimited periods and obtain free water as well. When possible, they selected berths on the sheltered north sides to obtain protection from storms coming up the harbour and to avoid pressing and pounding against the dock pilings. Each of the three main wharves could accommodate a half-dozen Tancook schooners end to end, the ordinary berthing procedure when in port. On crowded occasions, however, it was not unusual for the contingent of island coasters to tie up alongside each other to save space.[158]

Since municipal ordinance prevented schooners from selling their produce at the wharves,[159] the first order of business for boat captains was to arrange sales elsewhere in the city.* In this activity they were sometimes assisted by the owners of the cargoes, who often accompanied their cabbage to market as unofficial supercargoes. Island cabbage was sold to both wholesalers and retailers, and upon arrival in Halifax, the schoonermen immediately visited the wholesale district to ascertain whether the major buyers were accepting consignments.

The wholesalers were located on Barrington Street near the present Scotia Square, and in the 1920s and 1930s the most prominent were Nickerson and Crease, C.W. Outhit, R.J. Whitten, and B.A. Blakeney, wholesale/retail fruit and vegetable companies that dealt in a variety of produce and sold to local independent retailers as well as to the West Indies. These firms purchased cabbage by the dozen† and took only large lots of fifty to a hundred dozen at a time, accepting no boat cargoes until they had firm resale orders of their own. At that point, they delivered wooden crates to the waterfront, and the schooner crews unloaded their produce on the wharves and boxed it for reship-

---

* Direct retailing meant obtaining a license that permitted the boat owner to set up a table in the Halifax farmers' market, the only place where producers were allowed to deal directly with consumers. Just one island skipper, Stephen Alinard of the schooner *Green Bow II*, is known to have followed this practice. (*Source*: Interview, Thomas Mason, 1 October 1989.)

† Until World War II cabbages were always wholesaled loose by the dozen except for the small numbers shipped in barrels aboard coastal steamers prior to 1917, which were sold by the container. During the war, they began to be marketed by the pound and delivered in bags. (*Source*: Interviews, Thomas Mason, 30 September 1987 and 1 October 1989.)

ment. If bound for the Caribbean, the crated cabbage was trucked directly to the nearby CNS piers for export. Otherwise it was taken uptown to the Barrington Street warehouses, initially by horse and wagon and in later years by motor truck, a truckload amounting to two hundred dozen head or the full complement of a small schooner.[160]

Wholesalers commonly gave certain boats a preference in completing sales. Hovey Slauenwhite's *Tyrienne S.*, for instance, was said to have been favoured by Nickerson and Crease in the 1920s because the firm's operatives knew her skipper from his younger days as a crewman aboard the *White Birch*. A small bribe, such as a bottle of illicit liquor for the wholesale agent, occasionally speeded the transaction. Otherwise it was not unusual for a schooner to wait two or three weeks to be divested of her cargo, an inconvenience some skippers were willing to accept because of the minimal wharfage fee. Those who declined to remain at the beck and call of the wholesale merchants did have alternative recourse, however; they could deal with the multitude of retail grocers scattered throughout the city. By selling directly to the retailers, who offered the same price for cabbage as the large wholesalers, a schooner could usually peddle her cargo in just a few days. For their part, the retailers welcomed an opportunity to bypass the middleman who normally supplied them.[161]

In the early days of the cabbage trade, schooner masters canvassed the city grocers on foot to arrange sales, and grocery trucks subsequently appeared at the wharves to load prior purchases. Later, in the difficult years of the 1930s, skippers began to deliver produce themselves by handcart in order to more readily obtain badly needed sales and to beat out competing boats. It was labourious work, Thomas Mason of the schooner *Patavana* recalled long hours spent walking the streets of Halifax from one end of the city to the other in search of retail buyers, many of whom were needed to empty the vessel's hold. An average sale was just ten or fifteen dozen head of cabbage, and a large sale only twenty-five dozen, totals dwarfed by the transactions in the wholesale market. Until the flowering of the West Indies trade (ca. 1928), Tancook's deck boats, which routinely delivered cargoes belonging to as many as four growers, participated in selling to retailers along with the island's smaller schooners. The growers, who accompanied their crops to market, canvassed retailers themselves and sold their cabbage individually. In the late 1920s, however, the export demands of the CNS Line began to absorb the bulk of the deck boat cargoes, and door-to-door selling was left to Tancook's lesser carriers. It was a form of democratic enterprise well suited to small boat owners and small corner grocers alike.[162]

The marketing of Tancook sauerkraut differed slightly from that of cabbage. The 'kraut, first of all, was not transshipped to the West Indies. Except for small amounts sent to Newfoundland, it was consumed locally within the Halifax area. Like cabbage, 'kraut could be sold to wholesalers, some of whom – Pazant and King, John Tobin, Parker and Sawyer, and Howard Wentzell – specialized in its handling during the 1920s and 1930s. Unlike cabbage, however, most island 'kraut was delivered directly to the retailers, who because of its consumer appeal were willing to offer higher prices. Retail grocers purchased their 'kraut by the half-barrel, just as it came from Tancook, and sold it from the same container in their stores. It was retailed by weight and distributed, wrapped in paper, by the bag.[163]

Compared to cabbage, sauerkraut was a relatively stable commodity in terms of price structure. It wholesaled for $2 to $3 per half-barrel, usually bringing $2 or a little more during the postwar period. Cabbage prices, on the other hand, fluctuated widely from year to year, month to month, and even week to week, ranging from as high as $2.25 per dozen (in 1926) to as low as 50¢ per dozen (in 1931).[164] Island growers rarely knew quite what to expect from the wholesale cabbage market, whose supply and demand cycles were governed partly by the quality of the product and partly by its abundance. Small heads could depress the price, as could fine fall weather, which guaranteed a steady supply and glutted the market.[165] The schoonermen who delivered the crops at least had the security of a dependable income, small as it was, from one year to the next. The *Patavana*, which made a dozen voyages to Halifax in the course of an average year in the 1930s, earned a minimum of $25 per trip in freight money, or $300 per season.[166] That, combined with income earned fishing and shipping cattle, was enough to carry her owner and his family through the Depression.

CATTLE AND SHEEP

The Tancook cattle trade, though a relatively small part of the island's economy during the schooner era, merits mention as an indicator of the versatility of the vessels involved. Historically, islanders raised two types of animals for commercial purposes – sheep and beef cattle.* Sheep were marketed only in small numbers, being mostly main-

---

* Some sense of the numbers involved may be gleaned from the 1871 census, which reported that the Tancooks were home to 226 head of cattle (85 oxen, 53 bulls, and 88 milk cows) and 690 head of sheep that produced nearly 8,000 yards of wool cloth. The only other livestock deemed worthy of mention were the 89 pigs kept for slaughtering. (*Source*: Can.MsCen, 1871: Lunenburg County, Nova Scotia, town of Tancook.)

tained for their wool, which provided Tancook's population with socks, mittens, nippers (fishing gloves), long underwear, suspenders, and "wool beds" (the traditional heavy, thick blankets or quilts used for warmth on cold winter nights). Sheep were first raised on the main island, but were later kept (until the late 1930s) on smaller Flat Island off Southeast Cove, a partially cleared islet with fresh-water ponds, where the animals lived in the open year-round, sheltering in the woods and occasionally foraging for grass, bushes, kelp, and seaweed in lieu of their regular ration of hay. The herds were maintained by natural propagation, and the conditions of their existence produced a hardy breed noted for its thick wool coat.[167]

Island boats were used to transport sheared wool to mainland fulling mills (where it was cleaned and thickened)* and to periodically deliver hay to the herds on Flat Island in winter, but for the most part, sheep raising was a self-contained remnant of Tancook's purely agricultural era. Not so the island cattle trade. Tancook was nearly as well known for its good beef as it was for its cabbage and sauerkraut, and substantial amounts were shipped to Halifax aboard the perennial island coasters until the early 1920s, either on the hoof or as quartered carcasses.[168] A more important market, however, was in nearby Chester, whose tourist hotels turned the meat into prized steaks for their predominantly American guests. Tancook beef owed its reputation partly to the same rich growing soil responsible for the island's envied cabbage crop, which produced a superior forage hay that grew to twice the height of most hay found on the mainland. The quality of the beef was also enhanced by early slaughtering, a practice that resulted in unusually tender and succulent meat.[169]

By the 1930s, the abbreviated but unique island cattle trade was focused on Chester and on Glen Margaret in St Margaret's Bay, where there were meat markets and butchering facilities. The enterprise involved the annual shipment by schooner of up to a dozen young oxen, an undertaking monopolized for some years by Howard Mason's *Patavana*. This 43-foot semi-deck boat usually made two trips each summer at the end of the spring plowing and haymaking sea-

---

* This took place in late spring or early summer (usually June), following the annual shearing. Spring shearing was a social event of some import to islanders. Numbers of them went out to Flat Island for the one-day occasion to picnic, collect gull eggs (a local delicacy), and shear the animals that had survived the winter. Professional shearers from the mainland were sometimes hired and paid in wool. They gathered the herd in a fenced corral (a "pound") and performed their task on small tables made from poles and set in a rectangular arrangement. Shed of their coats, the sheep were allowed once more to roam freely through the woods and pastures that bordered the island's protected hay fields until the following year. (*Source*: Interview, Thomas Mason, 4 October 1988.)

son, carrying four or five live head of cattle each time. These animals had been purchased on the mainland* a year or two earlier, fattened on island hay and water, and used in the interim for plowing and hauling. When sold for butchering at the still-young age of three to four years, they dressed out at about eight hundred pounds and brought their owners between $100 and 200 apiece.

The loading of two tons of oxen aboard a small Tancook schooner required considerable care and ingenuity. First, the vessel's main fish hatches were removed and her hold filled with seaweed to provide footing for the live cargo. Two or three of the animals were then placed in the large forward hatchway between the masts, standing side by side. Farther aft, two more were tied on deck, arranged one on each side (like dories), lashed to the mainmast rigging, and secured with ropes around their necks and trunks. One of these ropes extended from shoulder level back to the cockpit area where it was fastened to the deck and served as a safety railing. Once under way with this precarious cargo, the schooner operated under power, using her tightly sheeted mainsail as a riding sail for steadying purposes.[170]

Until about 1940, the marriage between the semi-agrarian Tancook economy and the island's sailing schooners was a happy one. The Tancook schooner was admirably suited to the diverse, subsistence form of livelihood that existed in this and other South Shore outports between the world wars. It was sufficiently versatile to combine fishing with coasting and, if desired, to moonlight as a rum runner on the side. Small and maneuverable enough to perform effectively as a net or hand-line fishing boat near home, it was also large and seaworthy enough to visit the swordfishing grounds of Cape Breton, trawl the Gulf of St Lawrence for cod, or carry bulk cargoes on the winter run to Halifax. By the early 1940s, however, that special combination of features was no longer sufficient to perpetuate its survival, and within a decade the Tancook schooner, as a sailing working craft, was an artifact of the past.

---

* Usually at Blandford or along the Windsor Road on the outskirts of Chester.

4 Last Years

Hard-surfaced roads within Nova Scotia have now become a reality, and the province is beginning to reap the benefits of the reconstruction which had been carried on the past few years ... It has been said that there has never been a public works program of similar proportions in any other Canadian province.
A. S. MacMillan, Nova Scotia Minister of Highways, 1937

THE END OF COASTING

With the coming of the Second World War, two developments conspired to put an end to the Tancook schooner and the way of life it represented. Chief of these was the decline of the generations-old Halifax coasting trade, which owed its demise to several interrelated factors. The first blow was the withdrawal from service of the CNS Lady Boats beginning in 1939–40, which severely disrupted produce exports to the Caribbean. Several of the old steamers were lost to submarines in the course of wartime duty as troop and hospital ships, and when peace came in 1945, an insufficient number remained to fully reconstitute the West Indies runs in the manner prescribed by the trade agreement of 1925. The growing obsolescence of the surviving ships was an additional problem, as was postwar competition from commercial airlines. After several years of providing token service and operating at a loss, the last Lady Boats were finally retired in 1952.[1] The removal of the West Indies liners for the duration of the war and their subsequently restricted operating schedules effectively eliminated the export half of Tancook's cabbage market and sharply reduced shipments to Halifax.[2]

Meanwhile, other forces were at work that curtailed Tancook's remaining domestic trade. Until the end of the war, island growers retained a virtual monopoly on cabbage sales in Halifax. Somewhere between eighty and ninety percent of the city's cabbage arrived on Tancook schooners in the 1930s. After 1945, however, other parts of the province began to enter the market, including the fertile Annapolis Valley, and the island product suddenly faced severe competition. Simultaneously, cabbage itself lost some of its appeal to consumers. Cheap and nutritious, it had been an ideal staple during the long, difficult years of the Depression, but in the relatively prosperous period that followed, a more varied diet came within the reach of many, and cabbage, closely identified with hard times, declined in popularity.[3]

Even more critical to the destiny of Tancook's coastal trade (and that of the province as a whole) was the revolution in land transportation that took place in Nova Scotia between 1934 and 1940 under the auspices of A.S. MacMillan, minister of highways in the government of Premier Angus L. MacDonald. During that brief time MacMillan, acting to implement the platform of the newly elected Liberal Party, presided over the creation of a modern highway system that incorporated a thousand miles of paved roads, 980 more than when he took office in 1933.[4] What that accomplishment meant to commercial traffic and the movement of goods is not hard to imagine. MacMillan himself pointed to the welcome elimination of the bumps, ruts, sharp curves, dust, and flying stones so characteristic of the old gravel roads, which had been hard on vehicles and often impossible to keep fit for efficient travel during the non-summer months.[5]

The agricultural sector eagerly welcomed the new road system. Editorializing on behalf of better highways as early as 1916, *The Halifax Herald* had proclaimed: "Let every farmer in the province consider how much valuable time he loses each year in hauling his produce to a shipping point on account of sand and mud and ruts."[6] A decade later little had changed, and impassable country roads often held up overland shipments to the Halifax wholesale market.[7] Mud was a particular problem on the unpaved St Margaret's Bay highway, which connected the city to the South Shore and its agricultural hinterland. As late as the 1920s, marooned motor vehicles were a not uncommon sight on that key stretch of roadway.[8] Under such conditions, the produce trade by sea continued to thrive,* and the Tancook schooner realized its maximum potential as a coastal freight carrier.

Unfortunately for the schoonermen, the massive road building program of the 1930s totally altered their economic world. By the end of 1937, 677 miles of provincial highway had been paved, including Route 1 from Yarmouth to Halifax via the Annapolis Valley, which brought that rich and formerly distant agricultural area within easy reach of the metropolitan market. The following year, surfacing work was completed on Route 3, connecting the capital with Yarmouth by way of the South Shore, and Lunenburg County itself was opened to unrestricted auto and truck traffic for the first time.† Of special import to Tancook's produce trade was the Highway Department's firm commitment, beginning in 1936–37, to keep the new provincial road system open in winter. By the season of 1937–38, nearly four hundred miles of formerly impassable roadways were being regularly cleared of snow, a vast improvement over previous years.[9] Suddenly, winter freight no longer had to move by water or by rail.

As the 1930s drew to a close, the motor truck emerged as the primary means of delivering market garden produce throughout Canada,[10] and the South Shore of Nova Scotia was no exception. For all practical purposes, the coasting trade between Tancook Island and Halifax came to an end in the early 1940s, although the very last trip was not made until about 1954.[11] Howard and Stanley Mason, whose boats had dominated winter cabbage shipments for much of the depression decade, made their last voyages to the city in 1940 and 1942, respectively. Stanley Mason thenceforth ran his cargoes to nearby Chester and hired rental trucks to haul them to Halifax over the improved coast highway. Around 1946 he opened a wholesale store in Chester and began to ship from there in his own fleet of vehicles.[12] Stanley, and later his son David, monopolized what was left of the Halifax trade in the postwar period, but by then, cabbage raising had already passed its peak on Tancook. Improved prices enabled most islanders to turn once more to fishing for their chief livelihood – to the

---

* Nationally, only seven percent of Canada's farm products reached urban markets by way of motor trucks in 1924, and seven years later, in 1931, there was still only one truck for every fifteen Canadian farmers – a direct outgrowth of poor rural roads. (*Source*: Glazebrook, *Transportation in Canada*, 2:252.)

† A visitor to the county in 1937 reported that there were still only a few motorized trucks on the mainland and none at all on the offshore islands, where traditional hauling by oxen continued to prevail. (*Source*: Waters, "Bluenose and Codfish," 78.)

increasing neglect of farming.[13] Significantly, however, they did so not in their long-celebrated schooners, but in a new type of fishing craft, the Cape Island boats.

THE COMING OF THE CAPE BOATS

The Tancook schooner, which had served islanders so well for over three decades, finally succumbed to changing times in the 1940s. Its successor, the Cape Island boat (or simply "Cape boat"), represented the triumph at long last of motor power over sail in the local fisheries, a triumph that, however hard for some to accept, was probably overdue. Thirty years earlier, federal officials had remarked on the already accelerating replacement of sailing craft by gasoline-powered motor boats in the Nova Scotia fisheries, especially those of western Shelburne County.[14] By the late 1920s, the industry investment in all-gasoline boats nearly equalled that in vessels combining sails with auxiliary engines,[15] and a report on shipbuilding activity along the South Shore observed that "a notable feature of the work that has been done, is the fact that most of the craft are entirely power boats, where in former years the boats either were all sail or sail and power combined."[16]

Most of the new powered craft were based on a design that originated at Shelburne County's Cape Sable Island around 1910 and took the name of its place of origin.[17] The resultant Cape Islander, whose descendants still dominate the inshore fisheries of the Maritimes, was a flat and shallow but sharp-bowed boat of carvel construction that averaged 35' to 45' overall and depended entirely on its powerful gasoline engine for propulsion. Probably based on some early form of racing motorboat, it gradually became popular with fishermen because of its speed, which increased over time as engines grew in size and horsepower.[18]

Migrating eastward along the coast, the type appeared at the Tancooks shortly after World War I and was initially built (ca. 1920–21)* by Reuben Heisler and Stanley Mason.[19] By the 1930s, Cape boats were a common sight at the islands, though far fewer in number than the predominant schooners. About a dozen of substantial size were constructed for local ownership during the interwar period, including the huge 50-footers *Guinea Gold* (1927) and *Old*

---

* The first registered motor launch built at the islands and powered solely by a gasoline engine was the *Polly N.S.* (8 tons; 35.7' × 7.8' × 3.2'), launched by Henry Levy at Little Tancook in 1911. This craft may have been a primitive Cape Islander, but that is uncertain. (*Source:* Can.HCH, HalSR: register of motorboat *Polly N.S.*, 18 July 1911.)

Kentucky (1928) launched at the Mason yard in Southeast Cove.[20] Several Cape boats participated in the Cape Breton swordfishery and the Halifax coasting trade after 1930, accounting for as many as a quarter of the island cabbage shipments toward the end of the depression decade.[21]

The lines of the 40-footer *Here We Are*, modelled by Wesley Stevens, Sr, and built for his sons Raymond, Guy, and Wesley, Jr in 1939 (see fig. 28), show the early appearance of the Cape Islander as it evolved on Tancook. Considerably narrower than the Cape boat of later years, it incorporated the time-honoured 1 to 4 beam-length ratio of the island schooner that preceded it. A more modern design produced by Southeast Cove builder and fisherman Ervin B. Cross in about 1960 (see fig. 31) shows a boat substantially wider in proportion and featuring a much higher bow and more pronounced sheer. In terms of construction materials, the *Here We Are* was built much like a Tancook schooner: oak ribs, yellow birch keel, stem, and transom, and pine planking. She was powered by a converted truck engine (some boats favoured used automobile engines) that cost $35 and was obtained by making a down payment of potatoes and sauerkraut and paying the balance from the returns of a swordfishing trip. Unlike later Cape Islanders, which possessed fully enclosed cabins, the *Here We Are* had only a small, low cuddy and steered from the open. Nevertheless, equipped with a lookout spar for sighting swordfish, she managed several trips to the waters off Cape Breton.[22]

The Cape boat had several advantages over the traditional Tancook schooner. It was easier and cheaper to build, outfit, and operate. Rigging and ballasting could be dispensed with, and launching and hauling procedures were greatly simplified. The Cape boat was also faster under power and, since it went over rather than through the water, could go farther on a gallon of gasoline. The desirability of the new craft was reinforced on Tancook by a generational factor. The younger island fishermen who came to maturity in the late 1930s and 1940s were anxious to assert themselves and break with the past; inevitably drawn to the newer Cape boat, they adopted it as their own. It was the preceding generation, which had spent a lifetime in sail, that remained most loyal to the schooner through habit and familiarity. When these older men passed from the scene, their boats went with them.[23]

Nevertheless, despite the novelty of the Cape Islander and its undeniable practicality from the standpoint of operating ease and efficiency, the Tancook schooner remained the vessel of choice for most islanders until World War II. For one thing it was a better sea boat. Notwithstanding its speed and maneuverability, the excessively flat and shallow Cape boat was inherently unstable and susceptible to broaching-to and capsizing in a following sea.[24] Even barring such dire occurrences, which were admittedly rare, it was an unpleasant craft in which to spend long hours off shore, having a tendency to pound and toss about in a seaway, while a comparable schooner rolled easily in similar conditions. Some islanders, moreover, could not accommodate themselves to the total reliance on internal combustion that the Cape boats represented. Builder and fisherman Howard Mason remained in schooners throughout the 1930s and beyond simply because, as one of his sons put it, "He liked to sail."[25]

Beyond comfort, safety, and the psychic rewards of sailing there was, above all, a fundamental economic reason for the survival of the Tancook schooner as a work boat well into the 1940s. That was its superiority as a coasting vessel. Cape boats could engage in the Halifax produce trade with the addition of a portable after-house to shelter their cockpit cargoes, and a number did in the early fall, beginning in the 1930s. A 40-foot Cape boat, if properly enclosed, could in fact carry more cabbage than a comparably sized schooner. Its basic design, however, rendered it totally unsuited to coasting in the late fall and winter months. While schooners sat deep in the water, Cape boats sat on the surface, drawing barely enough to immerse their propellers. Consequently, while schooner cargoes, which were stowed below deck and mostly beneath the waterline, were naturally protected from cold and frost, semi-exposed Cape boat cargoes could be easily destroyed unless the inboard engines generated sufficient cockpit heat – an uncertainty at best.[26] Practically speaking then, the produce that moved from Tancook to the Halifax market between the crucial months of December and March, when export demands were at their height, needed to be transported in the holds of schooners. That fact prolonged the island's age of sail for at least a decade. It was only when the cabbage trade by sea ceased to be a key ingredient in the local economy after 1940 that the Tancook schooner lost its final economic rationale.

When the end came, it came quickly. Of the ten registered schooners still owned at Big and Little Tancook islands on the eve of the Second World War, only one remained in 1945. Some were sold to the eastward, finishing their days in the Eastern Shore or Cape Breton Island fisheries. Others were refurbished for yachtsmen, gaining a new lease on life for a few years more. Such was the fate of Howard Mason's venerable *Patavana*, which, after more than a decade of fishing and coasting, found her way into the Great Lakes pleasure fleet of Hamilton, Ontario, in 1943.[27]

With one or two exceptions, the few smaller schooners continuing to operate through the war years were cut-down and motor-driven versions that performed little of their work under sail.* They bore only marginal resemblance to the glorious Tancook schooners of the past, which were sailing vessels first and foremost, and looked the part. The 34-foot *Verna B.*, built backalong in the late 1930s by Murray Wilneff for fishermen Ainsley and Percy Baker, was one of these vestigial two-masters, and she was representative of the island schooner in its final stages of decline. Full bodied and short ended with heavy quarters and a shallow draft, this boat retained the deck arrangement of a traditional sailing Tancooker, but little else (see photo 30). Among the very last working schooners on the island, she survived as such until 1945, when her owners, too, replaced her with a Cape Island boat.[28]

The transition from sail to power exemplified by the *Verna B.* was mercifully brief and did nothing to dull the lustre or dim the memory of the true Tancook schooner at the height of its development a decade or so earlier. It lives still in the minds of those who knew it as something special, a thing of beauty in a mundane, workaday world.

---

* One throwback to the era of the pure sailing schooner was the *X10U8*, a 33-footer built in the spring of 1940 by Howard Mason of Southeast Cove for his sons Thomas and Murray (see figs. 29, 30 and photos 23, 24). This small knockabout fished for several seasons on the ridges before being sold to the Great Lakes as a yacht in 1945. (*Source*: Interviews, Thomas Mason, 25 September 1987 and 4 October 1988.)

Epilogue

The Tancook islands were truly a microcosm of coastal Nova Scotia in the decades leading up to the Second World War. Their economy of inshore fishing and subsistence farming was duplicated in numerous outports from Yarmouth to Canso, and their coasting trade with urban Halifax was, products excepted, not very different from that of any number of other isolated rural communities along the Atlantic shore. Similarly, their constant struggle to survive difficult times in a harsh environment in many ways reflected the hard-scrabble Maritime way of life of the period – albeit magnified by their sea-girt geography.

What set these islands apart throughout their history was the technological means by which they pursued their hard day-to-day existence. Their boats, lovingly crafted and duplicated nowhere else, expressed the unique genius of the Tancook Islanders. Those special watercraft, beginning with the fabled whalers of the nineteenth century and culminating in the unsurpassed schooners of the twentieth, were a perfect marriage of form and function. It is no exaggeration to say that they brought the small sailing work boat of North America to its pinnacle in both a practical and an artistic sense. That this feat was accomplished by a people of agrarian inheritance, limited formal training and education, and scant economic means living in an isolated corner of the continent is all the more remarkable. It represents nothing less than a triumph of the human spirit.

Figures

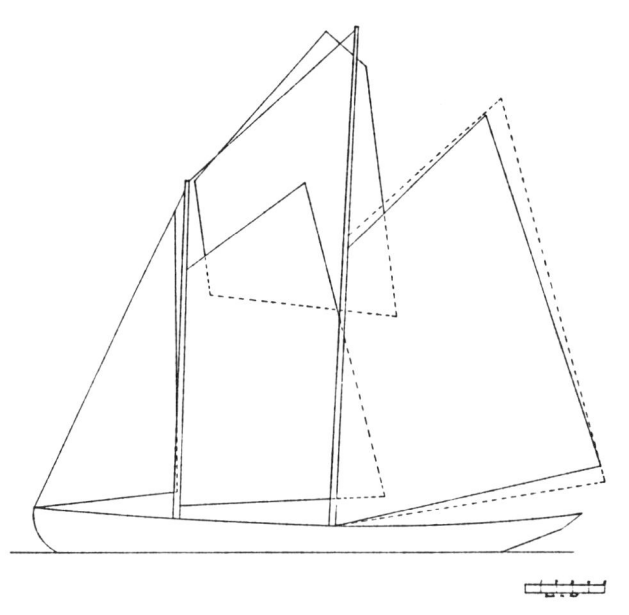

Fig. 1 Sail plan of an unidentified 35' schr built for Benjamin Levy of Little Tancook, probably by Amos H. Stevens, ca. 1905–09. Plan courtesy Harold W. Stevens. Redrawn by W.M. O'Leary from original by Randolph B. Stevens.

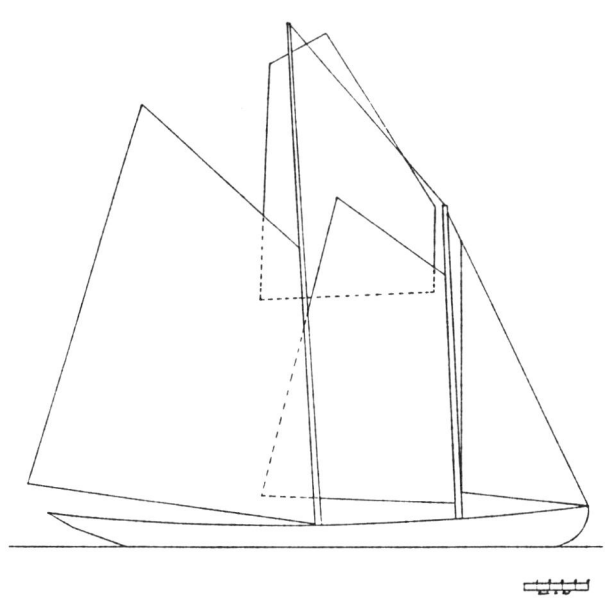

Fig. 2 Sail plan of 43' schr *Togo* [?], modelled and built by Amos H. Stevens, 1905. Plan courtesy Harold W. Stevens. Redrawn by W.M. O'Leary from original by Randolph B. Stevens.

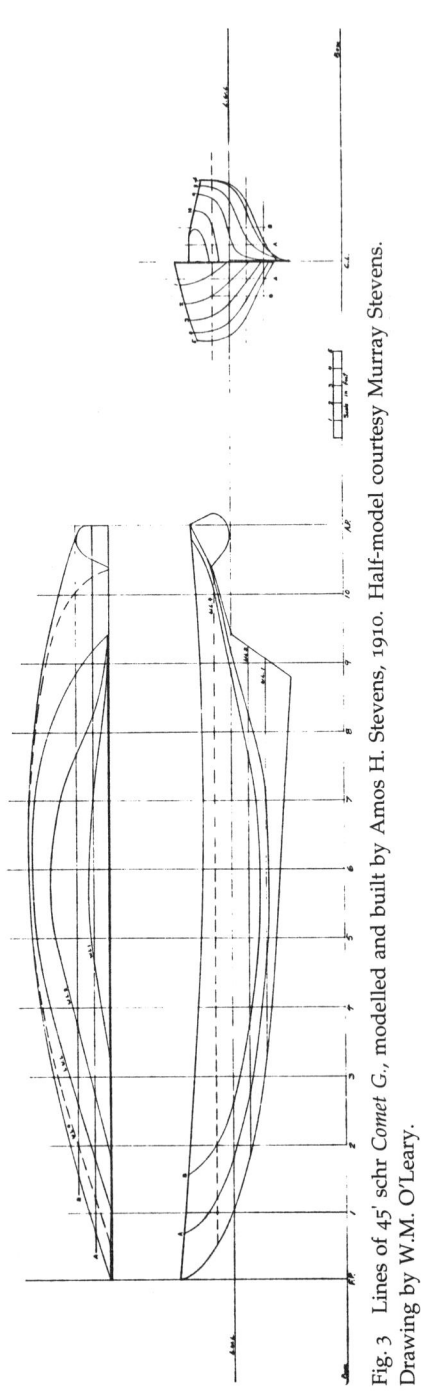

Fig. 3 Lines of 45' schr *Comet G.*, modelled and built by Amos H. Stevens, 1910. Half-model courtesy Murray Stevens. Drawing by W.M. O'Leary.

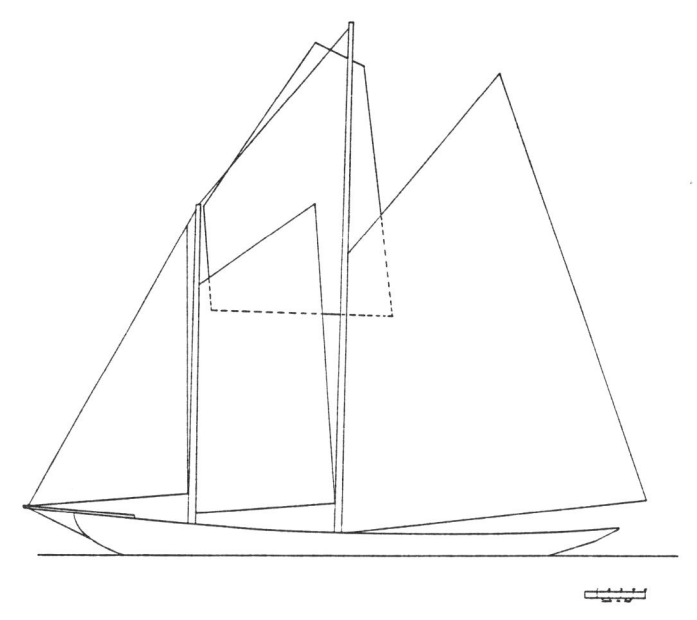

Fig. 4 Sail plan of schr *Comet G.*, 1910. Plan courtesy Harold W. Stevens. Redrawn by W.M. O'Leary from original by Randolph B. Stevens.

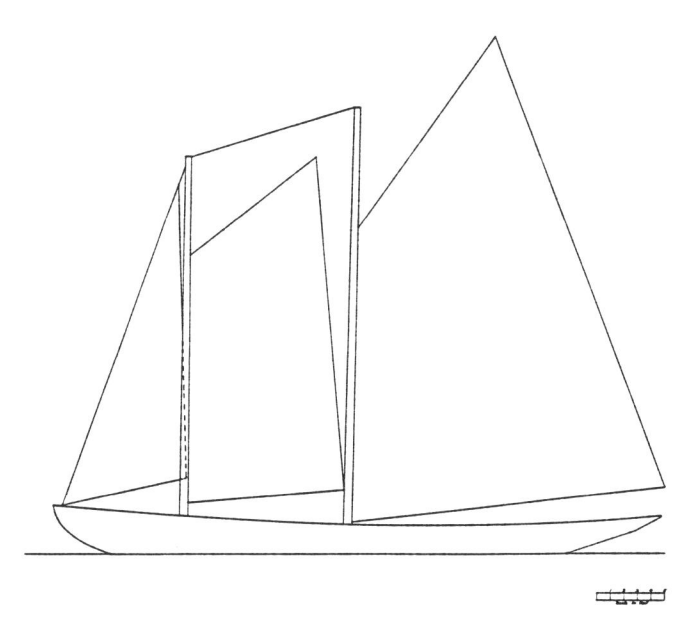

Fig. 5 Revised sail plan of schr *Comet G.*, 1916. Plan courtesy Harold W. Stevens. Redrawn by W.M. O'Leary from original by Randolph B. Stevens.

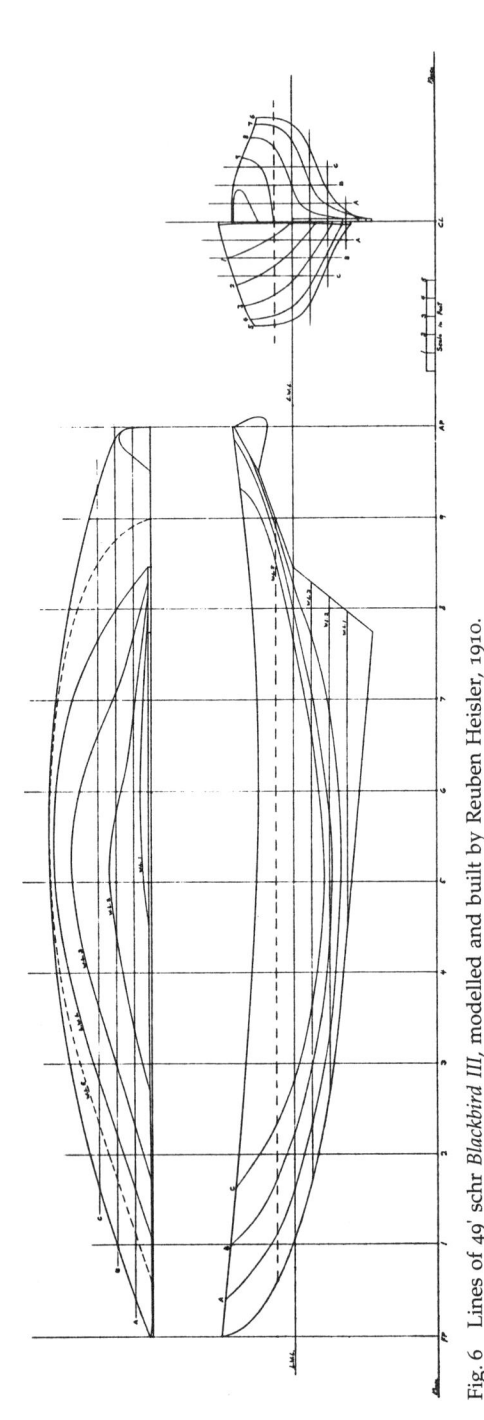

Fig. 6 Lines of 49' schr *Blackbird III*, modelled and built by Reuben Heisler, 1910. Half-model courtesy Mystic Seaport Museum (MSM 70.344). Drawing by W.M. O'Leary.

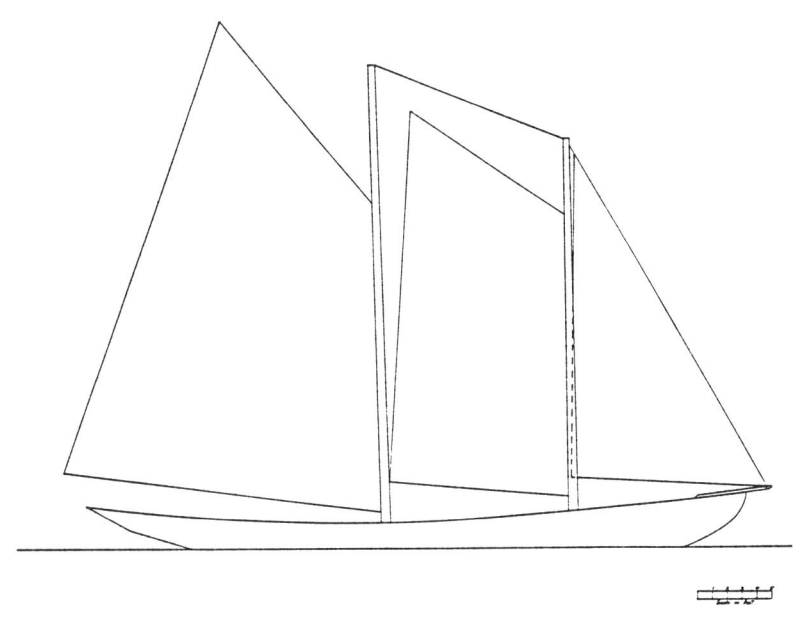

Fig. 7 Sail plan of 40' schr *Flosie*, modelled and built by Stanley G. Mason, 1912. Plan courtesy Harold W. Stevens. Redrawn by W.M. O'Leary from original by Randolph B. Stevens.

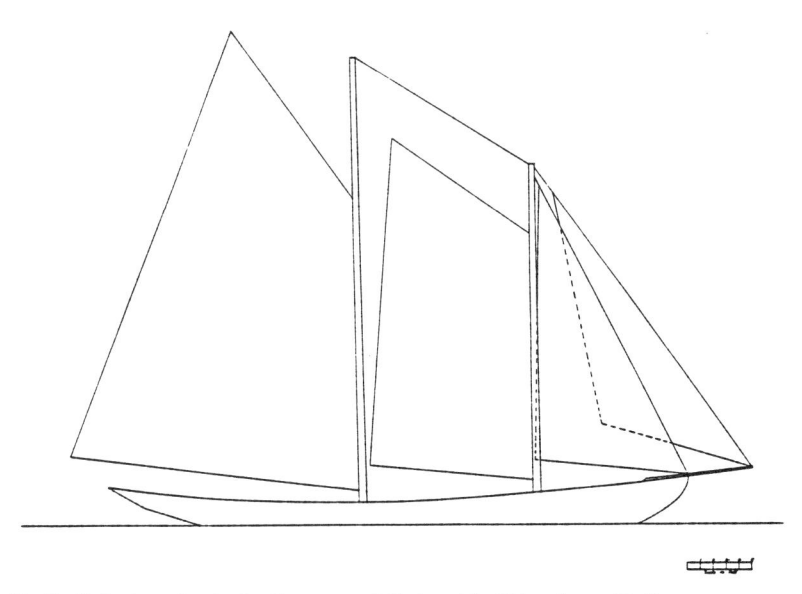

Fig. 8 Sail plan of 45' schr *Dagon*, modelled and built by Amos H. Stevens, 1912. Plan courtesy Harold W. Stevens. Redrawn by W.M. O'Leary from original by Randolph B. Stevens.

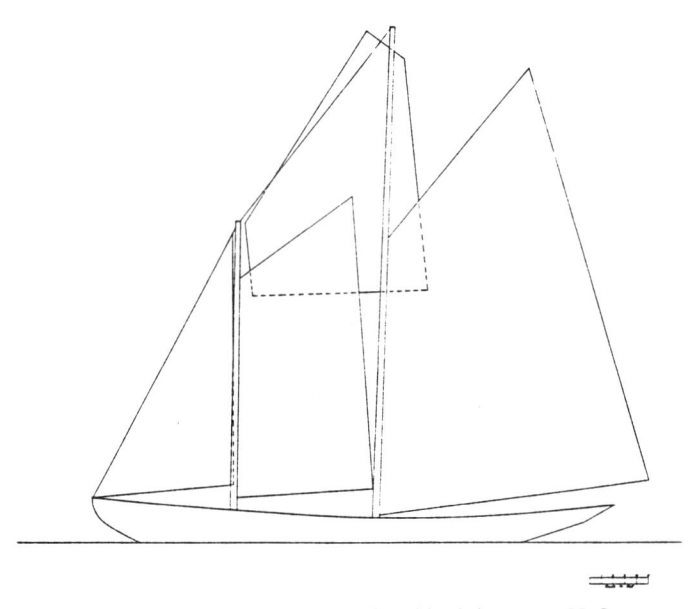

Fig. 9 Sail plan of 45' schr *Mianus*, modelled and built by Amos H. Stevens, 1912. Plan courtesy Harold W. Stevens. Redrawn by W.M. O'Leary from original by Randolph B. Stevens.

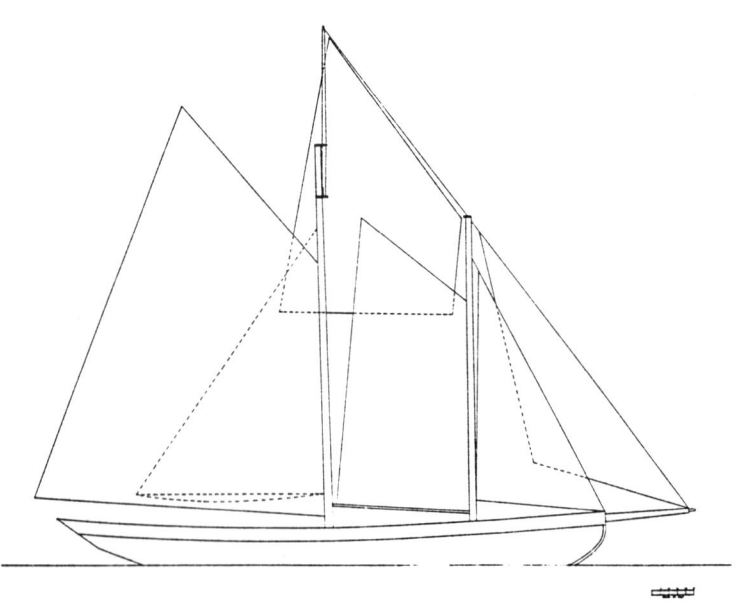

Fig. 10 Sail plan of 64' schr *Tancook*, modelled and built by Amos H. Stevens, 1914. Plan courtesy Harold W. Stevens. Redrawn by W.M. O'Leary from original by Randolph B. Stevens.

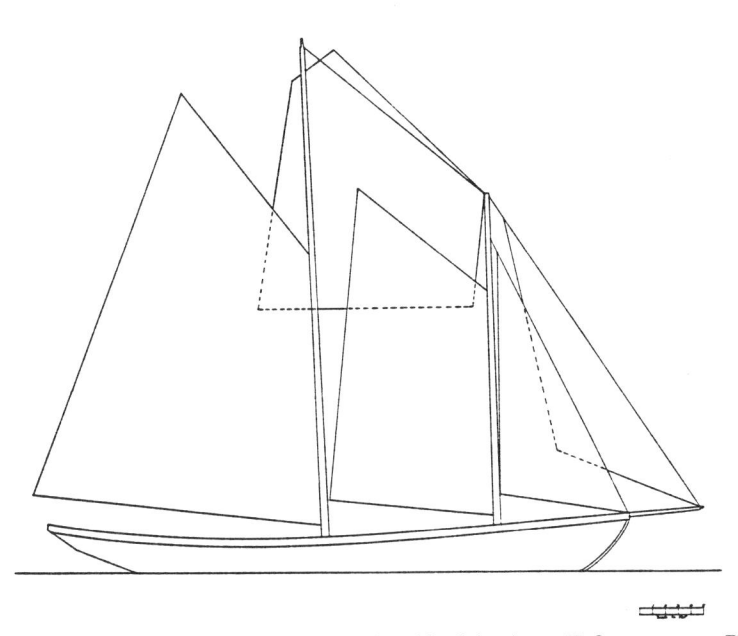

Fig. 11 Sail plan of 46' schr *Haig*, modelled and built by Amos H. Stevens, 1917. Plan courtesy Harold W. Stevens. Redrawn by W.M. O'Leary from original by Randolph B. Stevens.

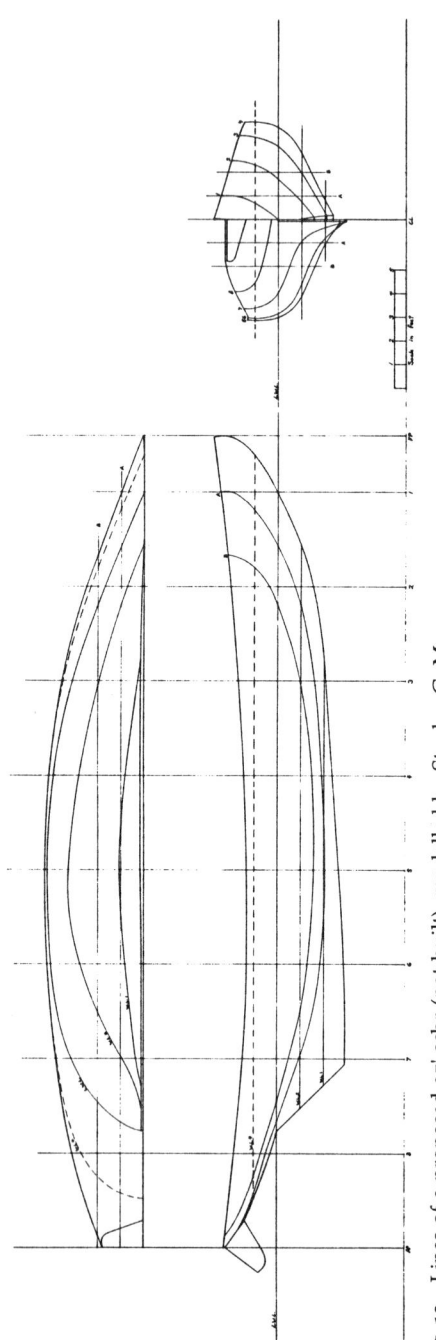

Fig. 12 Lines of a proposed 35' schr (not built), modelled by Stanley G. Mason, ca. 1910–20. Author's collection. Drawing by W.M. O'Leary.

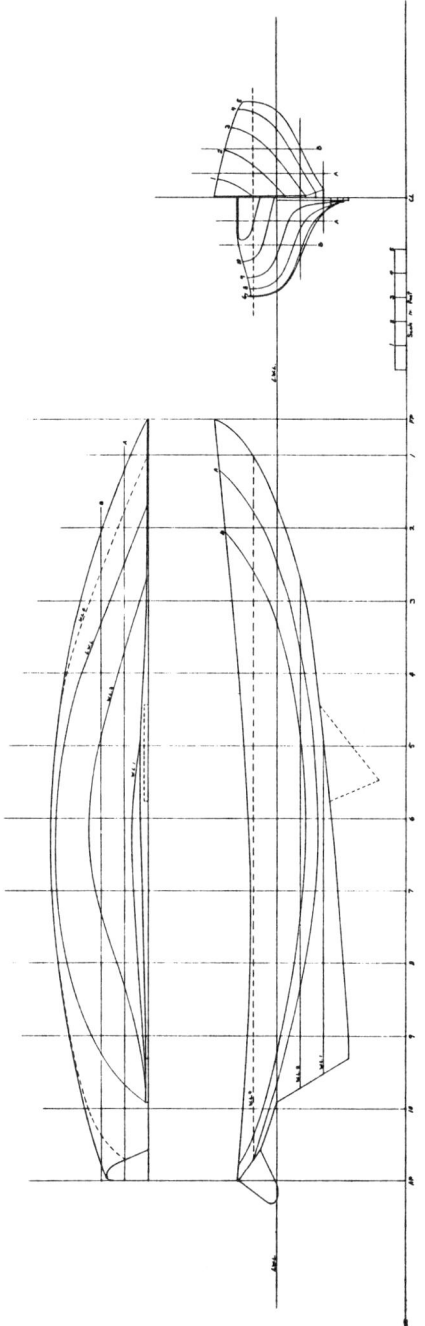

Fig. 13 Lines of 32' schr *Green Bow*, modelled by David W. Langille and built by Mason & Langille, ca. 1923. Author's collection. Drawing by W.M. O'Leary.

Fig. 14 Lines of 49' schr *Elsie B. Young*, modelled by David W. Langille and built by Mason & Langille, 1923. Schr *Bluebeard* built the same year from the same design. Half-model courtesy Leslie A. Mason. Drawing by W.M. O'Leary.

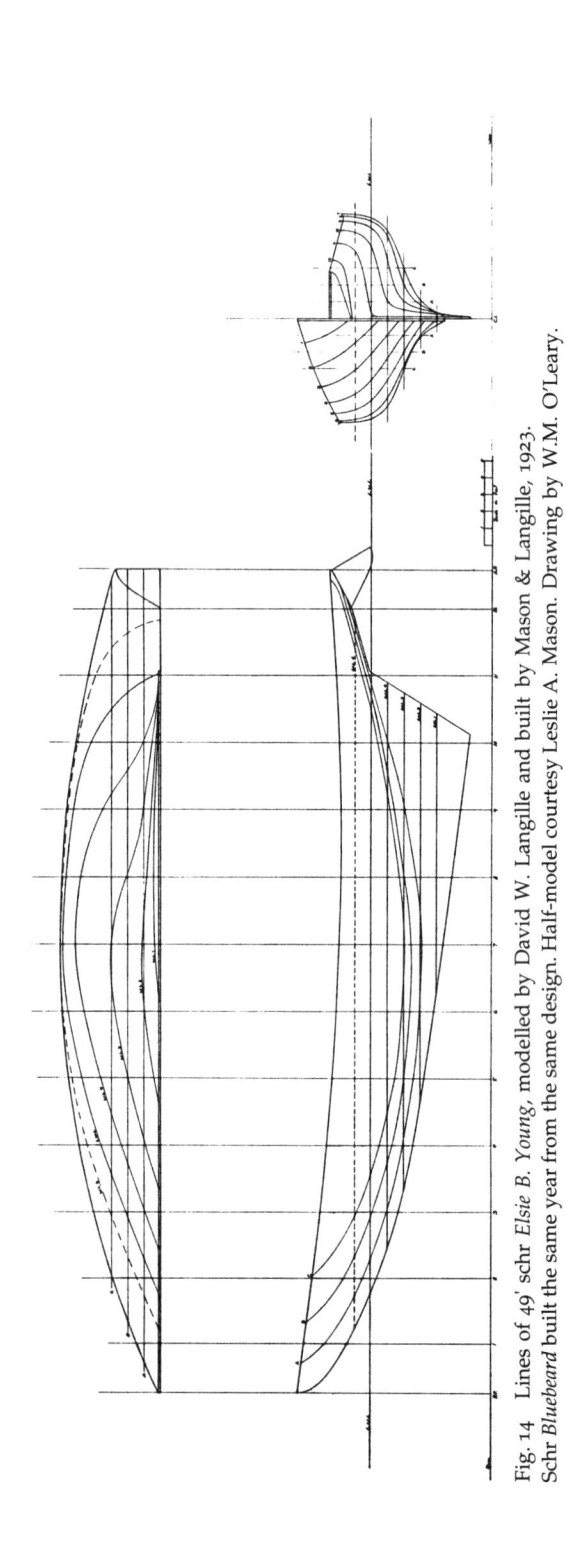

Fig. 15 Lines of 65′ schr *Sarah Pauline*, modelled by David W. Langille and built by Mason & Langille, 1924. Half-model courtesy Donald Langille. Drawing by W.M. O'Leary.

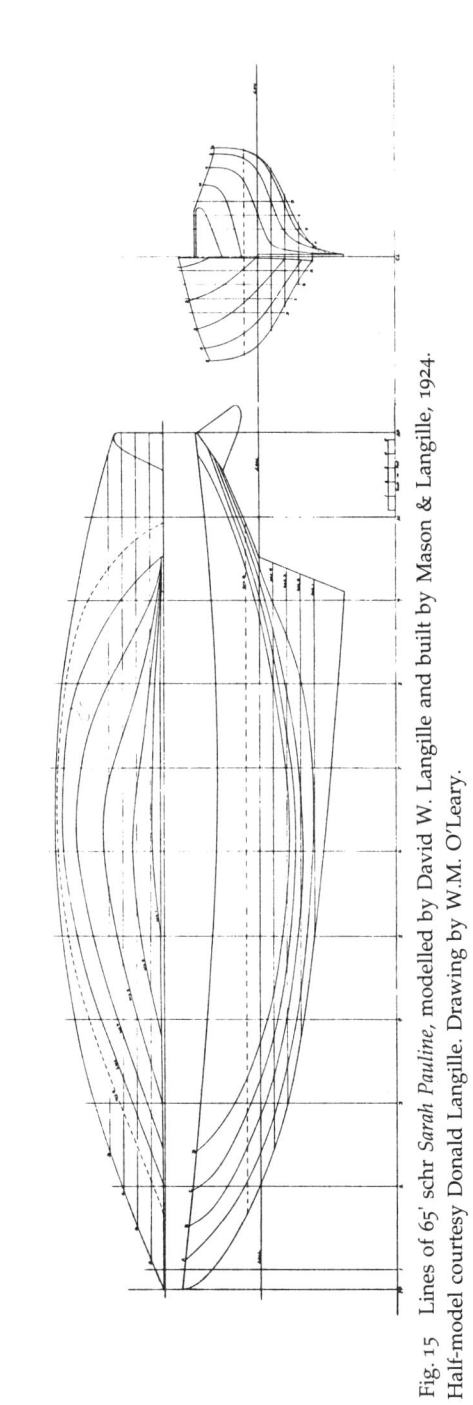

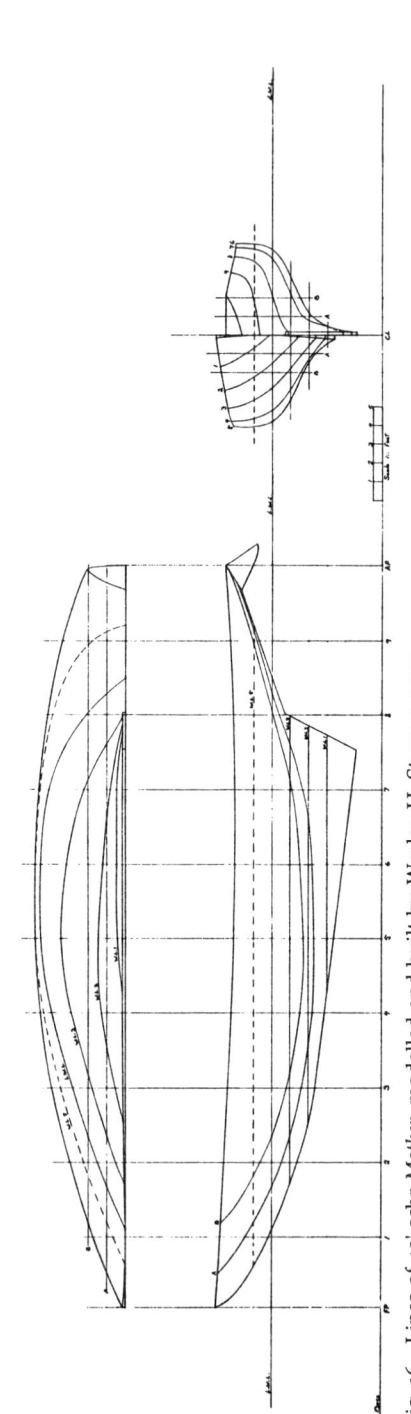

Fig. 16 Lines of 40' schr *Mother*, modelled and built by Wesley H. Stevens, 1924. Half-model courtesy Gerald L. Stevens. Drawing by W.M. O'Leary.

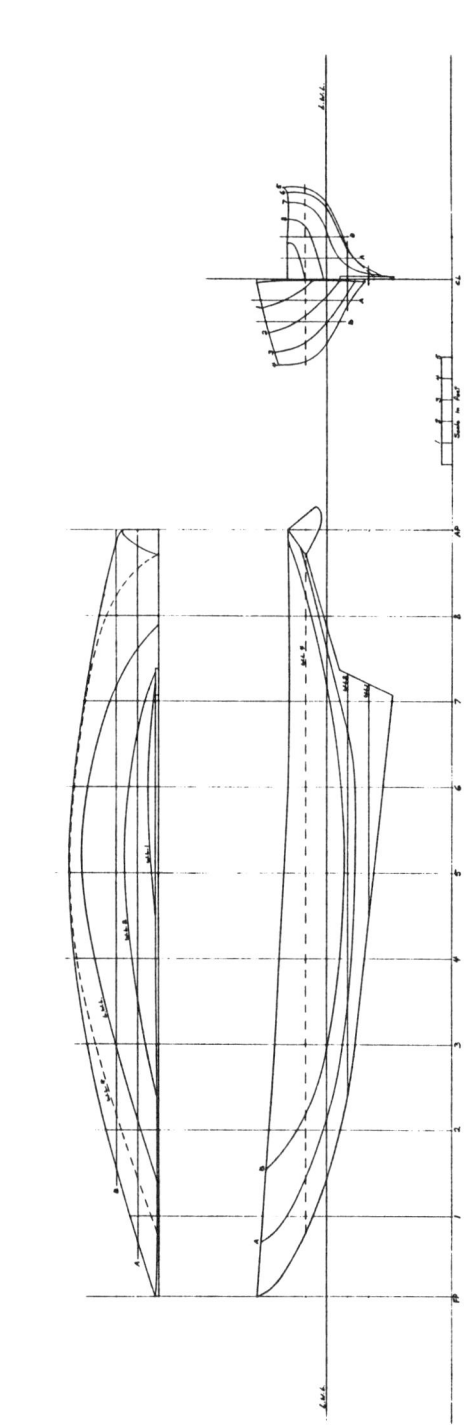

Fig. 17 Lines of 36' schr *Attaboy*, modelled and built by Wesley H. Stevens, 1928. Schrs *Catchalot* (1929), *Turret* (1930), *Glendora* (1931), and *Stormalong* (ca. 1936) built to the same design. Half-model courtesy Gerald L. Stevens. Drawing by W.M. O'Leary.

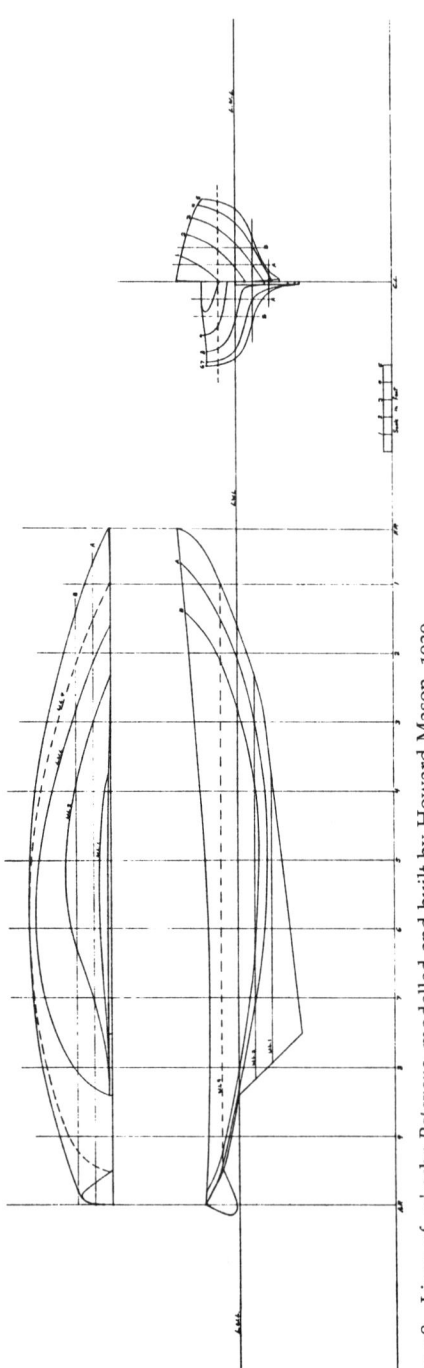

Fig. 18 Lines of 43' schr *Patawana*, modelled and built by Howard Mason, 1929. Half-model courtesy Thomas Mason. Drawing by W.M. O'Leary.

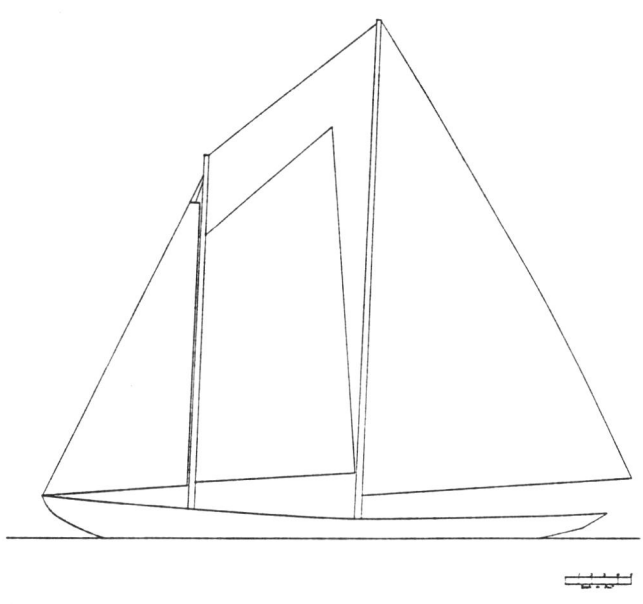

Fig. 19   Sail plan of schr *Patavana*, 1929. Author's reconstruction.

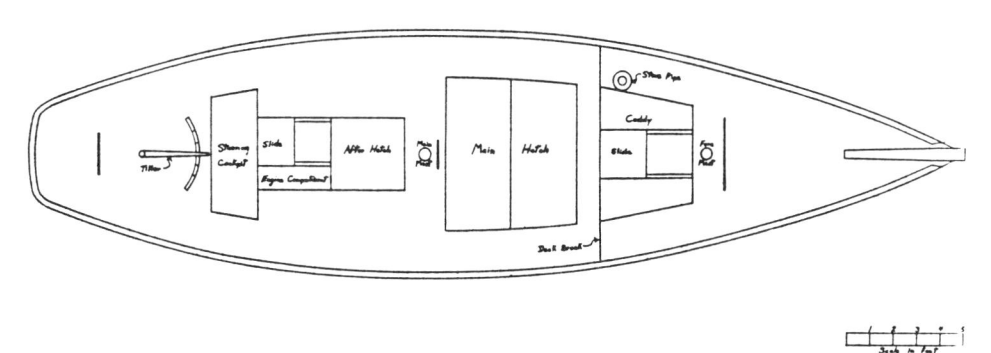

Fig. 20   Deck plan of a 40' Tancook semi-deck boat (after schr *Patavana*, 1929). Author's reconstruction.

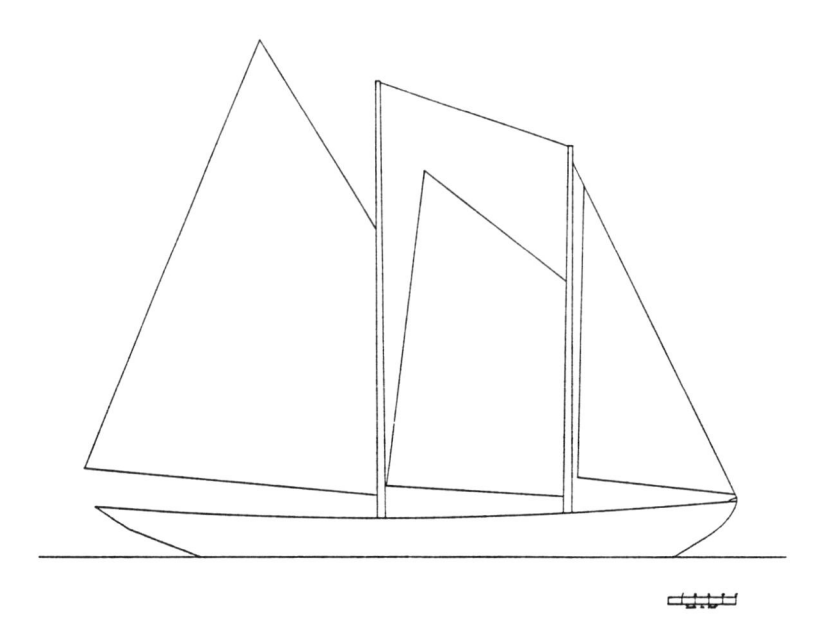

Fig. 21 Sail plan of 47' schr *Holly C.*, modelled and built by Manson W. Langille, 1929. Plan courtesy Harold W. Stevens. Redrawn by W.M. O'Leary from original by Randolph B. Stevens.

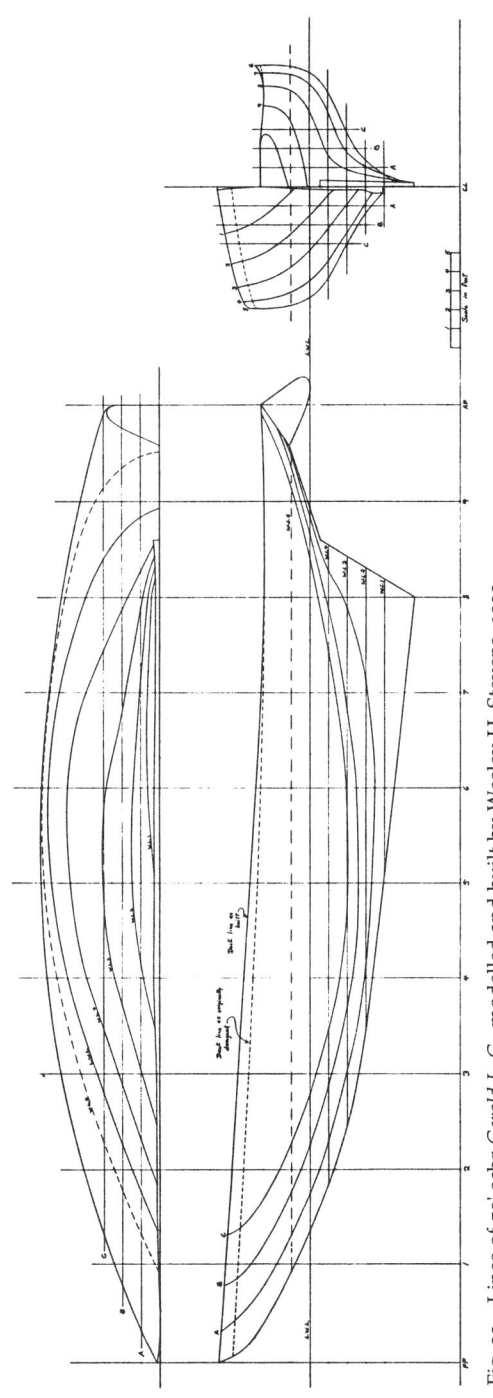

Fig. 22 Lines of 50' schr *Gerald L. C.*, modelled and built by Wesley H. Stevens, 1933. Half-model courtesy Gerald L. Stevens. Drawing by W.M. O'Leary.

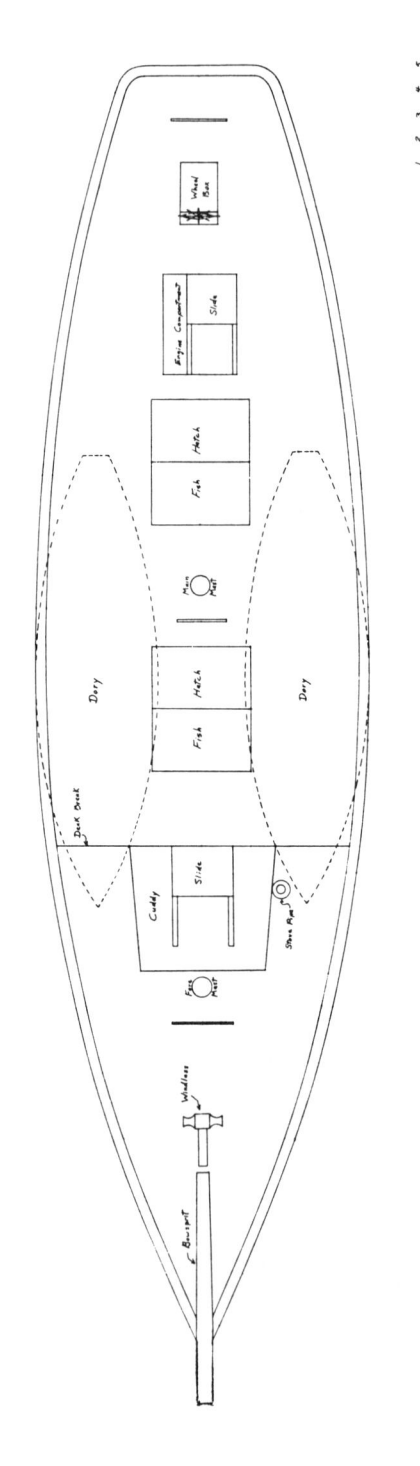

Fig. 23 Deck plan of a 50' Tancook deck boat (after schr *Gerald L. C.*, 1933). Author's reconstruction.

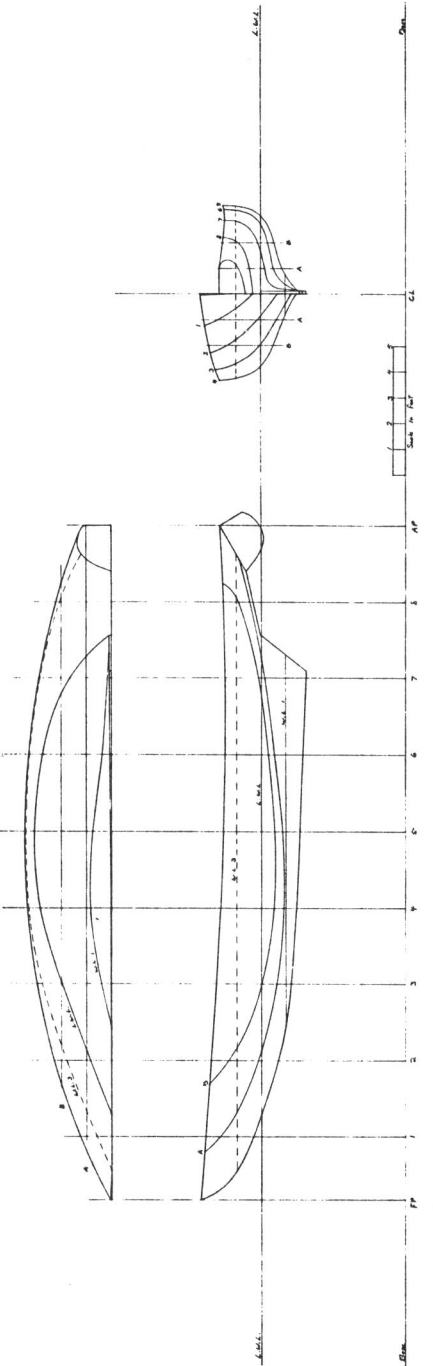

Fig. 24 Lines of 27' sloop *Polly Anna*, modelled by Howard Mason and built by Steadman S. Mason and Perry W. Stevens, 1934. Author's collection. Drawing by W.M. O'Leary.

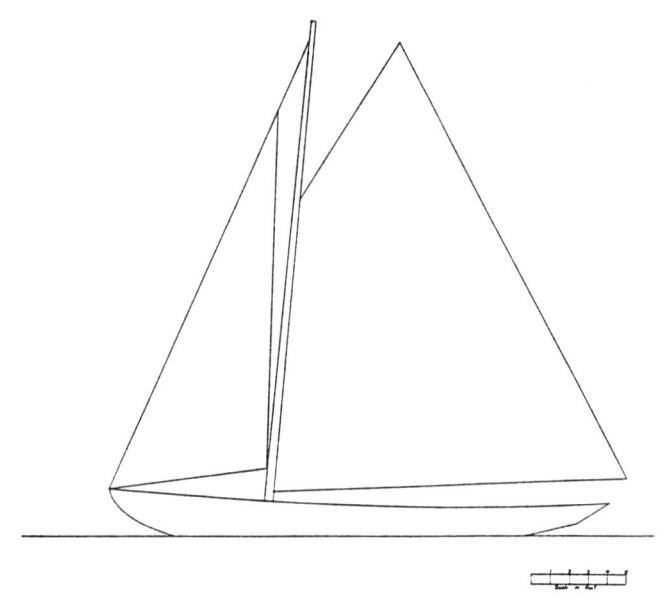

Fig. 25   Sail plan sloop *Polly Anna*, 1934. Plan courtesy Harold W. Stevens. Redrawn by W.M. O'Leary from original by Randolph B. Stevens..

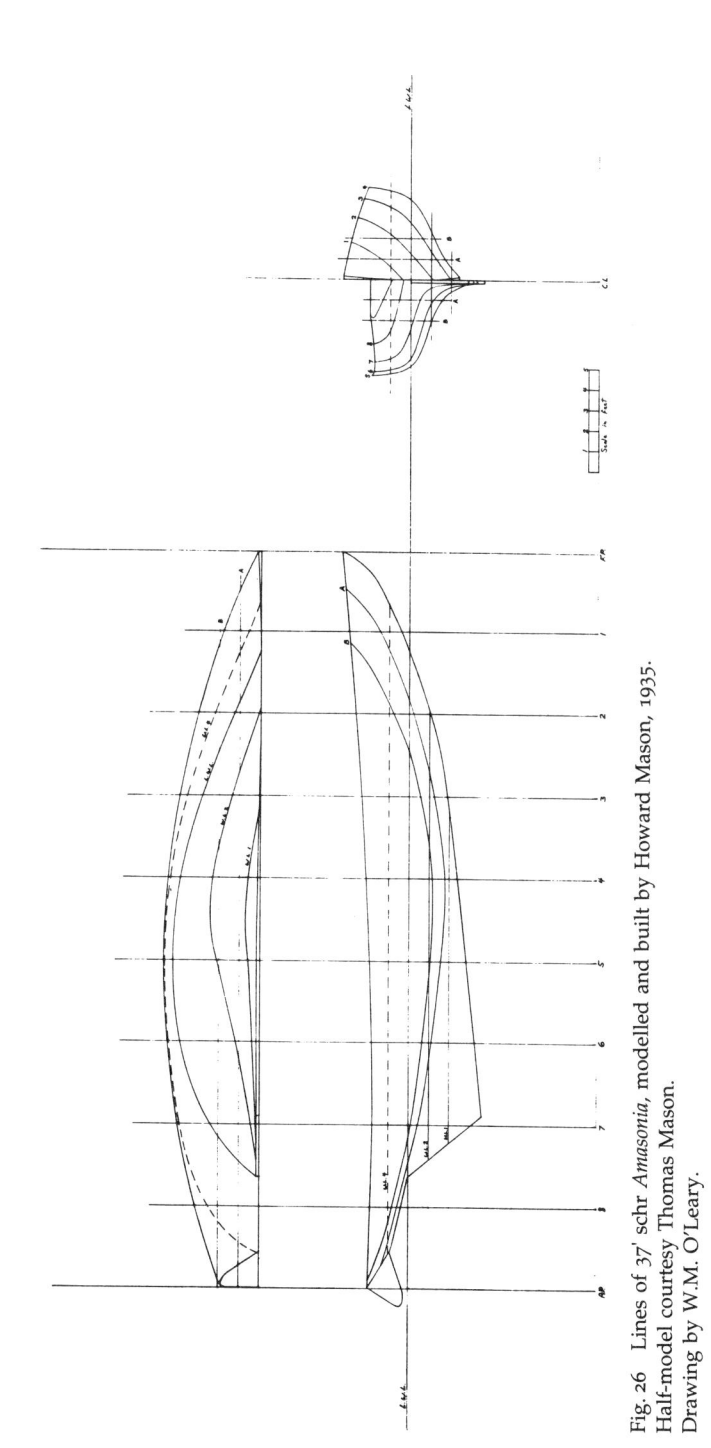

Fig. 26 Lines of 37' schr *Amasonia*, modelled and built by Howard Mason, 1935. Half-model courtesy Thomas Mason. Drawing by W.M. O'Leary.

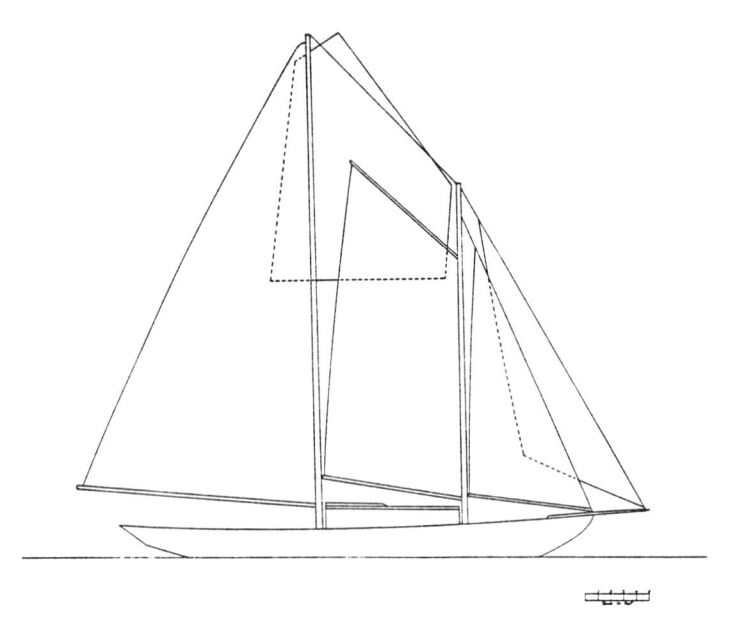

Fig. 27 Sail plan of schr *Amasonia*, 1935. Plan courtesy Harold W. Stevens. Redrawn by W.M. O'Leary from original by Randolph B. Stevens.

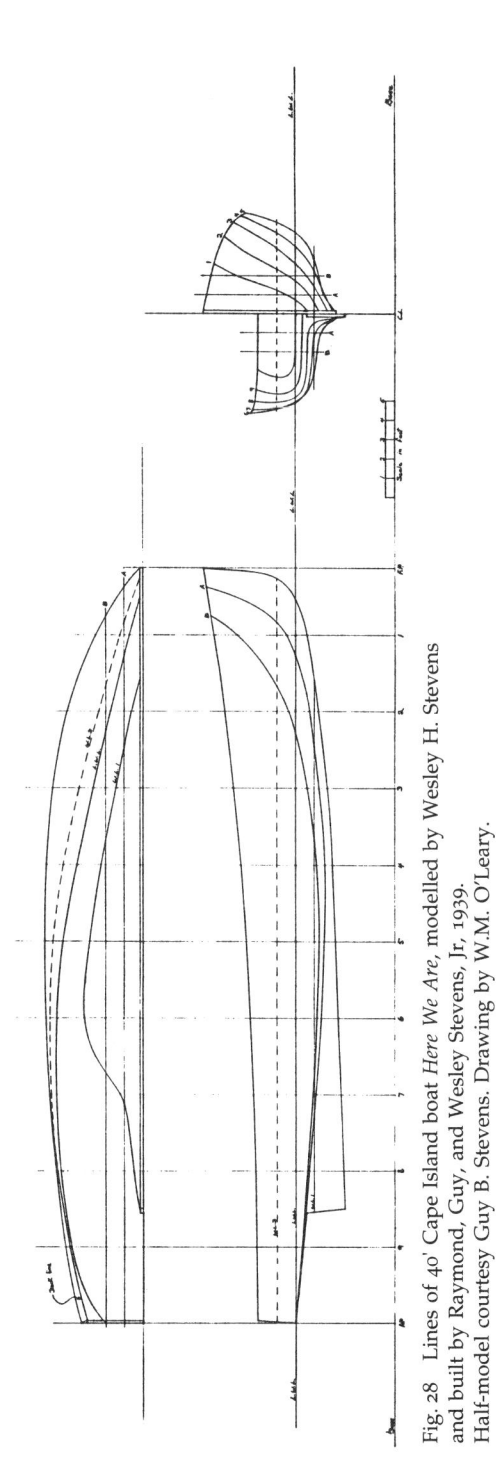

Fig. 28 Lines of 40' Cape Island boat *Here We Are*, modelled by Wesley H. Stevens and built by Raymond, Guy, and Wesley Stevens, Jr, 1939. Half-model courtesy Guy B. Stevens. Drawing by W.M. O'Leary.

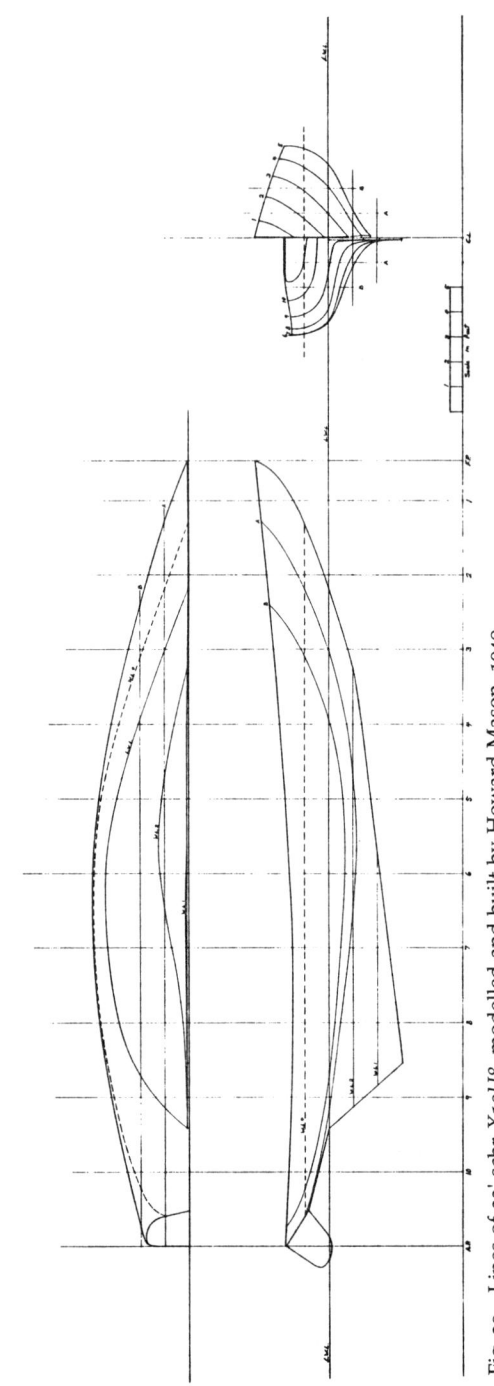

Fig. 29 Lines of 33' schr *X10U8*, modelled and built by Howard Mason, 1940. Author's collection. Drawing by W.M. O'Leary.

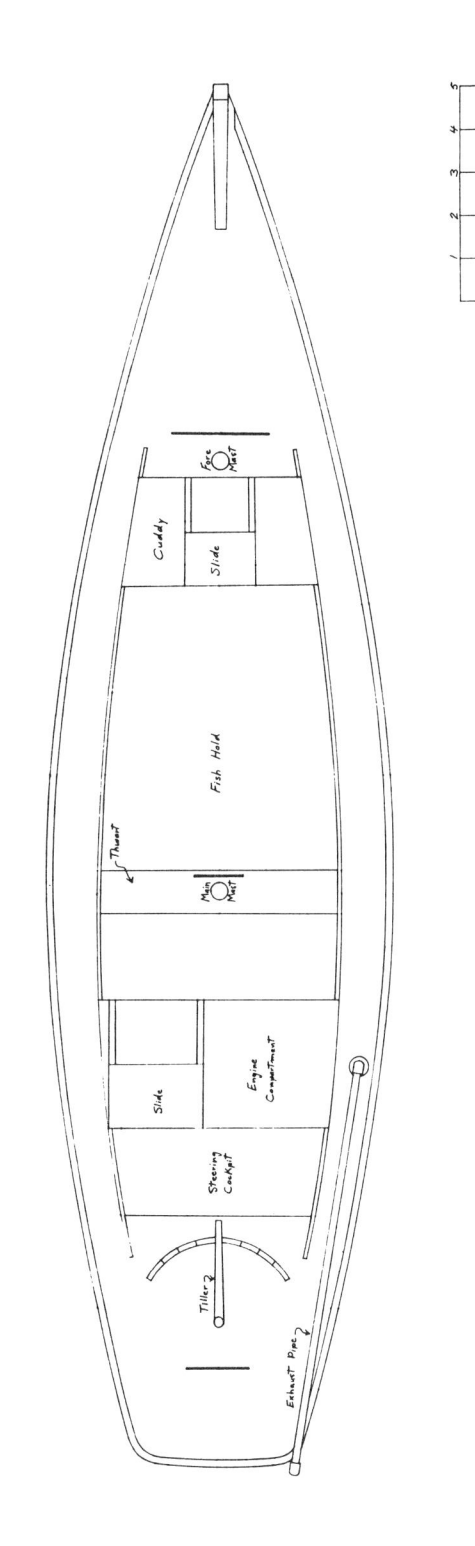

Fig. 30 Deck plan of a 30′ Tancook hatch boat (after schr X10U8, 1940). Author's reconstruction.

Fig. 31 Lines of a 32' Cape Island boat, modelled by Ervin B. Cross, ca. 1960. Author's collection. Drawing by W.M. O'Leary.

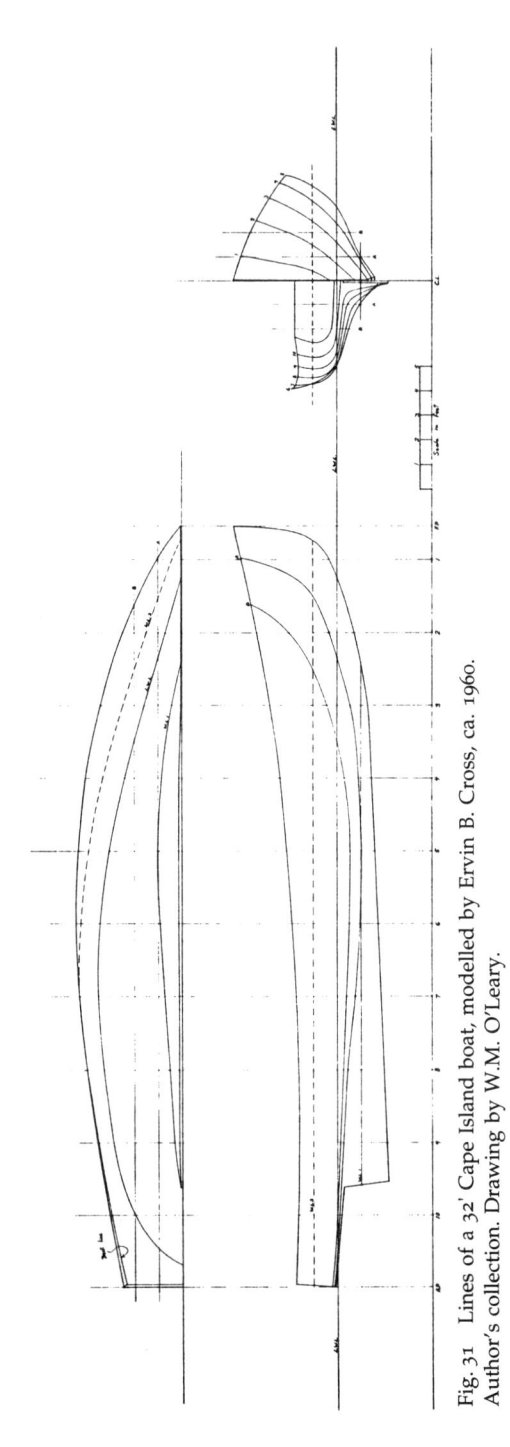

Appendices

APPENDIX ONE

A. LIST OF REGISTERED SCHOONERS BUILT AT BIG AND LITTLE TANCOOK ISLANDS, 1827–1936*

Name	Gr. Reg. Tonnage	Register Dimensions		Builder(s)	Original NS Home Port	Remarks/Disposition
THREE BROTHERS (ltr GOLDEN AGE)	29 (o.m.)	39'6" × 14' × 5'11"	1827	John Baker	Big Tancook	ss; sld Chester n.d.; reblt, new i.d.
LINNET	46 (o.m.)	46'4" × 15'7" × 7'4"	1832	John Gasper Young	Big Tancook	ss; brkn up 1843
LINNET II	38 (o.m.)	47.6' × 14.3' × 7.2'	1843	Peter Mason	Big Tancook	ss; sld St Mary's River 1845
SANDWICH	31 (o.m.)	50.3' × 15' × 6.9'	1845	Peter Mason	Big Tancook	ss; sld Halifax 1853
DOLPHIN	23 (o.m.)	39.5' × 12.3' × 6.1'	1848	George Baker	Big Tancook	ss; sld Peggy's Cove 1850
PATIENCE	42 (o.m.)	49' × 15.8' × 8.3'		unknown	Big Tancook	ss; reblt 1857
DARING	36	58' × 17.4' × 7.5'	1872	George Slauenwhite	Big Tancook	ss; wrkd 1886
GREEN LINNET	12	37' × 12' × 6'	1886	unknown	unknown	Regrd Canso 1900; brkn up Dover 1918
VALKYRIE	5	34.4' × 8.6' × 3.6'	1893	Amos H. Stevens	Halifax	W, Y, lap; brkn up 1910s

* *Sources: Can.LV; NA, LunSR; NA, HalSR; NA, ArISR; Can.HCH, HalSR; Can.LCH, LunSR; Can.SRD, CanSSR; Lloyd's Register of American Yachts.*

Note: For key to abbreviations, see end of list (p. 226).

Name	Gr. Reg. Tonnage	Register Dimensions	Builder(s)	Original NS Home Port	Remarks/Disposition
		1894			
VIGILANT	5	34.3' × 9' × 3.7'	Amos H. Stevens	Halifax	W, Y, lap; brkn up 1910s
		1903			
MINNIE J.	14	40' × 12.4' × 6.9'	unknown	Whitehaven	Brkn up Charlos Cove 1927
		1904			
LAURIE H.	16	42.8' × 12' × 7'	Amos H. Stevens	Indian Harbour	Sld PEI 1912
		1905			
BEULAH H.	12	40.3' × 10.2' × 5.2'	Amos H. Stevens	Big Tancook	cl; brkn up Tancook 1920
ELMA M.	10	40.2' × 10' × 5.2'	Alfred F. Langille	Stonehurst	W; reg. clsd 1916
GEORGE E.H.	10	39.8' × 9.9' × 5.3'	Alvin G. Stevens	Big Tancook	W; reg. clsd 1912
LUNENBURG	11	40.2' × 10.2' × 5'	Alvin G. Stevens	Cross Island	Sld Terence Bay 1920
TOGO	14	43.2' × 11' × 6.2'	Amos H. Stevens	Big Tancook	RF; sld PEI 1924
W. BAKER	10	39.6' × 9.9' × 5.2'	Alvin G. Stevens	Big Tancook	W; sld Port Joli 1916
		1906			
MATILDA H.	12	40' × 10.1' × 5.2'	Reuben Heisler	Big Tancook	Sld Terence Bay 1918
PAULINE L.	14	43.6' × 10.8' × 6.6'	Henry Levy	Little Tancook	Sld Lunenburg 1912
TACOMA (ltr ADARE)	11	40.2' × 10' × 5.2'	Reuben Heisler	Big Tancook	st; sld Halifax 1949 as Y
WILLIE ROY	12	44' × 11.8' × 5.6'	Henry Levy	Herring Cove	W; grnd & brkn up Mahone Bay ca. 1922
		1907			
ZORAYA	16	44.2' × 12.5' × 6.4'	Henry Levy	Big Tancook	Sld PEI 1934
ALMA M.	16	43.6' × 10.8' × 6.6'	Henry Levy	Eastern Point	Grnd & wrkd La Have 1942
BLANCHE S.	11	40.2' × 10.3' × 5.8'	Henry Levy	Blandford	W; sld Fox Point 1918
ENA T.	17	42.9' × 12.4' × 6.6'	Amos H. Stevens	Indian Harbour	Sld Whitehead 1917
FORTUNA	14	43' × 11.9' × 5.7'	Amos H. Stevens	Canso	Sld PEI 1928; brkn up 1930s
MILDRED BAKER	10	40.2' × 10' × 5.2'	Alvin G. Stevens	Lunenburg	W; reg. clsd 1919
SADIE H.	17	45.8' × 12.8' × 6.6'	Henry Levy	Blandford	Destrd Spry Bay 1928

UTOWANA	15	42.6' × 12.6' × 6.3'	Amos H. Stevens	Canso	Sld Sydney Mines 1926
VERNIE S.	10	38.5' × 9.9' × 4.8'	Albert Stevens	Big Tancook	cl; sld Blue Rocks 1915
			1908		
BONNIE B.	19	48.4' × 13' × 6.5'	Reuben Heisler	Blandford	Brkn up Peletier, Nfld 1949
DENTON S.	11	36' × 10.8' × 5.2'	Amos H. Stevens	Indian Harbour	Brkn up Indian Hbr 1920
DOROTHY G.	17	46.4' × 12.7' × 6.6'	Amos H. Stevens	Whitehead	Sld Canso 1910
HARPER	10	40.8' × 9.8' × 5'	Henry Levy	Blandford	W; sld Spry Bay 1917
HATTIE MAUD	16	44.7' × 12.4' × 5.4'	Amos H. Stevens	Canso	Brkn up n.d.
IRBESSA	17	41.6' × 12.4' × 6.5'	Reuben Heisler	Dover	Sld Canso 1911
M. UNITY	26	50.4' × 13.7' × 8'	Henry Levy	Blandford	Sld Cheticamp 1923
NINA S.	19	44' × 12.2' × 6.2'	Amos H. Stevens	Terence Bay	Brnd & snk nr Pennant Pt 1912
SEALER	12	40.4' × 10.4' × 5.4'	Joshua C. Langille	Cross Island	Brkn up Tancook ca. 1934
SHANT-ALEE	11	42.2' × 10.3' × 5.3'	Amos H. Stevens	Blue Rocks	Snk off W. Dover ca. 1932
STANLEY HUBLEY	18	45.8' × 12.6' × 6.4'	Amos H. Stevens	Indian Harbour	Sld No. Sydney 1926
VICTOR S.	12	40.2' × 10.3' × 5.8'	Reuben Heisler	Mill Cove	Brkn up & brnd Louisburg 1941
			1909		
C.L. MILLER	11	39.6' × 10.2' × 5.4'	Henry Levy	Northwest Cove	Sld W. Dover 1924
DAN PATCH	12	41.2' × 10.8' × 5.6'	Amos H. Stevens	Lunenburg	Cndmd W. Dublin 1925
ETHEL M.G.	11	41' × 10.3' × 5.3'	Amos H. Stevens	Indian Harbour	Cndmd Indian Hbr ca. 1938
EVA E.L.	11	39.6' × 10.2' × 5.4'	Henry Levy	Bayswater	Brkn up Dover 1920s
HATTIE M.J.	12	42.2' × 10.4' × 5.4'	Reuben Heisler	Mill Cove	Sld East Dover 1912
JOSEPH A.	15	44' × 10' × 6.6'	Amos H. Stevens	Petit de Grat	Sld Glace Bay 1926
LAURA M. LEVY	12	40.2' × 10.6' × 5.6'	Amos H. Stevens	Lunenburg	Sld PEI 1916
ORIOLE L.	10	39.4' × 10' × 5'	Alfred F. Langille	Little Tancook	Reg. clsd 1914
ROLAND A.T.	11	41' × 10.3' × 5.2'	Amos H. Stevens	Black Rocks	Brnd Stonehurst 1923
SHILOH	22	46.2' × 12.6' × 5.9'	Reuben Heisler	Terence Bay	Sld Lunenburg 1925; fndrd 1935
VIOLET F.	12	42.2' × 10.3' × 5.3'	Reuben Heisler	Indian Harbour	Sld Sydney 1918

Name	Gr. Reg. Tonnage	Register Dimensions	Builder(s)	Original NS Home Port	Remarks/Disposition
			1910		
ADANA C.	16	45' × 11.2' × 7'	Henry Levy	Bayswater	Sld No. Sydney 1924
BRENDA C.	12	41.4' × 10.3' × 5.3'	Mason & Langille*	Big Tancook	Sld W. Dover 1927
COMET G.	11	40.2' × 10.6' × 5'	Amos H. Stevens	Big Tancook	RF; sld Halifax 1920
EDNA H. (ltr PATROL BOAT #3)	17	47' × 12.9' × 6.2'	Reuben Heisler	Terence Bay	RR; szd 1923; snk Glace Bay 1930
ELLA M. YOUNG	12	42.4' × 10.8' × 5.4'	Alfred F. Langille	Dover	Reblt 1918; sld Pope's Hbr 1926
ELSIE C.	11	40.2' × 9.8' × 5'	Mason & Langille	Big Tancook	K; brkn up Tancook n.d.
FORMAN F.	15	42.4' × 10.9' × 6.2'	Henry Levy	Blandford	Sld River Bourgeois 1919
GLADYS G. HART	27	53.2' × 13.8' × 7'	Alvin G. Stevens	Sambro	Sld Liverpool 1917
HUGHIE V.L.	11	39.6' × 10.2' × 5.4'	Henry Levy	Little Tancook	Sld USA 1937
IRENE L.	11	39.6' × 10.2' × 5.4'	Henry Levy	Little Tancook	Grnd & brkn up PEI ca. 1943
JOSEPH EARLE	29	54' × 14.2' × 7.6'	Alvin G. Stevens	Terence Bay	Sld Nfld 1920
LAVINA B.	12	41.2' × 10.3' × 5.9'	Amos H. Stevens	Mill Cove	Brkn up L. Tancook 1929
LOTTIE B.L.	12	42' × 10.4' × 5.3'	Amos H. Stevens	Little Tancook	Sld Port Bickerton 1917
MADGE A.P.	11	44.8' × 10.2' × 5.2'	Alvin G. Stevens	Blandford	Grnd & brkn up Lingan 1934
MURIEL L.	15	44.6' × 11.2' × 7'	Henry Levy	Blandford	Brnd La Have 1931
PHOEBE M.	12	40.6' × 10.8' × 5.6'	Amos H. Stevens	W. Dover	Brkn up W. Dover n.d.
ROSIE L.	20	47.6' × 13.2' × 6.7'	Reuben Heisler	Terence Bay	Sld Ingonish 1919; wrkd 1938
VIOLET B. WYNACHT	11	42' × 10.2' × 5'	Amos H. Stevens	Stonehurst	Sld USA 1947
			1911		
A.L. CONRAD	12	40.4' × 10.6' × 5.2'	Mason & Langille	Rose Bay	Wrkd Liverpool 1938
ASAPH F.	15	43.6' × 10.8' × 6.6'	Henry Levy	Blandford	Brkn up Blandford 1930s
CUNNER	11	40.8' × 10' × 5.2'	Mason & Langille	Big Tancook	Grnd & wrkd Strait of Canso 1936

* Partners: Stanley G. Mason and Vernon R. Langille, 1909–11; Stanley G. Mason and David W. Langille, 1913–25.

DAISY Z.	11	39.6' × 10' × 5.4'	Henry Levy	Blandford	Cndmd Fisherman's Hbr 1937
DORA C.	12	40.4' × 10' × 5.6'	Henry Levy	Blandford	Sld Mushaboom Hbr 1930
FRANCES LENORE	13	41.6' × 10' × 5.6'	Albert Langille	Indian Harbour	Cndmd & brkn up Canso ca. 1940
GLADYS E.B.	24	47.2' × 13.2' × 7'	Reuben Heisler	Herring Cove	Sld Terence Bay 1919
H.C.R.	18	43.6' × 12.7' × 6.8'	Reuben Heisler	Canso	Sld Louisburg 1932
HAZEL C.	12	40.8' × 10.8' × 5.4'	Reuben Heisler	Indian Harbour	Brkn up Indian Hbr 1930s
HOLLO	12	42.8' × 10.1' × 5.5'	Alvin G. Stevens	Big Tancook	Sld Glace Bay 1924
JAMES L.	32	56.2' × 14' × 7.6'	Amos H. Stevens	Terence Bay	Sld Quebec 1918
JENNIE P.S.	33	59.2' × 14' × 7.6'	Alvin G. Stevens	Hackett's Cove	Sld Charles Cove 1924
LOTTIE M. BLANCHE	12	40.8' × 10.1' × 5.4'	Stanley Baker	E. Chester	Sld Indian Hbr 1923
MARGERY IRENE	12	40.2' × 10.2' × 5.3'	Reuben Heisler	Pennant Harbour	Brkn up Pennant Hbr 1929
OSWALD	20	45' × 13.6' × 6.8'	Alvin G. Stevens	Halifax	Sld Prospect 1912
PEARL BEATRICE H.	32	56.2' × 14' × 7.6'	Amos H. Stevens	Indian Harbour	Sld Nfld 1927
REBECCA M.L.	12	41.4' × 10.3' × 5.3'	Mason & Langille	Little Tancook	Sld Canso 1934; cndmd & brkn up 1945
RIGHT AWAY	21	45' × 13.3' × 6.8'	Alvin G. Stevens	Halifax	Grnd & brkn up No. Sydney 1942

1912

S.F. LEVY	12	40.4' × 10' × 5.6'	Henry Levy	Little Tancook	K; destrd L. Tancook n.d.
SADIE EVELYN	12	42' × 10.3' × 5.3'	Mason & Langille	Blandford	Brkn up W. Dover 1934
VERA MAY	23	46.6' × 13.4' × 6.8'	Reuben Heisler	Halifax	Sld Nfld 1931
WINNIFRED MARR	17	44.8' × 12.6' × 6.6'	Amos H. Stevens	Canso	Brkn up Canso 1940
ZOA H.	17	44.8' × 12.5' × 6.5'	Reuben Heisler	No. Sydney	Sld St. Pierre & Miquelon 1911
ALVIN S.	29	53.2' × 14.6' × 7.6'	Alvin G. Stevens	Halifax	Sld Quebec 1919
BERNICE	11	40.2' × 9.8' × 5'	Alfred F. Langille	Big Tancook	Brnd Margaree Hbr ca. 1937
BETTY B.	11	40.2' × 9.8' × 5.3'	Vernon R. Langille	Blandford	Cndmd Port Bickerton 1940
CECIL V.L.	12	41.4' × 10.4' × 5.5'	Vernon R. Langille	Big Tancook	K; sld River Bourgeois 1919
DAGON	13	45' × 10.4' × 5.8'	Amos H. Stevens	Big Tancook	Sld PEI 1921
DELIA H.	12	41.4' × 10.4' × 5.3'	Joshua C. Langille	Big Tancook	Sld Glace Bay 1941

Name	Gr. Reg. Tonnage	Register Dimensions	Builder(s)	Original NS Home Port	Remarks/Disposition
DRAMA	11	40.1' × 11' × 5.4'	Reuben Heisler	E. Dover	Snk Halifax Hbr 1941
EDITH ADELE	33	52.6' × 14.6' × 7.6'	Alvin G. Stevens	Ketch Harbour	Sld Nfld 1918
ELSIE S.	11	40' × 10' × 5.2'	Alvin G. Stevens	Blandford	Sld Chester Basin 1918
FLOSIE (ltr AEMAR)	11	40' × 10' × 5'	Stanley G. Mason	Big Tancook	Sld Halifax & renmd 1930
GLADYS IRENA	17	46.3' × 12' × 6.5'	Reuben Heisler	Terence Bay	Sld Quebec 1927; brkn up 1931
GWENDOLYN H.	12	41.4' × 10.4' × 5.5'	Vernon R. Langille	Indian Point	Cndmd & brkn up Halifax 1933
HOSIE	11	40' × 10' × 5'	unknown	Big Tancook	Sld Liverpool 1926
HOWKER	13	41' × 11.3' × 5.9'	Wesley H. Stevens	Lunenburg	Sld Three Fathom Hbr 1939
HURRAH	14	42.6' × 11' × 5.6'	Alvin G. Stevens	Big Tancook	Sld PEI 1928
LOIS M.C.	13	40.4' × 11' × 6'	Vernon R. Langille	Big Tancook	Brkn up Tancook n.d.
MARGARET E.	11	39.8' × 11' × 5.5'	Reuben Heisler	Ketch Harbour	Sld PEI 1918
MARONA	25	49.2' × 13' × 6.9'	Amos H. Stevens	Owl's Head	Wrkd Whitehead 1916; reblt & sld Sydney 1920
MATTAPEX	12	42' × 10.3' × 5.3'	Amos H. Stevens	Indian Harbour	RF; sld Clam Hbr 1926
MIANUS	15	45.2' × 10.8' × 6'	Amos H. Stevens	Indian Harbour	K; brkn up Indian Hbr n.d.
N.A.F.	24	48' × 13.5' × 7'	Reuben Heisler	Halifax	Sld Canso 1915; strmd 1930
NO-TOW	16	43.6' × 10.8' × 6.9'	Henry Levy	Blandford	Sld Indian Hbr 1915
OVILA	24	49.2' × 13.5' × 7'	Reuben Heisler	Sambro	Sld Fox Bay 1918; fndrd 1927
PETAWAWA	33	56.2' × 14.7' × 7.4'	Amos H. Stevens	Canso	hw; sld Nfld 1924
PLYMOUTH ROCK	24	48' × 13.5' × 7'	Reuben Heisler	E. Dover	Sld Arichat 1917
RAKWANA	12	40.2' × 10.5' × 5.7'	Stanley G. Mason	Cross Island	Sld USA 1936
SHIANNE	17	47' × 13.2' × 5.7'	Reuben Heisler	E. Dover	Sld Arichat 1915
THELMA C.	14	40.6' × 10.5' × 6.4'	Henry Levy	Southwest Cove	Sld Lunenburg 1927; brkn up 1934
THREE COUSINS	13	41.2' × 10.2' × 5.6'	Alvin G. Stevens	E. Berlin	Sld No. Sydney 1915
ZELMA T. YOUNG	16	43.6' × 10.8' × 6.9'	Henry Levy	Blandford	Sld Nfld 1915; lst in storm Deer Lake 1925

			1913		
ADONIA S.	19	46.8' × 12.4' × 6'	Amos H. Stevens	Terence Bay	Sld Nfld 1925
AZANETTA	35	59' × 15.8' × 9'	Henry Levy	Bayswater	Sld Nfld 1920
HOWARD STANLEY	16	43.8' × 12' × 6'	Vernon R. Langille	Big Tancook	Fndrd off Ingonish Is. 1939
LOBELIA L.	25	48.8' × 13' × 7.8'	Henry Levy	Little Tancook	Sld Nfld 1919; cndmd 1951
MALADA	22	47.2' × 13.3' × 7'	Reuben Heisler	Blandford	Sld No. Sydney 1930
MARY K.	15	45' × 11.4' × 5.8'	Reuben Heisler	Devil's Island	Sld Halifax 1926
SELMA M.	12	41.2' × 10.6' × 5.4'	Mason & Langille	Big Tancook	Sld Chester 1938
VALERIE S.	17	47.8' × 12.2' × 6'	Amos H. Stevens	Terence Bay	
			1914		
ELVA M.Y.	12	41.4' × 10.2' × 5.3'	Joshua C. Langille	Big Tancook	Sld Owl's Hd 1930; brkn up Canso n.d.
EUNICE F.	16	41.4' × 12' × 6'	Alvin G. Stevens	Ketch Harbour	Sld Nfld 1920
HELEN VIOLA	14	42.8' × 11.6' × 6'	Reuben Heisler	Sambro	Brkn up Murray Hbr PEI 1941
OLIVER TWIST	11	38' × 10.9' × 6.2'	Amos H. Stevens	Summerville	Brkn up Lunenburg 1926
PEGGY (ltr OUR NELLIE)	12	40.7' × 10.4' × 5'	Reuben Heisler	Chester	Y; 46'6" l.o.a., 58" dr; sld USA 1946
TANCOOK	38	59.4' × 16.4' × 7.6'	Amos H. Stevens	Big Tancook	mt; 64' l.o.a.; sld Nfld 1922
			1915		
AGNES G.R.	11	38.5' × 9.8' × 5.4'	Mason & Langille	Blandford	Sld Magdalen Is. 1946
AUGUSTINE B.	15	42.8' × 10.8' × 6.2'	Amos H. Stevens	Dominion	Sld Terence Bay 1931
ETTA L.	25	48.5' × 13.5' × 7'	Reuben Heisler	W. Liscomb	Sld Nfld 1925
GERTRUDE M.B. (ltr POLLY ANN)	18	42' × 12.8' × 6.5'	Reuben Heisler	Indian Harbour	Sld USA & renmd 1925
PEOLIA F. LEVY (ltr BAYSPORT)	13	43.8' × 10.4' × 5.4'	Amos H. Stevens	Lunenburg	Sld Sambro 1925; brkn up 1938
			1916		
ATTENTION	15	42.7' × 10.6' × 6.4'	Reuben Heisler	Blandford	Sld Baddeck 1944
BLEUCHER C.	12	41.4' × 10.7' × 5.6'	Mason & Langille	Big Tancook	Sld Liscomb 1917
HARRY P.	12	41.4' × 10.7' × 5.6'	Mason & Langille	Blandford	Sld Truro 1932; lst ca. 1941

Name	Gr. Reg. Tonnage	Register Dimensions	Builder(s)	Original NS Home Port	Remarks/Disposition
		1917			
GUARANTEE	11	40.2' × 10.3' × 5.3'	Reuben Heisler	Pennant Harbour	unknown
HAIG	15	45.4' × 11' × 5.6'	Amos H. Stevens	Big Tancook	Sld Nfld 1949
HURRY UP	17	43.5' × 12' × 6.3'	Alvin G. Stevens	Big Tancook	Sld Spry Bay 1928; strnd 1938
J.C. MARTIN	25	52' × 13.6' × 6.7'	Amos H. Stevens	Ketch Harbour	Sld Nfld 1928
JESSEN J.M.*	15	42.6' × 11.4' × 6.3'	Mason & Langille	Little Tancook	Sld USA 1946
SCAMPER	12	41.8' × 10.7' × 5.6'	Mason & Langille	Cross Island	Sld USA 1933
SILVER OAK	42	62.4' × 16' × 8'	Reuben Heisler	Big Tancook	hw; sld Nfld 1919; lst 1933
STEWARD D.S.*	13	42.2' × 11.4' × 5.6'	Mason & Langille	Big Tancook	Sld Stonehurst 1945
		1918			
BLANCHE M. STEVENS	25	49.6' × 13.8' × 7.2'	Amos H. Stevens	Big Tancook	Sld Nfld 1919; reblt 1927
ERSKINE B.	13	43.2' × 10.6' × 5.6'	Mason & Langille	Alberton, PEI	
OPAL JUNE	16	42.5' × 11.5' × 6'	Reuben Heisler	Big Tancook	RR; grnd & wrkd 1923
WHITE BIRCH	28	49.8' × 14.2' × 7.5'	Mason & Langille	Big Tancook	hw; sld St Pierre & Miquelon 1924, Nfld 1926
		1919			
L.H. FLEET	17	47.9' × 13' × 5.4'	Mason & Langille	Blandford	Brnd at sea 1923
LUCILLE B. YOUNG	18	44.2' × 12' × 6.1'	Amos H. Stevens	Big Tancook	RR; wrkd Halifax Hbr 1935
		1922			
VIOLET B.	12	40' × 10.8' × 5.1'	Reuben Heisler	Herring Cove	Sld Halifax 1929
		1923			
BLUEBEARD	16	47.8' × 13' × 6.2'	Mason & Langille	Big Tancook	Sld Glace Bay & lst at sea 1940
DOROTHY LUCILLE	17	46' × 12' × 6.5'	Reuben Heisler	Herman's Island	Sld Quebec 1933

* Sister ships.

Name		Dimensions	Builder	Year	Port	Notes
ELSIE B. YOUNG	16	43.4' × 12.9' × 6.2'	Mason & Langille		Big Tancook	RR; sld Nfld 1926; lst 1928
EQUITABLE II	12	43.5' × 11.1' × 5.6'	Reuben Heisler		Blandford	Brnd Indian Hbr 1927
RITA IRENE	12	41.2' × 11' × 6'	Mason & Langille		Big Tancook	Sld USA 1934
				1924		
GLORIA P.H.	20	45' × 13.9' × 6.9'	Mason & Langille		Big Tancook	RR; szd 1929; sld No. Sydney 1937
MOTHER	13	38' × 10.6' × 6'	Wesley H. Stevens		Big Tancook	Sld USA 1929
SARAH PAULINE	37	60' × 17' × 9'	Mason & Langille		Canso	RR; 65' l.o.a., 10' dr; szd & sld Nfld 1931
TYRIENNE S.	27	51.6' × 15.5' × 7.8'	Mason & Langille		Big Tancook	Strnd & lst 1930
				1925		
FRANCES M.R.	21	44.8' × 13.8' × 7'	Mason & Langille		Big Tancook	Sld Digby 1944
LOVALON	11	38' × 10.6' × 6'	Mason & Langille		Blandford	Sld Nfld 1945
OLD CHUM	20	43.8' × 13.8' × 7'	Mason & Langille		Big Tancook	Sld Nfld & USA 1950
PALAWANA	13	40' × 11.5' × 7.2'	Mason & Langille		Big Tancook	RR; sld PEI 1932; szd 1933
ROSE DOROTHY	23	51.6' × 13' × 7.6'	Mason & Langille		Indian Harbour	Sld Nfld 1929
				1926		
CARPATICA	15	40' × 11' × 6.8'	Stanley G. Mason		Blandford	Aband Ingonish Beach 1949
EILEEN E.	21	41' × 13' × 7'	Stanley G. Mason		Blandford	Sld Nfld 1945
ESSIE M.L.	20	44.4' × 13' × 7'	Stanley G. Mason		Big Tancook	Snk off Canso 1927
GLORIA SWANSON	20	54.6' × 14.6' × 5.6'	Stanley G. Mason		Big Tancook	RR; fndrd off Sambro 1927
				1927		
MARION C.	23	55' × 15' × 7'	Stanley G. Mason		Lunenburg	hw; wrkd Big Duck Is. 1947
				1928		
BLACK ROBIN (ex PEGGY)	14	40' × 10.1' × 5.4'	Alexander Wilson		Big Tancook	Reblt, new i.d.; sld Ontario & USA 1936
DIXIE ARROW	10	40.4' × 11.3' × 5.4'	Melvin H. Stevens		Big Tancook	Sld Louisburg 1941; cndmd & brkn up 1948
LOYALIST	15	45.6' × 12.6' × 6.4'	Stanley G. Mason		Indian Harbour	Sld Herring Cove 1948
MALABATA	16	45.6' × 12.6' × 6.6'	Stanley G. Mason		Blandford	Sld USA 1935
WILDCAT	26	54' × 15' × 7'	Stanley G. Mason		Big Tancook	RR; sld USA 1937

Name	Gr. Reg. Tonnage	Register Dimensions	Builder(s)	Original NS Home Port	Remarks/Disposition
		1929			
ADVANTAGE	10	40.6' × 11.6' × 5.2'	Melvin H. Stevens	Pennant Harbour	Sld Port Morien 1946; destrd by fire 1958
EMMELINE J.	14	48' × 13' × 7.6'	Stanley G. Mason	W. Dover	Sld Nfld 1945
EVELYN J.	15	45.6' × 12.2' × 6.4'	Stanley G. Mason	W. Dover	Sld USA 1936
HAROLD H. (ltr BLUE LAGOON & WINDSTARK)	16	45.6' × 12.5' × 6.4'	Stanley G. Mason	Blandford	49' l.o.a., 6' dr; reblt as Y, renmd, & sld USA 1935
HOLLY C. (ex ELIZA ANN)	17	46.6' × 12.4' × 6.6'	Manson & Langille	Big Tancook	K, RR; sld W. Dover 1929 & snk off Pennant Pt 1935
NELSON L.	40	60' × 17.2' × 9'	Stanley G. Mason	Canso	hw, 63' l.o.a., 9' dr; fndrd off Pt Bickerton 1938
PATAVANA	11	43' × 11' × 5.4'	Howard Mason	Big Tancook	K, mm; sld Ontario 1943
		1930			
DIXIE FLYER	13	40' × 11.8' × 6.6'	Stanley G. Mason	Big Tancook	Sld USA 1938
MORNING STAR II	31	60' × 16.5' × 8.5'	Stanley G. Mason	Canso	hw, mm; sld Nfld 1934
		1931			
DOROTHY AND ELLA	19	44.2' × 12.6' × 6.8'	Melvin H. Stevens	Big Tancook	Snk Pointe-du-Chene, NB 1952
ELIZABETH M.	21	47.4' × 14.5' × 6.8'	Stanley G. Mason	Lunenburg	Sld Digby 1935
NAOMI RUTH	20	49' × 13.3' × 6.4'	Stanley G. Mason	Indian Harbour	Sld No. Sydney 1947; destrd by fire 1950
SUNAPEE	20	49' × 13.5' × 6.4'	Stanley G. Mason	Indian Harbour	Sld USA 1956
SYLVIA PAULINE	13	44.5' × 11.9' × 6'	Stanley G. Mason	Big Tancook	Sld Nfld 1944, Glace Bay 1946
		1932			
MADELINE S.	10	39' × 10.7' × 5.4'	Harvey A. Stevens	Big Tancook	Sld foreign 1935
YAHOO	17	48' × 13' × 6.6'	Stanley G. Mason	E. La Have	Sld Nfld 1938

GERALD L.C.	17	48.6' × 13.6' × 7'	1933	Wesley H. Stevens	Big Tancook	Sld Glace Bay 1941
STREAMLINE	11	38' × 10.7' × 5.6'	1936	Warren Pearl, Jr.	Big Tancook	Sld Ontario 1943

B. PARTIAL LIST OF UNREGISTERED SCHOONERS BUILT AT BIG TANCOOK ISLAND, 1903–1949*
(Alphabetical)

Name	Building Date	Approximate Overall Length	Builder(s)	Original Ns Home Port	Remarks/Disposition
AMASONIA	1935	37'	Howard Mason	Chester	Y, mm, ld kl; reblt 1964
ATTABOY	ca. 1928	36'	Wesley H. & Archibald Stevens	Big Tancook	
BLACKBIRD III	1910	49'	Reuben Heisler	Chester	Y, ld kl; wrkd Halifax 1922
BLACK LIZE (or LIZA)	ca. 1905	38'	Amos H. Stevens	Big Tancook	st
BLACK NANCE	ca. 1903	38'	Amos H. Stevens	Big Tancook	RF, cl
CATCHALOT	1929	36'	Wesley H. Stevens	Big Tancook	tt
COCKAWEE	ca. 1910	32'	Amos H. Stevens	Chester	Y
GERALDINE B.L.	ca. 1935–39	35'	Warren Pearl, Jr	Big Tancook	tt, sld Quebec ca. 1934
GLENDORA	1931	36'	Wesley H. Stevens	Big Tancook	cb; fndrd off Dover 1928
GREEN BOW	ca. 1923	32'	Mason & Langille	Big Tancook	cb; reblt as Y 1949, ld kl, new i.d.
GREEN BOW II (ltr SEA WAY, AIRLIE)	1929	37'	Stanley G. Mason	Big Tancook	
IVANHOE	ca. 1923	34'	Mason & Langille	Big Tancook	
KATHLEEN B.Y.	ca. 1930–35	35'	Melvin H. & Byron Stevens	Big Tancook	
LORNE M.C.	ca. 1923	under 40'	unknown	Big Tancook	
MEEMIE	ca. 1910–12	45'	Reuben Heisler	Chester	Y, ld kl
NORMA PAULINE	1933	34'	Stanley G. Mason	Big Tancook	
ODA B.H.	ca. 1915–20	35'	Alvin G. Stevens	Big Tancook	
PEGGY† (ltr BLACK ROBIN)	ca. 1910–12	44'	Reuben Heisler	Chester	Y, im bal; reblt 1928, new i.d.
RITA	1920	36'	Howard Mason	Big Tancook	fndrd off Louisburg 1922
SALADA	ca. 1915–20	34'	Alvin G. Stevens	Big Tancook	
SEA GULL	ca. 1923	38'	Reuben Heisler	Big Tancook	cb

SEA WAY (ex GREEN BOW II [q.v.]; ltr AIRLIE)	1949	40'	Howard Mason	Chester	Y, mm, ld kl; renmd 1951
SQUANTO	ca. 1906–08	under 40'	Alfred F. Langille	Big Tancook	
STORMALONG	ca. 1936	36'	Wesley H. Stevens	Chester	Y
TAG	ca. 1917	under 40'	unknown	Big Tancook	
TURRET	1930	36'	Raymond & Wesley H. Stevens, Jr	Big Tancook	Modelled by Wesley H. Stevens, Sr
UTOPIA	ca. 1925–30	34'	Wesley H. Stevens	Big Tancook	
VERNA B.	ca. 1935–38	34'	Murray Wilneff	Big Tancook	
X10U8	1940	33'	Howard Mason	Big Tancook	K, mm; tt, sld Ontario 1945
ZAIDA	ca. 1910	under 40'	unknown	Halifax	K, Y

* Compiled from newspaper marine lists and personal interviews.
† Not to be confused with the PEGGY of 1914 (see Appendix 1).

Abbreviations Used in Appendix One

Descriptive Remarks

cb	centreboard
cl	clipper bow
dr	draft
ex	formerly
hw	hardwood-built
i.d.	identity
irn bal	iron ballast
K	knockabout
lap	lapstrake-planked
ld kl	lead keel
l.o.a.	length overall
ltr	later
mm	marconi mainsail
mt	main topmast
o.m.	old measurement
RF	racing fisherman
RR	rum runner
ss	square stern
st	straight stem
W	whaler
Y	yacht

Disposition

aband	abandoned
brkn up	broken up
brnd	burned
cndmd	condemned
clsd	closed
destrd	destroyed
fndrd	foundered
grnd	grounded
lst	lost
n.d.	no date
nr	near
reblt	rebuilt
reg.	register
regrd	registered
renmd	renamed
sld	sold
snk	sank
strnd	stranded
szd	seized by Crown
tt	tourist trade
wrkd	wrecked

APPENDIX TWO

REGISTERED SCHOONERS BUILT AT THE TANCOOKS, 1904–1936*
(By Locale)

	Northwest Cove	Southeast Cove	Little Tancook	Total
1904	1	0	0	1
1905	5 (2 w)†	1 (1 w)	0	6 (3 w)
1906	2	0	3 (1 w)	5 (1 w)
1907	4 (1 w)	1	3 (1 w)	8 (2 w)
1908	9	1	2 (1 w)	12 (1 w)
1909	8	1	2	11
1910	10	3	5	18
1911	14	5	4	23
1912	19	8	3	30
1913	4	2	2	8
1914	5	1	0	6
1915	4	1	0	5
1916	1	2	0	3
1917	5	3	0	8
1918	2	2	0	4
1919	1	1	0	2
1920	0	0	0	0
1921	0	0	0	0
1922	1	0	0	1
1923	2	3	0	5
1924	1	3	0	4
1925	0	5	0	5
1926	0	4	0	4
1927	0	1	0	1
1928	2	3	0	5
1929	1	6	0	7
1930	0	2	0	2
1931	1	4	0	5
1932	1	1	0	2
1933	1	0	0	1
1934	0	0	0	0
1935	0	0	0	0
1936	1	0	0	1
1904–36	105 (3 w)	64 (1 w)	24 (3 w)	193 (7 w)

* Compiled from *Can.LV*, various years, in conjunction with NA, LunSR; NA, AriSR; Can.LCH, LunSR; Can.HCH, HalSR; and Can.SRD, CanSSR: registers of Tancook-built schooners.
† "w" denotes whaler schooner; "5 (2 w)" indicates 5 schooners of which 2 were whalers.

APPENDIX THREE

REGISTERED SCHOONERS BUILT AT THE TANCOOKS, 1904–1936*
(By Disposition)

	Local Ownership	Outside Ownership	Total
1904	0	1	1
1905	4 (2 w)	2 (1 w)	6 (3 w)
1906	4	1 (1 w)	5 (1 w)
1907	1	7 (2 w)	8 (2 w)
1908	0	12 (1 w)	12 (1 w)
1909	1	10	11
1910	6	12	18
1911	4	19	23
1912	8	22	30
1913	3	5	8
1914	2	4	6
1915	0	5	5
1916	1	2	3
1917	5	3	8
1918	3	1	4
1919	1	1	2
1920	0	0	0
1921	0	0	0
1922	0	1	1
1923	3	2	5
1924	3	1	4
1925	3	2	5
1926	2	2	4
1927	0	1	1
1928	3	2	5
1929	2	5	7
1930	1	1	2
1931	2	3	5
1932	1	1	2
1933	1	0	1
1934	0	0	0
1935	0	0	0
1936	1	0	1
1904–36	65 (2 w)	128 (5 w)	193 (7 w)

* Compiled from *Can.LV*, various years, in conjunction with NA, LunSR; NA, AriSR; Can.LCH, LunSR; Can.HCH, HalSR; and Can.SRD, CanSSR: registers of Tancook-built schooners.

† "w" denotes whaler schooner; numbers are inclusive: "4 (2 w)" indicates 4 schooners of which 2 were whalers.

APPENDIX FOUR

REGISTERED SCHOONERS OWNED AT THE TANCOOKS, 1905–1945*

	Big Tancook	Little Tancook	Total
1905	4	0	4
1906	6	2	8
1907	6	1	7
1908	6	1	7
1909	7	1	8
1910	9	3	12
1911	11	6	17
1912	17	4	21
1913	16	4	20
1914	18	5	23
1915	17	4	21
1916	15	3	18
1917	14	4	18
1918	16	4	20
1919	12	4	16
1920	11	3	14
1921	9	3	12
1922	9	3	12
1923	12	3	15
1924	13	3	16
1925	16	3	19
1926	16	2	18
1927	16	2	18
1928	17	1	18
1929	15	1	16
1930	14	1	15
1931	14	1	15
1932	15	1	16
1933	16	1	17
1934	14	1	15
1935	13	1	14
1936	13	1	14
1937	13	1	14
1938	10	1	11
1939	9	1	10
1940	9	1	10
1941	9	1	10
1942	7	1	8
1943	7	1	8
1944	4	1	5
1945	1	0	1

* Compiled from NA, LunSR; Can.LCH, LunSR; and Can.HCH, HalSR: registers of Tancook-owned schooners.

APPENDIX FIVE

ANNUAL FISHERY CATCH AT THE TANCOOKS, 1876–1917*
(All Species)

	Processed Pounds[†]	Market Value
1876	194,000	$ 8,775
1877	620,250	27,248
1878	418,400	18,570
1879	1,042,000	54,828
1880	853,460	31,062
1881	275,500	8,653
1882	591,800	26,488
1883	1,359,400	31,448
1884	2,373,100	103,935
1885	1,090,375	38,945
1886	1,219,109	53,235
1887	1,256,370	57,142
1888	940,070	37,433
1889	958,535	37,414
1890	2,002,801	79,970
1891	1,918,780	75,681
1892	1,112,425	39,370
1893	1,554,500	46,265
1894	‡	‡
1895	1,115,625	76,471
1896	2,920,985	72,307
1897	443,100	13,203
1898	1,065,850	21,921
1899	1,468,600	31,671
1900	1,364,680	55,074
1901	1,433,520	41,389
1902	1,163,750	30,752
1903	1,187,000	27,450
1904	1,185,715	34,791
1905	552,720	14,186
1906	1,393,300	32,325
1907	1,459,600	33,893
1908	1,406,650	28,008
1909	947,210	28,092
1910	1,404,900	27,951
1911	1,016,000	35,175
1912	734,500	16,984
1913	1,500,200	41,379
1914	2,505,512	55,371
1915	1,399,060	49,691

231 Annual Fishery Catch at Tancooks

	Processed Pounds[†]	Market Value
1916	436,980	50,072
1917	1,083,100	[‡]

[*] Compiled and calculated from *Can.RFB*, 1876–1916/17, fishery inspectors' reports, Lunenburg County, Nova Scotia: annual returns of fish landings and catch values, Big and Little Tancook islands; and *Can.CenInd, 1917*, Pt 3: *Fisheries Statistics*, 18–25.
[†] Catch figures for preserved fish converted from hundred-weight and barrels to pounds on the basis of 1 cwt = 100 lbs and 1 bbl = 200 lbs.
[‡] Statistics are unavailable for 1894 and incomplete for 1917.

APPENDIX SIX

ANNUAL FISHERY CATCH AT THE TANCOOKS, 1876–1917*
(Selected Species)

	Dried Cod (cwt)	Dried Haddock (cwt)	Pickled Herring (bbls)	Pickled Mackerel (bbls)
1876	300	0	270	300
1877	700	1,200	450	1,700
1878	360	450	250	1,400
1879	350	250	2,800	2,000
1880	400	65	1,850	2,088
1881	300	150	700	250
1882	550	140	400	1,850
1883	900	210	6,000	200
1884	3,300	400	1,650	8,000
1885	5,007	0	1,900	910
1886	5,058	100	2,070	1,262
1887	2,071	636	1,900	2,458
1888	1,966	292	2,016	840
1889	1,605	0	2,400	920
1890	1,937	441	5,250	2,855
1891	945	475	5,450	2,695
1892	960	385	3,140	1,015
1893	1,170	370	5,000	1,325
1894	–	–	–	–
1895	1,850	545	3,600	170
1896	1,105	490	13,050	87
1897	2,000	325	420	25
1898	1,300	450	1,700	15
1899	2,100	700	2,300	120
1900	2,100	700	1,325	2,000
1901	2,200	910	1,320	1,000
1902	2,200	910	25	20
1903	2,310	912	450	250
1904	3,000	900	1,300	285
1905	240	500	700	150
1906	142	280	4,000	300
1907	145	350	4,000	350
1908	155	300	4,000	95
1909	31	280	4,000	0
1910	2,020	515	3,800	0
1911	4,500	900	1,800	0
1912	845	152	1,473	210
1913	740	175	5,040	550
1914	1,394	768	4,762	539
1915	2,051	852	4,000	478
1916	400	46	17	420
1917	3,015	650	1,150	925

	Dried Cod (cwt)	Dried Haddock (cwt)	Pickled Herring (bbls)	Pickled Mackerel (bbls)
Avg. 1870s	428	633	1,076	1,444
Avg. 1880s	2,116	249	2,189	1,878
Avg. 1890s	1,485	465	4,434	923
Avg. 1900s	1,252	604	2,200	431
Avg. 1910s	1,871	506	3,255	390

* Compiled from *Can.RFB*, 1876–1916/17, fishery inspectors' reports, Lunenburg County, Nova Scotia: annual returns of fish landings, Big and Little Tancook islands; and *Can.CenInd, 1917*, Pt 3: *Fisheries Statistics*, 19–22.

APPENDIX SEVEN

SELECTED MARINE GLOSSARY OF TANCOOK TERMS AND PHRASES

Aberdeen stem	– clipper bow
bastard dory	– a specially designed fishing dory of intermediate size used by Tancook's trawling schooners
boat rock	– large rectangular rock to which mooring gear was attached
bulky boat	– burdensome, short-ended craft with an overly long mid-section
Cape boat	– Cape Island-type motorized fishing boat
cranky boat	– one lacking stiffness or the ability to stand up to a strong breeze without heeling excessively
cutch	– catechu; a commercial wood extract used in tanning sails
deck boat	– a completely decked schooner of 50' to 65' overall length that was employed in dory trawling; a miniature banker
double rigging	– standing rigging consisting of two shrouds on each side of a mast (employed on Tancook schooners over 40' long)
doubling up	– a fishing arrangement in which a non-owning sharesman crewed aboard another man's boat in exchange for a percentage of the financial returns (mostly practised in the whaler era when boats normally had two-man crews)
droguing	– drift fishing with nets for herring or mackerel
dummy	– a sluggish boat that did not sail well
fan transom	– a narrow, straight-sided, triangular-shaped transom such as incorporated in the first counter-sterned Tancook schooners
filled to the gunnels (gunwales)	– said of a schooner so fully loaded with cargo that her deck was nearly awash
flat roofing	– reducing the sail plan of a schooner by shortening its masts and eliminating its staysail (common practice after the introduction of auxiliary motors)
frame	– removable framing mould used in schooner hull construction to shape the body of the vessel
hardwood-built	– said of a schooner planked with native hardwood rather than traditional pine

hatch boat	– an open, undecked schooner of 40' or less in length that was equipped with portable hatches and used primarily for net fishing
jolly boat	– a small, open, clinker-built sloop with transom stern used for inshore fishing; also called a lobster boat
knockabout	– a schooner with no bowsprit and a single stemhead jib (the usual headsail arrangement for small Tancook schooners under 40' long)
makes the water rough where she is	– said of a poorly designed boat that created excessive turbulence as she sailed
progy	– a chum or rising bait composed of chopped herring and fish oil and used in the hook-and-line mackerel fishery
ram boat	– a smaller, sloop-rigged version of the Tancook whaler
rib	– the permanent hull frame of a schooner (see also "timber")
scallop boat	– a small, counter-sterned fishing sloop on Tancook schooner lines used primarily for dragging scallop rakes
seamwork planking	– carvel or plank-on-edge construction
semi-deck boat	– a partially decked schooner of intermediate size measuring 40' to 50' in overall length and used for fishing and coasting
shifting board	– a wooden partition used to hold loose rock ballast in place aboard Tancook schooners
single rigging	– standing rigging consisting of one shroud on each side of a mast (employed on Tancook boats under 40' long)
slung right	– balanced properly (in reference to a vessel's sail plan and the positioning of her masts)
sweet water	– smooth, calm sea with small or nonexistent waves, as in a protected bay (thus, a "sweet-water boat" – one well adapted to such ideal sailing conditions)
timber	– the collective frames of a schooner hull (see also "rib")
transom stern	– counter stern with transom
tripped by the nose	– trimmed by the bow (in reference to adjusting a boat's load water line by forward ballasting)
whaler	– a double-ended, clipper-bowed schooner of under 45' overall length, built prior to 1910; generally used for herring fishing

Reference Abbreviations

NEWSPAPERS AND JOURNALS

- CF *Canadian Fisherman*
- CH *Chronicle-Herald* [Halifax]
- CM *Christian Messenger* [Halifax]
- DFP *Dartmouth* [NS] *Free Press*
- HH *Halifax Herald*
- HJ *Hants Journal* [Windsor, NS]
- HMS *Halifax Mail-Star*
- LP *Lunenburg* [NS] *Progress*
- MC *Morning Chronicle* [Halifax]
- MH *Morning Herald* [Halifax]
- NS *Nova Scotian* [Halifax]
- Ns *Novascotian* [*Chronicle-Herald* magazine insert]
- NYT *New York Times*
- PE *Progress-Enterprise* [Lunenburg, NS]

GOVERNMENT DOCUMENTS (series)

- Can.Cen Canada, Ministry of Agriculture, Census Office, *Census of Canada* (decennial).
- Can.CenInd Canada, Bureau of Statistics, *Census of Industry* (annual).
- Can.LV Canada, Ministry of Marine and Fisheries, *List of Vessels on the Registry Books of the Dominion* (annual).

238 Abbreviations

Can.MsCen Canada, Ministry of Agriculture, Census Office, Manuscript Census Schedules (decennial).
Can.RFB Canada, Ministry of Marine and Fisheries, *Annual Report of the Fisheries Branch.*
Can.RMB Canada, Ministry of Marine and Fisheries, *Annual Report of the Marine Branch.*
Can.RPW Canada, Ministry of Public Works, *Annual Report.*
Can.RS Canada, *Revised Statutes of Canada.*
Can.S Canada, *Statutes of Canada.*
NS.JPHA Nova Scotia, *Journal and Proceedings of the House of Assembly.*
NS.S Nova Scotia, *Statutes of Nova Scotia.*
US.SL United States, *Statutes at Large.*

GOVERNMENT REPOSITORIES (active records)

Can.HCH, HalsR Canada, Ministry of National Revenue, Department of Customs and Excize, Halifax [NS] Customs House, Shipping Registers for the Port of Halifax, Nova Scotia.
Can.LCH, LunsR Canada, Ministry of National Revenue, Department of Customs and Excize, Lunenburg [NS] Customs House, Shipping Registers for the Port of Lunenburg, Nova Scotia.
Can.SRD, CansSR Canada, Ministry of Transport, Department of the Coast Guard, Ship Registration Division, Ottawa, Shipping Registers for the Port of Canso, Nova Scotia.
NS.CLRC Nova Scotia, Department of Lands and Forests, Crown Lands Record Center, Dartmouth.
NS.LunRD Nova Scotia, Department of the Attorney General, Registry of Deeds, Municipality of the District of Lunenburg, Bridgewater.
NS.RG Nova Scotia, Department of Health, Office of the Registrar-General, Halifax.

ARCHIVAL COLLECTIONS

MSM, MSS G.W. Blunt-White Library, Mystic Seaport Museum, Mystic, Connecticut, manuscript collection.
NA, ArisR National Archives of Canada, Ottawa, Records of the Department of Marine (Record Group 42), Shipping Registers for the Port of Arichat, Nova Scotia.
NA, HalsR National Archives of Canada, Ottawa, Records of the Department of Marine (Record Group 42), Shipping Registers for the Port of Halifax, Nova Scotia.
NA, LunsR National Archives of Canada, Ottawa, Records of the Department of Marine (Record Group 42), Shipping Registers for the Port of Lunenburg, Nova Scotia.

PANS, Bus Public Archives of Nova Scotia, Halifax, Business Papers (Manuscript Group 3).
PANS, CC Public Archives of Nova Scotia, Halifax, Church and Community Records (Manuscript Group 4).
PANS, FI Public Archives of Nova Scotia, Halifax, Papers of Families and Individuals (Manuscript Group 1).
PANS, LA Public Archives of Nova Scotia, Halifax, Legislative Assembly Papers (Record Group 5).
PANS, LF Public Archives of Nova Scotia, Halifax, Lands and Forests Records (Record Group 20).
PANS, VS Public Archives of Nova Scotia, Halifax, Vital Statistics Collection (Record Group 32).

MAPS AND CHARTS

Can.HS Canada, Ministry of Energy, Mines and Resources, Hydrographic Service.
Can.SMB Canada, Ministry of Energy, Mines and Resources, Surveys and Mapping Branch.
HBT Halifax, Nova Scotia, Board of Trade.
US.HO United States, Department of the Navy, Hydrographic Office.

Notes

PROLOGUE

Epigraph: MacLennan, *Barometer Rising*, 119.

1 *Fishermen of the Atlantic, 1925*, passim; *Official Reference Book of the Fishermen's Union, 1927*, passim.
2 See *HH*, article, 29 February 1924, supp. 11.
3 Canada, Conservation Commission, *Sea Fisheries of Eastern Canada*, 97–8.
4 Waters, "Bluenose and Codfish," 78.
5 Holdridge, *Northern Lights*, 211.
6 Maury, *Saga of Cimba*, passim.
7 Interview, Thomas Mason, 1 October 1988; *Lloyd's Register of American Yachts, 1939*, 475; NA, LunSR: register of schr *Harold H.*, 1 May 1929. See also Hayden, *Wanderer*, 199–200, and Van de Water, *Real McCoy*, passim.
8 Allen, "Chester Yacht Club," 7; Finney, *Surgeon's Life*, 144–8.

CHAPTER ONE

Epigraph: *HH*, 25 March 1909, 9.

1 Can.SMB, Topographical Map of the Maritime Provinces (1968); see also Can.HS, Chart of the Southeastern Coast of Nova Scotia from Egg Island to West Ironbound Island (1967).
2 Can.SMB, Topographical Map of the Municipality of Lunenburg, Nova Scotia (1977).

3 Can.HS, Chart of Mahone Bay, Nova Scotia (1959).
4 Interview, Thomas Mason, 24 June 1988.
5 Waters, "Bluenose and Codfish," 78.
6 NS.CLRC, old plans, no. 12 (c): memorandum attached to survey map of the Tancook islands, 11 June 1788.
7 DesBrisay, *County of Lunenburg*, 310; DesBarres, *Atlantic Neptune*, vol. 2, ser. 4, pl. 17; Fergusson, *Place-Names and Places*, 664.
8 NS.CLRC, old grant bk 2, 93: grant to Patrick Sutherland, 12 September 1759; Bell, *Foreign Protestants*, 410–11, 431, 509, 565.
9 NS.CLRC, old registry bk, 67: register of grant to Patrick Sutherland, 25 September 1759. See also NS.CLRC, old grant bk 2, 71–3: grant to Jonathan Prescott, 17 September 1759.
10 DesBarres, 2, ser. 4, pl. 17; PANS, LA, ser. A., vol. 1b, no. 132: affidavit of Alexander Thompson, 11 December 1784.
11 NS.CLRC, old grant bk 19, 147: grant to John Henry Fleiger and George Grant, 17 December 1792; NS.CLRC, escheats, no. 120: Patrick Sutherland escheat, 22 October 1792. See also Atkins, *History of Halifax City*, 104, 129, 134, 140.
12 NS.LunRD, registry bks 4, pp. 167, 209, 278; 5, p. 243; and 7, p. 137: land deeds for Big and Little Tancook islands, 1796–1816. See also Stevens and Stevens, *Stevens Families of Nova Scotia*, 70–1.
13 Bell, *Foreign Protestants*, 95–102, 304–5. See also *Encyclopaedia Britannica*, 11th ed., s.v. "Montbéliard."
14 Bell, *Foreign Protestants*, 288–90; Stevens and Stevens, *Stevens Families of Nova Scotia*, 74–5, 184; Can.MsCen, 1861: Lunenburg County, Nova Scotia, town of Tancook, returns for population.
15 Compiled from Can.MsCen, 1861, 1871: Lunenburg County, Nova Scotia, town of Tancook, returns for population. See also Bell, *Foreign Protestants*, 288–90.
16 Medjuck, *Jews of Atlantic Canada*, 31.
17 Post, *Tancook Whalers*, 28; Zinck and Zinck, "Tancook Stevenses," 1.
18 *Can.Cen*, 1871, 1:326–7; 1881, 1:212–13; 1901, 1:308–9; 1921, 1:394–5; 1941, 2:334–5.
19 Bell, *Foreign Protestants*, 99–100, 388–90, 586–602, *passim*; see also Post, *Tancook Whalers*, 28, and Creighton, *Folklore of Lunenburg County*, 1.
20 DesBrisay, *County of Lunenburg*, 159, 281, 312. See also Church, *Topographical Township Map of Lunenburg County, Nova Scotia* (ca. 1883).
21 *Can.Cen*, 1871, 1, 234–7; 1891, 1, 246–7.
22 Can.MsCen, 1881: Lunenburg County, Nova Scotia, town of Tancook, returns for population.
23 Stevens and Stevens, *Stevens Families of Nova Scotia*, 77–8, 86, 103, 105.

243 Notes to pages 11–16

24 Langille, *South Shore Langilles*, 2–3, 48–9; Can.MsCen, 1871, 1881, 1891: Lunenburg County, Nova Scotia, town of Tancook, returns for population.
25 NS.LunRD, registry bks 5–13: land deeds for Big and Little Tancook islands, 1801–48.
26 Haliburton, *Historical and Statistical Account*, 2:128; Can.MsCen, 1861: Lunenburg County, Nova Scotia, town of Tancook, returns for population; *Can.Cen, 1941*, 2:61.
27 Haliburton, *Historical and Statistical Account*, 2:128.
28 NA, HalsR: register of schr *Three Brothers*, 18 October 1827.
29 Bell, *Foreign Protestants*, 101, 300, 316.
30 Ibid., 101, 193.
31 Ibid., 481, 505, 549.
32 NS.Lun.RD, registry bk 6, 83, 264: land deeds transferring farm lots and barns on Big Tancook Island from Jacob and Frederick Baker to David Langille and John Cross, 15 August 1808 and 11 January 1812.
33 Brebner, *Neutral Yankees of Nova Scotia*, 44.
34 PANS, CC, Lunenburg County: Canon E.A. Harris genealogies, Mason family; NS.LunRD, registry bk 4, 32: land deed transferring Knaut's Island from Benjamin Knaut to Peter Mason, 10 May 1794; registry bk 9, 99: land deed transferring Flat Island from Jacob Baker, Jr. to George Mason, 5 April 1828; interviews, Murray A. Mason, 16 June 1988, Thomas Mason, 4 October 1988.
35 *Can.Cen, 1871*, 3:95; *1881*, 2:27.
36 Can.MsCen, 1861: Lunenburg County, Nova Scotia, town of Tancook, returns for agriculture.
37 *Can.Cen, 1871*, 3:196–7; *1881*, 3:142–3; *1891*, 4:30–1.
38 MC, commercial news (imports), 29 December 1874, 3, and 29 November, 8 December 1875, 3.
39 Calculated from statistics in Can.MsCen, 1861: Lunenburg County, Nova Scotia, town of Tancook, returns for agriculture; *Can.Cen, 1871*, 3:26–7; *1881*, 3:94–5.
40 *Can.Cen, 1871*, 1:76–7; *1911*, 1:306.
41 Interview, Thomas Mason, 25 September 1987.
42 Interviews, Thomas Mason, 14, 15 June 1989.
43 Interview, Thomas Mason, 14 June 1989.
44 Brebner, *Canada*, 170.
45 Can.MsCen, 1871, 1881, 1891: Lunenburg County, Nova Scotia, town of Tancook, returns for population.
46 *Can.MsCen, 1861*: Lunenburg County, Nova Scotia, town of Tancook, returns for population and shipping; *Can.Cen, 1871*, 1:77, and 3:262, *1881*, 1:11, 3:278, *1891*, 1:138, *1901*, 1:48–9, *1911*, 1:68; Can.RFB, *1880*, 175, *1891*, 50, *1901*, 82, *1910/11*, 114.

CHAPTER TWO

Epigraph: DesBrisay, *County of Lunenburg*, 313.

1 Howard I. Chapelle, letter to the author, 11 September 1969.
2 NA, HalsR: register of schr *Three Brothers*, 18 October 1827.
3 See, for example: HH, article, 22 November 1952, 4; Fader, "Reminiscence," 5; Post, *Tancook Whalers*, 21.
4 NA, HalsR: registers of schr *Linnet*, 2 April, 15 August 1833.
5 Ibid.: register of schr *Linnet*, 14 June 1843.
6 Ibid.: register of schr *Sandwich*, 18 September 1845; NS.JPHA, *1851*, 2nd sess., app., 89.
7 NA, HalsR: registers of schrs *Dolphin*, 15 May 1848, and *Patience*, 9 September 1848.
8 Ibid.: registers of schrs *Ostrich*, 29 July 1846, and *Isidore*, 14 April 1848 and 6 May 1853. See also ibid.: registers of schrs *British Lady*, 12 August 1867, *J.A. Kirk*, 27 September 1876, and *W.E. Wier*, 18 January 1892; and NA, LunsR: registers of schrs *Sea Slipper*, 24 May 1858, *Sky Lark*, 7 June 1859, *Bella Young*, 2 June 1860, *Bella Barry*, 3 November 1866, *Highland Lass*, 6 August 1869, *Girl I Love*, 23 October 1872, *J.P. Corkum*, 13 January 1877, *Florence B.*, 2 June 1880, *Carrie M.C.*, 16 April 1888, and *Emily L.*, 24 April 1895.
9 NS.CLRC, old plans, no. 12 (c): memorandum attached to survey map of the Tancook islands, 11 June 1788.
10 PANS, LF, crown lands records: order of survey for Tancook, Little Tancook and Star islands, 29 November 1792.
11 Can.MsCen, 1871: Lunenburg County, Nova Scotia, town of Tancook, comment following returns.
12 Interviews, Thomas Mason, 4 October 1986 and 1 October 1987.
13 Interview, Thomas Mason, 19 August 1972.
14 Interviews, Thomas Mason, July 1969, 4 October 1986.
15 NS.RG: certificate of death for Alfred F. Langille, 10 May 1926.
16 Can.MsCen, 1861: Lunenburg County, Nova Scotia, town of Tancook, returns for shipping.
17 Interviews, Thomas Mason, July 1969, 30 September 1986, 25 September 1987, and 14 June 1989, Steadman S. Mason, 4 October 1986.
18 Interview, Thomas Mason, 30 September 1986.
19 Interview, Thomas Mason, 4 October 1986.
20 Can.MsCen, 1871: Lunenburg County, Nova Scotia, town of Tancook, returns for shipping.
21 See, for example, Post, *Tancook Whalers*; Bell, "Passing of the Tancook Whaler"; Lee, "Tancook Whaler-Evolution"; Chapelle, *American Small Sailing Craft*, chap. 3.

22 Jenson, *Fishermen of Nova Scotia*, 35; Bell, "Passing of the Tancook Whaler," 55; Holdridge, *Northern Lights*, 29; Lee, "Tancook Whaler – Evolution," 15.
23 Post, *Tancook Whalers*, 10, 13.
24 NS.JPHA, *1853*, app., 120–1.
25 Chapelle, *American Fishing Schooners*, 37, 51–7; Chapelle, *American Sailing Craft*, 131–2.
26 NA, HalsR: registers of Nova Scotia-built pinkies, 1839–53.
27 Ibid., 1843–47.
28 Ibid.; see also Chapelle, *American Fishing Schooners*, 37–57, passim.
29 Chapelle, *American Small Sailing Craft*, 166; Post, *Tancook Whalers*, 20; MacKean and Percival, *Little Boats*, 100. See also NA, LunsR: registers of Tancook-built whalers, 1911–13.
30 See illustrations in the following: Davis, *American Sailing Ships*, opposite 16–17 and 19, 164, 166–71; Chapelle, *American Small Sailing Craft*, 163–5; Chapelle, *American Fishing Schooners*, 38–57, passim.
31 Stackpole, *The Sea Hunters*, 41, 103–11, 123–30.
32 Hall, *Report on Shipbuilding*, 22; Chapelle, *American Small Sailing Craft*, 42.
33 Chapelle, *American Small Sailing Craft*, 41–3; Hall, *Report on Shipbuilding*, 23.
34 Chapelle, *American Small Sailing Craft*, 41–3; Hall, *Report on Shipbuilding*, 23; Goode, *Fisheries and Fishery Industries*, sec. 5, 2:241.
35 Chapelle, *American Small Sailing Craft*, 42; Goode, *Fisheries and Fishery Industries*, sec. 5, 2:240; Hall, *Report on Shipbuilding*, 24.
36 Perley, *Sea and River Fisheries*, 247.
37 Chapelle, *American Small Sailing Craft*, 139.
38 Ibid, 162.
39 Ibid., 137–8, 141–3.
40 Goode, *Fisheries and Fishery Industries*, sec. 5, 1:137–8.
41 Chapelle, *American Small Sailing Craft*, 143, 164–7.
42 Goode, *Fisheries and Fishery Industries*, sec. 5, 1:144–5; Audubon, *By Himself*, 227.
43 Sabine, *Principal Fisheries*, 78, 170.
44 Balcom, *Lunenburg Fishing Industry*, 3–4, 12, 17–19. See also HH, article, 21 November 1896, 1.
45 Reproduced in Post, *Tancook Whalers*, 8.
46 HH, article, 21 November 1896, 1.
47 LP, news item, 31 May 1881, 2.
48 Ibid.
49 Bell, "Passing of the Tancook Whaler," 56.
50 LP, news item, 31 May 1881, 2.
51 NA, LunsR: registers of schrs *Hattie*, 23 June 1903, *Ellwood*, 13 April 1905,

Anita, 11 April 1905, and *Hazel R.*, 27 January 1916. See also Chapelle, *American Small Sailing Craft*, opposite 174, and Post, *Tancook Whalers*, 16.
52 Chapelle, *American Small Sailing Craft*, 142.
53 Ibid., 162.
54 Post, *Tancook Whalers*, 15.
55 Pullen, "Old Schooners Never Die," 51.
56 Fader, "Reminiscence," 1; Langille, *South Shore Langilles*, xviii, 48.
57 Post, *Tancook Whalers*, 15.
58 Interviews, Thomas Mason, 15 June and 4 October 1986.
59 Can. MsCen, 1861, 1871, 1881, 1891: Lunenburg County, Nova Scotia, town of Tancook, returns for population and shipping; PANS, CC, Lunenburg County: Canon E. A. Harris genealogies, Baker family; *CM*, news item, 19 September 1860, 299; NA, HalSR; register of schr *Dolphin*, 15 May 1848; NS.LunRD, registry bk 20, 357–8: land deeds transferring lots of Big Tancook from Peter Wilneff and John Heisler to John Crooks, 25 June 1866; interviews, Thomas Mason, 24 September, 1 October 1987, Mary Baker, 3 October 1987.
60 Howard I. Chapelle, letter to the author, 11 September 1969; Chapelle, *American Small Sailing Craft*, 162.
61 Bell, "Passing of the Tancook Whaler," 56, 102; Fader, "Reminiscence," 1.
62 Howard I. Chapelle, letter to the author, 11 September 1969.
63 Chapelle, *American Small Sailing Craft*, 162.
64 Interviews, Thomas Mason, 1 October 1988; Murray A. Mason, 5 October 1988; David M. Stevens, 3 October 1988; Perry W. Stevens, 13 June 1986.
65 MacGregor, *Fast Sailing Ships*, 99–121; MacGregor, *The Tea Clippers*, 43–7.
66 MacGregor, *Fast Sailing Ships*, 116, 119.
67 DesBrisay, *County of Lunenburg*, 478; Wallace, *Wooden Ships and Iron Men*, 75–6.
68 Laurette, *John O'Brien*, 77. See also O'Brien's painting of the *Stag*, ibid., 76, and DesBrisay, *County of Lunenburg*, 482.
69 MacGregor, *Fast Sailing Ships*, 114–15.
70 Interviews, Thomas Mason, 5 February and 22 June 1986; see also Can.MsCen, 1891: Lunenburg County, Nova Scotia, town of Tancook, returns for population.
71 Interviews, Murray A. Mason, 16 June 1988, Thomas Mason, 14 June 1989.
72 Interview, Thomas Mason, 4 October 1986.
73 Interview, Thomas Mason, 30 September 1986.
74 Interviews, Thomas Mason, 4 October 1986, Murray A. Mason, 28 September 1987.
75 Interviews, Thomas Mason, 4 October 1986, Murray A. Mason, 28 September 1987.
76 Stevens and Stevens, *Stevens Families of Nova Scotia*, 103; PANS, VS, birth

records for Lunenburg County, 1871, and Halifax County, 1875: births of Wesley H. Stevens, 31 August 1871, and Ida E. and Laura J. Stevens, 7 December 1874; Ibid., marriage records for Lunenburg County, 1895: marriage of Reuben Heisler and Celest Stevens, 21 February 1895; interviews, David M. Stevens, 3 October 1988, Wesley H. Stevens, Jr, 22 June 1988; *CH*, article, 22 November 1952, 4.
77 Interview, Benjamin Heisler, 22 June 1989.
78 Interviews, Thomas Mason, July 1969 and 15 June 1989.
79 Chapelle, *National Watercraft Collection*, 250; Chapelle, *American Small Sailing Craft*, 162–3; Fader, "Reminiscence," 1; Lee, "Tancook Whaler – Evolution," 17; interviews, Thomas Mason, July 1969, Vernon R. Langille, July 1969; see also photo of whalers at Tancook Island, ca. 1905 (photo 4).
80 NA, HalsR: registers of schrs *Three Brothers*, 18 October 1827, *Linnet*, 2 April 1833, *Linnet* (2nd), 14 June 1843, *Sandwich*, 18 September 1845, *Dolphin*, 15 May 1848, and *Patience*, 9 September 1848.
81 Interviews, Thomas Mason, 29 September 1986 and 14 June 1989; Steadman S. Mason, 17 June 1989.
82 Chapelle, *Boatbuilding*, 445.
83 Greenhill, *Archaeology of the Boat*, 61; McGrail, "Viking Age Boatbuilding," 245; Nielsen, *Wooden Boat Designs*, 3; Hall, *Report on Shipbuilding*, 23–5.
84 Nielsen, *Wooden Boat Designs*, 2; Davis, *American Sailing Ships*, 6, 10.
85 Christensen, "Boatbuilding Tools," 252–3; Greenhill, *Archaeology of the Boat*, 64, 178.
86 Phillips-Birt, *Building of Boats*, 158–9; Nielsen, *Wooden Boat Designs*, 6; see also Parker, *Cape Breton Ships and Men*, 29, and Stephens, *Yachting*, 50–1.
87 Interviews, Thomas Mason, July 1969, Vernon R. Langille, July 1969.
88 Greenhill, *Archaeology of the Boat*, 296; Phillips-Birt, *Building of Boats*, 159; Christensen, "Boatbuilding Tools," 239.
89 Phillips-Birt, *Building of Boats*, 149; Greenhill, *Archaeology of the Boat*, 72.
90 Chapelle, *Boatbuilding*, 441.
91 Interviews, Murray A. Mason, 13 June 1986, Thomas Mason, 29 September 1986; *CH*, article, 29 October 1957, 24.
92 Chapelle, *American Small Sailing Craft*, 162–3; Bell, "Passing of the Tancook Whaler," 56; Post, *Tancook Whalers*, 17; Jenson, *Fishermen of Nova Scotia*, 35; Cabot, "New England Double Enders," 125.
93 Interview, Thomas Mason, 4 October 1988.
94 NA, LunsR: 1860–1920; NA, HalsR: 1860–1903; Can.HCH, HalsR: 1904–20.
95 Interview, Thomas Mason, 29 September 1987.
96 NA, LunsR: registers of schrs *St Kilda*, 13 August 1887, *Hattie*, 23 June

1903, *Nina*, 17 March 1903, *Oreda*, 4 April 1904, *Evelyn*, 6 April 1905, *Ellwood*, 8 April 1905, *Anita*, 11 April 1905, *Harper*, 11 July 1911, *Rosanna T.*, 21 July 1911, *George E.H.*, 16 August 1911, *W. Baker*, 18 August 1911, *C.W. Mason*, 13 July 1912, *P.L. Mason*, 13 July 1912, *DeWitt*, 15 July 1912, *Lola R.*, 29 July 1912, *Blanche S.*, 15 August 1912, *Leone G.*, 29 January 1913, *Austin B.*, 23 June 1913, *Elma M.*, 27 June 1913, and *Mildred Baker*, 31 July 1913; NA, HalsR: registers of schrs *Valkyrie*, 10 May 1893, and *Vigilant*, 20 May 1894; Can.HCH, HalsR: register of schr *Willie Roy*, 9 November 1912.
97 Interview, Murray A. Mason, 16 June 1988.
98 Fader, "Reminiscence," 1. See also Allen, "Chester Yacht Club," 2.
99 LP, news item, 18 July 1888, 3.
100 Ibid., 22 August 1888, 3.
101 DesBrisay, *County of Lunenburg*, 313, 483.
102 Allen, "Chester Yacht Club," 3, 5–7.
103 See Greenhill, *Archaeology of the Boat*, 72, and Chapelle, *Boatbuilding*, 45, 48.
104 NA, HalsR: registers of schrs *Valkyrie*, 10 May 1893, and *Vigilant*, 20 May 1894; DesBrisay, *County of Lunenburg*, 313.
105 Fader, "Reminiscence," 4–5.
106 Interviews, Vernon R. Langille, July 1969, Thomas Mason, 14 June 1989.
107 Fader, "Reminiscence," 5; see also Allen, "Chester Yacht Club," 6.
108 NA, LunsR: register of sloop *Falcon*, 12 April 1907.
109 Interviews, Thomas Mason, July 1969, 20 June 1986, 1 October 1988.
110 See, for example, Post, *Tancook Whalers*, 25, 27, and Chapelle, *National Watercraft Collection*, 250.
111 Interview, Thomas Mason, 29 September 1986.
112 Holdridge, *Northern Lights*, 29.
113 Interview, Thomas Mason, 25 September 1987.
114 NA, LunsR: registers of schrs *Harper*, 11 July 1911, *Elma M.*, 27 June 1913, and *Mildred Baker*, 31 July 1913.
115 Ibid.: register of schr *Sunny Day*, 5 July 1915.
116 Interview, Wesley H. Stevens, Jr, 22 June 1988.
117 NA, LunsR: registers of schrs *George E.H.*, 16 August 1911, and *W. Baker*, 18 August 1911.
118 Interview, Thomas Mason, 4 October 1986.
119 Interviews, Steadman S. Mason, 4 October 1986 and 22 June 1988.
120 PANS, VS, birth records for Lunenburg County, 1874: birth of Joseph Reuben Heisler, 21 June 1874; Chapelle, *American Fishing Schooners*, 79–80; Chapelle, *American Sailing Craft*, 89; National Museum of American History, Washington, Div. of Marine Transportation, USNM models no. 326522 and no. 326527: builders' half-models of unidentified

Mahone Bay, Nova Scotia, fishing schooners, 1871 and 1888; see also Armour and Lackey, *Sailing Ships of the Maritimes*, 165.
121 Fader, "Reminiscence," 4.
122 Ibid.
123 Chapelle, *History of American Sailing Ships*, 254; Chapelle, *The National Watercraft Collection*, 170, 226–8; Chapelle, *American Fishing Schooners*, 172–6; Chapelle, *American Sailing Craft*, 86–8.
124 Can.RFB, 1891–99, annual reports of the Fisheries Protection Service of Canada, passim, in conjunction with Chapelle, *American Fishing Schooners*, 172–212, passim; NA, LunsR: registers of various fishing schooners, especially schrs *Triton*, 7 May 1891, *Atlanta*, 4 April 1892, *Yucatan*, 9 November 1893, *Dora*, 3 May 1894, and *Athlon*, 25 September 1895; Armour and Lackey, *Sailing Ships of the Maritimes*, photographs and plans, 193, 195.
125 Interview, Perry W. Stevens, 13 June 1986.
126 Interview, Thomas Mason, 4 October 1988; Fader, "Reminiscence," 3.
127 Interviews, Thomas Mason, 25 September 1987 and 4 October 1988, Steadman S. Mason, 4 October 1986; NA, LunsR: registers of schrs *Beulah W.*, 19 August 1911, and *Vernie S.*, 19 June 1912.
128 Chapelle, "Speed Under Sail," 67–8; Chapelle, *History of American Sailing Ships*, 342; Stephens, *American Yachting*, 120, 129, 177, 190.
129 Herreshoff, *Capt. Nat Herreshoff*, 163.
130 Interviews, Thomas Mason, 4 October 1988, Steadman S. Mason, 4 October 1988; NA, LunsR: register of schr *Tacoma*, 15 August 1911; Can.HCH, HalsR: registers of schr *Tacoma* (later *Adare*), 28 April 1913 and 23 March 1920.
131 Interviews, Thomas Mason, July 1969 and 1 October 1988.
132 See Chapelle, *Boatbuilding*, 49.
133 See Chapelle, *National Watercraft Collection*, 227, 229–31, and Chapelle, *The American Fishing Schooners*, 174–5, 180–9, 197–201.
134 NA, LunsR: registers of various Lunenburg fishing schooners, 1891–1905.
135 Interviews, Thomas Mason, 12 June 1986 and 25 September 1987.
136 NA, LunsR: registers of Tancook-built schooners, 1904–11.
137 Interviews, Thomas Mason, July 1969 and 4 October 1988.
138 Howard I. Chapelle, letter to the author, 11 September 1969; see also Chapelle, *National Watercraft Collection*, 250.
139 Interviews, Benjamin Heisler, July 1969, David M. Stevens, 20 June 1988.
140 PANS, VS, marriage records for Lunenburg County, 1895: marriage of Reuben Heisler and Celest Stevens, 21 February 1895; interview, Benjamin Heisler, 22 June 1989.
141 Post, *Tancook Whalers*, 30. See also Stevens and Stevens, *Stevens Families of Nova Scotia*, 103.

142 Interview, Steadman S. Mason, 22 June 1988.
143 Interviews, Benjamin Heisler, July 1969 and 22 June, 4 October 1989; see also Keith, "Ben Heisler," 4-C.
144 Interviews, Vernon R. Langille, July 1969, Steadman S. Mason, 4 October 1988.
145 Interviews, David M. Stevens, 20 June and 3 October 1988, Perry W. Stevens, 16 June 1989, Thomas Mason, July 1969; *CH*, article, 6 April 1982, 10.
146 Holdridge, *Northern Lights*, 29.
147 Post, *Tancook Whalers*, 21.
148 Interviews, Benjamin Heisler, July 1969, David M. Stevens, 20 June and 3 October 1988.
149 Chapelle, *American Sailing Craft*, 96–8; Chapelle, *National Watercraft Collection*, 171; Chapelle, *American Fishing Schooners*, 215, 231, 234; *Can.RFB*, 1898–1900, annual reports of the Fisheries Protection Service of Canada, passim.
150 Chapelle, *American Sailing Craft*, 96, 98; Chapelle, *National Watercraft Collection*, 232; Chapelle, *American Fishing Schooners*, 219–20, 245.
151 Chapelle, *American Sailing Craft*, 99–104; Chapelle, *National Watercraft Collection*, 172, 233; Chapelle, *American Fishing Schooners*, 223–7.
152 *HH*, news item, 5 October 1906, 3; NA, LunSR: register of schr *Henry L. Montague*, 22 October 1906; Maritime Museum of the Atlantic, Halifax, painting no. M 73.10.1: schr *Henry L. Montague*.
153 *HH*, news items, 19 March 1908, 9, 4 June 1908, 9, and 31 December 1921, 13, photograph, 5 February 1923, 11; NA, LunSR: registers of schrs *Clintonia* and *Vivian C. Walters*, 27 March and 6 June 1908; Thomas, *Fast and Able*, 136.
154 *HH*, news items, 16, 18, 25 June 1908, 9; NA, LunSR: register of schr *Minnie H. Mosher*, 23 June 1908.
155 *HH*, news item, 31 December 1917, 20, article, 30 December 1922, 8, advertisement, 31 December 1920, supp., 11.
156 *HH*, news items, 31 December 1917, 20, 1 January 1918, 9, and 31 December 1920, supp., 13; *PE*, news item, 9 January 1918, 1; NA, LunSR: register of schr *General Haig*, 8 March 1918.
157 *HH*, news items, 31 December 1918, 15, 19 September 1919, 7, 11 December 1919, 11, AND 7 April 1920, 3; NA, LunSR: register of schr *Shepherd King*, 17 June 1918.
158 *HH*, news item, 5 April 1907, 2.
159 Interviews, David M. Stevens, 20 June and 3 October 1988.
160 Interviews, Benjamin Heisler, July 1969, Thomas Mason, 23 June 1988.
161 NA, LunSR: registers of schrs *Nova Zembla*, 12 February 1884, and *Hispaniola*, 7 April 1903; *Can.RFB*, 1884–1907, annual lists of vessels

receiving fishing bounties, Lunenburg County, Nova Scotia; *PE*, news item, 20 March 1907, 8.
162 Stevens and Stevens, *Stevens Families of Nova Scotia*, 129; interview, David M. Stevens, 3 October 1988.
163 *CH*, article, 21 December 1976, 21; NS.LunRD, registry bk 72, 257: land deed transferring lot on Big Tancook from Amos H. Stevens to Randolph B. Stevens, 19 February 1910; NA, LunSR: register of schr *Bonnie B.*, 12 June 1908; Can.SRD, CanSSR: register of schr *Irbessa*, 10 August 1908.
164 *Can.RFB*, 1902–09/10, annual reports of the Fisheries Protection Service of Canada, passim, in conjunction with Chapelle, *American Fishing Schooners*, 226, 249–52, 268–85, passim.
165 Howard I. Chapelle, letter to the author, 11 September 1969.
166 O'Leary, "Maine Sea Fisheries," 267–8.
167 *Can.RFB*, 1900, 269.
168 Chapelle, *American Fishing Schooners*, 292.
169 *Can.RFB*, 1900–06, annual reports of the Fisheries Protection Service of Canada, passim, in conjunction with Chapelle, *American Fishing Schooners*, 213–66, passim. See also vessels listed in Thomas, *Fast and Able*, 86–125, passim; Church and Connolly, *American Fishermen*, 179–90, passim; and O'Hearn, *New England Fishing Schooners*, passim.
170 Interview, Vernon R. Langille, July 1969.
171 NA, LunSR: register of schr *Togo*, 7 July 1905; Fader, "Reminiscence," 3.
172 Interview, Perry W. Stevens, 2 October 1989.
173 NA, LunSR: registers of schrs *Matilda H.*, 10 June 1911, and *Tacoma*, 15 August 1911.
174 Erhard, *First in its Class*, 66–8; Chapelle, *American Fishing Schooners*, 224; Hilchie, "Chester Yacht Club," 2; Allen, "Chester Yacht Club," 6.
175 *Can.RFB*, 1908/09, 355; 1909/10, 361. See also Chapelle, *American Fishing Schooners*, 269–72.
176 Interview, Thomas Mason, 4 October 1988; NA, LunSR: registers of schrs *S. F. Levy*, 18 July 1911, *Elsie C.*, 24 July 1911, *Mianus*, 20 March 1912, and *Cecil V. L.*, 15 June 1912.
177 Pugsley, "Chester, Nova Scotia," photo insert, 16–17.
178 *HH*, news item, 21 October 1910, 5.
179 Interviews, Thomas Mason, 15 June and 29 September 1986.
180 See Chapelle, *American Small Sailing Craft*, 166.
181 Interview, Thomas Mason, 29 September 1986.
182 *CH*, article, 29 October 1957, 24.
183 NA, LunSR, and Can.HCH, HalSR: registers of Tancook-built schooners, 1904–20.

184 Interview, Thomas Mason, 15 June 1989. See also Holdridge, *Northern Lights*, 28–9, and Stevens and Stevens, *Stevens Families of Nova Scotia*, 103–5.
185 Interview, Thomas Mason, 5 February 1989. For the general impact of the 1914–18 construction boom, see also Raddall, *Halifax*, 264.
186 Interviews, Vernon R. Langille, July 1969, Steadman S. Mason, 4 October 1988.
187 NA, LunSR: register of schr *Bernice*, 20 June 1912; Langille, *South Shore Langilles*, 48–9.
188 NA, LunSR; Can.HCH, HalSR; and Can.SRD: registers of Tancook-built schooners, 1904–45, including NA, LunSR: register of schr *Silver Oak*, 21 April 1917.
189 Interview, Thomas Mason, 4 October 1986.
190 Interviews, Murray A. Mason, 28 September 1987, Thomas Mason, 5 February, 22 June 1989.
191 Interviews, Thomas Mason, 20 June 1986 and 15 June 1989, Benjamin Heisler, 22 June 1989, Murray A. Mason, 16 June 1988.
192 Interviews, Benjamin Heisler, July 1969, Thomas Mason, July 1969, 4 October 1986, and 3 October 1989. See also Keith, "Ben Heisler," 4-C, and Women's Institute of Nova Scotia, *History of Chester*, 84.
193 Interviews, Steadman S. Mason, 4 October 1986, Perry W. Stevens, 16 June 1989, Benjamin Heisler, 22 June 1989. Mason and Heisler subscribed to the arson theory, while Stevens, who worked at the shop, credited the storage of flammable materials near a window facing the sun.
194 HH, news item, 22 November 1927, 13.
195 NA, LunSR; Can.HCH, HalSR; Can.LCH, LunSR; and Can.SRD, CanSR: registers of Tancook-built schooners, 1904–45.
196 Interviews, Thomas Mason, 30 September 1986 and 15 June 1989; Stevens and Stevens, *Stevens Families of Nova Scotia*, 103–5.
197 Interviews, Thomas Mason, July 1969, 20 June 1986, and 1 October 1987, Guy B. Stevens, 20 June 1988; NA, LunSR: register of schr *Mother*, 21 July 1924; Can.LCH, LunSR: registers of schrs *Dixie Arrow*, 12 May 1928, *Advantage*, 5 September 1929, and *Gerald L.C.*, 9 June 1933; Can.HCH, HalSR: register of schr *Dorothy and Ella*, 6 June 1931; Women's Institute of Nova Scotia, *History of Chester*, 58.
198 Interview, Steadman S. Mason, 4 October 1988.
199 Interviews, Thomas Mason, July 1969 and 25 June 1990. See also PE, article, 5 February 1964, 5.
200 Interview, Harold W. Stevens, July 1969; NS, article, 31 May 1986, 4; Stevens and Stevens, *Stevens Families of Nova Scotia*, 129; unidentified newspaper clipping in the possession of Perry W. Stevens.
201 Interview, Thomas Mason, 12 June 1986.

253   Notes to pages 67–71

202 Unidentified sail plan, Stevens sail loft, Second Peninsula, Lunenburg, Nova Scotia.
203 Interview, Thomas Mason, 19 August 1972.
204 Interviews, Guy B. Stevens, 20 June 1988, Wesley H. Stevens, Jr, 22 June 1988; HH, news item, 25 April 1931, 25.
205 Interviews, Murray A. Mason, 21 June 1989, Thomas Mason, 15 June 1989.
206 Post, *Tancook Whalers*, 21.
207 NA, LunSR; NA, AriSR; Can.HCH, HalSR; Can.LCH, LunSR; CanSRD, CanSSR: registers of Tancook-built schooners, 1904–32. See especially Can.SRD, CanSSR: registers of schrs *Sarah Pauline*, 23 April 1924, and *Nelson L.*, 9 July 1929; NA, LunSR: register of schr *Silver Oak*, 21 April 1917; and Can.LCH, LunSR: register of schr *Morning Star II*, 15 August 1930.
208 Interviews, Thomas Mason, 20 June 1986 and 1 October 1988, Murray A. Mason, 21 June 1989; CH, article, 29 October 1957, 24; NS., LunRD, registry bk 74, 98, 551: land deeds transferring lot at Southeast Cove, Big Tancook from Joshua Mason to Stanley G. Mason and Vernon R. Langille, 18 April 1911, and from Vernon R. Langille to Stanley G. Mason, 5 October 1911.
209 Interviews, Thomas Mason, 20 June 1986 and 22 June 1989.
210 NA, LunSR; Can.HCH, HalSR; Can.LCH, LunSR; and Can.SRD, CanSSR: registers of Tancook-built schooners, 1907–45.
211 Interviews, Thomas Mason, 20 June 1986 and 23 June 1988, Murray A. Mason, 1 October 1987, Hovey Slauenwhite, 30 September 1987. See also NA, LunSR: registers of schrs *White Birch*, 21 May 1918, *Bluebeard*, 30 June 1923, *Tyrienne S.*, 4 August 1924, and *Francis M.R.*, 2 May 1925; Can.HCH, HalSR: register of schr *Elsie B. Young*, 15 May 1923; and Can.SRD, CanSSR: register of schr *Sarah Pauline*, 23 April 1924.
212 Interview, Hovey Slauenwhite, 30 September 1987.
213 Interview, Murray A. Mason, 5 October 1988.
214 Interview, Thomas Mason, 29 September 1987.
215 Interviews, Hovey Slauenwhite, 30 September 1987, Sadie I. Langille, 18 June 1988.
216 NA, LunSR: registers of schrs *Cecil V.L.*, 15 June 1912, *Gwendolyn H.*, 28 June 1912, *Lois M.C.*, 12 July 1912, *Betty B.*, 6 August 1912, and *Howard Stanley*, 20 June 1913.
217 Interviews, Vernon R. Langille, July 1969, Hovey Slauenwhite, 30 September 1987; NA, LunSR: register of schr *Cecil V.L.*, 15 June 1912.
218 Interviews, Murray A. Mason, 28 September 1987, Thomas Mason, 20 June 1986, 24 September 1987, and 5 February 1989.
219 NA, LunSR: register of schr *Howard Stanley*, 20 June 1913.

220 Interviews, Thomas Mason, 4 October 1986, Cecil F. Langille, 4 October 1989; Langille, *South Shore Langilles*, 50; NS.LunRD, registry bk 81, 599: land deed transferring lot at Indian Point from Jacob Hiltz to Vernon R. Langille, 18 January 1917.
221 Interviews, Thomas Mason, July 1969 and 25 September 1987.
222 Post, *Tancook Whalers*, 20.
223 Interviews, Murray A. Mason, 16 June 1988.
224 HH, article, 31 December 1917, 21.
225 Interview, Thomas Mason, 25 September 1987.
226 Interview, Thomas Mason, 4 October 1988. See also Can.LCH, LunSR: register of schr *Patavana*, 28 November 1929.
227 HMS, editorial, 5 September 1962, 4; interview, Thomas Mason, July 1969.
228 NA, LunSR; NA, AriSR; Can.HCH, HalSR; Can.LCH, LunSR; and Can.SRD, CanSSR: registers of Tancook-built schooners, 1904–45.
229 Interview, Thomas Mason, 29 September 1986.
230 Interviews, Steadman S. Mason, 4 October 1986, Thomas Mason, 26 September 1987.
231 Interviews, Thomas Mason, 19 August 1972, 29 September and 4 October 1986, and 15 June 1989.
232 Interview, Thomas Mason, 25 September 1987.
233 Interviews, Thomas Mason, 1 October 1987, Murray A. Mason, 16 June 1988, Guy B. Stevens, 20 June 1988, Wesley H. Stevens, Jr, 22 June 1988; HH, news items, 27 August 1929, 13, and 25 April 1931, 25.
234 NA, LunSR; NA, AriSR; Can.HCH, HalSR; Can.LCH, LunSR; and Can.SRD, CanSSR: registers of Tancook-built schooners, 1904–45.
235 NA, LunSR; NA, AriSR; Can.HCH, HalSR; Can.LCH, LunSR; and Can.SRD, CanSSR: registers of Tancook-built schooners, 1904–45.
236 NA, LunSR; NA, AriSR; Can.HCH, HalSR; Can.LCH, LunSR; and Can.SRD, CanSSR: registers of Tancook-built schooners, 1904–45.
237 Interview, Thomas Mason, 29 September 1986.
238 NA, LunSR; NA, AriSR; Can.HCH, HalSR; Can.LCH, LunSR; and Can.SRD, CanSSR: registers of Tancook-built schooners, 1905–12, 1930–34.
239 Interview, Thomas Mason, 29 September 1986.
240 Interviews, Thomas Mason, 12 June, 30 September 1986.
241 Can.RFB, 1906–1912/13, fishery inspectors' reports, Lunenburg County, Nova Scotia: annual returns of fish landings, Big and Little Tancook islands.
242 NA, LunSR; NA, AriSR; Can.HCH, HalSR; Can.LCH, LunSR; and Can.SRD, CanSSR: registers of Tancook-built schooners, 1904–45, especially 1910–12.
243 *Can.RFB, 1911/12*, 118; *1912/13*, 116.
244 NA, LunSR: registers of schooners built and owned at the Tancooks, 1905–12.

245 Calculated from *Can.RFB*, 1910/11–1916/17, fishery inspectors' reports, Lunenburg County, Nova Scotia: annual returns of fish landings and catch values, Big and Little Tancook islands.
246 Canada, Ministry of Marine and Fisheries, *Report of the Royal Commission Investigating the Fisheries*, 33, 89–92; HH, article, 6 October 1914, 9.
247 NYT, article, 10 September 1913, 8–9; HH, news items, 10 October 1913, 11, and 6 January 1914, 13.
248 Barrett, "Development and Underdevelopment," 20; HH, articles, 30 December 1916, 24; Canada, *Report Investigating the Fisheries*, 124–5; CF, February 1917, 40.
249 Interview, Thomas Mason, 29 September 1986.
250 NA, LunSR; NA, AriSR; Can.HCH, HalSR; Can.LCH, LunSR; Can.SRD, CanSSR: registers of Tancook-built schooners, 1904–45, especially 1904–14.
251 Post, *Tancook Whalers*, 20; Jenson, *Fishermen of Nova Scotia*, 35.
252 Interviews, Thomas Mason, 29 September 1986 and 1 October 1988.
253 Interview, Thomas Mason, 29 September 1986; US.HO, Chart of the Southeast Coast of Nova Scotia (1918).
254 HH, article, 20 January 1915, 9.
255 Ibid., 1 January 1934, sec. 3, 1; Interview, Hovey Slauenwhite, 30 September 1987.
256 Can.HCH, HalSR; registers of stmrs *Grace*, 16 April 1907, *Seacrest*, 30 March 1908, and *Hilford*, 7 April 1908.
257 NA, LunSR: registers of schrs *Laura M. Levy*, 19 December 1910, *Dan Patch*, 30 January 1911, *Elsie C.*, 24 July 1911, and *Sealer*, 17 August 1911.
258 NA, LunSR; NA, AriSR; Can.HCH, HalSR; Can.SRD, CanSSR: registers of Tancook-built schooners, 1910–18; Interview, Thomas Mason, July 1969.
259 NA, LunSR; NA, AriSR; Can.HCH, HalSR; Can.LCH, LunSR; Can.SRD, CanSSR: registers of Tancook-built schooners, 1905–37; Women's Institute of Nova Scotia, *History of Chester*, 87.
260 Interviews, Murray A. Mason, 21 June 1989, Thomas Mason, 1 October 1989.
261 Post, *Tancook Whalers*, 43, 46.
262 Interviews, Thomas Mason, 29 September 1986 and 1 October 1989.
263 CH, article, 29 October 1957, 24.
264 HH, article, 20 January 1915, 9.
265 Calculated from *Can.RFB*, 1910/11–1916–17, fishery inspectors' reports, Lunenburg County, Nova Scotia: annual returns of fishing vessels, fish landings and catch values, Big and Little Tancook islands. See also *CanRFB, 1910/11*, 114, 126–7; *1914/15*, 142, 154–5.
266 Interview, Murray A. Mason, 16 June 1986.
267 Interview, Thomas Mason, 23 June 1988.

268 Interview, Thomas Mason, 1 October 1988.
269 Interview, Thomas Mason, 17 June 1989.
270 NA, LunSR; NA, AriSR; Can.HCH, HalSR; Can.LCH, LunSR; Can.SRD, CanSSR: registers of Tancook-built schooners, 1904–45. See also footnote, p. 87.
271 Interview, Thomas Mason, 29 September 1987.
272 Interviews, Thomas Mason, 15 June 1986, 24 September 1987, and 1 October 1988, Murray A. Mason, 16 June 1986.
273 Interviews, Thomas Mason, 19 August 1972 and 24 September 1987, Murray A. Mason, June 1985 and 16 June 1986.
274 Interviews, Thomas Mason, 29 September 1986 and 8 June 1989, Steadman S. Mason, 17 June 1989.
275 Sailmaker's sail plans, schrs *Comet G.*, *Mianus*, *Tancook*, and *Haig*, Stevens sail loft, Second Peninsula, Lunenburg, Nova Scotia; NA, LunSR: registers of schrs *Mianus*, 27 March 1912, *Comet G.*, 8 June 1912, *Tancook*, 30 April 1914, and *Haig*, 7 May 1917.
276 Can.HCH, HalSR: registers of schrs *Gladys E.B.*, 5 December 1911, and *Tacoma*, 28 April 1913.
277 Interview, Thomas Mason, 4 October 1988.
278 Ibid.
279 Sailmaker's sail plans, schrs *Mianus* and *Holly C.*, Stevens sail loft, Second Peninsula, Lunenburg, Nova Scotia; NA, LunSR: registers of schrs *Mianus*, 27 March 1912, and *Holly C.*, 1 August 1929; Can.LCH, LunSR: register of schr *Patavana*, 28 November 1929. See also figures 9, 19, 21, and photos 20, 22, 48.
280 Interviews, Thomas Mason, 25 September 1987 and 4 October 1988, Murray A. Mason, 18 June 1986.
281 Interviews, Thomas Mason, July 1969 and 26 September 1987.
282 Interview, Thomas Mason, 29 September 1986.
283 See plans in Post, *Tancook Whalers*, 17, 21, 24, 26, 46, and Chapelle, *American Small Sailing Craft*, 164, 167.
284 Interviews, Murray A. Mason, 18 June 1986, Thomas Mason, 1 October 1988.
285 Interviews, Thomas Mason, 25 September 1985 and 18 June 1986; sailmaker's sail plans, schrs *Amasonia*, *Comet G.*, *Flosie*, *Dagon*, *Mianus*, *Tancook*, *Haig*, and *Holly C.*, Stevens sail loft, Second Peninsula, Lunenburg, Nova Scotia. See also figure 19.
286 Herreshoff, *Capt. Nat. Herreshoff*, 279.
287 Carrick and Henderson, *John G. Alden*, 128–9, 134–6.
288 Interviews, Thomas Mason, 12 June 1986 and 1 October 1988.
289 Interview, Thomas Mason, 24 June 1988.
290 Interviews, Thomas Mason, 12 June 1986 and 23 June 1988.
291 Merkel and MacAskill, *Schooner Bluenose*, 15; Gillespie, *Bluenose Skipper*, 60.

257 Notes to pages 100–9

292 Interview, Hovey Slauenwhite, 30 September 1987. See also NA, LunSR: register of schr *Tyrienne S.*, 4 August 1924.
293 Based on an examination of existing half-models; also, interview, Thomas Mason, 19 August 1972.
294 Interviews, Thomas Mason, July 1969 and 22 June 1989, Murray A. Mason, 21 June 1989, Perry W. Stevens, 16 June 1989, Steadman S. Mason, 17 June 1989.
295 Interviews, Thomas Mason, July 1969 and 14, 15, 17, 22 June 1989, Murray A. Mason, 21 June 1989.
296 Interview, Thomas Mason, 25 June 1990.
297 Interviews, Thomas Mason, 25 June 1990, Murray A. Mason, 26 June 1990, Gerald L. Stevens, 25 June 1992.
298 Interviews, Thomas Mason, 19 August 1972 and 29 September, 4 October 1986.
299 Interview, Thomas Mason, July 1969.
300 Interviews, Thomas Mason, July 1969 and 29 September 1986. See also Can.SRD, CanSSR: registers of schrs *Petawawa*, 12 November 1912, *Sarah Pauline*, 23 April 1924, and *Nelson L.*, 9 July 1929; NA, LunSR: registers of schrs *Silver Oak*, 21 April 1917, and *White Birch*, 21 May 1918; Can.LCH, LunSR: registers of schrs *Marion C.*, 9 May 1927, and *Morning Star II*, 15 August 1930.
301 Interview, Thomas Mason, July 1969; NA, LunSR: register of schr *Bluebeard*, 30 June 1923; Can.LCH, LunSR: register of schr *Patavana*, 28 November 1929; and Can.HCH, HalSR: register of schr *Elsie B. Young*, 15 May 1923.
302 Interview, Guy B. Stevens, 20 June 1988.
303 Interview, Thomas Mason, July 1969.
304 Interview, Thomas Mason, July 1969 and 1 October 1988.
305 Interview, Thomas Mason, 1 October 1988.
306 Interviews, Thomas Mason, 25 June 1990, Gerald L. Stevens, 25 June 1992.
307 Interviews, Thomas Mason, 25 June 1990, Murray A. Mason, 26 June 1990, Gerald L. Stevens, 25 June 1992.
308 Interview, Thomas Mason, 25 June 1990.
309 Interviews, Thomas Mason, July 1969 and 24 September, 1 October 1987, Murray A. Mason, 17 June 1986.
310 Interviews, Thomas Mason, July 1969 and 24 September, 1 October 1987, Murray A. Mason, 13 June 1986.
311 Interviews, Thomas Mason, July 1969, 24 September 1987 and 1 October 1988, Murray A. Mason, 13 June 1986.
312 Interviews, Thomas Mason, 1 October 1987 and 1 October 1988.
313 Interview, Thomas Mason, 1 October 1988.
314 Interview, Thomas Mason, 29 September 1987.
315 HH, news items, 17 April 1924, 13, and 11 March 1930, 11.

316 Interview, Thomas Mason, 29 September 1987.
317 Interviews, Murray A. Mason, 29 September 1987, and Thomas Mason, 29 September 1987.
318 Fader, "Reminiscence," 1; Pugsley, "Chester, Nova Scotia," 3–4. See also Bell, "Passing of the Tancook Whaler," 55.
319 Interview, Thomas Mason, July 1969.
320 Ibid.

CHAPTER THREE

Epigraph: Creighton, *Folklore of Lunenburg County*, 83.

1 Blunt, *American Coast Pilot*, 105.
2 *Can.RFB*, 1876–1916/17, fishery inspectors' reports, Lunenburg County, Nova Scotia: annual returns of fishing gear and fish landings, Big and Little Tancook islands; interviews, Thomas Mason, 25 September 1987, Murray A. Mason, 21 June 1989.
3 *NS.JPHA, 1851*, 2nd sess., app., 89.
4 Perley, *Sea and River Fisheries*, 247.
5 US. HO, Chart of the Southwest Coast of Nova Scotia (1918).
6 *Can.RFB*, 1870, 297.
7 *Can.Cen*, 1871, 3: 262–3.
8 NA, LunsR: registers of schrs *Sea Slipper*, 24 May 1858, *Sky Lark*, 7 June 1859, *Bella Young*, 2 June 1860, and *Highland Lass*, 6 August 1869; Can.MsCen, 1871: Lunenburg County, Nova Scotia, town of Tancook, returns for shipping.
9 NA, HalsR and NA, LunsR: registers of Tancook-owned schooners, 1845–1905; *Can.RFB*, 1883–1905, annual lists of vessels receiving fishing bounties, Lunenburg County, Nova Scotia.
10 NA, LunsR: register of schr *Bella Barry*, 3 November 1866; *LP*, marine list, 5 August 1879, 3.
11 *HH*, article, 21 November 1896, 1.
12 *Can.RFB*, 1876, 234–5.
13 *MC, MH, HH*, commercial news (imports), September–December, 1879–99, passim.
14 Interviews, Thomas Mason, 19 August 1972 and 1 October 1987.
15 *Can.RFB*, 1870, 297.
16 *Can.RPW*, 1872, 24; 1873, 28, app., 51. See also DesBrisay, *County of Lunenburg*, 313.
17 *Can.RPW*, 1909, 46; interview, Thomas Mason, 24 June 1988.
18 Interviews, Thomas Mason, 1 October 1988, Wesley H. Stevens, Jr, 22 June 1988.
19 Interviews, Thomas Mason, 24 June 1988 and 25 June 1990.

20 Interviews, Thomas Mason, 24 June 1988 and 25 June 1990.
21 *Can.RFB, 1870*, 297.
22 *Can.s*, 45 Vict. (1882), chap. 18; *Can.RFB, 1883*, lxxiii–lxxiv.
23 Innis, *Cod Fisheries*, 372; Ryan, *Fish out of Water*, 82–3.
24 Calculated from *Can.RFB, 1881*, 38–9; *1882*, 34–5; *1883*, 52–3; *1884*, 116–17.
25 Can.MsCen, 1881, 1891: Lunenburg County, Nova Scotia, town of Tancook, returns for population.
26 *Can.RFB*, 1884–1914, fishery inspectors' reports, Lunenburg County, Nova Scotia: annual returns of fish landings (converted from cwts. and bbls. to lbs.) and catch values, Big and Little Tancook islands. See also, Grant, *Canadian Atlantic Fishery*, 22–5.
27 *NYT*, article, 10 September 1913, 8–9; *HH*, news items, 10 October 1913, 11, and 6 January 1914, 13. See also Innis, *Cod Fisheries*, 422, 431, and Balcom, *Lunenburg Fishing Industry*, 43.
28 *HH*, articles, 20 December 1916, 24, 31 December 1918, 15, and 31 December 1920, supp., 11; *CF*, January 1917, 10, and February 1917, 40; Canada, *Report Investigating the Fisheries*, 124–5. See also Barrett, *Development and Underdevelopment*, 20, and Grant, *Canadian Atlantic Fishery*, 30.
29 *HH*, article, 31 December 1918, 15.
30 *Can.RFB*, 1876–1916/17, fishery inspectors' reports, Lunenburg County, Nova Scotia: annual returns of fish landings, catch values, vessels and boats, and fishing gear and facilities, Big and Little Tancook islands; *Can.RFB*, 1883–1916/17, annual lists of vessels receiving fishing bounties, Lunenburg County, Nova Scotia. See also Canada, *Report Investigating the Fisheries*, 125.
31 *Can.RFB, 1914/15*, 142–3, 154–7, 362–5.
32 *HH*, articles, 31 December 1920, supp., 11, 17, and 31 December 1921, 13; Canada, *Report Investigating the Fisheries*, 44, 124–5. See also Grant, *Canadian Atlantic Fishery*, 31–2, and Balcom, *Lunenburg Fishing Industry*, 45.
33 *US.SL*, vol. 42 (1921–23), pt 1, chap. 356, sec. 1; *NYT*, article, 10 September 1913, 8–9; see also Canada, *Report Investigating the Fisheries*, 44.
34 Forbes, *Maritime Rights Movement*, 55–6, 65; Grant, *Canadian Atlantic Fishery*, 136; Innis, *Cod Fisheries*, 431.
35 *Can.Cen, 1911*, 1, 68; *1921*, 1, 255; *1931*, 2, 171.
36 NA, LunsR and Can.LCH, LunsR: registers of Tancook-owned schooners, 1905–36.
37 Canada, *Report Investigating the Fisheries*, 125; Nova Scotia, *Royal Commission, Provincial Economic Inquiry*, 147.
38 Interview, Thomas Mason, July 1969.
39 Balcom, *Lunenburg Fishing Industry*, 46, 48.
40 *Can.RFB*, 1876–1916/17, fishery inspectors' reports, Lunenburg County,

Nova Scotia: annual returns of fish landings converted to lbs., Big and Little Tancook islands; *Can. CenInd., 1917*, pt 3: *Fisheries Statistics*, catch returns for the Tancooks, 18–25, converted to lbs.

41 *Can.RFB*, 1876–1916/17, fishery inspectors' reports, Lunenburg County, Nova Scotia: annual returns of fish landings converted to lbs, Big and Little Tancook islands; *Can.CenInd, 1917*, pt 3: *Fisheries Statistics*, catch returns for the Tancooks, 18–25, converted to lbs.

42 Interviews, Thomas Mason, July 1969, 12 June 1986, and 14 June 1989, Murray A. Mason, 17 June 1986.

43 *Can.RFB*, 1876–1916/17, fishery inspectors' reports, Lunenburg County, Nova Scotia: annual returns of fish landings converted to lbs., Big and Little Tancook islands; *Can.CenInd, 1917*, pt 3: *Fisheries Statistics*, catch returns for the Tancooks, 18–25, converted to lbs.

44 Interviews, Murray A. Mason, 17 June 1986, 16 June 1988, and 21 June 1989, Thomas Mason, July 1969, 12 June 1986, and 17 June 1989.

45 Interviews, Thomas Mason, July 1969 and 5 October 1988.

46 Interviews, Thomas Mason, 5 October 1988 and 25, 29 June 1990.

47 Interviews, Murray A. Mason, 16 June 1988, and 21 June 1989, Thomas Mason, 24 June 1988 and 17 June 1989.

48 *Can.RFB*, 1876–1916/17, fishery inspectors' reports, Lunenburg County, Nova Scotia: annual returns of fish landings and catch values, Big and Little Tancook islands; *Can.CenInd, 1917*, pt 3: *Fisheries Statistics*, 18–25.

49 Interviews, Thomas Mason, 12 June 1986 and 1 October 1988.

50 Interviews, Thomas Mason, 20 June 1986 and 14 June 1989, Murray A. Mason, 21 June 1989. See also *Can.RFB, 1913/14*, 87.

51 Interviews, Thomas Mason, 4 October 1986, 24 September 1987, and 1 October 1988.

52 Interviews, Thomas Mason, 29 September 1986, 25 September, 1 October 1987 and 17 June 1989, Murray A. Mason, 28 September 1987.

53 Interviews, Thomas Mason, 4 October 1986 and 24 September 1987, Murray A. Mason, 21 June 1989.

54 *HH*, news item, 25 March 1920, 13.

55 Interviews, Murray A. Mason, 17 June 1986, Thomas Mason, July 1969.

56 Interviews, Steadman S. Mason, 21 June 1986, Hovey Slauenwhite, 30 September 1987; *Can.RFB, 1914/15*, 365.

57 Interview, Hovey Slauenwhite, 30 September 1987.

58 Interviews, Thomas Mason, 23 June and 5 October 1988, David M. Stevens, 20 June 1988, Benjamin Heisler, 22 June 1989.

59 Interviews, Thomas Mason, 12 June 1986 and 25 September 1987; see also NA, LunSR: registers of schrs *Silver Oak*, 21 April 1917, and *White Birch*, 21 May 1918.

60 Interviews, Thomas Mason, 13 June 1986, and Murray A. Mason, 13 June 1986.

61 Interviews, Thomas Mason, July 1969, 4 October 1986, 24 September 1987, and 17 June 1989.
62 Interview, Thomas Mason, 25 September 1987; NA, LunSR: registers of schrs *Tancook*, 30 April 1914, *Silver Oak*, 21 April 1917, and *Blanche M. Stevens*, 29 May 1918.
63 Interview, Thomas Mason, 17 June 1989.
64 Interviews, Steadman S. Mason, 21 June, 4 October 1986, and 17 June 1989.
65 *HH*, news item, 29 May 1931, 13.
66 *Can.RFB*, 1909/10, 39.
67 Ibid., 1909/10–1916/17, fishery inspectors' reports, Cape Breton, Victoria, Richmond and Inverness counties, Nova Scotia: annual returns of fish landings; *Can.CenInd*, 1917–20: *Fisheries Statistics*, returns of fish landings for Cape Breton Island and Nova Scotia.
68 *Can.RFB*, 1910/11–1915/16, fishery inspectors' reports, Lunenburg County, Nova Scotia: annual returns of fish landings and catch values, Big and Little Tancook islands.
69 *HH*, news item, 8 September 1922, 11, article, 20 August 1932, 7; interview, Hovey Slauenwhite, 30 September 1987.
70 *HH*, news item, 8 September 1922, 11, articles, 16 July 1932, 18, and 22 April 1933, 22.
71 *HH*, article, 22 April 1933, 22 news item, 18 December 1935, 19; *Can.CenInd*, 1917, pt 3: *Fisheries Statistics*, 9. See also Nova Scotia, *Provincial Economic Inquiry*, 185.
72 *HH*, news item, 11 August 1925, 9.
73 Ibid., 20 September 1921, 13; 14 July 1922, 13; 14 September 1932, 15; and 22 April 1933, 22.
74 Interviews, Murray A. Mason, 17 June 1986 and 28 September 1987, Hovey Slauenwhite, 30 September 1987, Wesley H. Stevens, Jr, 22 June 1988; *HH*, news items, 8 August 1928, 11, 1 August 1929, 15, 12 August 1931, 15, and 16 July 1932, 18, marine lists, July-August 1929, 1931, passim; see also Kuuisto, "Went with Our Living," 28.
75 Interviews, Thomas Mason, 24 September 1987 and 1 October 1988, Wesley H. Stevens, Jr, 22 June 1988; *HH*, news item, 1 August 1929, 15, marine list, 3 August 1929, 21.
76 Interviews, Murray A. Mason, 17 June 1986, and 28 September 1987, Thomas Mason, 1 October 1988, Steadman S. Mason, 17 June 1989; see also Kuuisto, "Went with Our Living," 28.
77 *Can.RFB*, 1909/10, 39; *HH*, news items, 29 August 1930, 13, and 12 August 1931, 15.
78 Goode, *Fisheries and Fishery Industries*, sec. 5, 1: 318–20. See also Church and Connolly, *American Fishermen*, 161–76.
79 Ackerman, *New England's Fishing Industry*, 109. See also *HH*, articles, 1 September 1923, 8, and 22 April 1933, 22.

80 HH, news item, 29 August 1930, 13, article, 20 August 1932. See also Goode, *Fisheries and Fishery Industries*, sec. 1, 1:345, 350-4.
81 Interview, Thomas Mason, 1 October 1988; MC, news item, 26 August 1922, 3.
82 Canada, *Report Investigating the Fisheries*, 124-5; Nova Scotia, *Provincial Economic Inquiry*, 147; Urquhart and Buckley, *Historical Statistics of Canada*, 394-5.
83 Interview, Steadman S. Mason, 17 June 1989.
84 Interview, Benjamin Heisler, 22 June 1989.
85 HH, news items, 12 August, 1931, 15, and 18 December 1935, 19, article, 22 April 1933, 22. See also Urquhart and Buckley, *Historical Statistics of Canada*, 394-5.
86 Interview, Wesley H. Stevens, Jr, 22 June 1988.
87 US Navy Hydrographic Office, *Nova Scotia Pilot*, 432-3; HH, news item, 30 September 1929, 13.
88 Stephens, *Iron Roads*, 15-16; *Nova Scotia Pilot*, 447-8.
89 Waters, "Bluenose and Codfish," 78.
90 Interview, Thomas Mason, 1 October 1987.
91 Strople, "Prohibition and Social Reform," 6, 95-7, 127, 132-3, 136, 145-51, 162-3, 168-9; Spence, *Prohibition in Canada*, 123-4, 221, 339-42, 487-8; Andrieux, *Prohibition and St Pierre*, 11-13. See also NSS, 10 Edw. VII (1910), chap. 2, and ibid., 20 Geo. V (1930), chap. 2.
92 Spence, *Prohibition in Canada*, 329-30; HH, article, 6 September 1924, 8.
93 Strople, "Prohibition and Social Reform," 6, 96; Andrieux, *Prohibition and St Pierre*, 77.
94 Grant, *Canadian Atlantic Fishery*, 33-4.
95 Bell, *Foreign Protestants*, 440, 598; DesBrisay, *County of Lunenburg*, 407-10, 485-6.
96 DesBrisay, *County of Lunenburg*, 411-12; Strople, "Prohibition and Social Reform," 96.
97 Hennigar, *Rum Running Years*, 8.5.
98 Interviews, Thomas Mason, 23 June 1988, and 15 June 1989, Wesley H. Stevens, Jr, 22 June 1988, Steadman S. Mason, 17 June 1989.
99 Baker, "Tancook Island," 42-3.
100 Robinson and Robinson, *By the Boat Load*, 136; Can.SRD, CansSR: register of schr *Sarah Pauline*, 23 April 1924; HH, news item, 10 September 1931, 3.
101 Interviews, Thomas Mason, July 1969 and 20 June, 30 September 1986; see also Hennigar, *Rum Running Years*, 123.
102 Can.HCH, HalsR: register of schr *Elsie B. Young*, 15 May 1923; NA, LunSR: register of schr *Gloria P.H.*, 19 May 1924.
103 Baker, "Tancook Island," 41.
104 Ibid., 42-3; Hennigar, *Rum Running Years*, 123; Patton, *Sinking of the*

I'm Alone, 35–6; see also NA, LunSR: register of schr *D.D. McKenzie*, 8 September 1920, and Parker, *Sails of the Maritimes*, 191, 203.
105 Robinson and Robinson, *By the Boat Load*, 35.
106 Patton, *Sinking of the I'm Alone*, 36; interview, Thomas Mason, 17 June 1989; NA, LunSR: register of schr *Holly C.*, 1 August 1929.
107 *Can.RPW*, 1872, 24; 1873, 28 and app., 51. See also DesBrisay, *County of Lunenburg*, 313.
108 MC, marine lists, 10, 13, 21, 23 December 1870, 3; NA, LunSR: register of schr *British Lady*, 12 August 1867.
109 MC, marine lists, 7 November and 15, 26 December 1871, 3, and 5, 26 January, 20 February and 5 March 1872, 3; NA, LunSR: registers of schrs *British Tar*, 10 June 1853 and 12 January 1859, *Sky Lark*, 7 June 1859, and *Bella Young*, 2 June 1860; *Can.LV*, 1886, 158.
110 MC, MH, HH, marine lists and commercial news (imports), 1 September-30 April 1872–99, passim; NA, HalSR and NA, LunSR: 1850–1900.
111 Interview, Thomas Mason, 14 June 1989. See also NA, LunSR: register of stmr *Kinburn*, 10 March 1911.
112 MC, MH, HH, commercial news (imports), 1 September-30 April 1874–79, passim.
113 MC, commercial news (imports), 29 December 1874, 3.
114 MH, commercial news (imports), 14 November and 10, 11, 12, 19 December 1890, 3, and 20 March and 9 April 1891, 3.
115 *Encyclopaedia Britannica*, 11th ed., s.v. "Cabbage"; *Encyclopedia Americana*, 1988 ed., s.v. "Cabbage."
116 Interviews, Thomas Mason, 14, 15 June 1989, Murray A. Mason, 28 September 1987.
117 Jacobs, *Food and Food Products*, 2: 1344–6; Chaney and Ross, *Nutrition*, 459–64.
118 Jacobs, *Food and Food Products*, 3: 1830; *Encyclopedia Americana*, 1988 ed., s.v. "Cabbage."
119 Bell, *Foreign Protestants*, 527, 549.
120 Blunt, *American Coast Pilot*, 111; DesBrisay, *County of Lunenburg*, 486; NS, news item, 2 November 1826, 5. See also Raddall, *Halifax*, 174.
121 *Encyclopedia Americana*, 1988 ed., s.v. "Cabbage"; DesBrisay, *County of Lunenburg*, 458; interview, Benjamin Heisler, 4 October 1989.
122 Interview, Thomas Mason, 25 September 1987; *Encyclopedia Americana*, 1988 ed., s.v. "Cabbage"; see also *Encyclopaedia Britannica*, 15th ed., s.v. "Cabbage."
123 Interviews, Thomas Mason, 25 September 1987, Murray A. Mason, 28 September 1987. See also Bird, *Off-Trail in Nova Scotia*, 165.
124 Interviews, Murray A. Mason, 17 June 1986 and 28 September 1987.
125 Interviews, Thomas Mason, 19 August 1972 and 25 September 1987, Murray A. Mason, 28 September 1987.

126 Interview, Thomas Mason, 14 June 1989.
127 Interviews, Thomas Mason, 30 September 1987 and 3 October 1989.
128 PANS, Bus, Zwicker Coll., MSS 174, 189: Ships' Account Books, 1871–76, 1876–83, outfits of schrs *Druid*, 1872, and *Sibyl*, 1877.
129 Interview, Thomas Mason, 25 September 1987; DFP, article, 22 October 1959, 3; HJ, 4 April 1973, 12. See also Jacobs, *Food and Food Products*, 3: 1910.
130 Interview, Thomas Mason, 4 October 1988; CH, article, 29 October 1957, 24.
131 HH, wholesale prices current, 28 February 1914, 15, and 6 January 1917, 6, news item, 14 November 1917, 9.
132 Ibid., marine lists, 11 October 1911, 9, 4 November 1911, 13, and 21 November 1911, 9; NA, LunSR: registers of schrs *Pauline L.*, 27 June 1911, and *S.F. Levy*, 18 July 1911.
133 HH, marine lists, 6 December 1913, 17; 13, 27 January 1914, 11; 9 February 1914, 11; and 25 March 1914, 13.
134 NA, LunSR: register of schr *Florence B.*, 2 June 1880; NA, HalSR: register of schr *W.E. Wier*, 18 June 1892; see also HH, marine lists, November 1898-March 1899, passim.
135 Interviews, Thomas Mason, 14 June and 1 October 1989; NA, LunSR: register of stmr *Kinburn*, 10 March 1911; Can.LV, 1917, 53; Can.RMB, 1916/17, supp.: *Steamboat Inspection Report*, 76.
136 Interviews, Thomas Mason, 30 September 1986 and 1 October 1989; NA, LunSR: registers of schrs *Tancook*, 30 April 1914, *Bleucher C.*, 28 July 1916, *Silver Oak*, 21 April 1917, *Steward D.S.*, 15 May 1917, *Hurry Up*, 21 June 1917, and *White Birch*, 21 May 1918; HH, marine lists, 14 October 1914, 9, 28 November 1916, 11, 14, 15 November 1917, 9, 11, and 26 November 1918, 9, news items, 14 November 1917, 9, and 15 November 1917, 11.
137 Raddall, *Halifax*, 264–5.
138 *Can.Cen*, 1941, 2:60.
139 Interview, Thomas Mason, 25 September 1987; HH, news items, 9 January 1918, 9, and 22 March 1920, 11.
140 Hill, *Canada's Salesman*, 80; MC, commercial news (imports), 20 October and 11 December 1879, 3.
141 Hill, *Canada's Salesman*, 84, 149–56, 272–7. See also Lockwood, *Canada and the West Indies*, 39, 63.
142 Hill, *Canada's Salesman*, 166, 278, 290.
143 Ibid., 85; HH, article, 31 December 1920, 10.
144 HH, marine lists, 1 September 1922–30 April 1923, passim.
145 Interviews, Thomas Mason, 25 September 1987, Murray A. Mason, 28 September 1987.
146 HH, news items, 17 August 1928, 11; 10, 29 September 1928, 15, 29; 1 October 1928, 15; 13, 28 December 1928, 17, 11; 11 January 1929, 13.

147 Ibid., 20 April 1927, 11; 10, 29 September 1928, 15, 29; 1 October 1928, 15; 24 October 1933, 13.
148 *HH*, article, 20 April 1927, 11.
149 Ibid., marine lists, October-April 1927–39, passim, in conjunction with interviews, Thomas Mason, 30 September 1986 and 25 September 1987.
150 *CH*, article, 29 October 1957, 24.
151 Interview, Thomas Mason, 30 September 1987.
152 Interviews, Thomas Mason, 25, 30 September 1987.
153 Interviews, Thomas Mason, July 1969, 19 August 1972, 25 September 1985, 12 June and 30 September 1986, and 29, 30 September 1987. See also *CH*, article, 29 October 1957, 24, and *HH*, marine lists, October-April 1925–27 and 1929–40, passim.
154 Interviews, Thomas Mason, 19 August 1972, 12 June 1986, and 1, 2 October 1989, Benjamin Heisler, 4 October 1989.
155 Interviews, Thomas Mason, July 1969, 19 August 1972, 12 June and 30 September 1986, and 25 September and 1 October 1987.
156 Interviews, Thomas Mason, July 1969 and 12 June 1986, Murray A. Mason, 13 June 1986.
157 Interviews, Thomas Mason, 19 August 1972, 25 September 1985, 25 September 1987, 1 October 1988, and 25 June 1990. See also HBT, *Plan of the City of Halifax, Nova Scotia* (ca. 1930).
158 Interview, Thomas Mason, 30 September 1987. See also *HH*, news item, 30 November 1923, 13.
159 *HH*, article, 24 October 1919, 13.
160 Interviews, Thomas Mason, 25, 30 September 1987. See also *Might's Halifax and Dartmouth Directories, 1935*, classified, 13, 20, 41.
161 Interviews, Thomas Mason, 30 September 1987, Hovey Slauenwhite, 30 September 1987.
162 Interviews, Thomas Mason, 19 August 1972, 25 September 1985, and 25, 30 September 1987.
163 Interviews, Thomas Mason, 30 September 1987. See also *Might's Halifax and Dartmouth Directories, 1935*, classified, 13, 21.
164 *HH*, news items, 14 November 1917, 9, 20 February 1926, 8, 27 November 1931, 12, 27 September 1932, 11, and 12 October 1937, 12. See also ibid., wholesale prices current, September-April 1925–38, passim.
165 Ibid., news items, 27 November 1931, 12, and 12 October 1937, 12, wholesale prices current, 2 December 1915, 9.
166 Interviews, Thomas Mason, 25 September 1985 and 30 September 1987.
167 Interview, Thomas Mason, 4 October 1988.
168 *MH*, commercial news (imports), 20 March and 9 April 1891, 3; *HH*, commercial news (imports), 31 March 1891, 7; interview, Thomas Mason, 24 September 1987.
169 Interviews, Thomas Mason, 19 August 1972 and 15 June 1989.
170 Interview, Thomas Mason, 24 September 1987.

CHAPTER FOUR

Epigraph: *HH*, 31 December 1937, sec. 2, 9.
1 Lockwood, *Canada and the West Indies*, 40, 67–8, 75.
2 Interviews, Thomas Mason, 25 September 1987, Murray A. Mason, 28 September 1987.
3 Interviews, Murray A. Mason, 28 September 1987, Thomas Mason, 30 September 1987.
4 Hawkins, *Angus L.*, 173–4, 210.
5 *HH*, article, 31 December 1937, sec. 2, 9. See also 1 January 1934, sec. 1, 2.
6 Ibid., editorial, 20 December 1916, 18.
7 Ibid., news item, 30 April 1927, 5.
8 Ibid., photo caption, 30 November 1921, 10.
9 Ibid., article, 31 December 1937, sec. 2, 9. See also Raddall, *Halifax*, 288.
10 Glazebrook, *Transportation in Canada*, 2:252.
11 Interview, Vincent Stevens, August 1972.
12 Interviews, Thomas Mason, 12 June 1986 and 25 September 1987, Leslie Mason, June 1988.
13 Interview, Thomas Mason, 30 September 1987.
14 *Can.RFB, 1909/10*, xxvi.
15 Canada, *Report Investigating the Fisheries*, 100.
16 *HH*, news item, 1 November 1927, 11.
17 Pope, "Cape Island Boat," 57–8.
18 Chapelle, "Practical Fishing Launches," 31–2.
19 Interview, Thomas Mason, July 1969.
20 Can.LCH, LunsR: registers of Tancook-built motorboats, 1927–37, including *Guinea Gold*, 21 March 1927, and *Old Kentucky*, 30 November 1928; interviews, Thomas Mason, July 1969 and 25 September 1987, Murray A. Mason, 28 September 1987.
21 Interview, Thomas Mason, 1 October 1987; *HH*, marine lists, October–April 1930–39, passim, especially 1937–39.
22 Interview, Guy B. Stevens, 20 June 1988.
23 Interviews, Thomas Mason, 25 September 1987, Murray A. Mason, 28 September 1987.
24 Chapelle, "Practical Fishing Launches," 32–3.
25 Interview, Thomas Mason, 29 September 1987.
26 Interviews, Thomas Mason, 25 September 1987, Murray A. Mason, 28 September 1987.
27 NA, LunsR: registers of schrs *Steward D.S.*, 15 May 1917, *Jessen J.M.*, 16 May 1917, and *Old Chum*, 8 June 1925; Can.LCH, LunsR: registers of schrs *Dixie Arrow*, 12 May 1928, *Patavana*, 28 November 1929, *Gerald L.C.*, 9 June 1933, and *Streamline*, 8 May 1936; Can.HCH, HalsR: registers of schrs *Sylvia Pauline*, 18 May 1931, and *Dorothy and Ella*, 6 June 1931.
28 Interviews, Murray A. Mason, 17 June 1986, DeWitt Baker, 21 June 1986.

Bibliography

ARCHIVAL AND MANUSCRIPT SOURCES

PUBLIC RECORD COLLECTIONS

Canada.
- Ministry of Agriculture. Census Office. Manuscript Census Schedules (decennial) for Tancook, Lunenburg County, Nova Scotia. 1861–91. [on microfilm, National Archives of Canada, Ottawa.]
- Ministry of National Revenue. Department of Customs and Excize. Halifax and Lunenburg, Nova Scotia, Customs Houses. Shipping Registers for Ports of Halifax (1904–45) and Lunenburg (1926–45).
- Ministry of Transport. Department of the Coast Guard. Ship Registration Division, Ottawa. Shipping Registers for the Port of Canso, Nova Scotia. 1886–1929. [on microfilm]
- National Archives of Canada. Records of the Department of Marine. Record Group 42. Shipping Registers for the Ports of Arichat (1916), Halifax (1817–1903), and Lunenburg (1849–1925), Nova Scotia. [on microfilm]

Nova Scotia.
- Department of the Attorney General. Registry of Deeds, Municipality of the District of Lunenburg, Bridgewater. Land Deeds for Lunenburg County. 1794–1917.
- Department of Health. Office of the Registrar-General. Vital Records for Tancook Township.
- Department of Lands and Forests. Crown Lands Record Centre, Dartmouth. Land Records for the Tancook islands. 1759–92.

Public Archives of Nova Scotia, Halifax:
  Business Papers. Manuscript Group 3. Zwicker Collection.
  Church and Community Records. Manuscript Group 4. Canon E.A. Harris genealogies, Baker, Langille, and Mason families.
  Land and Forest Records. Record Group 20. Crown surveys of the Tancook islands.
  Legislative Assembly Papers. Record Group 5. Affidavits on the settlement of the Tancook islands.
  Papers of Families and Individuals. Manuscript Group 1. Stevens family genealogies.
  Vital Statistics Collection. Record Group 32. Birth and marriage records of Tancook residents.

MISCELLANEOUS ITEMS

Chapelle, Howard I. Letter to the author, 11 September 1969.
Sail Plan Record Book. Handwritten register. Stevens Sail Loft, Second Peninsula, Lunenburg, Nova Scotia.
Unattributed notes of a conversation with Randolph B. Stevens, spring 1955. Typescript, dated 16 August 1955, in the possession of the Chester Yacht Club, Chester, Nova Scotia.
Unidentified newspaper clipping in the possession of Perry W. Stevens, Chester, Nova Scotia.

GOVERNMENT DOCUMENTS

SERIES

Canada. Bureau of Statistics. *Census of Industry* (annual). 1917–20.
Canada. Ministry of Agriculture. Census Office. *Census of Canada* (decennial). 1871–1941. [pub. Ottawa: Dominion Bureau of Statistics, beginning in 1921.]
Canada. Ministry of Marine and Fisheries. *Annual Report of the Fisheries Branch.* 1870–1916/17. [pub. Ottawa: Department of Naval Service, 1915–17.]
Canada. Ministry of Marine and Fisheries. *Annual Report of the Marine Branch,* 1916/17.
Canada. Ministry of Marine and Fisheries. *List of Vessels on the Registry Books of the Dominion* (annual). 1874–1930. [pub. intermittently until 1902, yearly thereafter.]
Canada. Ministry of Public Works. *Annual Report.* 1872, 1873, 1909.
Canada. *Revised Statutes of Canada.* 6 Edw. VII, 18 Geo. V (1906, 1927).
Canada. *Statutes of Canada.* 36, 45 Vict. (1873, 1882).
Nova Scotia. *Journal and Proceedings of the House of Assembly.* 1851, 1853.

Nova Scotia. *Statutes of Nova Scotia*. 10 Edw. VII, 20 Geo. V (1910, 1930).
U.S. *Statutes at Large*. Vols. 42, 46 (1921–23, 1930).

DEPARTMENTAL REPORTS AND MONOGRAPHS

Canada. Commission on Conservation. *Sea Fisheries of Eastern Canada*. Ottawa: Mortimer Co., 1912.
Canada. Ministry of Marine and Fisheries. *Report of the Royal Commission Investigating the Fisheries of the Maritime Provinces and the Magdalen Islands*. Ottawa: F.A. Acland, 1928.
Nova Scotia. Office of Lieutenant Governor. *Report of the Royal Commission, Provincial Economic Inquiry*. Halifax: King's printer, 1934.
U.S. Department of the Navy. Hydrographic Office. *Nova Scotia Pilot*. 7th ed. rev. Washington: Government Printing Office, 1930.

PUBLISHED AND UNPUBLISHED
SECONDARY SOURCES

Ackerman, Edward A. *New England's Fishing Industry*. Chicago: University of Chicago Press, 1941.
Allen, B. J. "A Brief Story of the Chester Yacht Club, 1900–1950." Typescript, dated 30 August 1952, in the possession of the Chester Yacht Club, Chester, Nova Scotia.
Andrieux, Jean-Pierre. *Prohibition and St Pierre*. Lincoln, Ont: W.F. Rannie, 1983.
Armour, Charles A., and Thomas Lackey. *Sailing Ships of the Maritimes*. Toronto: McGraw-Hill Ryerson, 1975.
Atkins, Thomas B. *History of Halifax City*. 1895. Reprint. Belleville, Ont: Mika, 1973.
Audubon, James J. *Audubon, By Himself*. ed. Alice Ford. Garden City, NY: Natural History Press, 1969.
Baker, Rosa. "Tancook Island: Tales of Rumrunning During the 20s and 30s." In *Lunenburg County Folklore and Oral History Project '77*, ed. Laurie Lacey. Ottawa: National Museums of Canada, 1979.
Balcom, Berton A. *History of the Lunenburg Fishing Industry*. Lunenburg, NS: Lunenburg Marine Museum Society, 1977.
Barrett, L. Gene. "Development and Underdevelopment, and the Rise of Trade Unionism in the Fishing Industry of Nova Scotia, 1900–1950." Master's thesis, Department of Sociology, Dalhousie University, 1976.
Bell, Ernest A. "The Passing of the Tancook Whaler." *Yachting* (February 1933): 55–6, 102.
Bell, Winthrop P. *The "Foreign Protestants" and the Settlement of Nova Scotia*. Toronto: University of Toronto Press, 1961.

Bird, Will R. *Off-Trail in Nova Scotia*. Toronto: Ryerson, 1956.
Blunt, George W., ed. *The American Coast Pilot*. 16th ed. New York: E. & G. W. Blunt, 1850.
Brebner, John B. *Canada: A Modern History*. Ann Arbor, MI: University of Michigan Press, 1960.
- *The Neutral Yankees of Nova Scotia*. 2d ed. Toronto: McClelland & Stewart, 1969.
Cabot, David. "The New England Double Enders." *The American Neptune*, 12 (April 1952): 123–41.
Carrick, Robert W., and Richard Henderson. *John G. Alden and His Yacht Designs*. Camden, ME: International Marine Publishing, 1983.
Chaney, Margaret S., and Margaret L. Ross. *Nutrition*. 7th ed. Boston: Houghton Mifflin, 1966.
Chapelle, Howard I. *American Sailing Craft*. New York: Kennedy, 1936.
- *Boatbuilding: A Complete Handbook of Wooden Boat Construction*. New York: Norton, 1941.
- *American Small Sailing Craft: Their Design, Development and Construction*. New York: Norton, 1951.
- "Practical Fishing Launches: The Design, Construction and Powering of Small Fishing Boats, Part 1," *Boats* (May 1954): 29–34, 73–4.
- "The Search for Speed Under Sail, pt 3: 1880–1903," *Yachting* (April 1955): 66–70, 112–14.
- *The National Watercraft Collection*. Washington, DC: Government Printing Office, 1960.
- *The American Fishing Schooners, 1825–1935*. New York: Norton, 1973.
Christensen, Arne E. "Boatbuilding Tools and the Process of Learning." In *Ships and Shipyards, Sailors and Fishermen: Introduction to Marine Ethnology*, ed. Scandinavian Maritime History Group. Copenhagen: Copenhagen University Press, 1972.
Church, Albert C., and James B. Connolly. *American Fishermen*. New York: Norton, 1940.
Creighton, Helen. *Folklore of Lunenburg County, Nova Scotia*. 2d ed. Toronto: McGraw-Hill Ryerson, 1976.
Davis, Charles G. *American Sailing Ships: Their Plans and History*. 2d ed. New York: Dover, 1984.
DesBarres, Joseph F.W. *The Atlantic Neptune*. 2 vols. 1774–80. Reprint. Barre, MA: Barre Publishing Co: 1966–70.
DesBrisay, Mather B. *History of the County of Lunenburg*. 2d ed. 1895. Reprint. Bridgewater, NS: Bridgewater Bulletin, 1967.
Erhard, Nancie. *First in Its Class: The Story of the Royal Nova Scotia Yacht Squadron*. Halifax: Nimbus, 1986.
Fader, Edmund A. "Reminiscence of an Old-Timer." Typescript [1959] in the possession of the Chester Yacht Club, Chester, Nova Scotia.

Fergusson, Charles B., ed. *Place-Names and Places of Nova Scotia*. Halifax: Public Archives of Nova Scotia, 1967.
Finney, John M.T. *A Surgeon's Life: The Autobiography of J.M.T. Finney*. New York: Putnam's, 1940.
Fishermen of the Atlantic, 1925. Boston: Fishing Masters' Association, 1925.
Forbes, Ernest R. *The Maritime Rights Movement, 1919–1927: A Study in Canadian Regionalism*. Montreal: McGill-Queen's University Press, 1979.
Gillespie, G.J. *Bluenose Skipper*. Fredericton, NB: Brunswick Press, 1955.
Glazebrook, G.P.deT. *A History of Transportation in Canada*. 2 vols. 2d ed. Toronto: McClelland & Stewart, 1964.
Goode, George B., ed. *The Fisheries and Fishery Industries of the Unites States*. 7 vols. 5 secs. Washington, DC: Government Printing Office, 1884–87.
Grant, Ruth F. *The Canadian Atlantic Fishery*. Toronto: Ryerson, 1934.
Greenhill, Basil. *Archaeology of the Boat*. London: A. & C. Black, 1976.
Haliburton, Thomas C. *An Historical and Statistical Account of Nova Scotia*. 2 vols. 1829. Reprint. Belleville, Ont: Mika, 1973.
Hall, Henry. *Report on the Shipbuilding Industry of the United States*. Washington, DC: Government Printing Office, 1882.
Hawkins, John. *The Life and Times of Angus L.* Windsor, NS: Lancelot Press, 1969.
Hayden, Sterling. *Wanderer*. New York: Knopf, 1963.
Hennigar, Ted R. *The Rum Running Years*. Hantsport, NS: Lancelot Press, 1981.
Herreshoff, L. Francis. *Capt. Nat. Herreshoff, The Wizard of Bristol*. 2d ed. Dobbs Ferry, NY: Sheridan House, 1981.
Hewitt, H.W. "History of Lunenburg County." Undated typescript. Public Archives of Nova Scotia, Halifax. Church and Community Records, Lunenburg County.
Hilchie, Harold J. "Chester Yacht Club." Handwritten memoir, dated 1953, in the possession of the Chester Yacht Club, Chester, Nova Scotia.
Hill, O. Mary. *Canada's Salesman to the World: The Department of Trade and Commerce, 1892–1939*. Montreal: McGill-Queen's University Press, 1977.
Holdridge, Desmond. *Northern Lights*. New York: Viking, 1939.
Innis, Harold A. *The Cod Fisheries: The History of an International Economy*. 2d ed. rev. Toronto: University of Toronto Press, 1954.
Jacobs, Morris B., ed. *The Chemistry and Technology of Food Products*. 3 vols. 2d ed. rev. New York: Interscience Publishers 1951.
Jenson, L. B. *Fishermen of Nova Scotia*. 2d ed. Halifax: Petheric Press, 1984.
Keith, David. "Ben Heisler: Nova Scotia Yacht Builder." *The National Fisherman* (September 1974): 4–5C.
Kuusisto, Kathy. "'It All Went with Our Living': Life Patterns of Tancook Families (Part 2)." *The Occasional: An Occasional Journal for Nova Scotia Museums*, 5, no. 1 (Spring 1978): 27–30.

Langille, Stewart C. *A History and Genealogy of the South Shore Langilles of Nova Scotia*. 4th ed. Bridgewater, NS: H. & B. Langille Co., n.d.

Laurette, Patrick C. *John O'Brien, 1831–1891*. Halifax, NS: Art Gallery of Nova Scotia, 1984.

Lee, Lance R. "Tancook Whaler – Evolution." *The Apprentice: The Rockport [Me.] Apprenticeshop Journal*, no. 4 (Winter 1985): 14–19.

Lloyd's Register of American Yachts, 1939, 1947. New York: Lloyd's Register of Shipping, 1939, 1947.

Lockwood, P.A., ed. *Canada and the West Indies Federation*. Proceedings of a symposium held at Mount Allison University, 8–10 August 1957. Sackville, NB: Mt Allison University, 1957.

McCreath, Peter L., and John G. Leefe. *A History of Early Nova Scotia*. Tantallon, NS: Four East Publications, 1982.

McGrail, Sean. "Further Aspects of Viking Age Boatbuilding." In *Archaeology of the Boat*, Basil Greenhill. London: A.&C. Black, 1976.

MacGregor, David R. *Fast Sailing Ships, Their Design and Construction, 1775–1875*. 2d ed. rev. Annapolis, MD: Naval Institute Press, 1983.

– *The Tea Clippers: Their History and Development, 1833–1875*. 2d ed. rev. Annapolis, MD: Naval Institute Press, 1983.

MacKean, Roy, and Robert Percival. *The Little Boats: Inshore Fishing Craft of Atlantic Canada*. Fredericton, NB: Brunswick Press, 1979.

MacLennan, Hugh. *Barometer Rising*. New York: Duell, Sloan and Pearce, 1941.

Maury, Richard. *The Saga of Cimba*. New York: Harcourt, Brace, 1939.

Medjuck, Sheva. *Jews of Atlantic Canada*. St John's, Nfld: Breakwater, 1986.

Merkel, Andrew, and W.R. MacAskill. *Schooner Bluenose*. Toronto: Ryerson, 1948.

Might's Halifax and Dartmouth [NS] City Directories, 1935. Halifax: Might Directories Atlantic, 1935.

Nielsen, Christian. *Wooden Boat Designs: Classic Danish Boats Measured and Described*. trans. Erik J. Friis. New York: Scribner's, 1980.

Nova Scotia Directory for 1871. 1871. Reprint. London, Ont: Genealogical Research Library, 1984.

Official Reference Book of the Fishermen's Union of the Atlantic, 1927. n.p., 1927.

O'Hearn, Joseph C. *New England Fishing Schooners*. Milwaukee: Kalmbach Publishing, 1947.

O'Leary, Wayne M. "The Maine Sea Fisheries, 1830–1890: The Rise and Fall of a Native Industry." Ph.D. diss., Department of History, University of Maine, 1981.

Parker, John P. *Sails of the Maritimes*. Aylesbury and Slough, England: Hazell, Watson & Viney, 1960.

– *Cape Breton Ships and Men*. 2d ed. Toronto: McGraw-Hill Ryerson, 1980.

Patton, Janice. *The Sinking of the* I'm Alone. Toronto: McClelland & Stewart, 1973.

Perley, M.H. *Reports on the Sea and River Fisheries of New Brunswick*. Fredericton, NB: J. Simpson, 1852.

Phillips-Birt, Douglas. *The Building of Boats*. New York: Norton, 1979.

Pope, Timothy S. "The Cape Island Boat." *The Rudder* (August 1960): 57–9.

Post, Robert C. *The Tancook Whalers: Origins, Rediscovery, and Revival*. Bath, ME: Maine Maritime Museum, 1985.

Pugsley, Edwin. "Chester, Nova Scotia, 1904–1936." Typescript [1970]. G.W. Blunt-White Library, Mystic Seaport Museum, Mystic, CT. MS RF-355.

Pullen, H.F. "Old Schooners Never Die – Not in Nova Scotia." *Popular Boating* (December 1962): 50–2.

Raddall, Thomas H. *Halifax: Warden of the North*. Toronto: McClelland & Stewart, 1948.

Robinson, Geoff, and Dorothy Robinson. *It Came by the Boat Load: Essays on Rum-Running*. Summerside, PEI: Alfa Graphics, 1984.

Ryan, Shannon. *Fish out of Water: The Newfoundland Saltfish Trade*. St John's, Nfld: Breakwater, 1986.

Sabine, Lorenzo. *Report on the Principal Fisheries of the American Seas*. Washington, DC: Robert Armstrong, 1853.

Spence, Ruth E. *Prohibition in Canada*. Toronto: Ontario Branch of the Dominion Alliance, 1919.

Stackpole, Edouard A. *The Sea Hunters: New England Whalemen during Two Centuries, 1635–1835*. Philadelphia: Lippincott, 1953.

Stephens, David E. *Iron Roads: Railways of Nova Scotia*. Windsor, NS: Lancelot Press, 1972.

Stephens, William P. *Traditions and Memories of American Yachting*. 2d ed. Camden, ME: International Marine Publishing, 1981.

Stevens, Robert K., and C.J. Stevens. *The Stevens Families of Nova Scotia*. Yonkers, NY: Oracle Press, 1979.

Strople, Margaret J. Campbell. "Prohibition and Movements of Social Reform in Nova Scotia, 1894–1920." Master's thesis, Department of History, Dalhousie University, 1975.

Thomas, Gordon W. *Fast and Able: Life Stories of Great Gloucester Fishing Vessels*. Gloucester, MA: Gloucester 350th Anniversary Collection, 1973.

Urquhart, M.C., and K.A.H. Buckley, eds. *Historical Statistics of Canada*. Toronto: MacMillan, 1965.

Van de Water, Frederic F. *The Real McCoy*. Garden City, NY: Doubleday, 1931.

Wallace, Frederick W. *Wooden Ships and Iron Men*. 1937. Reprint. Belleville, Ont: Mika, 1976.

Waters, Donald. "Bluenose and Codfish." *Motor Boating* (December 1937): 32–5, 77–8, 80.

Women's Institute of Nova Scotia, Chester Branch, ed. *History of Chester [NS]: 1759–1967*. Lunenburg, NS: Progress-Enterprise, 1967.
Zinck, Willis, and Lottie Stevens Zinck. "Genealogy of the 'Tancook Stevenses.'" Undated typescript. Public Archives of Nova Scotia, Halifax. Papers of Families and Individuals, vol. 1453, no. 1928.

NEWSPAPERS AND JOURNALS

Canadian Fisherman. 1917.
Christian Messenger [Halifax]. 1860.
Chronicle-Herald [Halifax]. 1952, 1957, 1976.
Dartmouth [NS] *Free Press*. 1959.
Halifax Herald. 1892–1940.
Halifax Mail-Star. 1962.
Hants Journal [Windsor, NS]. 1973.
Lunenburg [NS] *Progress*. 1879, 1881, 1888.
Morning Chronicle [Halifax]. 1862–79, 1922.
Morning Herald [Halifax]. 1884–91.
New York Times. 1913.
Nova Scotian [Halifax]. 1826, 1860–70.
Novascotian [*Chronicle-Herald* magazine insert]. 1986.
Progress-Enterprise [Lunenburg, NS]. 1907, 1964.

INTERVIEWS

DeWitt Baker. Tancook, Nova Scotia. 21 June 1986.
Mary (Mrs Percy) Baker. Tancook, Nova Scotia. 3 October 1987.
Benjamin Heisler. Chester, Nova Scotia. July 1969; 22 June, 4 October 1989.
Cecil F. Langille. Indian Point, Nova Scotia. 4 October 1989.
Sadie (Mrs Whitman) Langille. Martin's Brook, Nova Scotia. 18 June 1988.
Vernon R. Langille. Indian Point, Nova Scotia. July 1969.
Leslie A. Mason. Chester, Nova Scotia. June 1988.
Murray A. Mason. Halifax, Nova Scotia. June 1985; 13, 16, 17 June 1986; 28 September, 1 October 1987; 16 June, 5 October 1988; 21 June 1989; 26 June 1990.
Steadman S. Mason. Chester, Nova Scotia. 21 June, 4 October 1986; 22 June, 4 October 1988; 17 June 1989.
Thomas Mason. Chester, Nova Scotia. July 1969; 19 August 1972; 25 September 1985; 12, 13, 15, 18 June, 29, 30 September, 4 October 1986; 24, 25, 26, 29, 30 September, 1 October 1987; 23, 24 June, 1, 3, 4, 5 October 1988; 5 February, 8, 14, 15, 17, 18, 22 June, 1, 2, 3 October 1989; 25, 29 June, 12 August 1990.
Hovey Slauenwhite. Mahone Bay, Nova Scotia. 30 September 1987.

David M. Stevens. Second Peninsula, Lunenburg, Nova Scotia. 20 June, 3 October 1988.
Gerald L. Stevens. Chester, Nova Scotia. 25 June 1992.
Guy B. Stevens. Chester, Nova Scotia. 20 June 1988.
Harold W. Stevens. Second Peninsula, Lunenburg, Nova Scotia. July 1969; September 1986.
Perry W. Stevens. Chester, Nova Scotia. 13 June 1986; 16 June, 2 October 1989.
Vincent Stevens. Tancook, Nova Scotia. August 1972.
Wesley H. Stevens, Jr. Tancook, Nova Scotia. 22 June 1988.

MAPS AND CHARTS

Canada. Ministry of Energy, Mines and Resources (EMR). Hydrographic Service. Chart of Mahone Bay, Nova Scotia. Ottawa: Canadian Hydrographic Service, 1959. [author's collection]
Canada. Ministry of Energy, Mines and Resources. Hydrographic Service. Chart of the Southeastern Coast of Nova Scotia from Egg Island to West Ironbound Island. Ottawa: Canadian Hydrographic Service, 1967. [author's collection]
Canada. Ministry of Energy, Mines and Resources. Surveys and Mapping Branch. Topographical Map of the Maritime Provinces. No. MCR 38. Ottawa: EMR, 1968. [author's collection]
Canada. Ministry of Energy, Mines and Resources. Surveys and Mapping Branch. Topographical Map of the Municipality of Lunenburg, Nova Scotia. No. 21-A/8. Ottawa: EMR, 1977. [author's collection]
Church, Ambrose F. *Topographical Township Map of Lunenburg County, Nova Scotia.* Bedford, NS: A. F. Church & Co., ca. 1883. [copy held by Provincial Map Library, Nova Scotia Department of Natural Resources, Dartmouth]
Halifax [NS] Board of Trade. *Plan of the City of Halifax, Nova Scotia.* Halifax: Board of Trade, ca. 1930. [copy held by Public Archives of Nova Scotia, Halifax: map no. V6/239]
Nova Scotia. Office of Surveyor-General of Woods and Forests. Manuscript Survey Map of the Tancook islands, 11 June 1788. [original held by Crown Lands Record Centre, Nova Scotia Department of Lands and Forests, Dartmouth: old plans, no. 12(c)]
United States. Department of the Navy. Hydrographic Office. Chart of the Southeast Coast of Nova Scotia from Cape Sable to Sambro Island. Washington, DC: US Navy Hydrographic Office, 1918. [author's collection]

MODELS, PLANS, AND PAINTINGS

Fisheries Museum of the Atlantic, Lunenburg, Nova Scotia. Ship model collection. Half-models of Vernon R. Langille.

Maritime Museum of the Atlantic, Halifax, Nova Scotia. Ship model collection. Half-models of Vernon R. Langille.

Maritime Museum of the Atlantic, Halifax, Nova Scotia. Ship painting collection. Painting of schr *Henry L. Montague*. No. M73.10.1.

Mystic Seaport Museum, Mystic, Connecticut. Ship model collection. Half-model of schr *Blackbird III*. No. 70.344.

National Museum of American History [Smithsonian Institution], Washington, DC. Division of Marine Transportation. Ship model collection. Builders' half-models of Nova Scotia fishing schooners.

Private half-model collections: Donald Langille, Berwick, Nova Scotia; Leslie Mason, Thomas Mason, Gerald Stevens, Guy Stevens, Chester, Nova Scotia; Murray Stevens, Second Peninsula, Lunenburg, Nova Scotia.

Stevens Sail Loft. Second Peninsula, Lunenburg, Nova Scotia. Sailmaker's sail plans.

Index

Aberdeen, Scotland, 30
Aberdeen stems. *See* clipper bows
Acadia Gas Engine Company, 91
Adare. *See Tacoma*
Ada Westhover, 138n
Airlie. *See Green Bow II*
Albertina, 159
Alberton, PEI, 136, 137, 139
Alden, John G., 97
Alhambra, 138
Alinard, Steven, 93–4, 94n, 143, 170n
Alinard family, 9n
Amasonia, 75, 98, 111, 117, 118, 205–6
American Coast Pilot, 119
American fishing schooner design, 55–6, 59
American influences: on Tancook boatbuilding, 42; on Tancook boat design, 50, 50n, 51–2, 53, 56, 57–8, 59, 60–1, 73
Anderson, John, 27
Anglicans, Anglicanism, 10, 11, 133n
Anita, 27n

Annapolis Valley, 176, 177
Aranoka, 138n
architectural drawings, 42, 46, 100
Arethusa, 61
Arichat, 59
Artisan, 56n
Aspotogan Peninsula, 35
"Atlantic" engine, 91
Atlantic Fish Companies, 57
"Atlantic Fisherman" stove, 133
Attaboy, 99, 197
Audubon, John J., 26n
auxiliary engines. *See* engines, auxiliary; Tancook schooners, engines in; Tancook whalers, engines in

"Backalong," Big Tancook Island, 32, 35, 66
"backbone," 45n, 103
Baden-Durlach, Germany, 9
bait nets, 134
Baker, Adelaide. *See* Crooks, Adelaide (Baker)

Baker, Ainsley, 80, 181
Baker, Charles, 158
Baker, Daniel, 158
Baker, David, 44
Baker, George, 18, 28–9
Baker, Jacob, 17, 18
Baker, John, 17
Baker, John George. *See* Baker, George
Baker, Percy, 80, 181
Baker, Philip, 17
Baker family, 8, 9, 11, 134n
"bald-headed" cabbage. *See* Danish round-head cabbage
ballast, ballasting, 70, 93, 145
banks fishing, 25, 58–9, 138
Baptists, Baptist denomination, 10, 11, 133n, 154n
barns, used for boatbuilding, 32n, 64, 82, 101n
barrels, barrel makers, 135, 162, 168–9
Barrington, 23
"bastard" dories, 79, 139
Bay of Fundy, 22
beam-length ratios, 23,

26, 44–5, 46n, 62, 62n, 65, 179
Becker family. *See* Baker family
Beebe, 157
Bell, Ernest A., 26, 46n
Bell, Winthrop P., 8, 12
Bella Barry, 121
Bella Young, 121, 158
Bermudian mainsails. *See* marconi mainsails
Bernice, 64
Bernice Zinck, 138n
Beulah W., 51
Big Tancook Island, 85, 122, 134n, 229; boatbuilding at, 83, 115, 227; coasting trade of, 13, 163; description and characteristics of, 6–7, 12, 19, 108, 120, 122–3; location of, 6; naming of, 6, 7; population of, 1881, 9n; settlement and settlers of, 8–9, 11; views of, 35–9. *See also* Tancook: cabbage; cabbage trade; fisheries; islands; jolly boats; ram boats; sauerkraut; scallop sloops; schooners; sloops; whalers
billet heads, 18, 23
Birt, Douglas Phillips. *See* Phillips-Birt, Douglas
bituminous coal, 152, 152n
Black and Flinn's Wharf, Halifax, 169
Blackbird III, 53, 65, 188
Black Lize, 52, 104
Black Nance, 35, 37, 50–1, 104
Blakeney, B.A., 170
Blanche M. Stevens, 137n, 139
Blandford, 85, 122, 133n
Bleucher C., 164
Block Island boats, 43
blocks, block making, 51n, 106
Bluebeard, 70, 99, 103, 107, 194

Blue Lagoon. *See Harold H.*
Bluenose, 64, 95n, 99, 100, 112, 138n
boat plans. *See* architectural drawings
"boat rocks." *See* moorings
Boston, 121, 141, 142
bounties. *See* fishing bounties
bows. *See* clipper bows and round bows. *See also* plumb stems and straight stems
bowsprits, 18, 56, 95, 96, 148
Bras d'Or Lake, 140
British boatbuilding, 42
British influence on Tancook boatbuilding, 30
British Lady, 158
British Tar, 158
builders' models. *See* half-models
Burgess, Edward, 50

cabbage. *See* Lunenburg, cabbage raising at; Tancook cabbage
cabbage houses, 39, 159, 161, 168
cabbage trade. *See* Lunenburg, coasting trade of; Tancook cabbage trade
cabins. *See* cuddies
Canada-British West Indies Trade Agreement of 1925, 165, 175
Canada Shipping Act, 44n
Canada Temperance Act of 1878, 153
Canadian Department of Public Works, 122
Canadian Fisherman, 81, 90
Canadian fishing schooner design, 50n, 59
Canadian National Railway (CNR), 142, 164
Canadian National

Steamships (CNS), 165, 171, 175–6
Canadian National Steamships Act of 1927, 165
"Canadian Standard" engine, 91
"candlewick," 102, 117
Canso, 49, 50n, 57, 59, 61, 79, 85, 140
"Canvas Town," Big Tancook Island, 68
Cape boats. *See* Cape Island boats
Cape Breton County, 145
Cape Breton Island, 95, 138; coal trade, 146, 152; cod fishery, 137, 139–41; as a market for Tancook cabbage, 164; as a market for Tancook schooners, 51, 86, 180; swordfishery, 137, 139, 141–6, 148–9, 179
Cape Island boats, 80, 143n, 150, 166, 167, 178–80, 181, 207, 210
Cape North, 141, 142
Cape Sable Island, 178
Caribbean trade. *See* West Indies trade
carvel planking, 18, 24, 34, 42, 43–4, 43n, 45, 46, 47, 48, 72, 102, 121, 178
Catchalot, 197
catechu, 109
cat-ketch rig, 29
caulking, 69, 102, 117
Cecil V.L., 61, 71, 83n, 99, 139, 140
centreboards, 20, 23, 26, 27, 29, 62, 84, 92, 94, 94n
chain plates (for rigging), 106, 112
Chapelle, Howard I., 17, 24, 25, 26, 27, 28, 42, 54, 56n, 58, 59
Chester, 6, 10, 11, 38; boatbuilding at, 31, 42n, 47, 50, 65; influence of, on Tancook boatbuilding, 30, 32, 46; manu-

facture of marine engines at, 91; role of, in Tancook economy, 13, 31, 129, 129n, 173, 177; settlement and settlers of, 42n; yachting and yacht racing at, 4–5, 36, 45–7, 50, 51, 60n, 65
Chester Yacht Club (CYC), 4, 46, 47, 61, 93n
Church of England. *See* Anglicans, Anglicanism
Cimba, 4
clinker construction. *See* lapstrake planking
Clintonia, 56
clipper bows, 21, 23, 25, 30–1, 37, 49, 50–1, 52, 54, 72, 84
coal, coal trade, 19, 94, 146, 152, 167
cockpits. *See* steering cockpits
Collins, Joseph W., 24
Columbia, 99
Comet G., 46n, 71, 93, 94, 95, 97n, 186–7
Conrad, Edward, 27, 27n
contact boats, 155–7
counter sterns, 43–4, 48, 49–50, 50n, 53, 54, 62, 63, 64, 70, 71, 81, 84, 87, 88n, 98
Covey, Ernest, 137, 140
Cowes, England, 47
Cronan's Wharf, Halifax, 170
Crooks, Adelaide (Baker), 28–9
Crooks, John, 28–9
Crooks, Willis, 34n
Crooks family, 9n
Cross, Charles, 90, 121, 158
Cross, Ervin B., 179, 210
Cross, George, 121
Cross, John, 18, 121
Cross, Jordan, 138n
Cross, Reuben, 47
Cross, Sebastian, 61
Cross, Stephen, 47, 91
Cross, William, 90

Cross family, 8, 9, 11, 161
crosscut sails, 36
Cross Island, 134, 137n, 156
crosstrees, 79, 106
Crowninshield, Benjamin B., 56, 57, 59
cuddies, 20, 29, 103, 104, 105n, 106, 113, 114, 132, 179
"cutch." *See* catechu
cutwaters, 51

D. D. McKenzie, 156
Dagon, 97n, 189
Danish boatbuilding. *See* Scandinavia, boatbuilding in
Danish herring sloops, 43, 45n
Dan Patch, 90
Daring, 18n
Dartmouth, 23, 167
Dauphinee, Mary (Stevens), 66n
deadeyes, 79, 106
deadrise, 65
deck boats. *See* Tancook schooners, as deck boats
decks, decking, 53n, 63, 102, 103, 104, 104n, 113–14
Deep Cove, 122
Delawana-type schooner, 57
Demerara, British West Indies, 154, 155
Depression of 1930s, 86, 128, 145–6, 159n, 167, 176
depth-beam ratios, 62n
DesBrisay, Mather B., 24n
DeWolfe's Wharf, Halifax, 151, 169
Digby County, 22
Dimock, Daniel, 120, 122, 124
Dingwall, 142
Dolphin, 18, 28
Dominion Coal Company, 146
Donald L. Silver, 138n

dories, 21, 78, 79, 94n, 150; design and construction of, 139; fishing uses of, 58, 107, 108, 135, 137, 139, 140, 143, 147, 149, 164; non-fishing uses of, 109, 124, 168, 168n
Dorothy Adams, 138n
Dorothy and Ella, 66
double-ended sterns, 21, 21n, 23, 24, 26, 72, 81, 88, 88n
double-enders, 17, 20, 21n. *See also* Block Island boats; Danish herring sloops; Hampton boats; Labrador whalers; Lunenburg whalers; New England pinkies; New England whaleboats; Nova Scotia pinkies; Tancook ram boats; Tancook whalers
double rigging, 79, 106
"doubling up." *See* share systems
draft, 62, 93, 181
drawings. *See* architectural drawings
drift fishing. *See* droguing
drift nets, 131
droguers, droguing, 96, 107, 108, 130, 131–3, 134, 135, 147
Dunn's Ridge, 89
Dutch Reformed Church, 10, 11

Eastern Shore of Nova Scotia, 22, 85, 86, 131n, 164, 180
East Ironbound Island, 9n, 39, 122, 130, 134
elliptical transoms, 49, 52, 53, 54, 56, 98, 113
Ellwood, 27n
Elma M., 45, 62n
Elsie B. Young, 70, 99, 103, 107, 155n, 156, 194
Elsie C., 61, 90

engine manufacturers, 91
engines: auxiliary, 62, 72, 76, 80, 88–92, 94–5, 98, 104, 108, 112–14, 126, 129n, 131, 131n, 133, 136, 139, 143, 156, 163, 164, 169, 178, 181; non-auxiliary, 178–9, 178n, 180
English settlers, 9
Essie M.L., 151
European fisheries, 127
Evans, Harry, 91
eyebolts: for moorings, 124; for rigging, 106

Fader, Edmund A., 50
Fairbanks, John E., 24, 89n
"false topmast," 95n
fan transoms, 53, 98
fastenings, 71, 102
Fifty Acre Island, 134
Finney, John M.T., 5
fish dryers, 140n
fisheries. *See* European fisheries; Lunenburg, fisheries of; Lunenburg County, fisheries of; Nova Scotia, fisheries of; Scandinavia, fisheries of; South Shore, fisheries of; Tancook fisheries
"fisherman-carpenters," 81–3
"fisherman profile," 56
fisherman staysails, 29, 36, 37, 61, 94–5, 95, 95n, 106
"fisherman-type" schooners, 97n
fish houses, 35, 126, 127
fishing bounties, 18, 44n, 58, 84n, 120, 125, 126, 127
fish waste, 159
flake yards, 140, 140n
Flat Island, 12, 33, 173
"flat-roofing," 95, 106
Fleiger, John Henry, 8, 19
Florence B., 163
Flosie, 96, 97n, 189

Fordney-McCumber Tariff, 128
forefoot, 51, 71, 93
"Foreign Protestants," 8–9, 12
frames, framing, 42, 43, 45n, 101, 103, 115, 116, 117, 118
Frances M.R., 70, 80, 107n
Franche-Comté, France, 9
Frank Baxter, 138n
Frank J. Brenton, 138n
Freda, David, 47
Fredonia, *Fredonia* model, 50, 52n, 53, 56, 58
freeboard, 63, 72, 97n
French settlers. *See* Montbéliard, Montbéliardians
fresh fishing, 129, 132, 142

Gabarus, 51
gaff mainsails, 29, 73, 96–7
gammon knees, 23, 52n
General Haig, 57
Georges Bank, 143
Gerald L.C., 66, 201–2
German settlers, 9, 10, 162
Gilbert B. Walters, 138n
gill nets, 131, 133
Glace Bay, 136, 140, 142, 146, 148
Glendora, 67, 197
Glen Margaret, 173
Gloriana, 52n
Gloriana bow, 51–2
Gloria P.H., 155n, 156–7
Gloria Swanson, 155, 155n
Goode, George Brown, 24
Grace, 90
Grant, George, 8, 19
Gray Bear, 105
Great Depression. *See* Depression of 1930s
Great Lakes, 111, 180, 181n
Great Tancook Island. *See* Big Tancook Island
Green Bow, 94, 94n, 99, 143, 193

Green Bow II, 94, 94n, 112, 114, 116, 170n
Greenhill, Basil, 43, 112
Green Island. *See* Pearl Island
"gripe." *See* forefoot.
Guinea Gold, 178
Gulf of St Lawrence, 4, 95, 137, 164. *See also* Prince Edward Island
gunwales, 103, 108
Guysborough County, 22, 85, 142

Haig, 95, 97n, 137n, 191
"half barrel-head" transoms, 98
half-models, 42, 43, 46, 46n, 47–8, 99–100, 101n, 103–4
Haliburton, Thomas C., 11
Halifax, 6, 9, 10, 143, 157, 164n; British West Indies trade of, 151, 165–6, 170–1, 175; cattle trade of, 158–9, 160, 173; coal trade of, 152, 167; farmers' market at, 170n; fish trade of, 51, 122, 129n, 158; fishing grounds near, 131n, 137; growth of, as a consumer market, 164; liquor prohibition and, 153; as a market for Tancook schooners, 85; produce prices at, 159n, 162, 172; produce trade of, 13, 121, 122, 158–9, 160, 167, 176 (*see also* Tancook cabbage trade; Tancook sauerkraut); produce wholesalers at, 170, 172; registration of vessels at, 22; rum running and, 156; shipping lanes, 132; wharves, piers at, 151, 164, 169–70, 171; yachts and yacht racing at, 46, 52n, 60n, 61–2

Halifax and La Have Steam Packet Company, 163
Halifax County, 22, 85, 153
Halifax Herald, 126, 176
Haligonian, 99
Hamilton, Ont., 180
Hamm, Obed A., 44, 56, 101n
Hampton, NH, 24
Hampton boats, 24-5, 26n, 27, 30
Hampton whalers. *See* Hampton boats
hand-lining, 107, 108, 120, 130, 131, 134-5
"hardwood-built" schooners, 79, 103
Harold H., 4, 78, 84n, 98, 113
harpoons, harpooners, 143-4, 148-9
hatch boats. *See* Tancook schooners, as hatch boats
hatches, hatch covers, 107, 108, 114
Hatt family. *See* Hutt family
Hattie, 27n
Haussler family. *See* Heisler family
Hawboldt, Forman, 91
Hawboldt and Evans, 91
hawsepipes, 107
Hazel R., 27n
Hebb, Timothy, 121, 121n
Heckman's Island, 134
Heisler, Benjamin, 55, 91n
Heisler, Celest (Stevens), 54
Heisler, George, 11
Heisler, Joseph R. *See* Heisler, Reuben
Heisler, Reuben, 37, 41, 60n, 66, 68, 70, 71, 73, 81, 82, 92n, 94n, 138, 145, 155n, 178; career of, as a builder, 63, 64-5, 69, 69n, 252n.193; characteristics of, as a designer, 53, 61, 65; designing method of, 100; designs

of, 188; and introduction of counter sterns, 49, 50n; and introduction of half-models, 47; launching system of, 109; and round-bow controversy, 54-5, 57-8, 59, 61
Heisler, William, 64n
Heisler family, 9, 11, 54
Helen G. Thomas, 56
Helen M. Coolen, 138n
Henry Ford, 99
Henry L. Montague, 56
Here We Are, 143n, 179, 207
Hero, 158
Herreshoff, L. Francis, 52
Herreshoff, Nathaniel G., 51, 97
Herring Cove, 131n
herring drifters. *See* droguers, droguing
Hesse-Darmstadt, Germany, 9
Highland Lass, 121
Hilford, 90
Hillis Foundry Company, 132
Hirtle, Clyde, 155, 156
Hirtle, Ralph, 155, 156
Hirtle family, 155
Hispaniola, 58, 59, 138
Holdridge, Desmond, 4, 47, 55
Hollo, 35
Holly C., 96, 157, 200
Howard Stanley, 71
Hubley, Charles, 138n
Hurry Up, 164
Hutt, Charles, 143
Hutt, Henry, 18, 121, 158
Hutt family, 9, 11
Hutt's Pond, Big Tancook Island, 66

ice, ice houses, 127, 134
Indian Harbour, 85, 141
Indian Headers, Indian-Header stems, 56, 58, 59, 60, 99, 148

Indian Point, 71
Ingalls, Harry, 155
Irish settlers, 9
Ironbound Island. *See* East Ironbound Island
ironwork, 51n
Isabel J. Corkum, 138n
Isidore, 18
Isle Madame, 141

Jazz Vamp, 70
Jean Smith, 138n
Jennie S., 60n
Jewish settlers, 9
jibs, 29, 61, 73, 95, 96
jolly boats. *See* Tancook jolly boats
Jung family. *See* Young family
Juniata, 59

keels, 56, 84, 92-3, 93n, 103
keelsons, 103
Kelly, John, 157
ketch rig, 24, 26
Kinburn, 158
Knickle, Adam, 57-8, 59
knockabouts, knockabout rig, 36, 56, 57, 58, 61-2, 71, 74, 77, 85n, 94, 95-6, 112, 148, 157, 181n
Krass family. *See* Cross family
'kraut cabbage, 162

Labrador, 24-6, 27, 138
Labrador boats. *See* Labrador whalers
Labrador whalers, 24, 25-6, 27, 29, 30, 31, 34, 45n
"Lady Boats," 165, 166, 175-6
Lady Drake, 166
Lady Hawkins, 166
Lady Nelson, 166
La Have, 163
Langille, Albert, 138n
Langille, Alfred F., 11, 38, 47, 54n, 59, 62n, 69, 70n, 71; building techniques

of, copied, 32–3; career of, as a builder, 20–1, 31–2, 34, 45, 48, 63–4, 71; designing method of, 42; role of, in introducing Tancook whaler, 28, 28n, 31
Langille, Allen, 138n
Langille, Angus, 138n
Langille, Avery, 138n
Langille, Benjamin, 32n, 34, 101n
Langille, Bridget. *See* Mason, Bridget (Langille)
Langille, David W., 94, 96n, 98, 156; career of, as a builder, 67, 68–70; characteristics of, as a designer, 70; designing method of, 100; designs of, 193–5. *See also* Mason and Langille
Langille, Hibbert L., 69, 138
Langille, Irwin, 138n
Langille, James, 64, 138, 138n
Langille, John David (first), 11
Langille, John David (second), 34
Langille, Joshua C., 70, 81, 90
Langille, Leopold Frederick, 12n
Langille, Manson W., 96, 200
Langille, Owen, 59
Langille, Thomas, 81
Langille, Vernon R., 4, 41, 61, 70, 83n, 85n, 98, 99; career of, as a builder, 67, 68, 71; on round-bow controversy, 55
Langille, Willard, 138n
Langille family, 9, 11, 12, 14, 54
lanyards, 79, 106, 112, 114
lapstrake planking, 20, 21, 21n, 24, 26 34, 37, 42–5, 45n, 47, 48

launching sleds, 79, 82, 109
launching techniques, 82, 109
launchways, 37, 124n, 150, 168n
Laura M. Levy, 90
Lawrence, Charles, 7
Levy, Amos, 90
Levy, Basil, 138n
Levy, Benjamin, 60, 185
Levy, Charles, 163
Levy, Gaspar, 121
Levy, Gordon, 138n
Levy, Henry, 45, 61, 163, 178n; career of, as a builder, 32, 48, 63; characteristics of, as a designer, builder, 65n
Levy, Percy, 138n
Levy, Thomas, 138n
Levy family, 9n, 11, 134n
Liberal Party of NS, 176
lignum vitae, 106
Linnard family. *See* Alinard family
Linnet (first), 18
Linnet (second), 18
liquor prohibition: in Canada, 153; in Nova Scotia, 152–3, 157; in the United States, 154n
"Little Cod" stove, 132
Little Tancook Island, 85, 122, 134n, 229; boatbuilding at, 10, 48, 65, 83, 86, 227; coasting trade of, 163; population of, 1881, 9n; relationship of, to Big Tancook Island, 6, 9n; settlement and settlers of, 8, 10, 11; view of, 36. *See also* Tancook: cabbage; cabbage trade; fisheries; islands; jolly boats; ram boats; scallop sloops; schooners; sloops; whalers
Liverpool, 59
Lobelia L., 137n, 163
Lohnes, Frank C., 85
Lois A. Conrad, 138n

loose-footed foresails. *See* lug foresails
Louisburg, 136, 140; coal trade of, 146, 152n; swordfishery at, 141, 142, 143, 143n, 145
Loyalists, 10
Lucille B. Young, 155n
lug foresails, 23, 26, 29, 61, 62, 94, 95, 96, 97
Lunenburg, 6, 12, 14, 103, 138n; boatbuilding at, 25, 26–7, 47, 57; cabbage raising at, 160; coasting trade of, 13, 160; cold storage fish facilities at, 129, 132; fish prices (wholesale) at, 127, 128; fisheries of, 25, 26n, 136, 162; influences of, on Tancook boatbuilding, 30, 32, 53, 98, 104; as a market for Tancook schooners, 85; and the origin of the Tancook whaler, 26–8; as an outfitting centre, 26, 76, 106, 122, 139, 158; role of, in developing the Labrador whaler, 25–7; rum running at, 153, 156; sailmakers and sailmaking at, 67, 105; sauerkraut and, 162; schooner design at, 53, 55, 56–7, 98; settlers from, at Tancook, 8, 10, 11; share system at, 136; West Indies trade of, 121, 125, 135, 154; whalers, 27, 31, 44n, 44–5; as a wholesale fish market, 121–2, 127, 131–2, 135, 140, 158
Lunenburg County, 85, 102, 124; fisheries of, 89n, 126, 131n, 154; land transportation in, 177; liquor prohibition in, 153–4; produce trade of, 160; rum running in, 153; settlement and set-

tlers of, 8, 9, 10, 42n; ship and boatbuilding in, 22, 25, 31, 50, 52n, 81
Lunenburg Foundry Company, 91, 133
Lunenburg Progress, 45
Lunenburg South, 140n
Lutherans, Lutheranism, 10

McCoy, William, 4, 78
MacDonald, Angus L., 176
MacGregor, David R., 30, 31n
McGuire, Agnes, 81
McKay, John, 56
mackerel hooking, 120
McManus, Thomas F., 36, 55, 56, 56n, 58, 59, 60, 61, 99
McMillan, A.S., 176
Mahone Bay, 129n, 155; islands in, 6, 12, 38, 154; waters of, 46n, 120, 154
Mahone Bay fishermen's regattas, 35, 36, 45–6, 51
Mahone Bay township, 6, 47, 56, 81, 98, 102, 103
Maine, 24, 42n
Malabars, 97n
marconi mainsails, 74, 75, 76, 96–8
Marion C., 79, 103
Marion Elizabeth, 138n
Martin's River, 103
Mary H. Hirtle, 138n
Mason, Augusta. *See* Stevens, Augusta (Mason)
Mason, Benjamin, 121
Mason, Bridget (Langille), 54n, 67
Mason, Charles, 164
Mason, Daniel, 121, 158
Mason, David, 68n, 100n, 177
Mason, Earl, 116
Mason, Emery, 33n
Mason, Ephraim, 121, 158
Mason, Eustace, 116, 147
Mason, George (first), 11, 12, 17, 18

Mason, George (second), 121, 158
Mason, Howard, 28, 41, 51, 54n, 67, 70, 75, 77, 83n, 96n, 98, 112, 114, 116, 128n, 135, 138, 143, 145, 147, 173, 177, 180, 181n; building methods of, 62, 81–2, 82n, 103; career of, as a builder, 48, 65, 71, 81, 85, 94; characteristics of, as a designer, 71, 93, 99; designing method of, 83, 100, 101n; designs of, 198–9, 203–6, 208–9; introduces marconi rig on Tancook, 96–7
Mason, Howard, Jr, 147
Mason, Isaac, 121, 158
Mason, Joshua, 33n, 40, 47, 54n, 64, 71, 121, 158; career of, as a builder, 32, 45, 48; designing method of, 42; on first Tancook whaler, 28; as a sailmaker, 34
Mason, Murray A., 181n
Mason, Peter, 10, 13–14, 18, 33n, 34, 120
Mason, Stanley G., 4, 40, 63, 66, 70, 71, 78–9, 82, 91, 94, 96, 98, 99, 103, 112, 113, 115, 155n, 178, 179; career of, as a builder, 67–9, 85; characteristics of, as a designer, 69; designing method of, 100, 101n; designs of, 189, 192; launching system of, 109; and Tancook cabbage trade, 177; as Tancook's leading builder, 67–8. *See also* Mason and Langille
Mason, Steadman S., 49, 55, 138n, 140, 145, 203
Mason, Thomas, 77, 81, 116, 117, 132, 138n, 147, 171; on auxiliary engines, 91; on dangers of droguing, 132; on marconi mainsails, 96; on round-bow controversy, 55, 58; on Tancook's timber resources, 19; on whaler half-models, 47
Mason family, 9, 11, 12, 14, 54
Mason and Langille, 61, 69n, 80, 90, 94, 107n, 134, 155n, 156, 193–5; building methods of, 68–9, 103–4; designing methods of, 99–100; sailmaking methods of, 105. *See also* Mason, Stanley G.; Langille, David W.
Mason's Island, 12
Massachusetts, 42n, 56
Masson (Mason), Frederique, 12
Masson (Mason), Pierre, 12
Masson family. *See* Mason family
mastheadmen, 143, 144, 144n, 145, 148–9
masts, 37, 79, 82, 83n, 94–5, 95n, 97, 103, 105, 105n, 106, 114, 116, 145, 148
Maury, Richard, 4
Meemie, 5
Meisner's Island, 134
Methodists, Methodism, 10, 11
Mianus, 61, 95, 96, 97n, 148–9, 190
Micmac Indians, 7
Mildred Baker, 45
Minnie H. Mosher, 56
mixed-wood construction, 45n, 103, 179
Mömpelgard. *See* Montbéliard
Montbéliard, Montbéliardians, 9, 10, 12
moorings, mooring poles, 36, 37, 123–4
Morash, Solomon, 56

Morning Star II, 68n, 85, 96, 103
Moseley, Ebenezer, 30
Mosher, Jessen, 138n
Mother, 66, 83n, 107, 167, 196
motor-sailors, 80, 181
moulds, moulding, 42–3, 62, 70n, 100–1, 103

Nancy, 72
National Seafood Wharf, Halifax, 156
Nelson L., 68, 68n, 79, 85, 103
New Brunswick, 25, 86
Newburyport, MA, 24
New England: boatbuilding, 42; fishing schooners, 49, 50, 55–6, 59, 73, 99; migration to, from Maritimes, 128; pinkies, 21, 22; whaleboats, 21, 23–4, 27
New Englanders, 23, 42n
Newfoundland, 25, 86, 127, 139, 172
New Hampshire, 24, 42n
New York, 152
Nickerson and Crease, 170, 171
North Sydney, 79, 136, 142, 146
Northwest Arm, Halifax, 156
Northwest Cove, Big Tancook Island, 8; boatbuilding at, 32, 35, 48, 51–3, 53n, 62, 64–6, 64n, 69, 86, 227; breakwater at, 122, 157–8, 163; characteristics of, as a harbour, 7, 122–3, 124, 168; sailmaking at, 34, 66–7; views of, 35, 37
Northwest Range, 12
Nova Scotia: fisheries of, 24, 25, 88, 120, 126, 127–8, 141, 142, 178; fishing schooner design in, 50n, 59; highways, highway system of, 176–7;

pinkies, 22–3; temperance movement in, 152–3
Nova Scotia Highway Department, 177
Nova Scotia Liquor Commission, 153
Nova Scotia Schooner Association, 52
Nova Scotia Temperance Act of 1910, 153
Nova Zembla, 138

Oakland, 102
oars. *See* sweeps
O'Brien, John, 30
Ocean Bride, 30
Oda B.H., 143
Old Kentucky, 178–9
Old Sydney Mine, 146
Ontario, 86
Opal June, 155n
Oreda, 44n
Oriole L., 62n
Ostrich, 18
"otter" trawling. *See* steam dragging
Outhit, C.W., 170
oval transoms. *See* elliptical transoms
Ovens, the, 140n
overhangs, 56, 60, 99–100, 112
oxen, 13, 63n, 82, 152, 168, 172n, 173–4, 177n

Palatinate, Germany, 9
Patavana, 71, 74, 76, 81–2, 83n, 93, 96, 99, 102, 103, 107, 111, 112, 114, 131, 132, 134, 135, 147, 149, 168, 171, 173–4, 180, 198–9
Parker and Sawyer, 172
Parrel family. *See* Pearl family
Patience, 18
Pazant and King, 172
Pearl, John, 121, 163
Pearl, Joseph, 34, 66, 66n, 67
Pearl, Walter, 18

Pearl, Warren V., 143n
Pearl family, 9n
Pearl Island, 130, 134, 137n
Pearl M. Pettipas, 65
Peggy, 145
Peggy's Cove, 18
Perley, M.H., 24
Petawawa, 103
Phillips-Birt, Douglas, 43
Pickford and Black, 165
pinkies, 21, 22–3, 24
pink sterns, 23, 24
planking, 69, 81. *See also* carvel planking; lap-strake planking
plank keels, 92
plank-on-edge construction. *See* carvel planking
plans. *See* architectural drawings
plumb stems, 20, 30
Polly Anna, 203–4
Polly N.S., 178
Pontiac, 61
Port Hawkesbury, 137
Post, Robert C., 28, 55
Presbyterians, Presbyterianism, 10
Prince Edward Island, 86, 137–9, 167
"progy," 120n
Prohibition. *See* liquor prohibition
Publicover, Daniel, 48
Puerto Rico, 126
"pulpits," 144, 148–9

quarter rails, 79
Quebec, 86
Queen Charlotte's Island. *See* Big Tancook Island
Queen Mab, 97

"racing fisherman" profile, 99, 112
Rafuse Island, 156
rail caps, 105n, 108n
rails, 79, 140n, 107, 108, 113, 114
ram boats. *See* Tancook ram boats
Ramona II, 143n

Index

ratlines, 148
recession of 1920s, 127, 128, 146, 167
Red Huntz, 105
regattas. *See* Mahone Bay fishermen's regattas
registration of vessels, 22, 44, 84
Rhineland, 8–9
"ridges, the," 89, 120, 130, 131, 132, 134, 181n
rigging. *See* double rigging; single rigging; standing rigging; "triple rigging"
Rita, 143, 145
Rob Roy, 56, 59
Rodenhiser, Zenas, 94n
Rodenhiser family, 9, 11
Rothenhausser family. *See* Rodenhiser family
Roué, William J., 95n
round-bow controversy, 54–5, 57–8, 60–1
round bows, 36, 49, 53, 54–61, 63, 73, 75, 84, 95, 99, 148
rowing, rowing craft, 20, 29, 43n, 63. *See also* dories; sweeps
Royal George Island. *See* Big Tancook Island
Royal Nova Scotia Yacht Squadron (RNSYS), 46, 52n, 60n, 61–2
rubbing strakes, 147
rudders, 20, 23, 26, 72, 88
"rule-of-thumb" construction, 42, 103
"Rum Row," 154
rum running, 152–7
run, 27n, 44, 71

S.F. Levy, 61
Sacrifice Island, 134
Sails. *See* crosscut sails; fisherman staysails; gaff mainsails; jibs; lug foresails; marconi mainsails; sprit sails. *See also* cat-ketch rig; ketch rig; sail plans; sails, preservation of; schooner rig; sloop rig; Tancook schooners, sails and sail plans of; Tancook whalers, sails and sail plans of
sailmakers, sailmaking, 34, 51n, 58, 60, 66–7, 105
sail plans, 46n, 60–1, 67, 83n
sails, preservation of, 109
St Margaret's Bay, 141, 155, 169
St Margaret's Bay highway, 176
St Pierre and Miquelon, 86, 154, 155
Salada, 143
salt, salt trade, 76, 122, 135
salt fishing, 107, 108, 129, 130, 132, 137, 140
Sandwich, 18, 120
Sarah Pauline, 68n, 69n, 70, 85, 99, 103, 155, 195
sauerkraut. *See* Lunenburg, sauerkraut and; Tancook sauerkraut
scallop boats. *See* Tancook scallop sloops
scallop sloops. *See* Tancook scallop sloops
Scandinavia: boatbuilding in, 42–3; fisheries of, 90, 92
Schlagenweit family. *See* Slauenwhite family
schooner rig, 22, 23, 29–30, 31, 85, 95
schooners. *See* Lunenberg, schooner design at; Lunenberg whalers; New England fishing schooners; Nova Scotia, fishing schooner design in; pinkies; Tancook schooners; Tancook whalers
Scott Act. *See* Canada Temperance Act of 1878
Scottish settlers, 9
scrollheads, 23
Seabrook, NH, 24, 25

Seacrest, 90
Sea Gull, 94n
Sealer, 70n, 90
"seamwork" construction. *See* carvel planking
Sea Slipper, 121
Sea Way. *See Green Bow II*
Second Peninsula, Lunenburg, 60, 67, 140, 140n
semi-deck boats. *See* Tancook schooners, as semi-deck boats
semi-knockabouts, semi-knockabout rig, 56–7, 59, 67, 76
"shallow bow-deep heel" profile, 70, 93
Shanti, 116, 117
sharesmen, 135
share systems, 135–6
sheep raising, 12, 13, 172–3, 173n
sheer, 65, 70, 71, 99, 112
sheer legs. *See* sheer poles
sheer poles, 116
Shelburne, 56, 59
Shelburne County, 22, 178
shell construction, 42
Shepherd King, 57
shifting boards, 145
Shippegan, NB, 139
shrouds. *See* standing rigging
Silver Oak, 64, 68, 103, 137n, 139, 164
Silver's Wharf, Halifax, 169
single rigging, 106, 112
skeletal construction, 42
Sky Lark, 121, 158
Slauenwhite, Clements, 140, 143n
Slauenwhite, Evelyn. *See* Stevens, Evelyn (Slauenwhite)
Slauenwhite, Frederick, 18
Slauenwhite, George, 18n
Slauenwhite, Hovey, 70, 71, 99–100, 138, 140, 143n, 171

Slauenwhite family, 9, 11, 161
sleds. *See* launching sleds
"sleighs." *See* launching sleds
sloop rig, 20, 84
sloops. *See* Danish herring sloops; Tancook jolly boats; Tancook ram boats; Tancook scallop sloops; Tancook sloops
Smith, George, 65
Smith, W.C. and Company, 56
Smith and Rhuland, 56, 57
Smith family, 134n
Smoot-Hawley Tariff, 128n
Southeast Cove, Big Tancook Island, 119n, 134; boatbuilding at, 31–2, 51, 62, 63, 65, 68–9, 70n, 71, 86, 96, 98, 134n, 227; breakwater at, 105, 122–3, 163, 168; characteristics of, as a harbour, 7, 122–3, 168; sailmaking at, 34; views of, 37–9, 150
Southeast Cove beach, Big Tancook Island, 20, 105
Southeast Pond, Big Tancook Island, 105
Southern Head, Big Tancook Island, 6–7, 39, 119n
South Shore, Nova Scotia, 45n, 85, 86; agriculture and, 159, 166, 176, 177; fisheries of, 87, 88, 119, 131n, 140–1; land transportation on, 177; rum running on, 155, 157; ship and boatbuilding on, 22, 42, 50, 56, 103, 178; yachting on, 46, 94
Southwest Beach, Big Tancook Island, 124
Spanish settlers, 9

Spanish windlass, 124
spike rails, 107, 108n, 113, 114
spoon bows. *See* round bows
"spreaders." *See* crosstrees
sprit sails, 24, 29
Squanto, 59n
Squanto (American schooner), 59, 73
Squanto (Tancook schooner), 59
square sterns, square-stern schooners, 18, 28, 34, 121
Stag, 30
stanchion rails, 79, 107, 108n
standing rigging, 79, 106, 112
stationary nets, 107, 130, 131, 133
steam bending, steam-bent construction, 42, 45n, 101, 103, 115, 116, 117, 118
steamboats (coastal), 90, 158, 163, 164, 170n
steam dragging, 88
Steebing, John George, 8
Steebing family. *See* Stevens family
steering cockpits, 107, 113, 114, 169
steersmen, 144, 144n, 148
stern planks. *See* transoms
sternposts, 21, 23, 26, 70, 72, 88–9, 103
sterns. *See* counter sterns; double-ended sterns; pink sterns; square sterns; transom sterns; V-sterns
Steubing family. *See* Stevens family
Stevens, Albert, 51
Stevens, Alvin G., 35, 45, 53, 65, 66; career of, as a builder, 32, 34, 48, 63, 85, 90; designing method of, 101n
Stevens, Amos H., 35, 40,

45, 49, 52, 61, 65, 66, 66n, 68, 69n, 71, 82, 90, 95, 96, 99, 100, 137, 148, 155n; boatbuilding myths associated with, 18, 28; career of, as a builder, 32–3, 34, 46–7, 50–1, 63, 64, 68, 69, 85; characteristics of, as a designer, 46, 65; designing method of, 100, 101n; designs of, 185–7, 189–91; innovations of, 47, 50, 53, 60n, 63, 98, 101n; as leading builder at Northwest Cove, 49, 64; and round-bow controversy, 54–5, 57, 60–1
Stevens, Augusta (Mason), 33n, 54n
Stevens, Byron, 66
Stevens, Celest. *See* Heisler, Celest (Stevens)
Stevens, Charles, 33n
Stevens, David, 11, 34, 121, 158
Stevens, David M., 55, 57, 81
Stevens, Edward, 33n
Stevens, Ernest, 64
Stevens, Ervine, 64
Stevens, Evelyn (Slauenwhite), 58
Stevens, Foster, 143
Stevens, Guy B., 143n, 179, 207
Stevens, Harold W., 46n, 66n
Stevens, Harvey, 143
Stevens, Lindsay, 138n
Stevens, Mary. *See* Dauphinee, Mary (Stevens)
Stevens, Melvin H., 65, 66, 69
Stevens, Perry W., 50, 55, 65, 138n, 203
Stevens, Randolph B., 46n, 62, 64, 138; career of, as a sailmaker, 34, 58, 60n, 66–7, 105; and

knockabout schooner concept, 61; and round-bow controversy, 57–8, 59, 60–1; sail plans of, 185, 187 189–91, 200, 204, 206
Stevens, Raymond, 143, 143n, 179, 207
Stevens, Roland, 69
Stevens, Wesley H., 40, 70, 81, 83n, 138n, 179; building methods of, 104; career of, as a builder, 64, 66, 67, 85; designing method of, 100; designs of, 196–7, 201, 207
Stevens, Wesley H., Jr, 143, 143n, 146, 179, 207
Stevens, William, 45
Stevens family, 9, 11, 54
Steward D.S., 139, 164
Stormalong, 67, 197
stoves: home, 19, 152; marine, 132–3
straight stems, 40, 51–2, 54, 61, 73, 84. See also plumb stems
Strait of Canso, 137
Sutherland, Patrick, 7, 8
Swedish fisheries. See Scandinavia, fisheries of
sweeps, 23, 62, 89–90
swordfish, description and nature of, 141n, 144–5
Sydney, 142, 164
Sydney and Louisburg Railroad, 146

Tacoma, 52, 61, 73
Tancook, 95, 97n, 99, 137n, 137–8, 139, 140, 143n, 145, 163, 190
Tancook cabbage, 13, 14, 130, 159, 160–1, 162, 176
Tancook cabbage trade, 13, 122, 151, 157–72, 175–7, 179, 180
Tancook fisheries: bait supplies in, 120n, 131, 134; boat ownership patterns in, 136n; bounties in, 18, 120, 125, 126, 127; catches in, processing of, 107, 129, 132, 135, 140, 140n, 143–4, 147, sizes of, 137, 140, 145–6, unloading of, 107–8; cod in, 87–8, 107, 127, 129, 130, 131, 133–40, 147, 149; crew sizes in, 18, 21, 107, 120, 121n, 134–5, 136, 137, 140, 144, 148; dangers of, 132, 145; Depression of the 1930s and, 128, 145–6; dories used in, 79, 107, 108, 135, 137, 139, 140, 143, 147, 149, 164; drift fishing in (*see* droguing in); droguing in, 96, 107, 108, 130, 131–3, 147; drying catches in (*see* catches in, processing of); earnings in, 127, 145–6, 146n; engines in, 88–92, 126, 129n, 131n, 133, 136, 143, 178–9; equipment, facilities owned in, 121, 126, 127, 134; expansion of, 16, 124–7; flounder in, 129; fresh fishing in, 129, 132, 142; groundfish in, 107, 120, 121, 127, 130, 134, 135; haddock in, 127, 129, 131, 133, 135, 137; hake in, 129; halibut in, 21, 129; hand-lining in, 107, 108, 120, 130, 131, 134–5; herring in, 87, 96, 107, 108, 120, 125, 127, 129, 130–3, 147; insurance in, 145; line fishing in, 121, 129 (*see also* hand-lining in; trawling in); lobster in, 84, 127, 129, 130; mackerel in, 18, 107, 120, 127, 129, 130, 133; marketing in, 121–2, 127, 131–2, 135, 140, 144, 145–6; net fishing in, 107, 107n, 120n, 121, 129–30, 130n (*see also* droguing, stationary nets in, trap nets in); number of boats participating in, 21, 121, 127, 142; number of fishermen in, 15, 120, 125, 127, 128; "otter" trawling and (*see* steam dragging and); pollock in, 129, 133; postwar decline of, 127–8, 145; production in, 121, 125–6, 133, 230–3; profit-sharing in (*see* share systems in); salmon in, 119, 129; salt fishing in, 107, 108, 129, 130, 132, 137, 140; salting catches in (*see* catches in, processing of); scallops in, 51, 84, 127, 129 130; share systems in, 135–6, 144; shipboard life in, 132, 140, 143; start of, 15–16, 119–20; stationary nets in, 107, 130, 131; steam dragging and, 88; swordfish in, 94, 129, 130, 137, 137n, 139, 141–6, 148–9, 152, 167, 179; tariff policies and, 88n, 126, 127–8; Tom cod in, 129; trap nets in, 119–20, 130, 131, 133n, 134; trawling in, 107, 130, 134, 137, 139, 140, 147, 149, 164; value of, 88n, 92, 125n, 126, 230–1; weirs in (*see* trap nets in); World War I and, 88, 126–7, 164
Tancook islands:
– agriculture: animal husbandry in, 12–13, 172–4; crop rotation in, 161; crops raised in, 13, 161, 173; description of, 1870, 120; farm acreage in, 12, 13; growing soil for, 12, 159, 173; plant-

ing and harvesting seasons in, 130, 139, 160–1, 173; start of, 11–12.
See also Tancook cabbage; Tancook sauerkraut
– boatbuilding industry: barns used in, 32n, 64, 82, 101n; boat shops in, 32, 35, 64, 65, 68, 69n, 115, 252n193; building of large vessels in, 18, 19; decline of, 86, 167; local variations in, 32, 53, 53n, 65n, 98, 109; mechanization in, 68; overview of, 19, 85–6, 121, 227–8; start of, 16, 33–4; timber imports for, 19, 81, 102–3; wages in, 69; wood used in, 45n, 103, 179; yacht building in, 46–7, 50, 66, 94, 106.
See also Tancook: jolly boats; ram boats; scallop sloops; schooners; sloops; whalers
– coasting trade: cattle in, 158–9, 173–4; coal in, 94, 146, 152, 167; end of, 175–7, 180; fish in, 51, 121, 129n; produce in, 121, 122, 137, 157–9, 167; season of, 130, 137; shipboard life in, 132–3; start of, 13, 90, 157–8.
See also Tancook cabbage trade; Tancook sauerkraut
description and characteristics of, 6–7, 19, 27, 108, 109, 122–3; dwellings at, 13, 39, 152; emigration from, 128; fishing industry, overview of, 124–8 (*see also*

Tancook fisheries); granting of, 7–8; land distribution at, 13–14; launchways at, 37, 124n, 150, 168n; location of, 6; Loyalist myths associated with, 10; medical care at, 70; moorings at, 37, 123–4; population statistics for, 9, 11, 128; prohibitionist sentiment at, 154n; religious beliefs and influences at, 10–11, 133n, 154n; rum running at, 154–7; settlement and settlers of, 8–12; timber resources of, 7, 19, 152; wharves at, 108, 122–3, 126, 127, 150, 157–8, 163, 168
See also Big Tancook Island; Little Tancook Island
Tancook jolly boats, 19–21, 30, 34, 64, 84, 120, 120n
Tancook lobster boats. *See* Tancook jolly boats
Tancook ram boats, 84
Tancook sauerkraut, 158, 159, 160, 161–2, 163, 167, 167n, 168–9, 172. *See also* Tancook cabbage trade
Tancook scallop sloops, 36, 37, 84, 100, 105, 108, 122, 130, 130n, 203–4
Tancook schooners: ballasting of, 70, 93, 145; bows of, 36, 37, 40, 49, 50–2, 54–61, 63, 64, 70, 73, 75, 93, 99, 111, 112, 148; builders of, 63–6, 67–71, 81; building of, in barns, 81–2, outdoors, 69n, by part-time builders, 81–2, by professional builders, 82, 85, by subcontract, 81; carvel planking in, 43–4, 43n, 102; cen-

treboards in, 62, 92, 94, 94n; as coasters, 162–4, 167–9, 173–4, 180; as codfishermen, 87, 107, 134–40; compared to Cape Island boats, 179–80; construction of, 43n, 43–4, 48, 62, 68–9, 81–2, 101–4, 114–18; cost of, 92, 92n; average crew size of, 107, 134–5, 144; as deck boats, 79, 104, 106–7, 108, 108n, 109, 124, 132–3, 136, 136n, 137, 139, 142, 163–4, 164n, 167, 168–9; decks, decking of, 53n, 63, 102, 103, 104, 104n, 113–14; designing of, 47, 82–3, 100–1; engines in, 62, 76, 80, 88–92, 94–5, 98, 104, 108, 112, 113, 114, 133, 136, 143, 156, 163, 164, 169, 181; first of, built, 50–1, 53; "hardwood-built", 79, 103; as hatch boats, 76, 77, 80, 104, 107–9, 113, 124, 134–5, 167, 168, 209; as herring droguers, 107, 131–3; hull shapes of, 43–4, 46n, 52, 62–3, 65, 65n, 69, 70, 88; influence of fishing vessel design on, 50, 52n, 53, 55–61, 73, 98, 99–100; influence of yacht design on, 50, 51–2, 61, 96; inherited characteristics of (*see* similarity of, to whalers); introduction of, 54; keels of, 92–3, 93n, 103; last of, built, 68n, 94; launching of, 79, 82, 109; living aboard, 132–3; markets for, 51, 85–6, 180; masts of, 79, 82, 83n, 94–5, 95n, 97, 103, 105n, 105–6, 114, 116, 145; mooring gear on, 79, 107, 124;

number of, built, 3–4, 65, 83–4, 85, 86, 227; owned locally, 85, 127, 128, 228–9; ownership patterns of, 136n; painting schemes for, 94n, 104–5, 104–5n; profiles of, 62, 93, 93n, 112; proportions of, 62, 67, 87n, 93; racing of, 5, 35–6, 46n, 51, 60, 61–2, 93n, 94; rails on, 79, 104n, 107, 108, 113, 114; registration of, 83–4, 84n, 85; rigging of, 51n, 79, 105–6, 112, 114; round bow controversy and, 54–5, 57–8, 60–1; rudders on, 88; as rum runners, 152, 155–7; sailmaking for, 34n, 51n, 66–7, 105; sails and sail plans of, 36, 46n, 60–2, 73, 74, 75, 76, 77, 83n, 94–8, 106, 109; seaworthiness of, 4, 52, 179–80; as semi-deck boats, 107, 108, 114, 124, 135, 167–9, 199; significance of, 3–4, 48; similarity of, to whalers, 62–3, 65, 88, 93n, 94; size of, 84–5, 86–8, 87n; steering gear on, 77, 79, 107; sternposts of, 70, 88–9, 103; sterns of, 43–4, 48, 49–50, 52–3, 54, 62, 63, 64, 65, 70, 71, 73, 75, 81, 87, 88n, 98, 103, 111; sweeps used by, 62, 89–90; as swordfishermen, 142–5; transoms on, 49, 52–4, 88n, 98, 113; versatility of, 48; winter storage of, 108–9, 124n; wood used in building, 102–3; as yachts, 4–5, 60, 61–2, 66, 73, 75, 78, 93n, 94, 106, 112, 180, 181n
Tancook sloops, 60n, 84. *See also* Tancook scallop sloops

Tancook township. *See* Tancook islands
Tancook whalers: bows of 21, 23, 25, 30–1, 72; builders of, 32, 48, 70n; building of, in barns, 32n, 101n, on contract, 31, 45, on mainland, 31; carvel planking in, 44, 45, 47, 48, 72; centreboards in, 23, 25, 26, 29, 31, 92, 94; characteristics of, 21, 23, 25–6; as coasters, 108; compared to schooners, 48, 63; construction of, 42–3; 48, 81; average crew size of, 21, 135; designing of, 42–3, 47–8, 101n; design of, disseminated, 32–3; engines in, 72, 88, 139; first of, built, 28–9; first recorded appearance of, 21; as fishing craft, 19, 27, 48, 87, 120n, 131n, 139; hull shapes of, 21, 23, 26, 27n, 63, 65; keels of, 92, 93n; lapstrake planking in, 21, 24, 34, 37, 42, 43n, 44, 45, 47; last of, built, 44, 48; masts and rigging of, 37, 97, 106; moorings for, 123; numbers of, built, 44, 83; origin of, 21–7; painting schemes for, 37, 104; profiles of, 93n; proportions of, 23, 24, 26, 29, 45, 62, 62n; racing of, 36, 45–6, 51n; registration of, 83, 84n; rudders on, 26, 72, 88; sails and sail plans of, 23, 25–6, 29–30, 31, 36, 37, 61, 96, 97, 109; sailmaking for, 34, 67; size of, 44–5, 86; sternposts of 21, 26, 72, 88; sterns of, 72, 81, 88n; sweeps used by, 23, 29, 43n, 89; tillers on, 72; in tourist trade, 48; winter

storage of, 108; wood used in building, 45n
tanned sails. *See* sails, preservation of
tariffs, tariff policy, 88, 126, 127–8, 165–6
Terence Bay, 85
Thomas, Joseph, 39
Thomas family, 9n
Three Brothers, 17–18
three-mould system, 42, 48
tillers, 72, 77, 107
Tobin, John, 172
Togo, 60–1, 185
tongue-and-groove decking, 102, 114
topmasts, 95n, 145
trailboards, 23
transoms, 49, 52–4, 88n, 98, 113
transom sterns, 20–1, 84
trap nets, trap fishing, 119–20, 130, 131, 133n, 134
trawling, 58–9, 107, 130, 134, 137, 139, 140, 147, 149, 164
"triple rigging," 106
tuck, 81
Turk's Island, British West Indies, 135
turnbuckles, 106
Turret, 143, 146, 197
Tyrienne S., 70, 99–100, 171

Uktancook. *See* Big Tancook Island
Underwood-Simmons Tariff, 88, 126, 127–8
United Empire Loyalists. *See* Loyalists
United States, 86, 126, 128, 128n, 142

"V"-sterns, 53, 54, 73, 98
Verna B., 80, 181
Vernie S., 51
Victoria County, 142
Vikings, Viking ships, 21
Vivian C. Walters, 56

W.E. Wier, 163
Walker, Andrew, 50
Waters, Donald, 4
weirs. *See* trap nets
Wentworth, John, 8
Wentzell, Howard, 172
West Dover, 44
Western Banks, 57, 138; trawl fishery of, 58–9
Western Shore, 162
West Indies trade, 121, 125, 127, 135, 151, 154, 165–6, 170–1, 175–6
whaleboats. *See* New England whaleboats
whalers. *See* Labrador whalers; Lunenburg whalers; Tancook whalers
whaling, 23
wharves, 105, 108, 122–3, 126, 127, 150, 151, 157–8, 163, 164, 168, 169–70, 171
wheels, wheelboxes, 79, 107

White Birch, 69, 103, 137n, 139, 164, 171
Whitten, R.J., 170
Wildcat, 155, 155n
Willie Roy, 45
Wilneff, Murray, 181
Wilneff family, 11
Wilson, Alexander J., 52, 65
Wilson, Charles, 51
Wilson, Ellsworth, 138n
Wilson, Rufus, 69
Wilson, Wilfred, 138n, 155
Wilson family, 9n, 52, 155
windlasses (anchor), 79, 107
Windstark. *See* Harold H.
wood. *See* mixed wood construction
wool making, 172–3, 172n
Württemburg, Germany, 9

X10U8, 76, 77, 93, 99, 113, 181n, 208–9

Yachting magazine, 26

yachts, yachting, 4–5, 35–6, 45–7, 50, 51–2, 60, 60n, 61–2, 65, 66, 73, 75, 78, 93n, 94, 96, 97, 106, 111–12, 180, 181n
Yarmouth, NS, 22
yawl-boats, 20
Young, Clarence, 155
Young, Demus, 138n
Young, Edward, 121
Young, Eli, 138n
Young, Ernest, 155
Young, Freeman, 163
Young, Gurney, 138n
Young, Herbert (first), 30
Young, Herbert (second), 51
Young, John Gasper, 18
Young, Joshua, 157
Young, Perry W., 69, 138n, 155, 156
Young, Wesley, 51
Young family, 9, 11, 52, 155

Zaida, 61
Zwicker, A.C., 56